Computer Graphics and CAD

Computer Graphics and CAD

Dr C.S. Verma
Assistant Director, Academic Bureau,
All India Council for Technical Education
and
Former Assistant Professor
N.S.I.T. Dwarka, New Delhi

Dr Rajesh Purohit
Associate Professor
Mechanical Engineering Department
Maulana Azad National Institute of Technology
Bhopal, India

Dr Koyel Datta Gupta
Reader
Computer Science & Engineering
Maharaja Surajmal Institute of Technology
New Delhi

Ms Harsha Verma
Former Lecturer, N.S.I.T and
Bhaskaracharya College of Applied Science
Delhi University

CRC Press
Taylor & Francis Group
Boca Raton London New York

CRC Press is an imprint of the
Taylor & Francis Group, an **informa** business

Manakin
PRESS

First published 2025
by CRC Press
4 Park Square, Milton Park, Abingdon, Oxon, OX14 4RN

and by CRC Press
2385 NW Executive Center Drive, Suite 320, Boca Raton FL 33431

© 2025 Manakin Press Pvt. Ltd

CRC Press is an imprint of Informa UK Limited

The right of C.S. Verma, Rajesh Purohit, Koyel Datta Gupta and Harsha Verma to be identified as author(s) of this work has been asserted in accordance with sections 77 and 78 of the Copyright, Designs and Patents Act 1988.

British Library Cataloguing-in-Publication Data
A catalogue record for this book is available from the British Library

Print edition not for sale in South Asia (India, Sri Lanka, Nepal, Bangladesh, Pakistan or Bhutan).

ISBN13: 9781032789873 (hbk)
ISBN13: 9781032789880 (pbk)
ISBN13: 9781003490128 (ebk)

DOI: 10.4324/9781003490128

Typeset in Times New Roman
by Manakin Press, Delhi

Manakin
PRESS

Brief Contents

Detailed Contents

7. Surface Modelling and Surface Fitting   253–278

8. Solid Modelling and Animation   279–298

Preface

Today is the day of scientific and technological advances taking benefits of Computer System? Now Computer System is a backbone electronic machine for getting desired output for products and services design in every field. Therefore, in recent years it has become quite difficult, not to notice the proliferation of Computer Graphics and Computer Aided Design (CAD). Using Computer System, user can get information on the display screen both in textual and graphical form. Watching TV, movies and video games by different medium for a while, the likelihood is that you will see the magic touch of Computer Graphics and CAD in commercial.

This book can be used as a textbook for a semester at the undergraduate level (B.E/ B. Tech for all branches) and also in some Post graduate level (M. Tech., MCA and MSc computer science) because it is found that contents of syllabus for either Computer Graphics and CAD or Computer Graphic or CAD subject of all branches in all affiliating Universities are more and less same and this book is framed nicely to cover syllabus of all the Universities at all level. Each chapter of this book could be covered within one week of a semester (approximately three lecture hours), with extra time allocated to longer chapters such as Chapter 2, 5 and 9.

This book is drafted nicely like a story book. It starts from basics and each chapter of this book is well connected with previous ones. Chapter 1 introduces Computer Graphics and CAD. It starts from discussion on hardware and software of computer system required to understand Computer Graphics and CAD. Further, definition, need and benefits of Computer Graphics as well as CAD and its modelling practices along with CAM/CIM/CAE, Data communication and Internet, Animation and Multimedia, Simulation has been discussed. Chapter 2 discusses the fundamental concepts of Computer Graphics & Object Modelling. It provides an in depth understanding of various geometric shape generating algorithms and area filling techniques. The chapter also illustrates the coordinate representation techniques and explains its significance in 2D transformation. Further the concept of projection and clipping is explained with ample examples. Chapter 3 extends the discussion to 3D by introducing the theory of 3d object representation through hidden surface removal algorithms, illumination and rendering techniques. In addition, general projections, view volume and 3D object clipping are described in this chapter and it is ensured that the context is simple for understanding these concepts. Chapter 4 deals curves and surfaces and its different forms of representation required for geometric modelling. Chapter 5 focus on geometric modelling of different types of curves used in Industries for products design with examples in each section to understand how curve will generate and design graphically. After designing curves, different fitting techniques are discussed to make composite curve of different types in Chapter 6 and Chapter 7 focus on surface modelling and its fitting techniques. Chapter 8 deals with solid modelling by various techniques used in Industries. This chapter also include 2 and 3 dimensional animation, animation systems, the various techniques used in animation and the various application area of animation. Finally, finite element analysis comes in last Chapter which is important and indispensible part of the CAD and computer graphics. This chapter on FEM include basic concepts used in FEM, bending of beams, potential energy approach, finite element formulation, plain stress and plain strain problems, constant strain triangle (CST), isoparametric formulation and one dimensional steady state heat transfer analysis. A sufficient number of solved and unsolved problems have been provided for practice in all the chapters.

Thank you for choosing our book. May you find it stimulating and rewarding.

Authors

Computer Graphics and CAD

1

1.0 INTRODUCTION

The purpose of this book is to explore some of the basic ideas of realistic image generation. This means the creation of images that give the viewer the impression that he or she is looking at a photograph. So, techniques examined here are used in the necessary steps of creating a model of an object, transformation of objects whenever required, lighting that objects and rendering that objects to simulate a real results. This technique is not fully explored because of their sheer complexity; instead, solutions for simple situations are presented for the learners. Examination of techniques for creation of necessary graphs or images of objects come under computer graphics. Computer graphic started with the display of graphs on the screen of cathode ray tube (CRT) of the computer

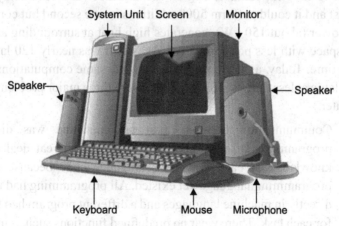

Fig. 1.1 Computer system

system where CRT is the most important elements of any computer graphics and Design. A computer system means working computer as shown in Fig. 1.1. The computer system includes not only the computer hardware and software but user (who operates computer) also. Therefore, in this chapter we will discuss about the silent feature of computer hardware and software and their functions which are useful for producing images in computer graphics and computer aided design (CAD). After then, introduction and related major elements (useful at this level) of computer graphics and CAD are discussed.

1.1   JOURNEY OF COMPUTER SYSTEM AND ITS SILENT FEATURE

Throughout history, human have attempted to design products/devices that would ease the burden of their labours for counting. The finger was the first method used for counting. For further perfection of counting and adding, a machine called ABACUS was invented in china about 400B.C. Until the 19th century, these devices could help only with physical work.

First electronic device without physical work was proposed by British mathematician Charles Babbage (1792-1871). They worked for Royal Astronomical Society. During working in 1822, he proposed the "Difference Engine" and after 10 year "Analytical Engine". Thus, Babbage is considered the "Father of modem computing". Ada king and some employee of U.S. defense department had been working to improve Babbage proposed machine or inventing new machine for many years. It is generally agreed that the first generation of modern computing began in the early 1940s (1940-1955) with the invention of device ENIAC (Electronic Numerical Integrator and Computer) at Moore School of Engineering. Weight of ENIAC was about 27 tons occupied a room 15 m×9 m, contains 18,000 vacuum tubes and 1500 relays. Its speed was fast and it could perform 5000 additions in one second but consumed very high power (about 150 kW), generates high heat at surrounding and occupied more space with less portability. ENIAC's cost was nearly 120 lacs of rupees at that time. Today, a micro processor with the same computational efficiency is available at less that Rs. 50,000. There were three major problems with early computer.

1. Communication between man and machine was difficult. The programming of early computers required a great deal of skill and knowledge of each machine's language code because no standard programming language yet existed. All programming had to be written directly in machine languages and a different program had to be written for each task. There wear no predefined functions such as mathematical symbols to indicate mathematical operations.

2. Maintenance was high and reliability was low.

3. The computer generated tremendous heat.

The second generation computers (1956-1963) took advantage of the invention of transistor in 1948. This small device made the vacuum tube absolute and the size of electronic machinery has been shrinking ever since. This transistor is first applied to computers in 1956. The second generation computer system included components like printer, tape, memory unit, operating system and stared programs etc. These features gave computers the flexibility to widespread use in business and others areas.

The third generation computers (1964-1971) had still great problem of the great of the amount of heat generated, which damaged the computer's sensitive part. In 1958, the Integrated Circuit (IC) solved this problem, which is made by small silicon disk and developed by Jack kilby, Texas Instrument Engineer.

The fourth generation of computing applies to the years between 1971 and the present. By the 1980s, million of components could be squeezed onto a very small size chip by using Large Scale Integrated Circuit (LSIC). Consequently computer continued to get even smaller, cheaper, more powerful, more efficient and more reliable. Today, the microchips stores more information, performs calculation 20 times faster, and is cheaper to manufacture than the previous generation devices. The macro processor has revolutionized the computer world and has made computers affordable for almost every one.

Fifth generation computers are yet to come for every one use which will contain Artificial Intelligence (AI). These computers can understand normal human speech, make a dialogue, learn from their own experience, use visual input, imitate human reasoning and perform inductive and deductive thinking. Japanese research is going on using Ultra Large Scale Integration (ULSI) technology for developing super chip.

1.2 COMPUTER SYSTEM

Computer system is not only fascinating machines but also gives very useful work. Computers are now influencing every sphere of our life in one way or other. Computers are making human life easier and comfortable at every locations. With the help of Computers, one can design, analyse, manupulate and manufacture the product with short span of time accurately in industrial applications. A computer is designed in such a way that it can automatically accept and store input data, process them and produce output results under the directions of a stored program called software. Thus, computer is a tool to increase productivity in our life.

Not all computers are visible. In some machines, small dedicated computers are fitted (called as embedded computers) that are not visible. These embedded computers work behind the curtains in sports and luxury cars, lathe machines, washing machines, televisions and so on. Among the visible computer, the most popular one's are the personal computer, in short known as PC. Computer systems that are available at affordable price and occupy less space is called Personal Computer (PC). Computer is an electronic data processing machine/device that accepts informations, stores it until the information is needed, process the information according to the instruction provided by user and finally returns to the results to the user. In other word, computer has four functions *i.e.*, (*i*) accepts data (*ii*) processes data (*iii*) produces output (*iv*) store results/output for future use. Thus, computer can read, write, compute, compare, store and process large volume of data with high speed, accuracy and reliability but computer cannot think. It stores the instructions given to it and then executes them at a very high speed automatically without manual intervention. It works on stored program concept. Once the data and instruction set called program is fed into computer memory, it reads the instruction and executes them to produce the desired result. Computer consists of two things which are hardware and software.

1.2.1 Hardware and Software

All physical parts of the computer system that we can touch and see also are known as Hardware. Thus, all internal and peripheral devices are called hardware such as CPU, memory devices, input/output devices and peripheral devices etc. Important hardware is discussed in this chapter. Hardware professionals deal with manufacturing, maintenance and repair of computer.

Software is a set of computer programs where program is the set of instructions for the computer system for the effective operation. This program is stored in the memory unit of computer. Software makes "intelligence" to the computer. One can see that without software, hardware is of no use. Thus, software runs computers. Software engineers or programmer or system analyst develop and maintain software. There are three types of software discussed in later sections of this chapter.

1.2.2 Classification of Computers

The computers come in a variety of sizes and shapes and with a variety of processing capabilities. The previous computers are quite large and costly because of a crude technology used. Now with the advent of new technology, the overall size and cost of computer begin to shrink. Today, the complete CPU can be made smaller than a postage stamp. Computer can be classified on the basis of sizes, processor speed, work and brands. Computer can be grouped into following categories as per descending order of sizes:

- Super Computer,
- Mainframe Computer,
- Minicomputer,
- Micro Computer,
- Workstations.

Currently supercomputer is the word's fastest and most powerful. Generally those computers which work with the speed of 5 to 100 million instructions per second (MIPS) can fall under super computers. Super computer are generally used for networking of computers for scientific computations, control of space satellite, banks, railway and flight traffics and reservation etc. For examples, account in a branch bank available in different locations can be controlled by a supercomputer placed in head office. Similarly Airlines and railways traffics control and its reservation are simplified by supercomputer.

The mainframes computer is a large generally housed in controlled environments which are often used to solve complex engineering and scientific problems such us dynamic of fluid, transfer of heat and stress-strain analysis. With the use of special work station mainframe can be used for running machines in built with CAD software shown in Fig. 1.2. IBM mainframe is 50 year old today.

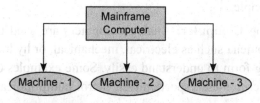

Fig. 1.2 Mainframe computer for running CAD machines.

The main difference between a super computer and a mainframe is that super computers can execute a single program faster than a mainframe and mainframes can support more simultaneous programs at a time.

Minicomputers lie between micro computer and mainframes in size and power. The mini computer is less powerful than a mainframe but it is capable to support 4 to about 200 users simultaneously. As compare to micro computer, mini computer is 5 times faster than micro computer having CPU speed of approximately 100 to 500 kilo instruction per second.

Micro computers are presently available in following three types:

(*i*) **Desktop Computer:** A personal or micro-mini computer sufficient to fit on a desk (Fig 1.1).

(*ii*) **Laptop Computer:** A portable computer complete with an integrated screen and keyboard. It is generally smaller in size than a desktop computer and larger than a notebook computer (Fig 1.3).

Fig. 1.3 Laptop Computer

(*iii*) **Palmtop Computer:** These computers are the hand-sized computers. Digital Diary, Notebook and PDAs are also coming in this category. Palmtops have no keyboard but the screen serves both as an input like key board and output device like monitor.

Workstations mean a desktop computer generally available in offices and banks. Workstations can be classified by following category on the basis of working principle.

(*a*) **Analog Computer:** Analog computers are used to convert physical phenomena such as electrical, mechanical, or hydraulic quantities into analog form to understand easily. Some examples of analog computer are thermometer, speedometer, petrol pump indicator and multimeter etc.

(*b*) **Digital Computer:** Digital computer performs any calculations and logical operations in terms of quantities which is represented as digits, usually in the binary number system (Fig 1.1 and 1.3).

(*c*) **Hybrid Computer:** This is a combination of analog and digital computers. Hybrid computer are capable to perform both in digital and analog signals. A hybrid computer offers a cost effective method for performing complex simulations.

Today's, personal computers are now fulfilling the real challenge to mainframe computers. Personal computers are now using to run Computer graphic and CAD software. The basic configuration used in CAD to operate machine for producing desired products is shown in Fig 1.4. CNC Lathes, CNC Milling, CNC Grinding, CNC EDM, CNC Boring, Drilling etc. are some of the CAD machines.

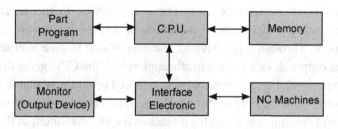

Fig 1.4 CAD Operation

1.2.3 Motherboard

Motherboard is the main circuit board that all the internal components connect to it. Mother board (Fig. 1.4a) provides as sub straight upon which other core component of a system such as CPU, memory devices (RAM, ROM etc.), chip set and expansion slots can reside. It also provides electrical connection between various components directly in the system. Other components may be found directly on the motherboard or connected to it through a secondary connection. The other important word in computer is computer's bus which is a collection of wires through which data is transmitted from one part of a computer to another.

Fig. 1.4(a) Mother Board

1.2.4 Processor: Central Processing Unit (CPU)

The CPU is the hardware device in a computer that executes all of the instructions from the software and called processor in computing system. In terms of computing power, the CPU is the most important element of a system.

The main function performed in the CPU is arithmetic and logic functions. The CPU is the device that interprets and executes instructions received through inputs devices and communicates the results to the external world through output devices/peripheral devices. These are similar to the sensory organs of human being which control activities of human body with the outside environment. Through input devices, the user is able to give instruction to the CPU. The output device is a means through which the CPU gives the results of the computations. The computer works on stored program available in memory of computer. With the help of this program, sequence of operation is generated by CPU and continues to do so till it reaches the end statement of the program. The flow of information in the CPU is shown in Fig 1.5.

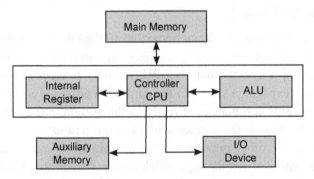

Fig. 1.5 Basic Configuration of CPU.

CPU contains three main parts which are controller units, ALU (Arithmetic and logic unit) and internal resisters. Controller unit (CU) is an electronic circuit which selects, interprets and executes instructions with the help of ALU and registers. Controller unit extracts instructions from memory and decodes and executes them, calling on the ALU when necessary. ALU is an also electronic circuit which performs arithmetic (*i.e.,* calculation etc) and logic operations (*i.e.,* comparisons etc.). In other words, ALU works like brain works in human being, therefore, in broader sense, CPU is called brain of computer. ALU of CPU works at very high speed and executes millions of instructions per second (MIPS), therefore in broader sense, the speed of the CPU operation is traditionally measured in terms of MIPS. The CPU also contains a number of internal registers to store data temporarily during the execution of the program. The number of registers differs from processor to processor. CPU is generally terms as processor. Depending upon the type of CPU, these registers could be 8, 16, 32 or 64 bit long word size where 64 bits word-size register is the most popular in Computer graphics and CAD. Register can also control the electricity consumption and heat dissipation.

The CPU is inserted directly into a CPU socket, pin side down, on the motherboard. With the advance in LSI and VLSI technology it becomes possible to build the whole CPU on a single 1C. A CPU of a digital computer fabricated as a single circuit (called chip) is termed as microprocessor. Intel 4004 (4-bit) was the first microprocessor developed by the Intel Corporation. The important aspect to be considered with the microprocessor is the speed with which they operate, termed the system clock rate. Clock rate for microprocessor are ranges from 1 MHz to 1 GHz. The world first 8-bit microprocessor *i.e.,* Intel 8008 was developed again by Intel Corporation. Other microprocessor manufacturing organizations are IBM, silicon graphics, Hewlett packed and Sun Ultra etc.

For typical CAD/CAM computers, microprocessor should be atleast 32 bits, but 64 bit size is preferred, with a clock rate above 600 MHz.

1.2.5 Storage Devices in Computer System

Storage devices is a hardware devices that are used for the storage of data called memory. For execution of programs, computer uses this data. Memory can be classified as given below (Fig 1.6).

1. Primary or main memory.

2. Secondary or auxiliary memory.

Primary or main memory is just a part of Central Processing Unit (CPU) whereas the secondary or auxiliary memory is external to the CPU. Primary memory or main memory of the computer is a semi-conductor memory. It stores programs and data which are currently needed by the CPU. Secondary, or auxiliary memory is a magnetic memory such as hard disks and floppy disk etc. The secondary memory is employed for bulk storage of programs, data and other information. It has much larger capacity than the main memory.

1.2.5.1 Primary or Main Memory

Traditionally, main memory cell are formed by small magnetic core of about 15 mm in size which was would around thin material of wires. By magnetizing, they obtain a specific orientation, which would not be erased even when the electric supply is put off. However, above type of memory system is very expensive and is now hardly used in computer system due to the availability of semi-conductor memory for same purpose with less size. In semi-conductor memory, the memory locations are organized as a series of small on/off switches. Advancement of technology in the semi-conductor industry has decreased the cost of the memory units, alongwith raising their capacity for storage. There are two types of primary memory or main memory *i.e.,* RAM and ROM and its detailed classification are shown in Fig 1.6.

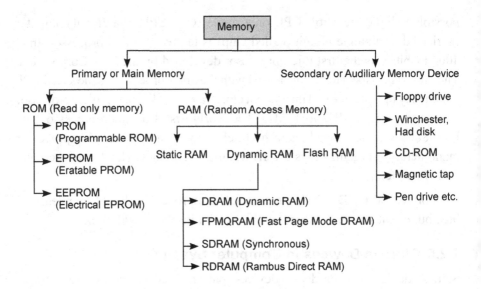

Fig. 1.6 Storage Devices (Memory).

1.2.5.1.1 RAM (Random Access Memory/Read-Write Memory)

RAM (*Random Access Memory*) is where data is stored that's being accessed by the CPU. RAM chips may be either static or dynamic or flash. In static RAM, the information is to written only once whereas in dynamics RAM (DRAM), written information can be continuously refreshed even though there may be no change in it. There are four types of DRAM in which synchronous dynamic RAM (SDRM) is generally used in PC because it is cheap and fast. RAM is a

Fig. 1.7 RAM storage devices.

volatile memory unit. It gets washed out the moment when the machine is going switched off (Fig. 1.7). RAM is used as a temporarily data storage device which need to be updated or erased several times. Professional persons work generally on RAM for writing, storing and updating data in computers and for running part programs in-manufacturing industries. Part programs for running CNC lathes or CNC milling are stored in RAM because part program will be different for manufacturing of different products. The machine should be equipped with enough RAM to store and process longest possible programs. In addition to RAM, the machine also contains hardware and software necessary to read and interpret the coded program for obtaining the desired movements in the machine.

1.2.5.1.2 ROM

Read Only Memory (ROM): Fig. 1.8 is a type of storage medium of any personal computers (PCs) and other electronic devices that can permanently store data and applications within it. ROM is an integrated circuit programmed with specific data for future use when it is manufactured. Thus ROM is a non-volatile memory. It stores information permanently which can be read any number of times unless the information is deliberately erased or overwritten. There is no need of power supply to retain the information fed into ROM. Therefore, ROM is used for store information for repetitive functions such as on online help, default parameters and operating instruction (operating software). This information is stored in ROM at the time of manufacturing the computer machine in the factory. Thus, most of the system software is normally provided in the ROM. They remain available to the user for the life time of the machine even if power is removed or the machine is down. This is the reason why permanent information is stored in ROM. Data stored in ROM is unchangeable and requires a special operation to change.

Fig. 1.8 ROM storage device.

1.2.5.2 Secondary Memory or Auxiliary Memory

Secondary memory is used for the permanent storage of data required for computers. There is no need of power supply to retain the data. Data stored in secondary memories can be used in future. One can take his data from one place to another with the help secondary memory. Some of the secondary storage devices (Fig. 1.9) are discussed below.

1.2.5.2.1 Floppy Diskette

The floppy disk is made from flexible plastic material is shown in Fig. 1.9. The base is coated with an iron oxide which is recording materials. Data is recorded as tiny magnetic spots. The read/write head of a floppy disk comes under direct contact during processing with the help of floppy drive and that's why floppy disk gets worn due to frequently use. The floppy disk can store upto 10M bytes per floppy. The standard sizes available now-a-days are 5.25 inch and 3.5 inch.

1.2.5.2.2 Hard Disk or Magnetic Disk

Storage capacity of hard disk is very much higher than floppy disk. The hard disk (Fig. 1.9) is a spindle of magnetic disks, thus it is also called Magnetic Disk. Magnetic characteristic in hard disk is responsible to record and store information. Information recorded to the hard disk remains intact after turn the computer off because the data is stored magnetically. This is one of the important differences between the hard disk and RAM. Hard disk in a PC is often called the C drive. When we install programs or save data on computer, the information is typically written and stored on C drive *i.e.,* hard disk. Hard disk has been extensively used because of its low access time, low cost and compact sizes. Storage size of hard disk presently available is from 6GB to 180 GB. Data is stores on both surfaces in a number of invisible concentric circles which are called tracks. Each track can store a fixed number of bytes. The hard disk *i.e.,* C-drive is housed inside the hard drive in the computer system. Thus, hard drive is used to transmits data back and forth between the CPU and the hard disk. Winchester hard disk is more popular.

1.2.5.2.3 Magnetic Tape

Magnetic tape (Fig. 1.9) is a long and narrow plastic strip coated with thin magnetic material. Nearly all recording tape is of this type, whether used for recording audio or computer data storage. Devices that record and playback audio using magnetic tape are generally called tape recorders. A device that stores computer data on magnetic tape can be called a tape drive. The greatest limitation of magnetic tape is the serial nature of storage, necessitating all the tape to be wound before accessing any inside information. Due to this, the magnetic tape can be used only for data exchange or back-up. A 10.5 -inch reel of magnetic tape can store about 180MB of data.

1.2.5.2.4 Compact Disk

Previous storage devices are generally based on magnetic principal. Advancement of new technology, very large capacity storage devices are developed based on the optical technology. Compact disc (CD) is one of them. The major disadvantage of this technology is that once the disk is written, it cannot be erased. For evaporation of data, a high density laser is required which is very difficult to provide in computer system and also it will be expensive.

As a result, it becomes like a ROM and hence one device is CD-ROM. In this technology, a small aluminium compact disk of 12 cm in diameter contains a number of pit in the range of about 1.5 microns. Disk thickness and center hole diameter are 1.2 mm and 15 mm respectively. Each pit can store data. There are various formats of CD such as Audio CD, CD-ROM and Video-CD (VCD) etc. CD-ROM can be used for storage where writes once and read much information are required. Thus, these devices cannot used as a regular auxiliary device with the computer but can used for only data base purpose. Presently, commercial drives are available which can be store 650-680 MB.

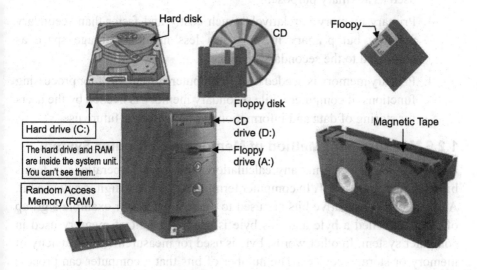

Fig. 1.9 Auxiliary memory or secondary memory device.

1.2.5.2.5 Digital Video Disk (DVD)

Now-a-day, recently developed storage medium *i.e.*, DVD (digital video disk) is becoming popular. DVD is similar to CD in size, thickness and looking, but its storage capacity is increased upto 17GB and even higher than this by reducing track pitch, pit length etc. Both CD and DVD are optical discs, which mean that the data stored on them is read by a laser. The laser goes over the pits and lands embedded onto the disc surface, and communicate a signal to the reading device that turns it into a digital code of 1s and 0s. CD is coated with one layer of polycarbonate followed by metal layer while DVD consists of 2 polycarbonate discs glued together, each 0.6 mm thick (0.6+0.6 mm =1.2mm). DVD technology uses a much thinner laser, which results in smaller and narrower pits. This allows packing more pits and lands onto surface of a DVD compared to a CD. This is the reason, DVD has more storage capacity than CD and used for holding cinemas, games, business information, eventually replacing CD-ROM. Memory card is also a secondary memory storage device.

1.2.5.2.6 Difference between Primary Memory and Secondary Memory

1. Primary memory is purely made of electronic devices (such as either by transistor or capacitor) while secondary memory is not purely made of electronic devices (such as either by transistor or capacitor).

2. Primary memory is called main memory because it can directly communicate with CPU while secondary memory is called auxiliary memory because it cannot directly communicate with CPU and it is used as auxiliary purpose.

3. Primary memory is relatively much costly and faster than secondary memory but primary memory has less memory storage space as compared to the secondary memory.

4. Primary memory is needed by the computer system itself for processing functions of computer while secondary memory is needed by the users for storing of data and information permanently for future use.

1.2.6 Measurement Method of Memory in Computer System

Digital computer performs any calculations and logical operations in terms binary digits *i.e.,* 0 and 1. In computer terminology, binary digit is called a bit. A number of consecutive bits are used to make a byte. For example a group of 8 bits is called a byte and this byte is used as a unit of memory used in computer system. In other words, byte is used for measurement of capacity of memory or storage devices. The number of bits that a computer can process at a time in parallel is called its word length. The 8, 16, 32 or 64 bits are commonly used word lengths. Computer with longer word length are more powerful, it means word length of a 32-bit computer is more powerful than 8 and 16 bits computers. These days, 64 bits word size is the most popular in computer graphic and CAD/CAM. Size/capacity of memory is represented by byte or KB or MB or GB and some useful representation is given below

$$1 \text{ Kilobyte (KB)} = 1024 \text{ bytes} = 2^{10} \text{ bytes}$$

$$1 \text{ Megabytes (MB)} = 1024 \text{ KB} = 1024 \times 1024 \text{ bytes} = 2^{20} \text{ byte}$$

$$1 \text{ Gigabytes (GB)} = 1024 \text{ MB} = 1024 \times 1024 \times 1024 = 2^{30} \text{ bytes}$$

1.2.7 Input/output and Peripheral Devices

Input, output and peripheral devices are also known as hardware of computer system. The input devices generally used for data inputs are the keyboard, mouse, trackball, joystick, light pen, scanner, digital camera, web camera, touch pad/screen, bar code reader available in general store, microphone, biometric devices, optical mark reader (used for answer sheet marking purpose), Bluetooth, magnetic card reader (used in colleges, shops, stations etc.), magnetic ink character reader (used in banks) and the digitizer etc. This input device controls the cursor in single execution. The keyboard is the most basic input device for all computers is shown in Fig 1.10. Keyboard has a controller (like 8042 or 8048) to check any key is pressed or released. If any key remains pressed for more than half a second, the controller sends a repeat signals at specific intervals to the processor (CPU) and images can be seen in the monitor similar to image pressed in key.

The mouse is a pointing or locating hardware device shown in Fig 1.1. Other pointing or locating devices are tablets, trackball and joystick etc which are now-a-day rarely used. Mouse is classified on the three basis of principal of operation *i.e.,* mechanical, optical and opt-mechanical operation. The mechanically operated mouse contains a free floating ball on the underside. When mouse is moved on a plane surface by hand, the ball would also be able to follow the motion of the hand. The motion of the ball is resolved into X and Y direction by means of two rollers pressed against the ball inbuilt in mouse. They in turn control the cursor position to reach at desired point or at icon available on the screen of computer, which can then be used for any desired application by clicking the buttons on the mouse. The LEDs present inside the optically operated mouse (in place of the rubber ball) would reflect the number of grid lines crossed in the X and Y direction. Number of grid line crossed indicate the distance moved by the mouse which in turn motion of the cursor on the screen of the computer. The life of the optical mouse is high due to no moving parts required for motion of cursor. Light pen is shaped like a pen with a wire connected to it to interact directly with the monitor screen. These locating or pointing input devices can be used for positioning a cursor and selecting the icon from the menu displayed on the screen. Now days touch screens are used. Touch screen are even more direct input devices than other devices even than light pens. They are used by simply touching monitor screen with one's finger or pointing devices.

Scanner (Fig 1.11) are used for direct entry of data into the computer. Scanner eliminates the duplication of human effort required to get data into the computer because reduction in human intervention. Two types of scanner *i.e.,* Optical scanners and magnetic ink character readers are generally available.

Important output devices are monitor, plotter, printer, cameras inbuilt in monitor etc. Monitor is a visual display device (shown in Fig 1.1) and most popular output device used for interactive processing. Once the output is finalized on the display device, it can be transferred into hard copy *i.e.,* on papers using printer for future use. Two types of printer *i.e.,* impact and non-impact are available on the basis of operation. Dot matrix and drum printer is impact printer. Inkjet and Laserjet printer is non impact printer shown in Fig. 1.12. Some other useful output devices are speaker and microphone (Fig 1.1).

The important peripheral devices used in computer system are modem/ internet adapter, switches/hub, router and TV tuner card etc.

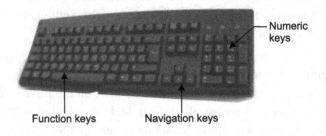

Fig 1.10 Keyboards.

Fig. 1.11 Scanner.

Fig. 1.12 Printer.

1.2.8 Computer Graphics Display Devices and Image Terminology

Display devices (*i.e.,* output devices) are the most important element for CAD and Computer graphics and used for presentation of information in visual or tactile (*i.e.,* touchable) form. Tactile electronic devices displays special kind of letter or text called Braille Display are usually intended for the blind people. Tactile electronic devices use electro-mechanical parts to dynamically update a tactile image (usually of text) so that the image may be felt by the fingers of blind people. Now-a-day's two and three dimensional display devices are commonly used. Two dimensional displays that cover a full area generally in a rectangle are called video displays and examples are Television sets, Computer monitors (Fig. 1.13). Head-mounted display, Broadcast reference monitor, medical monitors etc. Some of the operational techniques used in display devices are discussed below.

1. Cathode ray tube (CRT) display.

2. Plasma panel display.

3. Liquid crystal display (LCD).

Of above three, the CRT displays are extensively used in CAD and Computer graphics inspite of their bulkier size.

Fig. 1.13 Display device used in CAD and Computer graphic.

1.2.8.1 Cathode Ray Tube (CRT) Display

In CRT display as shown in Fig. 1.14, cathode is first heated using current which emits elections, the stream of electron are then accelerated with the help of accelerating system (also called accelerating anodes) and are focussed finally with the help of focusing systems (called focussing anodes) and deflectors onto a point on the display screen coated with phosphorus which gets illuminated when the speeding electrons hit the surface, displaying the point or images. The electron beam is controlled with the help of deflection systems for accessing any point on the surface of the display screen. Changing the current intensity changes the electron beam intensity which in turn changes the intensity of the spot created on the screen. Current intensity and resulted electron beam intensity is controlled by setting voltage levels on the control-grid, which is a metal cylinder that fits over the cathode shown in Fig. 1.14. Since the intensity of light emitted by the phosphor coating coated on screen depends on the number of electrons striking that screen, thus the brightness of a display can be controlled by varying the voltage on the control grid.

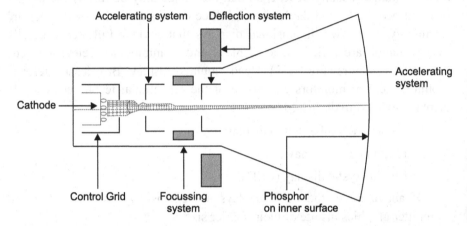

Fig. 1.14 Cathode Ray Tube (CRT) operations.

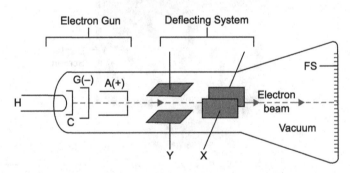

Fig. 1.15 Operation of an electronic gun

Basically two types of image drawing techniques used in graphic displays are given below:

(*i*) Stroke-writing,

(*ii*) Raster scan.

Stroke writing is also called stroke or vector graphics because the display is sent voltage point pairs (X, Y point pairs) and the beam in the CRT draws a line in one stroke from the last point to the current point [Fig 1.16 (*a*)]. Intensity of a point will be proportional to the amplitudes of the input signals. As shown in Fig 1.16 (*a*), we have five pairs of *X*, *Y* point only to define the shape (in this case star) so little memory required but there is need of a computer to generate the points that define the shape to send to the display. Thus, there is need of digital-to-analog converter inbuilt in computer system to convert these digital points to voltages for the CRT which is generally an expensive device. Stroke writing display device is expensive because their digital-to-analog converter contains complex analog circuits that must be trimmed periodically and also contains temperature dependent components that may be damaged soon in overheating. Thus, the stroke graphics method is favoured only when money is no issue. Of course one can prepare a low-cost stroke graphics display using 8-bit digital-to-analog but it will never compete with the digitally derived displays such as raster scan.

Raster scanning techniques is a most popular method for graphics displays in computer graphic and CAD/CAM. Today, all television sets also rely on this technique. In raster scanning, the electron beam emits in CRT is deflected in a weaving pattern that sweeps across the screen of the display device and down many times per second (Fig 1.16 b). The whole display surface is divided into a matrix of small dots called pixel. Pixel is the smallest element for picture element in computer graphic and pixel work as a shorthand (or stenography). A pixel is one location in an image on the computer screen (or in a printout). The pixels of an image are organized into a two-dimensional grid on the screen of display device that is called a frame buffer. In other words, the frame buffer is used as a two dimensional array of pixels in display system. Now graphics hardware of computer system is made for enough memory storage capacity to store multiple frame buffers, which is useful for animation and game programs. All frame buffers can be used simultaneously as and when required. The electrons beams scan (observe/judge) the whole display surface area line by line and sensitize the pixels according to lines/images to be drawn. There are upto 512 of horizontal lines on the TV screen. Upto 1024 points/pixels can be defined on a single one horizontal line. It means, 1024×512 (=524288) pixels are available on the TV screen. If the computer is properly synchronized to the sweeping electron beam, it can turn it on at any point in the displays *X*, *Y* plane and thus form a dot on the screen. Thus, the raster scanned television (TV) screen can be imagined as a super dense matrix of about 1024 dots by 512 lines that are sent to the TV screen line by line. Thus, if the electron beam is turned on at specific locations on the screen one can get a shape made of tiny points. Raster scan method of drawing graphics/images may seem even more complex than stroke graphics, but it turns out that raster scanning seriously reduces the need for analog circuits (digital-to-analog converter) which is very costly and allows a totally digital display to be built. Raster scanning requires much more memory than stroke writing because in raster scanning all the dots must be store that makes up a shape rather than just the end points of vectors as in stroke graphics. However, price of memory device is reducing drastically every year; therefore, raster scanning is becoming best approach for low-cost graphics displays. When programs render (refer/prepare/translate) an image that image will not fill the entire screen of the monitor but instead will be drawn in a window opened for that purpose. The pixel within this window is addressed based on their location, instead of their location on the screen. This way program can refer to a particular pixel address and that will always access the same place in the image, even if the user moves the window to a different location on the screen. If an image has no colours it is called gray scale image, and each pixel has one value. If an image has colour, each pixel will use three values to store the range of intensities for the red, green and blue (RGB) color. The screen of the monitor may be divided into large horizontal and vertical divisions by generally 320 divisions and 200 divisions respectively is called screen resolution of 320×200. Screen resolution of 640×200, 760×480 and 1024×760 etc. are also available. During drawing of an inclined line AB on the raster scan monitor, the adjacent pixels closer to the path of the line are addressed and the resulting line appears like a staircase (Fig 1.17) because of less resolution. If the resolution is more, then the line appears smooth. Drawing of horizontal or vertical lines will appear smooth irrespective of the resolution of the screen.

1.2.8.1.1 Frame Buffer

A frame buffer (refresh buffer) is used as memory devices in raster CRT graphics device. The definition of picture can be stored in frame buffer. In the simple case, there may be one memory bit for each pixel in the raster. The picture is built in the frame buffer one bit at a time. The memory bit can be either in 0 or 1 state as shown in Fig. 1.18 for the case of same inclined line drawing as shown in Fig. 1.17. This digital form on the buffer frame is converted into analog form on screen with the help of analog converter. A single bit plane yields a black and white display and colour display can be achieved by using additional bit planes. Fig. 1.19 shows 4 bits plane frame buffer. Since there are four bit planes, there can be 2^4 (=16) combinations. The resulting binary number is interpreted as an intensity level between 0 and $2^4 - 1$ (=15). This is converted into a voltage by the digital to analog converter between 0 (dark) and 15 (full intensity). This means, this arrangement can represent 16 grey levels of color shades. Generally, different colors can be obtained by mixing three primary colors *i.e.,* Red (R), Green (G), and Blue (B). Each bit buffer plane can be used for individual colors (either for Red or Green or Blue). Thus, the arrangement with three bit planes can lead to eight colors as given in Table 1.1 on the screen. To generate more color shades, additional bit planes can be used for each of the three color guns. In a 24 bit plane, 8 bit planes are used for each colour (*i.e.,* $8 \times 3 = 24$). This arrangement can generate $2^8 = 256$ intensities of red, green and blue colors. This when combine together can results in $(2^8)3 = 16,1777,216$ or 16.7 million possible colors.

Aspect ratio in raster scan is the ratio of vertical points to the horizontal points. It helps to produce equal length lines in both directions on the screen.

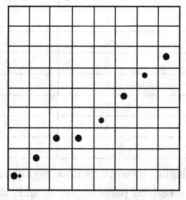

Fig. 1.17 Inclined line on screen with analog state.

0	0	0	0	0	0	0
0	0	0	0	0	0	1
0	0	0	0	0	1	0
0	0	0	0	1	0	0
0	0	0	0	1	0	0
0	0	1	1	0	0	0
0	1	0	0	0	0	0
1	0	0	0	0	0	0

Fig. 1.18 Incline line on buffer frame with digital state.

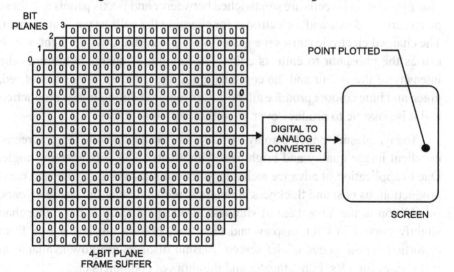

Fig. 1.19 4-bit plan frame buffer for producing colour.

Table 1.1 colour code.

1.	Black	0	0	0
2.	Red	1	0	0
3.	Green	0	1	0
4.	Blue	0	0	1
5.	Yellow	1	1	0
6.	Cyan	0	1	1
7.	Magenta	1	0	1
8.	White	1	1	1

Though CRT display monitor is now highly refined but it is extremely bulky because it has various parts bigger in size, thus CRT Display monitor is not portable. Emitting electrons from cathode requires more current means more heating which create problem to other parts also. Thus, now-a-day's flat screen gets favourable for customers. For small and flat screen, the plasma panel has been found to be useful where plasma is used to display the image.

1.2.8.2 Plasma Panel Display

Plasma Panel Display (PDP) is also called gas discharge display. Plasma is a gas containing a large number of negatively-charged electrons and positively-charged atoms, called ions. A plasma display panel is a collection of very small fluorescent-type lamps called cells. These tiny cells are full of inert ionized gas (a mixture of xenon and neon) and are lined with phosphor. Three cells make up one pixel where one cell has red phosphor, one green phosphor, and one blue phosphor. The cells are sandwiched between x and y-axis panels and these panels are used as x and y electrodes for charging the cells as per requirement. The charged electrode causes the gas in the cell to emit ultraviolet light, which causes the phosphor to emit its color. The amount of charge determines the intensity of the colour and the combination of the different intensities of red, green and blue colours produce all the colors required during image production and it is possible to produce over 16 million different colors.

Today, plasma panel displays (PDP) are available with large screens, excellent image quality and brightness with greater than 160° viewing angle. Due to application of advance technology for manufacturing of PDP and mass production, its cost and thickness/slimness is reducing over the last few years. In addition to the advantage of slimness, a plasma display is flat rather than slightly curved in CRT display and therefore, plasma display is free from distortion on the edges of the screen. Plasma displays are now available in many sizes for TVs, home theater and monitors of computers etc.

1.2.8.3 Liquid Crystal Display (LCD)

Solid, liquid, and gas are the three common states of matter. Liquid crystal is a fourth state of matter that can enter into under the right conditions. In solids, the molecules have both positional and orientation order but in liquids, the molecules do not have any positional or orientation order.

The liquid crystal phase exists between the solid and the liquid phase. In liquid crystal, the molecules have not positional order, but they have a certain degree of orientation order. There are many kinds of liquid crystal. *Nematic* liquid crystal is a common type. Liquid crystal has a number of unique characteristics that makes it very suitable for use in displays. Most of these characteristics that the liquid crystal is an *anisotropic* material, meaning that the properties of the liquid crystals differ depending on what direction they are measured or on what direction electric or magnetic fields are applied.

A liquid crystal display is special thin flat panels that can let light go through it, or can block the light. The panel is made up of several blocks, and each block can be in any shape. Each block is filled with a thin film of liquid crystal and is placed between two plates of glass or transparent plastic typically made of indium tin oxide. Tin oxides make possible to apply an electric field across small areas of the film of liquid crystal. Polarizing filters are usually placed on one or both sides of the glass to polarize (*i.e.,* to restrict) the light entering and leaving the liquid crystal. These polarizers are usually crossed so that no light can be passed through the display. The liquid crystal can modify the polarization of the light in some way that is dependent on the electric field being applied to it. Therefore, it is possible to dynamically create spots where light will get through and spots where light will not get through. Thus, the image on an LCD screen can be created by sandwiching an electrically reactive substance between two sheets of polarizing material/ electrodes. One of the best possible electrically reactive substances is liquid crystal solution. An electric current passed through the liquid crystals causes the crystals to align so that light cannot pass through them. Therefore, each crystal is like a shutter, either allowing light to pass through or blocking the light. The colour of this substance can be changed by increasing or reducing the electrical current intensity.

Liquid crystal displays are often used in battery-powered devices, such as digital watches, because they use very little electricity. LCDs are super-thin displays device that are used in laptop computer screens and flat panel monitors. Smaller LCDs are used in handheld TVs, calculator, digital watches, mobiles, portable computer, notebook computer and video game devices etc. The main advantage of LCD displays is that they take up less desk space and are lighter. Currently, however, they are also much more expensive.

The LCDs are light weight and consume less power than CRT which makes them attractive for portable computers. However, their display being dependent on the ambient light, they are still not used extensively in CAD and computer graphics applications.

In addition to above display devices, research is also going on for development of Carbon nanotubes display, Quantum dot display, Interferometric modulator display. In some places, the multiplexed display technique is used to drive most display devices. Similar to 2-dimensional displays, some of the 3-dimensional display devices are swept-volume display, varifocal mirror display, emissive volume display, laser display, holographic displar, light field display and volumetric display

1.3 TYPES OF SOFTWARE

Software refers to a set of programs (made in programming language of computer) for the effective operation of a data processing of computer system. In other words, computer software consists of the instructions and data that the computer manipulates to perform various data processing tasks. Types of software are shown in Fig 1.18.

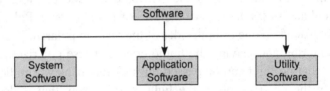

Fig. 1.18 Types of Software.

1.3.1 System Software

System software of a computer consists of a collection of programs designed to control the operation of the computer system. System software is an indispensable part of computer system. Its function is to compensate for the difference that exists between users needs and the capability of the hardware. The program included in a systems software package is referred to as operating system which is used to manage all the resources and operations of the computer. It also takes care of hardware functioning. On the basis of facility and functioning provided by them, operating system can be classified as follows.

(*a*) Single user operating system,

(*b*) Multi user operating system.

Single user operating system allow only one user to work at a time on the computer such as MS-DOS (Microsoft disc operating system) but multi user operating system allow more than one user at the same time to work on the same computer such as UNIX, XENIX; LINUX, VMS, Windows NT etc. This operating system allocates memory in such a way that many users can work simultaneously without disturbing each other. It also allocates the processing time in such a way that all user gets a very quick response from the machine. This is the reason; it is also called time sharing operating system.

1.3.2 Application Software

Application software refers to program or set of programs that perform specific processing applications such as preparation of marks sheets, payroll packages, and inventory control procedures. There are many application software used for different purposes some are as follows:

(*a*) World processing software such as MS-WORD, WORDSTAR, SOFTWORD etc.

(*b*) Spread sheet software such as LOTUS, MS-EXCEL, and SOFT-CALC. etc.

(*c*) Data base management software such as ORACLE, FOXBASE etc.

(*d*) Graphics software such as AUTOCAD, PHIGHS, etc.

(*e*) Some CAD/CAM software are Solidworks, Pro-E, CATIA and CNC simulator. MATLAB (programming, modelling and simulation tool designed by Mathworks), Hyperworks and Autocast (metal casting and simulation software) are also application software.

1.3.3 Utility Software

Utility software is used for the maintenance of the system software. This software helps in the better utilization of our software. Some of the utilities are Backup, Defrag and Scandisk.

1.4 PROGRAMMING LANGUAGES

The next important segment of the software is programming languages, through which the software development takes place. Normally, people interact with each other through communication and communication with each other is carried out through languages like English and Hindi etc. On the same pattern, communication with the computers is carried out through a language made in such a way that computer machine can understand and accordingly perform functions. Here, the language must be understood both by the user and the machine. Computer runs on the basis of set of programs (called software) and that program is made using suitable language. Therefore, language used for preparing program to run the computer is called programming language. Just as every language like English, Hindi, Tamil, and Punjabi has its grammatical rules, similarly every computer language must be bound by rules known as the SYNTAX. The meaning given for a particular SYNTAX in programming language can be defined as SIMANTIC. The programming language may be classified as shown in Fig 1.19.

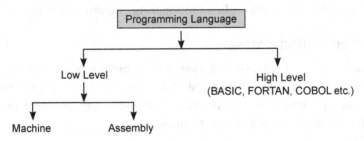

Fig. 1.19 Programming language.

Machine and assembly language comes under low level language. Machine language is called lowest level language because processor (CPU) itself uses this language directly to handle operations. Assembly language is also low level as it is very close to machine language. Thus, Lower level languages can be called very operation based languages. Low level languages were developed first, and high level languages came along later.

1.4.1 Low Level Language (LLL)

(*a*) Machine language is the only language understood directly by the computer because programming made by this language is written by only binary numbers *i.e.,* 0's and 1's. LLLs are always static, and never have garbage collection. LLLs have the advantage that the programmer is able to tune the binary machine code to be smaller. Binary machine-code instructions are very hard to remember, write down, or correct that they represent. Therefore, programmers use either an assembly language or a high-level language for programming.

(*b*) An assembly language contains the same instructions as a machine language while programming but the instructions and variables have some names (such as letters and symbols called mnemonics) instead of being just binary numbers. Thus, assembly language makes programming simpler and less time consuming than machine language. It is easier to locate and correct errors in assembly language. When a program is written in language other than machine language, the computer will not understand this; therefore, it must be translated into machine language before it is executed. The task of translation is done by software. A program (called software) which translates an assembly language program into machine language program is called an assembler.

1.4.2 High Level Language (HLL)

This language uses english letters, symbols, and numeric data called statement to make a program. Thus, program written in HLL is easy to understand. The program written in HLL must be translated into machine language which the computers understand. It can be done by either by using interpreter or compiler. Both interpreter and compiler are the programs, placed in the computer system to translate high level language into machine language. An interpreter reads one statement at a time to translate it into machine code, execute it and then goes to the next statement of the program. On the other hand, compiler is a larger program and occupies more memory space because it reads entire program once or twice and then translate it. Thus, it is costlier program than interpreter. HLL are computer independent, therefore, programming becomes very simple. These languages are problem oriented and offer readability, portability, easy debugging (process of removing errors), easy software development etc.

Some of the HLL are BASIC (beginners all purpose symbolic instruction code), COBOL (common business oriented language), FORTRAN (formula translation), PASCAL, PROLOG, C, C+, JAVA etc., which have higher levels of abstraction and structure than LLL.

1.5 BOOTING IN COMPUTER SYSTEM

Booting is the initial set of operations sequence that the computer performs when it is switched on (turned on) in order to diagnose particular hardware errors and non-volatile storage devices such as ROM in order to run softwares loaded in computer system. There is cold and warm booting in computer. If the computer is in off state and one boot the computer by pressing the power switch 'ON' from the CPU box then it is called as cold booting and if the computer is already 'ON' and any one restart it by pressing the 'RESET' button from the CPU box or Ctrl, Alt and Del key simultaneously from the keyboard then it is called warm booting.

1.6 COMPUTER GRAPHICS AND CAD

There is need to explain why Computer Graphic and CAD are important. Today, manufacturing industry is witnessed for not only a huge modernization in technology but also for acceptance of information and computer technology in large scale. Companies of mobiles, automobile and fashion designing are facing significant challenges to remain competitive in market supplying innovative collections of products at the right price by enhancing their brand image, customer loyalty and business horizons. To open the creativity of the component designers, CAD Technology and Automation is being used more and more in manufacturing industry. Today, with the introduction of CAD/

CAM and 3D technologies with its many software capabilities and Internet tools, the possibilities are now endless.

Manufacturing of free formed/sculptured surfaces of the objects is an important issue in modern industry. Products are designed with sculptured surfaces to make them either look better or function better or both of them. free formed/sculptured surfaces of the computers, laptops, mobiles, telephones, toys, utensils, statue etc., are designed to give better appearance while free formed/sculptured surfaces of aerodynamic parts such as turbine blades, airplane wings are designed to meet functional requirements. The former type of surface is called an aesthetic surface and latter is called functional surfaces. In many cases both aesthetic and functional factors are given either equal importance or one more or less for the products such as body of car is designed to resist wind load as well as to look better for customer satisfaction. Sculpture surface of the products is designed by using geometric modelling. The term geometric modelling is the activity of generating mathematical equations from the description of shape usually given in the form of engineering drawing or stored in the wire frame form in graphics software.

Once a geometric model is generated, according to which suitable algorithm is constructed then it is converted into the program (detailed set of instructions) with the help of programming languages. Program can be written for drawing and design and also for manufacturing with the help of programming languages understandable by computer. These programs are

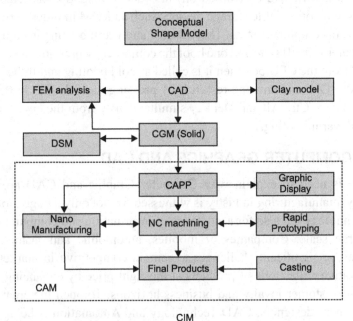

CIM

Fig. 1.20 CIM environments for curved object manufacturing.

called software which is tool to run the computer system. There are CAD/ CAM software also readily available provided CAD/CAM software developer industries for drawing, design and manufacturing of products. In case of CNC (Computer Numerical Controlled), a series of NC codes (like FANUC) generated manually or by the use of CAD software like Idea, CATIA, Proe, Solid works etc. in order to machine the surface of products on CNC machine tools. In case of Rapid Prototyping Machine recently developed, the program made for manufacturing of product is converted in STL (Stereo Lithography) file with the help of converter inbuilt in Rapid Prototyping Machine to make model or pattern for final product by casting/printing process etc. Final products are generally manufactured in CIM (Computer Integrated Machine) environments in modern industry as shown in Fig. 1.20.

Here our problem is to construct a Computational Geometric modelling (CGM) from a describable shape model (DSM) not from conceivable shapes. The term DSM is used for that geometric entity which can be described in terms of simple geometric entities on a drawing or on a CRT screen. There

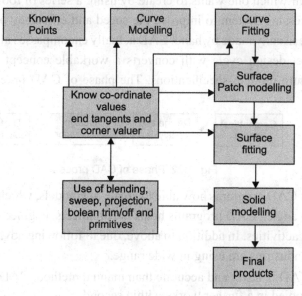

Fig. 1.21 Procedure for Computational geometric modelling of solid.

are four types of geometric entities in a DSM which are point, curve, surface and solid. These geometric entities must be described in terms of exact numeric values as much as possible. This numeric values must be converted into graph and finally object on CRT screen by the use of computer graphics software. In latter chapter, we will first understand the role of computer graphics for generating, manipulating and transformation different shapes/objects. Then we will start from curve modelling and reach upto the solid modelling by following steps as shown in Fig. 1.21. If this solid modelling is accomplice with the use computer then it is called computational geometric modelling.

Modern Industries are using AUTO-CAD software for drafting, CAD/ CAM software (like Ideas, Pro-E, CATIA etc.) for product design and manufacturing. This software has infinite solutions for just giving the end conditions either by mouse or by requesting command by CAD/CAM software in computer system.

1.6.1 CAD/CAM/CIM/CAE

CAD means Computer Aided Design that is a project assisted by a computer. CAD is the use of computer technology to aid in the design of a product. Design means creating something new product by enhancing existing design, altering them to perform new function or simply introducing new concepts. A CAD system permits to develop project functions, mainly based on the design of the item which one wants to create by using a series of tools provided by a data processing system to improve the speed and efficiency of the operations which are usually made by hand. CAD actually encompasses all those activities of product design cycle with converts a workable concept into a ready to manufacture product specifications. The phase of CAD process is shown in Fig. 1.22.

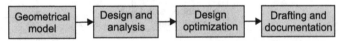

Fig. 1.22 Phase of CAD process.

Most CAD programs now able to create 3D models, which may be viewed from any angle. CAD programs helps the architects, engineers, and designers in design activities. In addition to above, due to following advantages of CAD, modern industries are using in wide range.

1. CAD is faster and accurate than manual method. CAD drawing can be copied in a further works within second.

2. Manipulation of attributes and dimensions of drawing elements is possible. Geometric properties of products can be calculated

3. Animation, simulation and Analysis (FEA) of object are possible.

4. It can create data base for manufacturing like CNC programming program of Robots, process, planning etc.

Today, CAD systems exist for Windows, Linux and UNIX etc.

CAM (Computer Aided Manufacturing) is the use of software to control the machine tools and related machinery for manufacturing of products. CAM can be used in all range of production such a mass production, batch production and job shop production. Traditionally, CAM has been considered as a numerical control (NC) programming tool, wherein 2D or 3D models of components generated in CAD software are used to generate G-code to drive computer numerically controlled (CNC) machine tools for manufacturing of components. Thus, a CAM system employ computer for two basic purposes:

(*i*) Monitoring and control

(*ii*) Supporting applications for Manufacturing

The phase of CAM process is shown in Fig. 1.23.

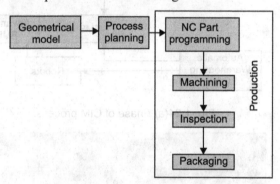

Fig. 1.23 Phase of CAM process.

CAM improves productivity and reliability which provides greater design freedom and operating flexibility, reduce lead time, maintenance, scrap and rework, allow better management control. All the above advantages when properly translated would mean a lower total cost and consequently higher final earnings.

CIM (Computer-integrated manufacturing) is the integration of all computers involve in the individual processes to exchange information with each other and initiate actions. Through the integration of computers, manufacturing can be faster and less error-prone, although the main advantage is the ability to create automated manufacturing processes. In CIM environment, the initial design is often modified several times based on the data from analysis and optimization. Typical phase and environment of CIM in Industry is shown in Fig. 1.24(*a*) and (*b*) respectively.

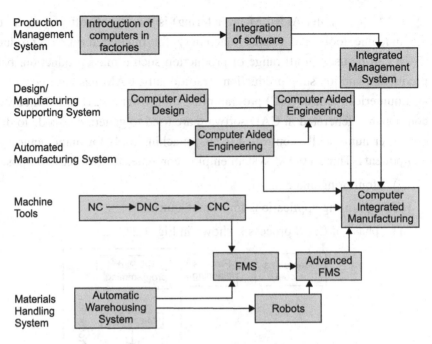

Fig. 1.24(*a*) Phase of CIM process.

Fig. 1.24(*b*) CIM environment in Industry.

CAE (Computer-aided engineering) is the broad usage of computer software to aid in engineering analysis tasks. Engineering analysis includes Finite Element Analysis (FEA), Computational Fluid Dynamics (CFD), Multi body dynamics (MBD) and optimization. This analysis is used to find that design of products which are acceptable for both producers and users with their satisfaction.

Now many industries are fully automated using CAD, CAM, CIM and CEA modules. Thus, automation involves all the processes of conceptualizing, designing, prototyping, analyzing and actual manufacturing with Computer's assistance without direct human activity in the process.

1.6.2 Geometric Modelling in CAD and Computer Graphics

Geometry is pure mathematics of points, lines, curves and surfaces and geometric modelling is the collection of methods used to define the above said shapes and other geometric characteristics of an object. In geometric modelling, we make mathematical model to define the shape of a real object or to simulate some process by the use of computer. Thus, it is a computer aided operation. The major components or architecture of geometric modelling are:

1. A computer hardware and Software for Geometric modelling (including the model builder).
2. A user interface graphic devices and a display generator for creating the graphic output.
3. A data base for storing the model and
4. Application programs etc.

The term geometric modelling was first use in the early 1970s with the rapid development of CAD and CAM. Now it is applying most effectively in above areas. In addition to above, robotics, computer vision and artificial intelligence are also applying geometric modelling capabilities.

Generally, we classify geometric elements into two ways, first are nameable elements (describable shapes) and second are un-namable (free form/sculptured shapes and conceivable shapes). The nameable elements are classical geometry like straight lines, planes, circles, spheres, parabola, hyperbola, ellipses etc. These shapes are easily defined by classical mathematics. But classical mathematics does not provide adequate methods for creating new free form or sculptured curves and surfaces that will satisfy various design criteria for producing complex objects. Today, there is need of special properties of shapes such as smoothness, fairness (means absence of kinks) and continuity. These types of non classical and un-namable curves and surfaces are frequently using to create today's products. To avoid difficulties of classical method, another method is come into use which is geometric modelling. In geometric modelling, we describe the curves or surfaces into parametric polynomial vector value form which can be use to define all kind of geometric elements including complex elements discussed in chapter 4-8.

There are three distinct aspect of geometric modelling. First aspect is representation of curves and surfaces discussed in chapter 4, in which physical shapes of a non-existent object are given and compute a mathematical approximation once. In this, model must be suitable for analysis and evaluation. Second is design/modelling of curves, surfaces and solids discussed in chapter 5-8, in which new shape is created to satisfy some operational or aesthetic objectives. After selecting a specific design, use its geometric model to guide the manufacture for production of objects. Third aspect is rendering, in which at any point, the geometric model provides information for rendering visual images of the object, including engineering drawings and computer graphics displays.

The geometric modelling are using in CAD/CAM where computers is used to compute and control the cutter motions of machine tools during machining. For these, special language is required which is computer compatible format to define shape of an object. This descriptive shape information is then transformed into instruction for computer controlled machine tools. This machine tool is called numerical controlled (NC) machine. For these various scientists worked to develop methods to define shapes of objects.

1.6.3 Geometric Modelling Methods

Generally, two types of modelling methods are adopted for product design, first an additive and second subtractive. Additive modelling is the process of building the block by assembling many simpler objects. Subtractive modelling is the process of removing pieces from a given object to create new objects. For example, creating a cylindrical hole in a sphere or a cube is subtractive modelling. Both modelling are adopted by CAD software. Geometry of objects created by above said method is defined by geometric modelling. It is again noted that geometric modelling is the mathematical representation of curves and surfaces. These techniques have been implemented with computers. Objects are described analytically with respect to a coordinated system and are manipulated in space to obtain the desired form, shape and view of objects. Typical pictorial representation of the curves, surfaces and solids is shown in Fig 1.25.

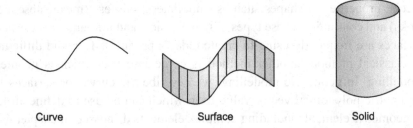

Curve   Surface   Solid

Fig. 1.25 Representation of curve, surface and solid.

To yield accurate representations of engineering models with intricate details of objects, we need to use mathematical tools to provide a concise description of the object. Here geometric modelling provides a means of representing part geometry in graphical representation. The introduction of computer controlled fabrications systems, especially Numerical Controlled Machine (CNC) tools some 40 year ago, created the need for electronic representation of product data. There are varieties of geometric modelling methods available and used in the industry for the variety of functions. They are listed below:

1. Wire frame modelling
   (*i*) 2D wire frame modelling,
   (*ii*) 3D wire frame modelling,
2. Surface modelling
3. Solid modelling

1.6.3.1 Wire Frame Modelling

In this method, an objects is represented by its edges only. In other words, a wire frame model is simply an appropriate collection of inter connected wires or slander sticks.

1.6.3.1.1 2D Wire Frame Modelling

This is first generation CAD tools used for 2D drafting which is similar to drawing used by draftsmen in the drawing office. This modelling method is used to represent 2D graphic primitives such as lines, arcs, text, symbols etc. in an electronic format. This is perhaps most popular and easiest way to model simple parts because it is easy to understand. The main disadvantage of 2D wire frame modelling is the inability to define more complex 3D objects and to handle real industrials design problems.

1.6.3.1.2 3D Wire Frame Modelling

This method is used for modelling of both 2D and 3D complex objects. In this, complete object is represented by a number of lines with their end point coordinates (x, y, and z) and connectivity relationships. This method overcomes the difficulties faced in 2D wire frame modelling. It appears simple but there is an ambiguity possible in three dimensional representations of objects as shown in Fig. 1.26. This figure shows three passages through the object. Another deficiency is the lack of contour or profile information for surfaces inferred between the wire frame lines and curves. Again wire frame model do not contain volume data, which makes them unsuitable for RP and CNC machine which are adopted in modern industries.

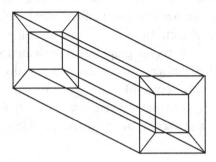

Fig. 1.26 Wire frame Ambiguity.

1.6.3.2 Surface Modelling

Surface modelling creates 3D objects by joining surfaces together. Surface modelling requires wire frame primitives to generate surfaces. The user enters the vertices of lines as in wire frame models to define the boundaries of each surface, and then surfaces are filled within boundaries. Surface modelling's are less ambiguous and more complete representations than their wire frame counter parts. Solid represented by surface modelling gives clear understanding for manufacturing point of view *i.e.,* can generate cutter path for NC machine easily. Unfortunately, surface models define only the outside geometry of objects. They do not store any information about their topology and can only by regard as a set of surfaces belonging to one object. Thus, if one edge is common to two surfaces, this information is not store in the model. This leads to the existence to gaps between the surfaces which mean that surface models cannot define closed volumes. To use surface models for NC machining and RP machines tools, these gap must be removed, which can be very difficult or even impossible in surface modelling. Surface modelling also does not give the interior information and properties of objects such as mass and type of materials etc. which are necessary for NC machining. Thus, this model as a complete technique for constructing a solid is extremely tedious and is not generally attempted.

But, these facilities would be frequently used in modelling for specific non-analytical surfaces called sculptured surfaces which is used in the car bodies, ship hulls and aerodynamic parts. There are a number of mathematical techniques available for handling these surfaces such as Spline, Bezier, B-Spline, NUB, NURBS, Coon patches etc. discussed in later chapters.

Surface modelling is different from solid modelling. Surface modelling deals only with individual surfaces whereas solid modelling deals with entire solid shapes. A box created by surface modelling comprises six surfaces whereas by solid modelling comprises a solid object with six sides. Surface models cannot be unioned or subtracted as can solid models. Surface modelling is particularly well suited for drawing complex 3-D meshes as might be found on a surface profile map, or for the transition area between an airfoil and the fuselage on an aircraft.

1.6.3.3 Solid Modelling

Solid modelling is a relatively new comer. It is intended to overcome the limitations of the 2D /3D wire frame and surface modelling when representing and analyzing 3D objects. The aim of solid modelling is to create unambiguous objects and its complete geometric representation. Solid construction technique in 3D is called Solid Modelling or primitive Instancing or constructive solid geometry (CSG). In this method, a number of 3D solids are provided as primitives. Some typical primitive are blocks, wedges, cylinders, cones, tours, pipes and so on. Using solid modelling software, solid models are created by joining together or unioning above basic primitive shapes or by defining a shape as a polyline and extruding it into solid shapes. Solid primitives may also be subtracted from one another. For example, to create a hole in a solid box, draw a solid cylinder of suitable length and diameter, then subtract by cylinder of same length and small diameter from the box. The result will be an open volume in the shape of a hole. Thus, complex objects can create by adding subtracting the primitive. To make a complex objects, Boolean operations like union, intersection and differences are also used. The advantage of solid modelling is that each body is represented as a single object and not as a complex collection of surfaces. As information is stored in their database, due to which there models are complete and unambiguous. Detailed description of solid modelling is given in chapter 8.

1.6.4 Need of Geometric Modelling

In product design, the concept of a product originates in the mind of design engineer's. If it is to be translated into reality, he needs to present it in a relevant form for the manufacturing engineer so that manufacturing engineer can understand and carry out the necessary operations on it for its production. For this purpose, design engineer generate a geometric model for object which must be clear for manufacturing. This geometric model can perform various functions.

1. Drafting for products such as image production, provide dimensions etc.

2. Design analysis such as calculation of areas, volumes, mass etc.

3. Analysis of assembles, finite element, mechanics, tolerances etc.

4. Manufacturing analysis such as process, NC data generation etc.

5. Production requirement planning analysis such as material, resources, scheduling requirement.

6. Inspection and quality control of products.

From above function of geometric modelling we see that study of geometric modelling is very important and here design of shapes and finite element analysis using geometric modelling are discussed in the coming chapters.

1.7 COMPUTER GRAPHICS AND ITS BENEFITS

One of the important works in CAD system is to manipulate geometric elements or drawings by the use of computer graphics software and hardware. Some of the required components of the computer graphic display with manipulation techniques and its facilities are discussed in this book.

Computer graphics is the use of computer to define, store, manipulate, interrogate and present pictorial output on monitor or screen. The computer prepares and presents stored information to an observer in the form of pictures by the use of graphics technique. Thus the end product of computer graphics is a picture. Here picture is used in its broadest sense to mean any collection of lines, points, texts etc. which is displayed on a graphics device such as monitor. There was no control by the observers over the pictures being presented in earlier computer graphics devices. Advance computer technologies have made interactive computer graphics a practical tool. In interactive graphics, the observer can influence the picture as it is being presented *i.e.,* the observer interacts with the picture in real time. Interactive graphic is an important component of CAD providing a window through which the communication with the computer can be realized. Such systems which enable communication between the human operators and the computer are called "user friendly" computer. In an interactive graphics session, the user constructs a geometric model or figures by specifying points, lines, arcs, and circles on the screen. When command is used, the software will request additional data if needed. There is always a help feature which the designer can consult if he is in doubt. Today, in almost all areas, computer graphics are used such as CAD/ CAM, arts, advertisements, education and training, entertainment, functioning government organization, business, industries, science and technology etc.

A major use of computer graphics is in design process particularly in CAD. CAD is the creation and manipulation of pictures on a computer to assist the engineer in design process. With help of computer graphics, CAD is not only used in designing, analyzing and manufacturing but it is also useful in Finite Element Analysis (FEM), Animations and Simulations. CAD software is used to design and develop products by the use of graphics technique called geometric modelling. Geometric modelling also includes scaling, rotation, translation and geometric representation of products. Similarly, CAM software is used to run machine tool to manufacture products with the help of computer. For these CNC machine tools, rapid prototyping machines etc. are developed.

In addition to above benefits, there are other areas for benefits of computer graphics also. Suppose, we have to show the performance of one steel industry such as Steel Authority of India Limited related with profit since from 1970. We required large number of pages to store their huge information of data's of each year regarding production costs, sales costs, fixed cost etc. This large number of pages requires more time to understand it or represent it. This information can easily be represented and understood with the help bar chart or pie chart created by computer graphic tools.

1.8 DATA COMMUNICATION AND INTERNET

Computers need to communicate with printers, terminals and other computers. Some popular devices for transferring digital data are parallel interface device (computer to printer), modems (from one computer to another computer through telephone connection), server, connecting cables using LAN system etc.

The internet is essentially a large number of connected computers through telephone wires and satellites. A computer on the internet can be located anywhere in the world, so you can communicate with someone over the internet no matter where that person lives. The internet contains several different types of information, including newsgroups, World Wide Web, mail check facilities. The information about any thing from any location on screen of monitor through internet in the web is called web pages. A group of web pages is called web site. The first page of a web site is often called the home page.

1.9 ANIMATION AND MULTIMEDIA

Animation is the technique of showing pictures in the form of motion. Animation is the process of design, drawing and layout of pictures for production of photographic sequence that are incorporated in the multimedia products in order to give it a smart appearance. In other words, animation involves the manipulation of still images to create the illusion of movement.

Using computer technology, a sequence of staggered images captured in related positions are made to appear as if they are really moving. Animators may use 2D or 3D animations for gaming, instructional programs etc. Animators must have strong drawing skills.

Multimedia is very combination of text, graphic art, sound, animation and video delivered to us by computer or other electronic means. Technically the term multimedia can be used to refer any combination of visual and audio material from a range of sources into a single presentation. More specifically the term multimedia is used for the combination of materials within a format or medium that can be used by a computer, including CD-ROM or digital video, interactive touch screen monitors, internet or web technology, streaming audio or video and data projection system etc. Modern cinema has gained great heights by absorbing the gift of multimedia in Hollywood and Bollywood blockbusters *viz.*, Jurassic park and Krish etc. Television advertisements, cartoon serials, presentations and model design are no exception.

1.10 SIMULATION

A simulation is similar to an animation for some real thing. Simulation is the representation of a real life system by another system, which depicts the important characteristics of the real system and allows experimentation on it. In other word, simulation help to prepare us for real life situations so we will know what to do if we have a similar experience in some particular atmosphere. With the help of simulation, traffic flow at particular location can analyze to get answer for smooth flow and to minimize accidents. Though the formal use of the simulation techniques is not very old, simulation has long been used by the researchers. In our day-to-day life, we use simulation, even without realizing it. Simulation is effectively used in video games (available in computer and mobiles), in flight training for more economical and safety, in clinical education program, in testing of automobile engines for their mileage, life and to ensure no deformation under normal operating conditions, in space shuttle for judgement of placing and handling problems if any etc. Flight simulators are often used to train pilots to operate aircraft in extremely hazardous situations such as landings with no engines or complete electrical or hydraulic failures.

There are different ways for simulation. Scale models of various machines and structures are used to simulate the plant layouts. A model airplane suspended in the wind tunnel can be used to simulate a real sized plane moving through the atmosphere for training and to study the aerodynamic characteristics. A planetarium (a theatre built primarily for presenting educational and entertaining shows about astronomy and night sky) represents a beautiful simulation of the planetary system. Environments in a geological park and in a museum of natural history are other example of simulation.

A computer simulation is an attempt to model a real-life or hypothetical situation on a computer so that it can be studied to how the system works. By changing variables predictions may be made about the behaviours of the system. Simulation software is based on the process of modelling a real phenomenon with a set of mathematical formulas. Several software packages exist for running computer based simulation modelling (*e.g.*, Monte Carlo Simulation and Stochastic modelling etc) that makes the modelling almost effortless. Using CAD/CAM in production units, sheet metal forming simulation software utilizes mathematical models to replicate the behavior of an actual metal sheet manufacturing process. This simulation prevents metal factories from defects in their production lines and reduces testing and expensive mistakes thereby improving efficiency in the metal forming process. Similarly, metal casting simulation software is designed as a defect-prediction tool for the foundry engineer, in order to correct or improve their casting process, even before prototype trials are produced. Some CAD/CAM software used for simulation is Solidworks, Pro-E, CATIA and CNC simulator. Other simulation software generally used are MATLAB (programming, modelling and simulation tool designed by Mathworks), Hyperworks and Autocast (metal casting and simulation software). Now, vehicle dynamic computer simulation software is developed which has now become an acceptable tool to aid in the improving of vehicle's design. Before manufacturing sports cars, production cars, military or the commercial transportation, an understanding of how the vehicle performs under multiple conditions is a requirement for companies to remain competitive. Thus, Computer simulations have the advantage of allowing a student and researchers to make judgments and also to make error and its correction.

Simulation is often used in the training of civilian and military personnel where use the real equipment in the real world is expansive or simply too dangerous to allow trainees. In such situations they will spend time for learning valuable lessons in a safe virtual environment. Simulation is also used in healthcare problems such as blood draw, to laparoscopic surgery and trauma care etc. Medical simulations of this sort will often use 3D or MRI scans of patient data to enhance realism. Simulations are also in robotics and to integrate CAD, CAM and CAE. The use of simulation throughout the product life cycle, especially at the earlier concept and design stages, has the potential of providing substantial benefits. Thus, the use of simulation we can increase the productivity.

In the real system, the change we want to study may take place too slowly or too fast to be observed conveniently. Computer simulation can compress the performance of a system over years into a few minutes of computer running time. In some systems like nuclear reactors where millions of events take place per second, simulation can expand the time to required level.

1.10.1 Limitations of Simulation

Simulation can be difficult because most natural phenomena are subject to an almost infinite number of influences. Due to this, Simulation does not produce optimum result when the model deals with uncertainties. Simulation is by no means a cheap method of analysis. Even small simulation takes considerable computer time.

❑❑❑

2

Principal of Computer Graphics and Object Modelling

2.0 INTRODUCTION

The manipulation and display of geometric information is the core of several computer applications and graphical displays form an important part of modern human-machine communications. In general sense, Computer graphics is the procedure of artificially generating a picture or image using the computer. There exists two major ways to create pictures, one in which programs are written to produce an image and other is by capturing a photograph with a camera. In this chapter, the former method is discussed. Simple picture or image can be produced by the potential available in contemporary word processors and spread sheets. However, lines can be coded for creating more precise image for complex objects. Geometric modelling can be used to create images of any shapes. The geometric modelling is a collection of techniques used to define points, lines, curves, surfaces and other geometric characteristics of an object. To describe the spaces of real object or to simulate some process by the use of computer, this modelling scheme builds mathematical model in vector form which is subsequently converted into program (a set of such programs are called software which is essential for the effective operation of a input data). The program is transformed into raster form (*i.e.*, pixel position) equivalent to its corresponding vector form. Electronic devices such as CRT (in-built in computer systems) are used to display on the monitor, the image of the objects as generated by these pixels. One of the important task in Computer Aided Design technique is to design some objects by drawings or by geometric modelling which includes geometric representation of products, their designing and transformation (such as scaling, rotation, translation etc,) discussed in this chapter. With the advent of modern computer graphics software and hardware, one can create, save, manipulate, evaluate current picturesque output on monitor or screen.

Thus, the final outcome of all computer graphics methods is a picture. It is evident that computer graphics is an essential pre-requisite of CAD. Designing, analyzing and manufacturing as well as Finite Element Analysis (FEM), Animations and Simulations, all can be done using CAD.

2.1 COMPUTER GRAPHICS HARDWARE AND SOFTWARE

With the rise in the utility and demand of computer graphics in almost all fields, various graphics hardware and software systems are now available for designing 2D and 3D scenes. Computer Graphics hardwares have been discussed in the previous chapter.

With personal computers, one can use a wide variety of interactive input devices and graphics software. In the previous chapter we have discussed that raster scan display techniques are widely used for display on monitors. Therefore, there is need of graphic software which can convert vectorial information of the picture or drawing into its equivalent raster format (*i.e.*, equivalent pixel position). Therefore, efforts are being made worldwide for development of an accepted standard for computer graphics software. Graphical Kernel System (GKS) was conceptualised and implemented for maintaining a standard for graphics based system. This system was adopted as the first graphics software standards by the ISO and ANSI. Although GKS was initially designed as 2D graphics packages, a 3D GKS extension was subsequently developed. After sometimes, second software PHIGS (Programmer's Hierarchal Interactive Graphics Standard) was developed which is extension of GKS and approved by ISO and ANSI. PHIGS provides the facilities of object modelling, surface rendering with specific colours, picture manipulations, simulation, animation and mechanism design etc.

2.2 CO-ORDINATE REPRESENTATION

In computer graphics, local modelling co-ordinate systems are used to represent the shape of objects and subsequently placed within the overall world co-ordinate scene. World co-ordinate in the range of 0-1 are understood by machine. At the concluding step, each device drivers transfer the normalized co-ordinate representation of the picture to the output system for display.

The modelling co-ordinate position (x_{mc}, y_{mc}) can be transferred to a device co-ordinate position (x_{dc}, y_{dc}).

$$(x_{mc}, y_{mc}) \rightarrow (x_{wc}, y_{wc}) \rightarrow (x_{nc}, y_{nc}) \rightarrow (x_{dc}, y_{dc})$$

A general purpose graphics software offers variety of functions for developing and modifying 2D and 3D images. The basic building blocks for picture constitute of design functions; transformation functions; attribute functions and viewing functions. The various graphics techniques can change the contour, dimension, location and orientation etc., of an object within a scene using geometric transformation.

2.3 TYPES OF COMPUTER GRAPHICS

There are two types of computer graphics:

1. **Raster graphics:** In this technique, each pixel is defined separately for formation of object, which is represented by patterns of individual pixel (dots). Large numbers of objects or elements are used for generating a picture by appropriate modification (as in a television and digital photograph etc).

2. **Vector graphics:** In this method, lines and contours are drawn using mathematical formulas. The elements are then perceived at the observer's end to produce the final image. Unlike, raster graphics, here, objects are interpretted as group of lines, rather than as patterns formed by individual. Vectors are suitable for representing simple pictures as it creates infinitely sharp graphics and often generates in smaller sized files. However, for complex picture representation, vectors take more time to render and generate larger size files than a raster equivalent.

2.4 SCAN CONVERSION/RASTERIZATION OF OUTPUT PRIMITIVES POINTS, LINES, CIRCLES AND ELLIPSES

In the previous chapter we have discussed that raster scan display techniques are widely used for display on monitors. Therefore, there is a need of a graphic software which can convert vector information of a picture or drawing into its equivalent raster format (*i.e.*, equivalent pixel position). This conversion process is called rasterization or scan conversion. The purpose of creating realistic image is to compute a collection of pixels according to the description of a scene provided in a data file. The graphic based algorithms discussed in the subsequent sections ensure a good outcome with limited available resources (like computation power) and specific time. Pictures are constituted as a collection of graphical primitives such as points, lines, curves, ellipse, filled polygon etc. The two most common forms of geometric elements are lines and circles. The other forms can be converted into either of these forms. Hence, the algorithms developed for scan conversion of line, circles and ellipse may be sufficient to discuss for graphical display purposes. In certain cases like drawing of a vertical line requires a large amount of computation when scan conversion of its vectorial information into its equivalent pixel positions is done. Hence, there is a requirement of simple methods or algorithms which can perform such tasks in less time with little computing overhead. Finally, the procedure from data processing to image creation on a computer monitor is called the graphics pipeline. This image generation or graphics pipeline is characterized by three stages-modelling, rendering and display as shown in [Fig. 2.1 (*a*), (*b*) and (*c*).

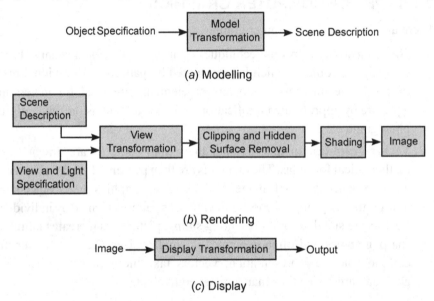

(*a*) Modelling

(*b*) Rendering

(*c*) Display

Fig. 2.1 (*a*, *b* and *c*) The graphics pipeline.

The **modelling** stage develops an internal representation (or object specification) of the objects in the scene. The internal representation comprises of the object colour, the material the object is made of, the appearance of the object as shiny or transparent, or translucent, and texture of the object. The selection of parameters should be specified in the algorithm. Depiction of the contour of an object depends on its complexity. Simple shapes can be represented by few parameters like a radius and a centre can define the shape of a sphere. On the contrary several parameters are required to describe a complex shape like the statue of God or a tree or a piece of cloth. In this chapter, we look at how to specify the simple shapes of the objects and how to scan convert them to determine what pixels they cover in an image. Object modelling procedures are also discussed in chapter 3 (2D and 3D geometric transformation, Chapter 4 (curves and surfaces representation), chapter 5 (geometric modelling for curves), chapter 6 (composite curve fitting), chapter 7 (Geometric modelling for surfaces and surface fittings), chapter 8 (solid modelling)

The rendering stage converts that scene description into image of that scene. Once, the data file has been read and an internal model of the scene has been created, the program now renders that data and produces the image of the scene. In addition to this, the rendering process also simulates the flow of light through the scene as it interacts with the objects. Thus, there needs to be a model for the light. To include the light factor in scene various illumination modes have been developed. The presence of light enables an observer to view the world. The effect of Illumination model may be diverse on different objects based on the texture of the object. If an illumination model fails to inculcate the effect of object's texture or material in the calculations, then objects of two different types can appear to be same. Therefore, the final image is influenced by both the object appearance parameters and the illumination model. Another factor is object visibility. In a complex scene, parts that are far away can be obscured (*i.e.*, covered/masked) by parts that are closer. The rendering algorithm must account for these obstructions for it to accurately render the scene. Therefore, this chapter also deals with some rendering algorithms also such as area or region filling algorithms, clipping algorithm and hidden lines and surfaces algorithms. Additional rendering issues including and the object's texture and shadows the objects casts, requires complex algorithms is not discussed here.

The display stage portrays the image on an output device/monitor as discussed in chapter 1. One concern with the display of a scene is diverse capabilities of different output devices. A computer monitor or a colour printer are manufactured with different components which may be exclusive for each company. Those components vary the output they produce.

2.4.1 Scan Conversion of a Line and Line Generation

The following criteria have been demanded for line drawing displays

1. Line should appear straight.
2. Line should be generated quickly.
3. Line should have consistent density.
4. Line density should not depend on factors like length and angle.
5. Line should terminate properly.

If co-ordinates of end points of the line segment are known, there are several methods for choosing the pixels between the end points. One method for drawing a line segment is the digital differential analyzer (DDA) algorithm.

2.4.1.1 DDA Algorithm for Line Drawing

The DDA algorithm is an incremental scan conversion method where we do calculation at each step using results from preceeding steps. In simple case, we sample the line at unit intervals in one co-ordinate and determine corresponding integer values nearest the line path for the other co-ordinates.

Algorithm:

Step 1: Read the end point co-ordinates (x_f, y_f) and (xl, yl) for a line where subscript f and l stands for first and last point of line.

Step 2: $dx = x_l - x_f$

$$dy = y_l - y_f$$

Step 3: If absolute (dx) > absolute (dy) then

$$\text{Step} = abs\ (dx)$$

Otherwise

$$\text{Step} = abs\ (dy)$$

Step 4: $x_{increment} = \dfrac{dx}{step}$

$$y_{increment} = \dfrac{dy}{step}$$

Step 5: Assign $x_0 = x_f$

$$y_0 = y_f$$

Put pixel $(x, y$ colour)

Step 6: $x_{i+1} = x_i + x_{increment}$

$$y_{i+1} = y_i + y_{increment} \text{ for } i = 0, 1, 2, ...$$

Put pixel $(x, y$ colour)

Step 7: Repeat step 6 until $x = x_1, y = y_1$

DDA algorithm is quicker than direct implementation of the straight line equation *i.e,* $y = mx + C$. Since, it calculates points on the line without any floating point multiplication. In other words, DDA algorithms eliminate multiplication process by addition process. DDA algorithm uses floating point which makes DDA algorithm slower but more accurate than Breshman's algorithm discussed in next section.

Example 2.1: Using DDA algorithm, rasterize line from (2, 2) to (6, 7)

Solution :

Step 1: Let

$$x_f = 2$$
$$y_f = 2$$
$$x_1 = 6$$
$$y_1 = 7$$

Step 2:
$$dx = x_1 - x_f = 6 - 2 = 4$$
$$dy = y\,y_1 - y_f = 7 - 2 = 5$$

Step 3: $abs\,(dy) > abs\,(dx)$

So, $step = abs\,(dy) = 5$

Step 4: $x_{inc} = \dfrac{dx}{step} = 0.8$

$$y_{inc} = \dfrac{dy}{step} = 1$$

Step 5: Assign first points $x_0 = x_f = 2$

$$y_0 = y_f = 2$$

Step 6: Other points are

$$x_1 = x_0 + x_{inc} = 2 + 0.8 = 2.8$$
$$y_1 = y_0 + y_{inc} = 2 + 1 = 3$$
$$(x_1, y_1) = (2.8, 3)$$
$$x_2 = x_1 + x_{inc} = 2.8 + 0.8 = 3.6$$
$$y_2 = y_1 + y_{inc} = 3 + 1 = 4$$
$$(x_2, y_2) = (3.6, 4)$$
$$x_3 = x_2 + x_{inc} = 3.6 + 0.8 = 4.4$$
$$y_3 = y_2 + y_{inc} = 4 + 1 = 5$$
$$(x_3, y_3) = (4.4, 5)$$
$$x_4 = x_3 + x_{inc} = 4.4 + 0.8 = 5.2$$
$$y_4 = y_3 + y_{inc} = 5 + 1 = 6$$
$$(x_4, y_4) = (5.2, 6)$$
$$x_6 = x_5 + x_{inc} = 5.2 + 0.8 = 6$$
$$y_6 = y_5 + y_{inc} = 6 + 1 = 7$$

Where $x_f = 6$

$$y_f = 7$$

From above points, we can plot lines as shown in Fig. (2.2).

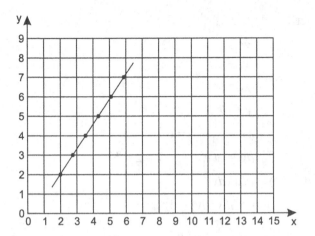

Fig. 2.2 Rasterization of line using DDA algorithm.

Above example suggest that DDA algorithms has following disadvantage.

1. Accumulation of round off errors in successive addition of floating point increment can (*a*) Result in drifting away of the estimated pixel positions from the actual path along the line segment. (*b*) Produce uneven or staircase manifestation unless the line are vertical or horizontal one.

2. This is still more expressive in terms of the total computation time since a large number of points need to be calculated for each of the line segment.

2.4.1.2 Bresenham's Algorithm for Line Drawing

The algorithm is an improvement over DDA algorithms. This algorithm can completely eradicate the floating point arithmetic expect for the preliminary computations. All other computation are fully integer arithmetic and hence this algorithm is more useful for rasterization. This algorithm can be discussed for two cases, one for slope $|m| < 1$ and another for slope $|m| \geq 1$.

Algorithm: Bresenham's algorithm works on the principle of finding the optimum raster locations to represent the straight line. The basic idea behind this Algorithm is to find the decision variable (the error term) which is equal to the difference between the distance of pixels which are lying above the expected line and the distance of pixels which are lying below the expected line.

Case 1 for $|m| < 1$ where $|m| = \dfrac{|dy|}{|dx|}$

Step 1: Assign (x_f, y_f), and (x_1, y_1) as the end-points co-ordinates where

$$x_0 = x_f, y_0 = y_f$$

Step 2: $\quad d_x = x_i - x_f$

$$dy = y_i - y_f$$

Step 3: We will initially set the decision variable

$$p_i = 2|dy| - |dx| \qquad i = 0$$

Step 4: If $\quad p_i < 0$ and $(x_f < x_i)$ then

$$x_{i+1} = x_i + 1$$

else $\qquad x_{i+1} = x_i + 1$

$$p_{i+1} = p_i + 2|dy|$$

otherwise

if $\qquad\qquad (y_f < y_i)$ then

$$y_{i+1} = y_i + 1$$

else

If $\qquad\qquad (x_f < x_1)$ then

$$x_{i+1} = x_f + 1$$

else $\qquad x_{i+1} = x_i - 1$

$$p_i + 1 = p_i + 2\,[|dy| - |dx|]$$

Step 5: Put pixel for second point $(x_i, y_i, \text{colour})$

Step 6: Repeat steps 4 and 5 until, last computer point is equal to x_1

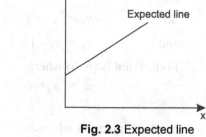

Fig. 2.3 Expected line generation

Case 2: For slope $|m| \geq 1$ where $|m| = \dfrac{|dy|}{|dx|}$

Step 1 : Assign (x_f, y_f) and (x_1, y_1) as the end points co-ordinates where

$$x_f = x_0, y_f = y_0$$

Step 2: $\qquad dx = x_i - x_f$

$$xy = y_i - y_f$$

Step 3: We will initially set the decision variable as

$$p_i = 2|dx| - |dx|$$

$$p_i + 1 = p_i + 2\,(|dy| - |dx|)$$

$$= 1 + 2\,[2 - 3]$$

$$p_i = -1$$

$$pi < 1$$

Step 5:

(1) Second Point is (4, 7)

(2) $P_i < 0$

So $\qquad x_2 = x_1 + 1 = 4 + 1 = 5$

and $\qquad y_2 = y_1 = 7$

Third point is $(5, 7)$

$$P_i + 1 = P_i + 2|dy|$$
$$= -1 + 2\,(2) = 3$$

(3) $\qquad P > 0$

So $\qquad x_3 = x_2 + 1 = 5 + 1 = 6$

and $\qquad y_3 = y_2 - 1 = 7 - 1 = 6$

Forth Point is $(6, 6)$ where

$$x_1 = x_3 = 6$$
$$y_1 = y_3 = 6$$

Stop computation where points after rasterization are $(3, 8)$, $(4, 7)$, $(5, 7)$ and $(6, 6)$.

Example 2.2: Using Bresenham's algorithm, rasterize line from $(2, 2)$ to $(5, 7)$

Solution : Assign

Step 1: $\qquad x_f = x_0 = 2$

$\qquad\qquad x_1 = 2$

$\qquad\qquad y_f = y_0 = 5$

$\qquad\qquad y_1 = 7$

Step 2: $\qquad dx = x_2 - x_1 = 5 - 2 = 3$

$\qquad\qquad dy = y_2 - y_1 = 7 - 2 = 5$

$\qquad\qquad |m| = |dy| \,/\, |dx| = 5/3$

Step 3: $\qquad$ If $|m| > 1$ then

$\qquad\qquad P_i = 2|dx| - |dy|$

$\qquad\qquad\quad = 2(3) - 5 = 1$

Step 4: $\qquad$ if $i > 0$ and

if $\qquad\qquad (x_f < x_l)$ then

$\qquad\qquad x_i + 1 = x_i + 1$

$\therefore \qquad\qquad x_1 = x_0 + 1 = 2 + 1 = 3$

if $\qquad\qquad (y_f < y_l)$

$\qquad\qquad\qquad y_i + 1 = y_i + 1$

$\qquad\qquad\qquad y_1 = y_0 + 1$

$\qquad\qquad\qquad\quad = 2 + 1 = 3$

$$P_i + 1 = P_i + 2 [|dx| - |dy|]$$
$$= 1 + 2(3 - 5) = -3$$

Step 5 : (1) Second point is (3, 3)

(2) $\qquad\qquad\qquad i < 0$

So $\qquad\qquad\qquad x_2 = x_1 = 3$

and $\qquad\qquad\qquad y_2 = y_1 + 1 = 3 + 1 = 4$

Third point is (3, 4)

$$P_i + 1 = P_i + 2 |dx|$$
$$= -3 + 2(3) = 3$$

(3) If $P > 0$ then

$$x_3 = x_2 + 1 = 3 + 1 = 4$$
$$y_3 = y_2 + 1 = 4 + 1 = 5$$

Forth point is (4, 5)

$$P_i + 1 = P_i + 2 [|dx| - |dy|]$$
$$= 3 + 2(3 - 5) = -1$$

(4) If $P < 0$ then

$$x_4 = x_3 = 4$$
$$y_4 = y_3 + 1 = 5 + 1 = 6$$

Fifth point is (4, 6)

$$P_i + 1 = P_i + 2\{dx\}$$
$$= -1 + 2(3) = 5$$

(5) If $P > 0$ then

$$x_5 = x_4 + 1 = 4 + 1 = 5$$
$$y_5 = y_4 + 16 + 1 = 7$$

Sixth point is (5, 7) where

$$x_1 = 5, y_1 = 7$$

So, stop computation. Thus, points after rasterization are (2, 2) (3, 3) (3, 4) (4, 5) (4, 6) and (5, 7)

2.4.2 Scan Conversion of a Circle

The circle can be defined and drawn by two methods, one is polynomial method and second is trigonometric method. In polynomial method, circle is expressed as $x^2 + y^2 = r^2$.

Where r is the radius of circle and $y = \sqrt{r^2 - x^2}$. To draw a quarter circle, we can increment x from 0 to r in unit steps and estimate the value of $+y$ at each step. The remaining quarter can be drawn by symmetry. Even though this method is simple and easy to implement but as it involves the square and square-root functions, it makes the method inefficient.

In second method, co-ordinates of each point in circle can be expressed as

$$x = r \cos \theta + x_c$$
$$y = r \sin \theta + y_c$$

where (x_c, y_c) is the centre of the circle, r and θ is the radius and angle of the circle. For one quarter circle, putting $\theta = 0$ to 90 degree gives different value of x and y. Though method is easy and simple, but the inclusion of trigonometric function makes it inefficient. Using eight point symmetry, we can draw a circle *easier than above.*

2.4.2.1 Circle Generating Algorithms Using Eight-point Symmetry

Using this method we can improve previous method by taking advantages of the symmetry in a circle. For this first we assume, the circle centre lies at the origin. If we have a point (x, y) on the circle, then the remaining seven points can be estimated in the following manner [Fig. 2.4(a)].

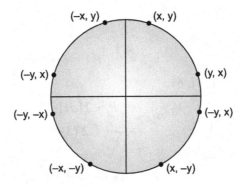

Fig. 2.4 (a) Eight-point symmetry of circle.

Above Fig (2.4)(a) suggests that there is need to compute only 45° arc. To describe the circle completely, all the points on the circle can be displayed by plotting eight pixels successively at the same time.

Put pixel (x, y colour)

Put pixel (x, $-y$ colour)

Put pixel ($-x$, $-y$ colour)

Put pixel (y, x, colour)

Put pixel ($-y$, x colour)

Put pixel ($-y$, $-x$ colour)

Then repeat above procedure for all points for $q = 0°$ to $45°$ or unit $x < y$. This method is again inefficient *because large procedure required.*

2.4.2.2 Bresentham's Circle Generation Algorithm

This method is most efficient for drawing the circle, as

1. It avoids the use of trigonometric and power functions.
2. It performs the computations with integer, simple addition and subtraction. Bresentham's circle algorithm works on the basic theory of acquiring the next pixel values by means of decision variable P_1 and generates the circle with eight symmetry property. Refer Figure 2.4(*b*) where P_1 having co-ordinate $(x_i - y_i - 1)$ which is boundary of circle, P_2 having $(x_i - 1 + 1, y_i + 1 + 1)$ which is within the circle and P_3 having $(x_i + 1 + 1\ y_i - 1)$ which is outside the circle, where r is the radius of circle.

Let $\quad P_A =$ distance of P_3 from origin^2 – radius of circle ^{2}

$\qquad P_B =$ distance of P_2 from origin^2 – radius of circle^2

Bresentham's method proceeds with finding the decision variable

$$P_i = P_A + P_B = 2x^2_i - 1 + 4x_i - 1 + 2y^2_{i-2}y^2_{i-1}\ 2y_i - 1 + 3 - 2r^2$$

Now for the the first point *i.e.*, p_0 $(x = 0, y = r)$, $P_i = 3 - 2r$

Algorithm for circle is given below.

Algorithm:

Step 1: Read radius r

Step 2: Assign $x = 0$

$\qquad y = r$

$\qquad P_i = 3 - 2r$

Step 3: If $P_i < 0$

$\qquad x_{i+1} = x_i + 1$

$\qquad y_{i+1} = y_i$

$\qquad P_{i+1} = P_i + 4x + 6$

Otherwise

$\qquad y_{i+1} = y_i - 1$

$\qquad x_{i+1} = x_i + 1$

$\qquad p_i + 1 = P_i + 4(x - y) + 10$

Step 4: Put pixel $(x, y$ colour)

Step 5: Repeat steps 3 and 4 unit $x < y$

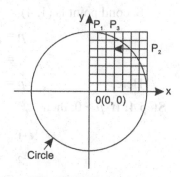

Fig. 2.4 (*b*) Bresenham's circle generation.

This algorithm can plot an arc for $45°$. To plot a complete circle, we have to use eight point symmetry method which is already discussed in the previous section.

Example 2.3: Using Bresentham's algorithm calculate the points to draw a circle having radius 4 and center is (0, 0)

Solution :

Step 1: Read Radius $r = 4$

Step 2: Put $x_0 = 0,$

$$y_0 = r$$

$$p = 3 - 2r$$

$$= 3 - 2(4) = -5$$

Here, $p = -5 < 0$

Step 3 : If $P < 0$ then

$$x_{i+1} = x_i + 1$$

$$x_i = x_0 + 1 = 0 + 1 = 1$$

And $y_{i+1} = y_i$

$$y_i = y_0 = 4$$

Second point is (1, 4)

$$p = p + 4x_1 + 6$$

$$= -5 + 4.1 + 6 = 3$$

Here, $p = 5 > 0$

Step 4: If $p > 0$, then

$$x_{i+1} = x_i + 1$$

$$x_2 = x_i + 1$$

$$\therefore \qquad = 2$$

$$y_{i+1} = y_i - 1$$

$$y_2 = y_0 - 1$$

$$y_2 = y_0 - 1 = 4 - 1 = 3$$

Third point (2, 3)

$$p = p + 4(x - y) + 10 = 5 + 4(2 - 3) + 10 = 11$$

$$P > 0$$

$$x_{i+1} = 3, \qquad y_{i+1} = 2$$

Fourth Point (3, 2)

2.4.2.3 Mid Point Circle

To use the midpoint circle method, the equation.

$$f_{\text{circle}}(x, y) = x^2 + y^2 - r^2$$

is used.

By evaluating the circle function at sampling position, the decision parameter can be evaluated.

$$P_x = f_{\text{circle}} = \left(x_{K+1}, y_K - \frac{1}{2} \right)$$

$$\therefore \qquad = (x_{K+1})^2 + \left(y_K - \frac{1}{2} \right)^2 - r^2$$

if $P_k > 0$ this midpoint is outside the circle

Plot (x_K, y_{K-1})

else

Plot (x_{K+1}, y_{K-1})

$$P_{K+1} = f_{\text{circle}} \left(x_{K+1} + 1, y_{K+1} - \frac{1}{2} \right)$$

By computing the circle function at the start position, the initial decision parameter is acquired.

$$P_0 = f_{\text{circle}} \left(1, r - \frac{1}{2} \right) = \frac{5}{4} - r \, 1 - r$$

Here, rounding is equal to one therefore, every increments must be integers.

Algorithm:

Step 1: Put circle centre $(x_c, y_c) = (0, r)$

Step 2: Initial value of the decision parameter is computed as follows:

$$P_0 = 1 - r$$

Step 3: At each x_K point, starting at $K = 0$, the following test is conducted:

If $P_K < 0$, the next point with centre $(x_c = 0, y_c = 0)$, along the circle is (x_{K+1}, y_K) and

$$P_{K+1} = P_K + 2x_{K+1} + 1$$

Otherwise the next point along the circle is (x_{K+1}, y_{K-1}) and

$$P_{K+1} = P_K + 2(x_K + 1) + 1 - 2y_{K+1}$$

where $\qquad 2x_{K+1} = 2x_{K+2}$

and $\qquad 2y_{K+1} = 2y_K - 2$

Step 4: Calculate points of symmetry in the other seven octants.

Step 5: Move every computed pixel point (x, y) into the circular path centred on (x_0, y_0) and plot and co-ordinate value $x = x + x_c$ and $y = y + y_c$.

Step 6: Repeat step 3 to 5 until $x > y$.

Example 2.4: Using midpoint circle algorithm plot a circle whose radius = 20 units.

Solution : Here $r = 10$

Put $(x_0, y_0) = (0, r) = (0, 10)$

Then initial decision parameter

$$P_0 = 1 - r = -9$$

Now, performing test whether $P_K < 0$

$$-9 < 0$$

Then next point will be (x_{K+1}, y_K) which will be $(1, 10)$

and $P_{K+1} = P_K + 2x_{K+1} + 1$

$$P_{0+1} = P_0 + 2x_{0+1} + 1 = 9 + 2.1 + 1$$

$$P_1 = -6$$

Since, above $P_1 < 0$, therefore, next point will be $(2,1)$ and next point $P_1 + i = P_1 + 2x_{1+1} + 1 = -6 + 2.2 + 1 = -1$.

Again since above $P_2 < 0$, therefore, next point will be $(3, 10)$ and $P_3 = 6$.

Since, new $P_3 > 0$, then the next point will be $(x_{K+1}, y_K - 1)$ $i.e.$, $(3 + 1, 10 - 1)$ or $(4, 9)$ and

$$P_{K+1} = P_K + 2x_{K+1} - 2y_{K+1}$$

$$P_4 = P_3 + 2.4 + 1 \, 2.9 = -13$$

again since $P_4 > 0$, therefore, next point will be $(6, 8)$ and

$$P_6 = P_5 + 2.6 + 1 = 5.$$

Again since $P_6 > D$, therefore, next point will be $(7, 7)$ Now we will stop here because $x = y$.

2.4.3 Ellipse Generation Algorithm

This algorithm is also called scan converting method of an ellipse. Similar to circle, the ellipse also shows symmetry. The symmetry factor of an ellipse is four. There are two method to define a ellipse.

2.4.3.1 *Polynomial Method of Defining an Ellipse*

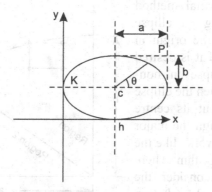

Fig. 2.4 (*c*) Polynomial
description of an ellipse.

Refer Fig. 2.4(*c*) expression of ellipse is represented as

$$\frac{(x-h)^2}{a^2}+\frac{(y-k)^2}{b^2}-1=0$$

where (*h*, *k*) are ellipse centre, a and *b* are length of major and minor axis respectively. Then

$$y = k + b\sqrt{1-\frac{(x-h)^2}{a^2}}$$

This method is very since the square of (*x* − *h*) and a must be established. In subsequent steps the floating point division of (*x* − *h*)^2 by a^2 and floating point multiplication of the square root of $\sqrt{1-\frac{(x-h)^2}{a^2}}$ by *b* must be executed.

2.4.3.2 *Trigonometric Method of Defining an Ellipse*

Refer Fig. 2.4(*d*), expression of an ellipse is represented as $x = a\cos\theta + h$ and $y = b\sin\theta + k$ where centre co-ordinate is *c* (*h*, *k*) and angle of point *P* (*x*, *y*) is *P* (*a* cos θ + *h*, *b* sin θ + *k*).

Here value θ varies from zero to $\frac{\pi}{2}$ radians.

The remaining points are found by symmetry. This method is also inefficient because of large number of trigonometric values are required which increases the cost of computer memory. But now-a-days high cost of computer memory has been overcome making this method is now quite acceptable.

2.4.3.3 Midpoint Ellipse Algorithm

This is an incremental method for scan converting an ellipse that is centered at the origin in standard position. If it is desired to display the ellipse in non-standard position, then the ellipse can be rotated about its centre co-ordinate to re-align the major and minor axis. It works like the midpoint circle algorithm. There is a requirement to consider the entire elliptical Fig. 2.4 (*d*) Two regions of the ellipse curve in first quadrant in two defined by the 45° tangent parts because of the four-ways symmetry

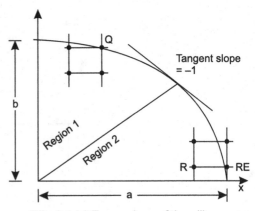

Fig. 2.4 (*d*) Two regions of the ellipse defined by the 45° tangent.

property. To apply the midpoint method, first we define an ellipse function [refer Figs 2.4 (*e*) and (*d*)].

$$f_{\text{ellipse}}(x, y) = b^2 x^2 - a^2 y^2 - a^2 b \text{ where}$$

$f_{\text{ellipse}}(x, y) \geq 0$, if point (x, y) is inside the ellipse boundary < 0, if point (x, y) is inside the ellipse boundary,

Thus, the ellipse function $f_{\text{ellipse}}(x_m, y)$ provides the decision parameter P_i. At each sampling position, the subsequent pixel along the ellipse path is choosen based on the sign of the ellipse function applied at mid-point between the two primary pixels.

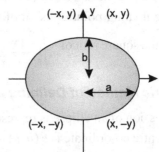

Fig. 2.4 (*e*) Ellipse.

function evaluated at $\left(x_p + 1, y_p - \dfrac{1}{2} \right)$ midpoint between the two co-ordinate pixel is located at (x_p, y_p), 1 if the current pixel is located at (x_p, s_p), then the decision variable for region 1, P_1 is $f_{\text{ellipse}}(x, y)$ evaluated at the midpoint Q and QE. We now repeat the process we used for deriving the two Δs for the circle

For a more to Q, the next midpoint is only adding 1 to x. Then

$$P_{old} = f_{ellipse}\left(x_p + 1, y_p - \frac{1}{2}\right) = b^2(x_p + 1)^2 + a^2\left(y_p - \frac{1}{2}\right)^2 - a^2 b^2$$

$$P_{new} = f_{ellipse}\left(x_p + 2, -\frac{1}{2}\right) = b^2(x_p + 2)^2 + a^2\left(y_p - \frac{1}{2}\right)^2 - a^2 b^2$$

$P_{old} + b^2(2x_p + 3)$, the increment $\Delta Q = b^2(2x_p + 3)$

For a move of QE the next midpoint is one increment over in x and one increment down in y. Then

$$P_{new} = f_{ellipse}\left(x_{P+2}, y_P - \frac{3}{2}\right)$$

$$= b^2(x_P + 2)^2 + a^2\left(y_P - \frac{3}{2}\right)^2 + a^2 b^2$$

$$= P_{old} + b^2(2x_p + 3) + a^2(-2y_p + 2)$$

where the increment $\Delta QE = b^2(2x_p + 3) + a^2(-2y_p + 2)$

Similarly, in region 2, if the current pixel is at (x_P, y_P) the decision variable P_2 is $f_{ellipse}$ (x, y) evaluated at $\left(x_P + \frac{1}{2}, y_P - 1\right)$, the midpoint between R and RE. Calculations similar to those given for region I may be done for region 2.

We must also calculate the initial condition. Assuming integer values a and b, and ellipse starts at $(0, b)$, and the first midpoint to be calculated is at $\left(1, b - \frac{1}{2}\right)$. Then

$$f_{ellipse}\left(1, b - \frac{1}{2}\right) = b^2 + a^2\left(1, b - \frac{1}{2}\right)^2 - a^2 b^2 = b^2 + a^2\left(-b - \frac{1}{4}\right)$$

At every iteration in region 1, we must not only test the decision variable P_1 and update the Δ function, but also see whether we should switch regions by evaluating the gradient at the midpoint between Q and QE. When the midpoint cut-through over into region 2, the choice of the two pixels is altered to compare from Q and QE to RE and R. At the sametime, the decision variable P_2 for region 2 is set to the midpoint between RE and R. That is, if the last pixel chosen in region one is located at (x_P, y_P), then the decisions variable P_2 is initialized at $\left(x_P + \frac{1}{2}, y_P - 1\right)$. We stop drawing the pixel in region 2 when the y values of the pixel is equal to 0.

Example 2.5 : Determine raster position across the ellipse path when major length $a = 8$ and minor length $b = 6$.

Solution : We can start with region 1.

The initial point of the ellipse centered on the origine is

$$(x_0, y_0) = (0, b) = (0, 6)$$

Then initial parameter

$$P_1 = f_{ellipse}\left(1, b - \frac{1}{2}\right) = b^2 + a^2\left(-b + \frac{1}{4}\right)$$

$$= 6^2 - 8^2 \cdot 6 + \frac{1}{4}8^2 = -332$$

Now check for $P_1 K < 0$, the next point will be (x_{K+1}, y_K) *i.e.* (1, 6) and

$$P_{1_{K+1}} = P_{1_K} + 2b^2 (x_{K+1}) + b^2$$

$$= -332 + 2.36 (1) + 36 = -224$$

Since $-224 < 0$, next point will be (3, 6) and

$$P_{1_{K+1}} = -44 + 2.36. (3) + 36 = 208$$

Here 208 > 0 then next point to be plotted is

$$(x_{K+1}, y_{K-1}) = (4, 5)$$

and $$P_{1_{K+1}} - 2a^2 y_{K+1} + b^2$$

$$P_{1_{K+1}} = 208 + 2 (36).4 - 2.(64).5 + 36 = -108$$

Again $-108 < 0$, then next point is (5, 5) and

$$P_{1_{K+1}} = -108 + 2.36.5 + 36$$

$$= 288 > 0$$

Next point will be (6, 4) and

$$P_{1_{K+1}} = 288 + 432 + 36 - 512 = 244$$

again   244 > 0

next point to plot will be (7, 3) and

$$P_{1, K+1} = 244 + 504 - 384 + 36 = 400$$

but here we see that

value of $2b^2 x_{K+1} = 504$

and $2a^2 y_{K+1} = 389$

i.e., $2b^2 x_{K+1} > 2a^2 y_{K+1}$

Hence, we move out of region 1.

Now calculating for region 2,

For region 2, $(x_0, y_0) = (7, 3)$

The $\quad P_2, 0 = b^2 \left(x_0 + \dfrac{1}{2} \right)^2 + a^2 (y_0 - 1)^2 + a^2 b^2$

$\qquad\qquad = -23 \text{ (here } k = 0)$

here $-23 < 0$, then the next point will be (x_{K+1}, y_{K-1}) i.e. $(8, 2)$ and

$$P_{2, \, k+2} = P_{2K} + 2b^2 x_{K+1} - 2a^2 y_{K+1} + a^2$$
$$= 361$$

Again $361 > 0$ then next point will be (x_K, y_{K-1}) i.e., $(8, 1)$ AND

$(P_2, k+1)$ new $= P_2, K + $ old $-2b_2 \times K + 1 + a^2$
$$= 361 - 2 \, (36). \, 8 + 64 = -151$$

2.5 AREA OR REGION FILLING

The earlier display devices for example plotter and vector refresh display were basically line drawing devices. Here raster display system can display solid object such as polygon, cylinder, sphere and alongwith lines they can also be used as primitive to graphics devices. Area filling is the process of "colouring in" a definite image area or region. Area or region may be defined at the pixel or geometric level. At the pixel level, we describe an area or region either in terms of the boundary pixels that outline it or as the totality of pixels that comprise it. In the first case the area or region is called boundary defined and the collection of algorithms used for filling such area or region are collectively called boundary fill algorithm.

In the second case, the term "interior" refers to the area or region enclosed by surface boundary and the algorithms used for filling such a bounded area, are collectively called flood fill algorithms. It is quite evident that initially for both flood fill algorithm and boundary fill algorithm, a starting pixel inside the bounded region is required. This starting pixel is called seed. Therefore, both boundary and flood fill algorithm can be classified under seed algorithm.

At geometric level, a region is defined as group of connected lines and curves, forming a closed figure. If region is made by a series of sequentially connected lines then this region is called polygon. Therefore, there are three types of algorithm. (1) Flood fill (2) boundary fill and (3) scan line polygon fill algorithm. These can be used for region or an area filling but here we will discuss about boundary fill and flood fill algorithm which are comparatively simpler than scan line algorithm. With the help of boundary fill and flood fill algorithm, we can fill different polygons also.

2.5.1 4-Connected and 8-Connected Approach to Fill Region

There are two methods in which pixels are considered to be connected to each other to form a continuous boundary as given below.

1. 4-Connected

2. 8-Connected

In 4-connected method a pixel may have upto four neighbours pixels [see Fig. 2.4(*f*)*i*]. Similarly, in 8-connected method, a pixel may have upto eight neighbour [see Fig. 2.4(*f*)*ii*].

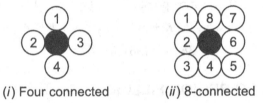

(*i*) Four connected   (*ii*) 8-connected

Fig. 2.4 (*f*) 4-connected and 8-connected.

All inner pixels can be used to fill with a given colour using either-4 connected or 8-connected approach. In 8-connected algorithm there are four other diagonal directions apart from left-right, up-down direction.

2.5.2 Seed Fill Algorithm

In this algorithm, the pixels of an area are assumed to be stored in the display memory and that atleast one pixel within the polygon area is known. As discussed previously we have to discuss two types of seed fill algorithms. (1) Boundary Fill (2) Flood Fill.

2.5.2.1 A Boundary Fill Algorithm

Boundary fill algorithm is simplest area filling algorithm. Here, boundary has specified colour. It starts with seed (called starting pixel with solid colour) which is inside the region. This algorithm checks to see if this pixel is a boundary pixel or has already been filled. If the answer is no, it fills the pixel with desired colour and continue inspect to identify the surrounding pixels to right and left of starting pixel called seeds, till the left most and the right most boundary pixels colour is achieved. Thus, this is similar to scan converting a line. The algorithm then finds the pixels above and below the line just drawn and repeat the process for the next horizontal line to fill. This process is terminated when all the pixels have been considered and all the pixels upto the boundary colour have been tested.

Steps

Input: Co-ordinates of an interior point (x, y), a fill colour, and a boundary colour.

1. Starting from (x, y), the procedure evaluates whether the colour of neighbouring positions are same as boundary colour.

2. If not, they are painted with the fill colour, and their successive neighbours are tested.

3. This process is terminated, once all pixels within the area upto the boundary colour have been tested.

In this method, we see that it can take time and more memory to execute, due to potentially high number for recursive calls, specially when the size of the region is relatively large. For example, in this algorithm the number of recursive call at any particular time is merely N when the current line is N scan lines away from the initial seed. The boundary fill algorithm is particularly useful when the region to be filled has no uniformly colour boundary.

2.5.2.2 Flood Fill Algorithm

To fill the area of all connected pixels at one specified colour, this algorithm can be used which is modification of boundary fill algorithm. Either 4-connected or 8-connected approach can be used to fill all interior pixels with a given colour.

Like boundary fill algorithm, it also starts from the given initial interior pixel called seed. From this seed, the group of algorithms inspects all the surrounding 8-connected pixels (in some cases 4-connected) to see whether the boundary extent is reached. If reached, it fills the pixel with colour. This process is repeated till all the interior pixels are inspected.

Input: node, fillcolor, target_colour

1. If target_colour is equal to fillcolor, return.

2. If the colour of node is not equal to target_colour, return.

3. Set the colour of node to fillcolor.

4. do Flood-fill (one step to the left of node, fillcolour, target_colour).

   do Flood-fill (one step to the right of node, fillcolor, target_colour).

   do Flood-fill (one step to the up of node, fillcolor, target_colour).

   do Flood-fill (one step to the down of node, fillcolor, target_colour).

5. Return.

Demonstration of above algorithm can be understand by following example.

Let polygon *PQRS* shown in [Fig. 2.2. (g)] is to be filled where *P* (0, 0), *Q* (4, 0) *R* (0, 4) with initial seed as (2, 2).

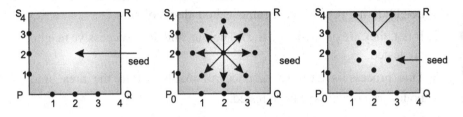

Fig. 2.4 (g) Flood fill method.

Algorithm starts from seed (2, 2), [Fig. 2.4 (g)], flood fill method which inspects all the eight points surrounding the seed that are (1, 1) (1, 2) (1, 3), (2, 3) (3, 3) (3, 2) (3, 1) and (2,1). Since, these are not on the boundary, each will be filled with colour. Now each of above right points or pixels becomes the seed. The algorithm continues in this fashion to fill region, which has the same colour. Triangle region can be filled by 4-connected approach using this algorithm.

2.6 ANTI-ALIASING-LINES

The lines drawn by various algorithms have a common problem. They have jagged or staircase appearance and unequal brightness of lines of different origin. Above undesirable effects are called aliasing. The application of techniques that can reduce or eliminate aliasing is referred as anti-aliasing.

The images or curves or primitives generated using anti-aliasing techniques are said to be anti-aliased. The effect will be more pronounced in the case of the line with small angles as shown in [Fig. 2.5 (a)]. It is possible to improve the appearance by increasing the screen resolution shown in [Fig. 2.5(b)].

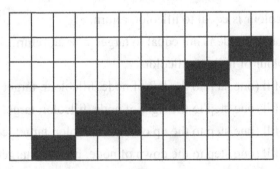

Fig. 2.5 (a) Staircase effects of pixels when drawing inclined line.

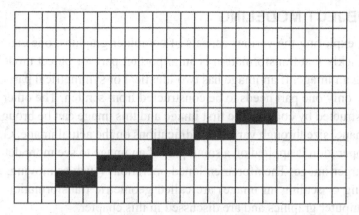

Fig. 2.5 (b) The staircase effect of pixels decreases when drawing inclined lines with increased resolution.

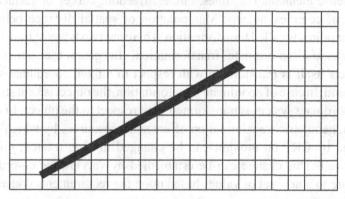

Fig. 2.5 (c) Anti-alisasing of pixels proportional to the portion of pixel occupied by the line.

But increasing resolution is an expensive solution that only determine the problem of jaggies, it does not eliminate the problem. There are other antialiasing techniques which are less costly and produces significantly better image given below.

(a) Unweighted area sampling

(b) Weighted area sampling.

(c) Gupta-sproull antiliased line

In sampling theory, the area of the pixel covered by the line thickness determines the pixel intensity. The pixel with different areas is overlapped by the finite line thickness as shown in Fig. 2.5(c). Though this improves the appearance of the line, but this is computationally more intensive. This problem can be again improved by Gupta-sprouall anti-alising line techniques (Ref. standard book of computer Graphics) and suitable other techniques.

2.7 OBJECT MODELING

During exploring the various aspects of computer graphics, one can discover very quickly that transformation is an important part for object modelling for creating an image. If an image has two identical or symmetrical parts, such as wheels, only one part needs to be constructed from scratch. The other one can be constructed by copying the first image and this image can be brought to the right shape, size through various modifications on the actual image. Generally, zoom operation is applied on a small part of an image to see more details or to see a larger image. The aforementioned operations (such as moving, rotating, reflecting or scaling an image) are called geometric transformation in CAD and computer graphics and are discussed in this chapter.

In CAD/CAM system, different techniques are used for manipulation of geometric elements (*i.e.* lines, circles, freedom curves or surface etc.) or drawing of complex objects. Manipulation of spatial distance between two objects or points is called transformation. There are two types of transformation Geometric and co-ordinate transformation. In geometric transformation, the objects itself is transformed with respect to a fixed coordinate system or background. In case of coordinate transformation, the object is kept still or fixed while coordinate system is transformed with respect to the object. In computer graphics, geometric transformation offers some resources by which an image generated by CRT on monitor can be changed in size, rotated, reflected or even moved. This change can be established by varying the co-ordinates of the picture to a new set of values based upon the requirements concerning the controlling of each point of an object in computer graphics. The subsequent topics to be discussed are geometric transformation of 2D and 3D objects.

2.7.1 Representation of a Point In Matrix Form

In co-ordinates system, a point P_0 is representation by its co-ordinates like P_0 (x_0, y_0) in case of two dimension and P_0 (x_0, y_0, z_0) in case of three dimension. In matrix form, 2D point P_0 is represented by position vector either by

$$[\vec{P}] = [x_0, y_0] \text{ called row vector or}$$

$$[\vec{P}] = \begin{bmatrix} x_0 \\ y_0 \end{bmatrix} \text{ called column vector or}$$

For 3D, P_0 point is represented by

$$[\vec{P}] = [x_0, y_0, z_0] \text{ called row vector or}$$

$$[\vec{P}] = \begin{bmatrix} x_0 \\ y_0 \\ z_0 \end{bmatrix} \text{ called column vector or}$$

This matrix is called position vectors of a point. This position vector of a point can be stored as a row matrix or column matrix format. In the book, we will use row matrix format. In some cases column matrix is also used. A series of points, each with a position vector relative to some co-ordinate system is stored in a computer as a matrix. The position/location of these points can be controlled by manipulating the matrix which defines the points. By suitably relocating the points, one can generate straight lines or curves or surface or finally objects.

To transform a point or picture in computer graphics, a known transformation matrix is required referred as $[T]$. The matrix $[T]$ used to perform geometric operation which forms the foundation of mathematical transformation in computer graphics. After applying geometric operation on $[\vec{P}]$

We obtain Transformed P.

$$[\vec{P_0}][T] = [\vec{P_1}] \qquad \qquad ...(1)$$

Where geometric transformation matrix is represented by

$$T = \begin{bmatrix} a & b \\ c & d \end{bmatrix} \text{ for } 2D$$

$$T = \begin{bmatrix} a & b & p \\ c & d & q \\ t_x & t_y & s \end{bmatrix} \text{ for } 3D \qquad \qquad ...(2)$$

Where a, b, c are geometric operations.

2.7.2 Two Dimensional Transformation

Using transformation we can change the size of a polygon or any object and also change its position or rotate it. In 2D, consider a point $P_0(x_0, y_0)$ to be transformed to another point P_1. Here, we can use a general transformation matrix $[T]$ in the following way as

$$[\vec{P_0}] [T] = [\vec{P_1}]$$

i.e., $$[x_0 \, y_0]\begin{bmatrix} a & b \\ c & d \end{bmatrix} = [ax_0 + cy_0 \;\; bx_0 + dy_0] \qquad \qquad ...(3)$$

$$= |x_1 \, y_1|$$

where $\qquad\qquad x_1 = ax_0 + cy_0 \text{ and } y_1 = bx_0 + dy_0$

Equation (3) shows that the initial co-ordinate x_0 and y_0 of a point P_0 is transformed to x_1 and y_1.

2.7.2.1 Translation and Rotation

In this section, the general procedures for applying translation, rotation, and scaling parameters to reposition and resize 2D objects are discussed.

A translation operation when applied to an object, repositions it in the direction of a straight path from one co-ordinate location to another. A two-dimensional point is translated/relocated by adding translation distances, t_x and t_y, to the original co-ordinate position $P_0(x_0, y_0)$, to shift the point to a new position (x_1, y_1).

$$x_1 = t_x + x_0$$
$$y_1 = t_y + y_0 \qquad\qquad\qquad \dots (4)$$

The translation values are termed as a translation vector or shift vector.

The translation equation 4 can be expressed in terms of a single matrix equation by using column vectors to represent co-ordinate positions and the translation vector

$$\begin{bmatrix} x_1 \\ x_2 \end{bmatrix} = \begin{bmatrix} x_0 \\ y_0 \end{bmatrix} + \begin{bmatrix} t_x \\ t_y \end{bmatrix}$$

Rotation of a Point about Origin

A 2D rotation is performed on an object by aligning it along a circular path on the xy plane. When a 2D point $P_0 (x_0 \, y_0)$ is multiplied by transformation matrix $[T]$ such that point $P_0 (x_0 \, y_0)$ will rotate counter clockwise by angle θ about origin as shown in [Fig. 2.6 (a)], the resulting point $P_1 (x_1, y_1)$ is expressed (note here counter clockwise rotation is taken positive) as :

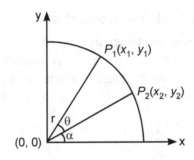

Fig. 2.6 (a) Rotations of point about origin

$$x_1 = r \cos (\theta + \alpha) = r \, [\cos \theta \cos \alpha - \sin \theta \sin \alpha]$$
$$= \cos \theta . \, r \cos \alpha - \sin \theta . \, r \sin \alpha$$
$$= x_0 \cos \theta - y_0 \sin \theta$$

Similarly, $\quad y_1 = r \sin (\theta + \alpha)$
$$= r \, (\sin \theta + \sin \alpha)$$

$$= r (\sin\theta \cos\alpha + \sin\alpha \cos\theta)$$

$$= x_0 \sin\theta + y_0 \cos\theta$$

$$[x_1 \, y_1] = [x_0 \, y_0] \begin{bmatrix} \cos\theta & \sin\theta \\ -\sin\theta & \cos\theta \end{bmatrix}$$

Above equation offer rotation of point P.

2.7.2.2 Scaling Reflection and Shearing

Let the point P_0 ($x_0 \, y_0$) is transformed to point $P_1(x_1, y_1)$. The steps for transformation of the point are discussed below:

1. Effect of diagonal terms: when off-diagonal terms of a transformation matrix are zero *i.e.*, $b = c = 0$ and $a = d = 1$, the transformation matrix is reduced to identity matrix. Then, by applying this transformation matrix on the point P_0 we obtain the following equation or results.

$$[\vec{P_0}][T] = [x_0 \, y_0] \begin{bmatrix} 1 & 0 \\ 0 & 1 \end{bmatrix}$$

$$= [x_0 \, y_0] = [x_1 \, y_1] = [\vec{P_1}] \qquad \dots (5)$$

Equation (5) shows that no change in co-ordinates of point P_0 occurs when $a = d = 1$ and $b = c = 0$.

2. Again, if $b = c = 0$ and $d = 1$, the transformation operation will give following results or equation

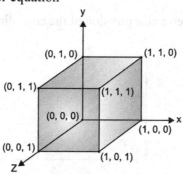

Fig. 2.6 (*b*) Scaling in *x*-direction.

Here, equation (5) shows that $x_1 = ax_0$, produce a scale change *i.e.*, magnification in the position vector's (of point P_0) x component. The outcome of this transformation is demonstrated in [Fig. 2.6 (*b*)]. Thus, when $a \neq 1$, $d = 1$ and $b = c = 0$ the transformation procedure will offer scaling effect (either magnification or reduction) along x-axis. Similarly, when $a = 1$, $d \neq 1$ and $b = c = 0$ the scaling of P_0 will take place along y-axis.

$$[x_0\,y_0] = \begin{bmatrix} a & 0 \\ 0 & d \end{bmatrix} = [ax\ dy]$$

$$= [x_1\,y_1] = [\vec{P_1}] \qquad\qquad\qquad ...(6)$$

Thus equation (6) gives a scaling of both the x_0 and y_0 co-ordinates of the original position vector $[\vec{P_0}]$ as shown in [Fig. 2.6 (c)]. Summary of this transformation operation is given below.

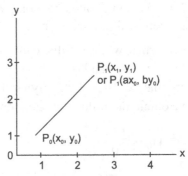

Fig. 2.6 (c) Scaling in xy plane.

If $a \neq d$, the scaling along x-axis and y-axis are not equal.

If $0 < a = d > 1$, then a pure enlargement of the co-ordinates of point P_0 occurs.

If $0 < a = d < 1$, then a compression of the co-ordinates of point P_0 occurs.

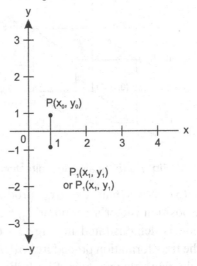

Fig. 2.6 (d) Refection through x-axis.

(*i*) If , $a = 1\ d = -1$, then

$$[x_0\ y_0]\ [T] = [x_0\ y_0] \begin{bmatrix} 1 & 0 \\ 0 & -1 \end{bmatrix} = [x_0 - y_0] = [\vec{P_1}] \qquad \qquad ...(7)$$

Equation (7) shows the reflection through *x*-axis shown in [Fig. 2.6 (*d*)].

(*ii*) if $a = -1$, $d = 1$, $b = c = 0$, then

$$[x_0\ y_0] \begin{bmatrix} -1 & 0 \\ 0 & 1 \end{bmatrix} = [x_0 - y_0] = [\vec{P_1}] \qquad \qquad ...(8)$$

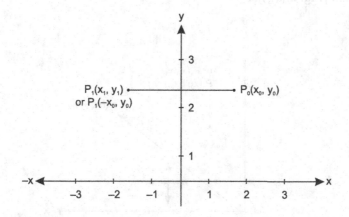

Fig. 2.6 (*e*) Reflection Through Y-axis.

(*iii*) if $a, d < 0$, but $a = d = -1$ then

$$[x_0\ y_0] \begin{bmatrix} a & 0 \\ 0 & b \end{bmatrix} = [x_0\ y_0] \begin{bmatrix} -1 & 0 \\ 0 & -1 \end{bmatrix}$$

The result to above operation shows that point $[\vec{P_0}]$ is reflected along origin as shown in [Fig. 2.6 (*f*)]

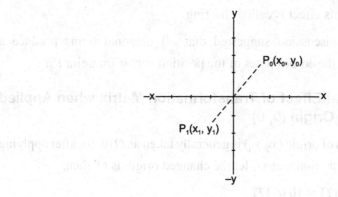

Fig. 2.6 (*f*) Reflection through origin.

II. Effect of off diagonal terms of transformation matrix when its terms is not zero. This will discuss as following ways.

(*i*) If $a = d = 1$ and $c = 0$, then

$$[x_0 \ y_0]\begin{bmatrix} 1 & b \\ 0 & 1 \end{bmatrix} = [x_0 \ (bx_0 + y_0)] = x_1 \ y_1 = [\vec{P_1}] \qquad \qquad ...(9)$$

Equation (9) shows that position vector $[\vec{P_0}]$ of point is unchanged in x co-ordinate but its y co-ordinates change linearly. This effect is called SHEAR as shown in [Fig. 2.6(*g*)].

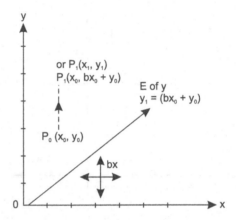

Fig. 2.6 (*g*) shear effects of a point.

(*ii*) if $a = d = 1$ and $b = 0$, then

$$[x_0 y_0]\begin{bmatrix} 1 & 0 \\ c & 1 \end{bmatrix} = [(x_0 + (y_0 \ c) \ y_0] = [x_1 \ y_1] = [\vec{P_1}] \qquad \qquad ...(10)$$

This suggests that y co-ordinate is unchanged but x co-ordinate change linearly because it depends on both x and y and change graphically as shown in [Fig. 2.6(*g*)]. This effect is called shearing.

Thus, above discussion suggested that off diagonal terms produce a shearing effect on the co-ordinates of the position vector for point P_0.

2.7.2.3   Special Effect of Transformation Matrix when Applied to the Origin (0, 0)

Since co-ordinates of origin (x_0, y_0) is generally taken as O (0, 0), after applying geometric transformation matrix, let the changed origin is O' then,

$$[x_0 \ y_0] \ [T] = [0 \ 0] \ [T]$$

2.7.2.4 Homogenous Transformation for Scaling Shearing Reflection, Rotation Translation and Projection of 2D Points and on

From equation (1), we know that co-ordinate of origin remains unchanged when multiplied by transformation matrix *i.e.*, origin remains same, here origin is invariant under the geometric transformation matrix. But in various cases in designing product, while using graphics software the changing of the origin is frequently required. This limitation (*i.e.*, origin is invariant under geometric transformation matrix) will be will be overcome by the use of homogenous co-ordinates. However, it is important to alter the position of the origin *i.e.*, to transform each point in the 2D plane. This can be achieved by translating the origin (or any other point) in 2D plane by the modification of equations (2) and equations (3) in following way *i.e.*,

$$x_1 = ax_0 + cy_0 + t_x$$
$$y_1 = bx_0 = dy_0 + ty$$

Where t_x and t_y are translation constants.

Unfortunately, it is not possible to introduce the constant to translation t_x, t_y into the generally 2×2 transformation matrix because there is no room.

This difficulty can also be overcome by introducing homogeneous co-ordinates antes. In homogeneous co-ordinates, we add third co-ordinate to a point. Instead of being represented by a pair of numbers $(x_0 \ y_0)$, each point is represented by $(x', y', h',)$. Thus, homogeneous co-ordinates of a point in vector varied form is represented as $[x] \ [y] \ h$ where $x_0 = \dfrac{x'}{h}, y_0 = \dfrac{y'}{h}$ and h is any real number.

From above homogenous vector origin can be shifted or projected into the plane $h = 1$ in three-dimensional space. Here, $[x_1 \ y_1 \ h]$ is called three dimensional homogeneous co-ordinates can be of the form $[x, y_1]$. This form is selected to denote the position vector of point $(x_0 \ y_0)$ in the physical x, y plane. Thus, $[x_0 \ y_0]$ and $[hx_0 \ hy_0]$ represent the same two-dimensional point $(x_0 \ y_0)$ if $h = 1$. The rest of the homogeneous co-ordinates are of the form $[h_x \ h_y \ h]$ There is no unique homogenous co-ordinates, *i.e.* [6 4 2], [912 8 40], [3 2 1] where all represent the physical point P_0 (3, 2). For 2D, we can use 3D homogeneous vector like $[x, y, 1]$ for changing the position of all points even origin. Similarly, in homogeneous representation, an n dimensional space is mapped into ($n + 1$) dimensional space. This will help to perform computer graphics operations and even for concatenation of matrix. In other words, it helps in multiple transformation of points or objects combined.

Therefore, $\begin{bmatrix} a & b \\ c & d \end{bmatrix}$ produce a linear transformation in the form of scaling.

Shearing, reflection, rotation either individually or any composite form $2D$ and $3D$ transformation or all of them depending on the value of a, b, c. Here, t_x and t_y are translation parameters, p and q are projecting parameters represented compression co-ordinates by 3×3 matrix as shown below for $2D$ points.

$$[T] = \begin{bmatrix} a & b & p \\ c & d & q \\ t_x & t_y & s \end{bmatrix}$$

Above transformation matrix is capable to transform an object by scaling shearing, translation, reflection, rotation and projection etc. individually or in a combined form. p and q offer projections and s results in overall scaling (*i.e.* signs can or camp session). The pure $2D$ translation matrix for changing the point (x_0, y_0) to let (x_1, y_1) will be

$$\begin{bmatrix} a & b & 0 \\ b & d & 0 \\ t_x & t_y & 1 \end{bmatrix} \text{ where } p = q = 0 \text{ and } s = 1$$

Then, $p[x_1 \, y_1 \, 1] = [x_0 \, y_0 \, 1] \begin{bmatrix} a & b & 0 \\ c & d & 0 \\ t_x & t_y & 1 \end{bmatrix}$

$$= [ax_0 + cy_0 + t_x \, bx_0 + dy_0 + ty_1] \qquad ...(12)$$

From equation (12) we notice that now every points in the two-dimensional plane can be transformed. Even origin $(x_0 = y_0 = 0)$ also, can be transformed about any other point by t_x and t_y on plane $h = 1$ (in this case position vector of changed origin is $[t_x \, t_y \, 1]$). Similarly, effects of following types of homogeneous transformation matrix when applied on points $[x_0 \, y_0 \, 1]$ are :

1. When $[T] = \begin{bmatrix} 1' & 0 & 0 \\ 0 & 1 & 0 \\ t_x & t_y & 1 \end{bmatrix}$ This will give pure translation of co-ordinates of

any point or origin. We can translate it means shift it in new position by adding t_x in x and t_y in where t_x and t_y are the translation factors.

2. When $(T) = \begin{bmatrix} S_x & 0 & 0 \\ 0 & S_y & 0 \\ 0 & 0 & 1 \end{bmatrix}$. This will give scaling of co-ordinates of any

point or origin.

3. $[T] = \begin{bmatrix} \cos\theta & \sin\theta & 0 \\ -\sin\theta & \cos\theta & 0 \\ 0 & 0 & 1 \end{bmatrix}$ This will give rotation of any point counter

clockwise by angle θ.

4. $[T] = \begin{bmatrix} 1 & 0 & 0 \\ S_{hx} & 1 & 0 \\ 0 & 0 & 1 \end{bmatrix}$. This will give shear along the x-direction.

5. $[T] = \begin{bmatrix} 1 & S_{hy} & 0 \\ 0 & 1 & 0 \\ 0 & 0 & 1 \end{bmatrix}$ This will give shear along y-axis.

6. $[T] = \begin{bmatrix} 1 & S_{hy} & 0 \\ S_{hx} & 1 & 0 \\ 0 & 0 & 1 \end{bmatrix}$ This will give shear along x and y direction respectively.

Shearing is the distortion in the shape of the object.

7. $[T] = \begin{bmatrix} 1 & 0 & 0 \\ 0 & 1 & 0 \\ 0 & 0 & s \end{bmatrix}$. This will give overall scaling (reduce or magnify) of the

shape of object.

If $s > 1$, compression occurs

$s < 1$, expansion occurs,

Because $[x_1 \, y_1 \, 1] = [x_0 \, y_0 \, 1] \begin{bmatrix} 1 & 0 & 0 \\ 0 & 1 & 0 \\ 0 & 0 & s \end{bmatrix}$

$$= [x_0 \, y_0 \, s]$$

Here, $x_1 = x_0$, $y_1 = y_0$ and $h = s$. After normalizing this yield co-ordinate $\left(\dfrac{x_0}{s}, \dfrac{y_0}{s}\right)$. Here, $h \neq 1$. Plane is parallel to the $h = 1$ plane, this means co-ordinates of object is now changed from $h = 1$ to $h \neq 1$ plane.

8. $[T] = \begin{bmatrix} 1 & 0 & p \\ 0 & 1 & q \\ 0 & 0 & 1 \end{bmatrix}$. This will give projection of objects or points on that

plane where $h = px_0 + qy_0 + 1$

2.7.2.5   Concatenation or Compounding or Composition of Transformation

Many times, it becomes necessary to combine the individual transformation like translation, scaling, reflection or rotation etc., in order to accomplish the requisite outcome. This combination is called concatenation or compounding or composition of transformation. The combined transformation matrix $[T]$, in such cases, can be obtained by multiplying the respective transformation matrices where care should be taken that the order of the matrix multiplication to be done. Thus, the concatenated transformation matrix may be

$$[T] = [T_n] [T_n-1] [T_n-2] - - - - [T_2] [T_1]$$

Thus, it is observed that, the basic purpose of merging multiple transformation operations is to gain efficiency by applying one compound transformation to a point rather than applying a sequence of transformation operation subsequently. Its advantages is clearly explained in following example.

Rotation of a Point About an Arbitrary Point

Previously counter-clockwise rotation has been discussed and the rotation is performed about the origin. But the section 2.10.2.4 suggested that homogeneous co-ordinates provides a mechanism for accomplishing rotation about points other than origin. This is accomplished using following procedures.

1. Translation given parts to the origin using suitable translation matrix.

2. Performing the required rotation and using suitable rotating transformation matrix again suitable translating matrix.

Thus, using concatenating rotation of a point whose position vector is $[x_0 y_0 1]$, about arbitrary point $[t_r, t_y]$, through arbitrary angle in the accomplished as (b) reflection of an object through an arbitrary line.

$$[x_0 \, y_0 \, 1] = [x_0 \, y_0 \, 1] \begin{bmatrix} 1 & 0 & 0 \\ 0 & 1 & 0 \\ -t_r & -t_y & 1 \end{bmatrix} \begin{bmatrix} \cos\theta & \sin\theta & 0 \\ -\sin\theta & \cos\theta & 0 \\ 0 & 0 & 1 \end{bmatrix} \begin{bmatrix} 1 & 0 & 0 \\ 0 & 1 & 0 \\ t_x & t_y & 1 \end{bmatrix}$$

In the previous section, we noticed that the reflection of a point is done through lines that passed through the origin. But reflection of an object through a line that does not pass through the origin is also required in various cases. When reflection of a point or objects through an arbitrary line is required, the following procedure can be used:

1. The line and the point or the object is translated so that the line crosses the origin.

2. The line and the object is rotated about the origin until the line overlaps with one of the co-ordinate axes.

3. Reflection is performed along the co-ordinate axes.

4. Inverse rotation is performed about the origin.

5. The object is translated back to the original location.

2.7.3 Representation of Objects in Terms of Position Vectors

For convenience, we can take simple objects such as straight line, triangle and square etc., that can extent for complex objects. For making straight line, if co-ordinates of starting point P_0 and end point P_1 are (0, 1) and (2.3) respectively then the position vectors of points P_0 and P_1 will be represented

$$[\vec{P_0}] = [0, 1] \quad [\vec{P_1}] = [2, 3]$$

More compactly the line may be represented by $[\vec{P_0}] = \begin{bmatrix} \vec{P_0} \\ \vec{P_1} \end{bmatrix} \begin{bmatrix} 0 & 1 \\ 2 & 3 \end{bmatrix}$ as shown is [Fig. 2.6 (h)]

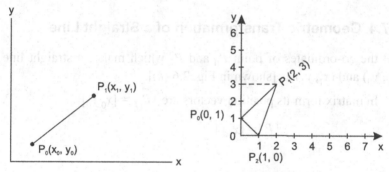

Fig. 2.6 (h) Straight line.   **Fig. 2.6 (i) Triangle.**

Similarly, if another point to make a triangle is P_2 and its co-ordinates is (1,0) then the triangle as shown in [Fig. 2.6 (i)] is represented by

$$\begin{bmatrix} \vec{P_0} \\ \vec{P_1} \\ \vec{P_2} \end{bmatrix} = \begin{bmatrix} 1 & 1 \\ 2 & 3 \\ 1 & 0 \end{bmatrix}$$

Also, a square can be depicted in terms of position vector, graphically shown in [Fig. 2.6 (j)].

$$[\text{Square}] = \begin{bmatrix} 1 & 1 \\ 1 & 4 \\ 4 & 4 \\ 4 & 1 \end{bmatrix} i.e., \begin{bmatrix} \overrightarrow{P_0} \\ \overrightarrow{P_1} \\ \overrightarrow{P_2} \\ \overrightarrow{P_3} \end{bmatrix} = \begin{bmatrix} 1 & 1 \\ 4 & 0 \\ 4 & 4 \\ 1 & 4 \end{bmatrix}$$

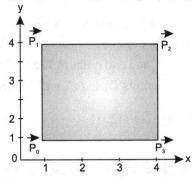

Fig. 2.6 (*j*) Rectangle representation.

2.7.4 Geometric Transformation of a Straight Line

Let the co-ordinates of point P_0 and P_1 which makes a straight line $\overrightarrow{P_0}\overrightarrow{P_1}$ be (x_0, y_0) and (x_1, y_1) as [shown in Fig. 2.6 (*k*)].

In matrix form its position vectors are $[\overrightarrow{P_0}]_1 = [x_0 \ y_0]$

$$[\overrightarrow{P_1}] = [x, y]$$

Fig. 2.6(*k*) Straight line.

    The orientation as well as the location of the line connecting these two points can be altered by operated either separately or combining these two position vectors of points by transformation matrix.

Let $\quad [T] = \begin{bmatrix} a & b \\ c & d \end{bmatrix}$

Then $\quad [\vec{P_0}][T] = [x_0 \, y_0] \begin{bmatrix} a & b \\ c & d \end{bmatrix} = [ax_1 + cy_1 \; bx_1 + dy_1]$

$$= [P_0^*] \qquad \qquad ...(13a)$$

And $\quad [\vec{P_1}][T] = [x_1, y_1] \begin{bmatrix} a & b \\ c & d \end{bmatrix} = \left[\overline{ax_1 + cy_1} \; \overline{bx_1 + dy_1} \right]$

$$= [P_1^*] \qquad \qquad ...(13b)$$

Equations 13(a) and 13(b) can also be represented as

$$\begin{bmatrix} \vec{P_0} \\ \vec{P_1} \end{bmatrix} [T] = \begin{bmatrix} x_0 & y_0 \\ x_1 & y_1 \end{bmatrix} \begin{bmatrix} a & b \\ c & d \end{bmatrix}$$

$$= \begin{bmatrix} ax_0 + cy_0 & bx_0 + dy_0 \\ ax_1 + cy_1 & bx_1 + dy_1 \end{bmatrix} = \begin{bmatrix} P_0^* \\ P_1^* \end{bmatrix} \qquad ... (14)$$

2.7.4.1 Transformation of Midpoint of Straight Line

From Equation (14) the midpoint of transformation line $P_0^* \, P_1^*$

$$(x_m^*, y_m^*) = \left[\frac{(ax_0 + cy_0) + (ax_1 + cy_1)}{2} \; \frac{(bx_0 + dy_0) + (bx_1 + dy_1)}{2} \right]$$

$$(x_m^*, y_m^*) = \left[a\left(\frac{x_0 + x_1}{2}\right) + c\left(\frac{y_0 + y_1}{2}\right) b\left(\frac{x_0 + x_1}{2}\right) + d\left(\frac{y_0 + y_1}{2}\right) \right]$$

Similarly, from the original line (shown in Fig 2.4 (I) the midpoint is

$(x_m \, x_y) = \left[\dfrac{x_0 + x_1}{2} \; \dfrac{+y_0 + y_1}{2} \right]$ and using $[T]$ the transformation of the

midpoint of the original line $P_0 \, P_1$ is

$$(x_m^* \, y_m^*) = \left[\frac{x_0 + x_1}{2} \; \frac{+y_0 + y_1}{2} \right] \begin{bmatrix} a & b \\ c & d \end{bmatrix} \qquad ...(16)$$

$$= \left[\frac{x_0 + x_1}{2} \; \frac{+y_0 + y_1}{2} \right] \begin{bmatrix} a & b \\ c & d \end{bmatrix} \qquad ...(17)$$

Comparing equations (15) and (17) show that they are same. This outcome is that any straight line can be transformed into any other straight line in any position by simply transforming its end points and the line between the end points is re-drawn, this is the one advantage of computer graphics approach. In a similar way, it is observed that a pair of parallel lines remain parallel after transformation operation and intersecting non-perpendicular lines when transformed may result in intersecting perpendicular lines and *vice-versa*. This effect can have disastrous geometric in CAD and graphics. To avoid this situation transformation of a pair of non perpendicular interesting line is accomplished by using pure rotation because angle between interesting line are taken into account in pure rotation. Further point of intersection of two parallel lines is termed to be a point at infinity.

Example 2.6: The position vectors of the end points of straight line AB are $[P_0] = [0,1]$, $[P_1] = [3 \quad 4]$. What will be effect of transformation matrix $[T] = \begin{bmatrix} 1 & 2 \\ 3 & 1 \end{bmatrix}$.

Solution: Straight line $\overrightarrow{P_0P_1}$ is drawn in [Fig. 2.4 (*m*)]. Then straight line P_0P_1 is represented in matrix form as

$$\begin{bmatrix} \overrightarrow{P_0} \\ \overrightarrow{P_1} \end{bmatrix} = \begin{bmatrix} 0 & 1 \\ 3 & 4 \end{bmatrix}$$

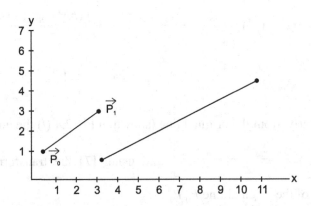

Fig. 2.6 (*l*) Straight line shearing.

Applying transformation matrix $= \begin{bmatrix} \overrightarrow{P_0} \\ \overrightarrow{P_1} \end{bmatrix} [T] = \begin{bmatrix} 0 & 1 \\ 2 & 3 \end{bmatrix} \begin{bmatrix} 1 & 2 \\ 3 & 1 \end{bmatrix}$

$$= \begin{bmatrix} 0.1+1.3 & 0.2+1.1 \\ 2.1+3.3 & 2.2+3.1 \end{bmatrix}$$

$$= \begin{bmatrix} 3 & 1 \\ 11 & 7 \end{bmatrix} = \begin{bmatrix} \overrightarrow{P_0^*} \\ \overrightarrow{P_1^*} \end{bmatrix}$$

Fig. 2.6(l) indicate transformation matrix $[T]$ increase the length of line and changes its orientation, thus producing shearing effects.

2.7.5 3D Geometric Transformation and Projection

Every enterprise has to design a products to satisfy customer needs. Generally, products are three-dimensional objects. In CAD, there is a need to change the orientation, position and sizes of object for complete understanding. In other word, the capability to denote or display 3D objects is fundamental to the perception of the profile of that object. This can be accomplished with the use of computer graphics. To understand this, the 2D analysis has to be extended to 3D.

2.7.5.1 Geometric Representation and Interpretation of 4 × 4 Transformation Matrix on Three-Dimensional Points or Objects

Previous experience reveals that one can use homogeneous co-ordinates of point to take advantages to transform any point even origin points to any other points. Let us have a three-dimension point P_0 whose co-ordinates is (x_0 y_0 z_0) then it be represented by a four-dimensional position vector (homogenous co-ordinates) as

$$[x_0 \, y_0 \, z_0 \, 1] \text{ or } [hx_0 \, hy_0 \, hz_0 \, h] = [x \, y \, z \, h]$$

In computer graphics every time a homogenous vector $[x \, y \, z \, h]$ is encountered, its cartisian co-ordinates $x_0 \, y_0 \, z_0$ are recovered by dividing the first three elements x, y, z by the last element h.

That is (x, y, z, h) converted to $\left(\dfrac{x}{h}, \dfrac{y}{h}, \dfrac{z}{h}, 1 \right)$ when a geometric interpretation of the homogenous vector is needed. This conversion is called normalization. The basic significance of normalization is that a surface or curve or objects developed using homogenous co-ordinate vectors is actually projected onto the plane $h = 1$ in a four-dimensional space. By the use of homogenous vectors any points even origin can be shifted to any other points or planes.

By definition, two homogenous vector $(x_0 \, y_0 \, z_0 \, 1)$ and $(hx_0 \, hy_0 \, hz_0 \, h)$ denotes the same three-dimensional point $(x_0 \, y_0 \, z_0)$ if $h \neq 0$.

To transform homogenous co-ordinates of any point to other point, 4×4 transformation matrix is required. The general 4×4 transformation matrix is represented as

$$[T] = \begin{bmatrix} a & b & c & p \\ d & e & f & q \\ g & i & j & r \\ t_x & t_y & t_z & s \end{bmatrix} \qquad ...(18)$$

Above transformation matrix can be partitioned into four parts where $\begin{bmatrix} a & b & c \\ d & e & f \\ g & i & j \end{bmatrix}$ produce a linear transformation in the form of scaling, shearing, reflection and rotation either separately or any combinations or all them depending upon the values of a, b, c, d, e, f g, i and j $\begin{bmatrix} p \\ q \\ r \end{bmatrix}$ produces a parallel or perspective transformation (projection), t_x t_y, t_z produces translation of origin or other points to any other point on plane. And s produces overall scaling *i.e.*, all components of the position vectors are equally scaled. If $s < 1$, then a homogeneous compression occurs. The alter to above homogenous transformation matrix can be clearly perceived by examples given in next section of this chapter.

2.7.5.2 Three-Dimensional Transformation of a Points

Suppose we have a three-dimensional point P is P_0 $(x_0, y_0\, z_0)$. It is represented by three-dimension homogenous vectors as

$$= [x_0\, y_0\, z_0\, 1]$$

Using transformation matrix (eq. 18) refection and overall scaling transformed point be

$$(x'\, y\, z\, h) = [x_0\, y_0\, z_0\, 1]$$
$$= ax_0 + dy_0 + gz_0 + t_x,\ bx_0 + ey_0 + iz_0 + t_y,$$
$$cx_0 + fy_0 + jz_0 + t_z\, p + q + r + s$$

where
$$x' = ax_0 + dy_0 + gz_0 + t_x$$
$$y' = bx_0 + ey_0 + iz_0 + t_y$$
$$z' = cx_0 + fy_0 + jz_0 + t_z$$
$$h = p + q + r + s$$

Effect of different form of 4 × 4 homogeneous transformation matrix are given below

(A) when $[T] = \begin{bmatrix} 1 & 0 & 0 & 0 \\ 0 & 1 & 0 & 0 \\ 0 & 0 & 1 & 0 \\ t_x & t_y & t_z & 1 \end{bmatrix}$ then its effect will be 3D point translation.

(B) when $[T] = \begin{bmatrix} s_x & 0 & 0 & 0 \\ 0 & s_y & 0 & 0 \\ 0 & 0 & s_z & 0 \\ 0 & 0 & 0 & 1 \end{bmatrix}$ then its effect will be 3D local scaling.

(C) when $[T] = \begin{bmatrix} 1 & 0 & 0 & 0 \\ 1 & c & s & 0 \\ 0 & -s & c & 0 \\ 0 & 0 & 0 & 1 \end{bmatrix}$ then its will give rotation around x-axis in

counterclockwise by angle θ, where $c = \cos\theta$ and $s = \sin\theta$ similarly

when $[T] = \begin{bmatrix} c & 0 & -s & 0 \\ 0 & 1 & 0 & 0 \\ s & 0 & c & 0 \\ 0 & 0 & 0 & 1 \end{bmatrix}$ then it will give rotation around y-axis and

when $[T] = \begin{bmatrix} c & s & 0 & 0 \\ -s & c & 0 & 0 \\ 0 & 0 & c & 0 \\ 0 & 0 & 0 & 1 \end{bmatrix}$ the it will give rotation around z-axis.

(D) when $[T] = \begin{bmatrix} 1 & 0 & 0 & 0 \\ 0 & 1 & 0 & 0 \\ 0 & 0 & 1 & 0 \\ 0 & 0 & 0 & s \end{bmatrix}$ then it will give overall scaling.

If $s > 1$, a uniform expansion of the position vectors occurs. It $s < 1$. a uniform compression of the position vectors occurs. Above matrix is called orthogonal matrix.

(E) when $[T] = \begin{bmatrix} 1 & s & 0 & 0 \\ 0 & 1 & 0 & 0 \\ 0 & 0 & -1 & 0 \\ 0 & 0 & 0 & 1 \end{bmatrix}$ gives reflection through the xy plane.

Similarly, when $[T] = \begin{bmatrix} -1 & 0 & 0 & 0 \\ 0 & 1 & 0 & 0 \\ 0 & 0 & 1 & 0 \\ 0 & 0 & 0 & 1 \end{bmatrix}$ gives reflection through the yz plane.

When $[T] = \begin{bmatrix} 1 & 0 & 0 & 0 \\ 0 & -1 & 0 & 0 \\ 0 & 0 & 1 & 0 \\ 0 & 0 & 0 & 1 \end{bmatrix}$ gives reflection through the xz plane.

Example 2.7: Rectangular parallelepiped with co-ordinates at each point is shown in [Fig. 2.6(i)]. Represent this parallelepiped in homogenous position vectors.

Solution : With reference to parallelopiped shown in [Fig. 2.6(i)], it will be represented in homogenous position vector $\vec{P}$ as.

$$[\vec{P}] = \begin{bmatrix} \vec{P}_0 \\ \vec{P}_1 \\ \vec{P}_2 \\ \vec{P}_3 \\ \vec{P}_4 \\ \vec{P}_5 \\ \vec{P}_6 \\ \vec{P}_7 \end{bmatrix} = \begin{bmatrix} 0 & 0 & 3 & 1 \\ 5 & 0 & 3 & 1 \\ 5 & 7 & 3 & 1 \\ 0 & 7 & 3 & 1 \\ 0 & 0 & 0 & 1 \\ 5 & 0 & 0 & 1 \\ 5 & 7 & 0 & 1 \\ 5 & 7 & 0 & 1 \end{bmatrix}$$

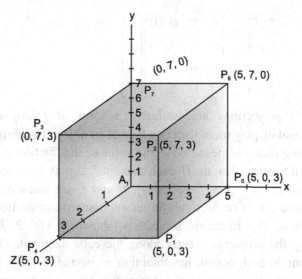

Fig. 2.6(*i*) Parallelepiped

2.7.5.2.1 General Projections

Projection is defined as the technique to display 3-D objects in a scene onto 2D view-plane after the world coordinate description of the object has been converted to view co-ordinate.

There are two types of projections:

(*i*) *Parallel Projection:* In parallel projection, object positions are transformed to the view plane along parallel lines. Relative sizes of the objects are preserved and parallel lines remain parallel.

(*ii*) *Perspective Projection:* In perspective projection, co-ordinate positions are transformed to the view plane along converging lines referred as the projection reference point sometimes also called centre of projection. Objects placed far away from view plane seem to be smaller than the objects located nearer to the view plane.

The parallel projections are further categorized as Orthographic parallel projection, Oblique parallel projection and Axonometric projection.

2.7.5.2.1.1 Parallel Projection

In orthographic parallel projection, the object co-ordinates are transformed perpendicularly to the view plane [shown in Fig. 2.7 (*a*)].The orthographic transformation matrix for homogenous co-ordinates is given as:

$$T_{\text{ortho}} = \begin{bmatrix} 1 & 0 & 0 & 0 \\ 0 & 1 & 0 & 0 \\ 0 & 0 & 0 & 0 \\ 0 & 0 & 0 & 1 \end{bmatrix}$$

$$\begin{bmatrix} x' \\ y' \\ z' \\ 1 \end{bmatrix} = \begin{bmatrix} 1 & 0 & 0 & 0 \\ 0 & 1 & 0 & 0 \\ 0 & 0 & 0 & 0 \\ 0 & 0 & 0 & 1 \end{bmatrix} \begin{bmatrix} x \\ y \\ z \\ 1 \end{bmatrix}$$

Axonometric projections are basically a form of orthographic parallel projections that display more than one face of an object. In computer graphics, foreshortening factor is measured as the value of the fraction of the projected length and the actual length. If each principal axis is foreshortened by the same amount *i.e.*, $f_x = f_y = f_z$ (where f_x, f_y and f_z are foreshortening factors along *x*, *y* and *z* axis respectively)in an axonometric projection, it is called isometric view. The isometric projection (shown in Fig. 2.7*b*) is obtained by arranging the projection vector along the cube diagonal. There are eight positions, one in each octant, for obtaining an isometric view. In addition an axonometric projection may have different scaling factors across the three principal directions. In case of diametric projection any of the two principal axis are foreshortened by same amount *i.e.* $f_x = f_y$ or $f_x = f_z$ or $f_y = f_z$. In trimetric projection, $f_x \neq f_y \neq f_z$.

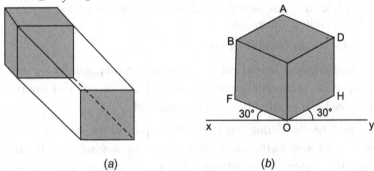

(a)   (b)

Fig. 2.7 Parallel projection of a unit cube.

(*a*) Orthographic

(*b*) Isometric

An oblique projection is obtained by projecting points that are not perpendicular to the projection plane but are parallel to one another. Fig. 2.8 shows the point (*x*, *y*, *z*) is projected to point (x_{vp}, y_{vp}) on the view plane. Co-ordinates of orthographic projection are at point(*x'*, *y'*) on the plane [shown in Fig. 2.8). The line on the projection plane that connects (x_{vp}, y_{vp},) and (*x'*, *y'*)] and the oblique projection line from (*x*, *y*, *z*) to (x_{vp}, y_{vp}) makes an angle α. This *L* length line is at an angle β with the projection plane along the horizontal direction in. The projection co-ordinates can be represented in terms of *x'*, *y'*, L, and β and the transformation matrix is given as follows

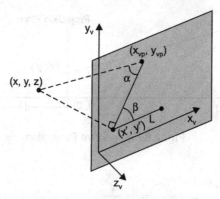

Fig. 2. 8 Oblique projection of point (x,y,z).

$$L = \frac{z}{\tan \alpha} = zL_1$$

$$x_{vp} = x' + L \cos \beta = x' + zL_1 \cos \beta$$

$$y_{vp} = y' + L \cos \beta = y' + zL_1 \cos \beta$$

$$T_{obl} = \begin{pmatrix} 1 & 0 & L_1 \cos\beta & 0 \\ 0 & 1 & L_1 \sin\beta & 0 \\ 0 & 0 & 0 & 0 \\ 0 & 0 & 0 & 1 \end{pmatrix}$$

Now, if $\alpha = 45°$ the oblique projection is called cavalier projection and for $\alpha = 63.4°$, the oblique projection is referred as cabinet projection (Fig. 2.9).

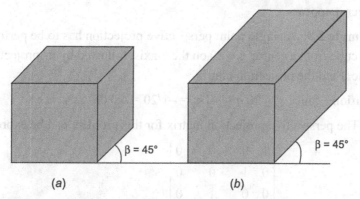

Fig. 2.9 (a) Cabinet projection of a unit cube (b) Cavalier projection of a unit cube.

2.7.5.2.1.2 Perspective Projection

Perspective projection can be one point, or two points or three points. Suppose the centre of projection is set at position $z = -d$, in direction of the z, axis and the view plane passes through $(0, 0, 0)$ (Fig. 2.9).

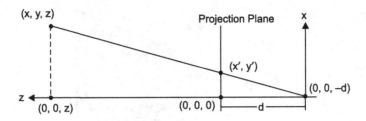

Fig. 2.9 Perspective Projection.

Then,

$$\frac{x'}{d} = \frac{x}{z+d} = \frac{x}{z/d+1}$$

$$\frac{y'}{d} = \frac{y}{z+d} = \frac{y}{z/d+1}$$

where x' and y' are projected points

and .
$$T_{\text{pers}} = \begin{bmatrix} 1 & 0 & 0 & 0 \\ 0 & 1 & 0 & 0 \\ 0 & 0 & 1 & 0 \\ 0 & 0 & 1/d & 1 \end{bmatrix}$$

In perspective projection the dimension of the projected object is determined by the distance between the object and the projection plane or view plane. The nearer the object lies with respect to the projection plane, the bigger it appears.

Example 2.8: A single point perspective projection has to be performed on a unit cube from a centre $z_c = 20$ on the z-axis, followed by its projection on z=0 plane. Find the projection matrix.

Solution: Since $z_c = 20$, $r = -1/z_c = -1/20 = -0.05$

The perspective projection matrix for this problem can be expressed as

$$\begin{bmatrix} 1 & 0 & 0 & 0 \\ 0 & 1 & 0 & 0 \\ 0 & 0 & 1 & 0 \\ 0 & 0 & -0.05 & 1 \end{bmatrix}$$

Example 2.9: The co-ordinates of a points P, Q, R of triangular lamina are $P(2, -1)$, $Q(3, 1)$ $R(1, 1)$ respectively. Then find new co-ordinate and effects of the triangle when applied to following transformation matrix.

(1) $[T] = \begin{bmatrix} 0 & 1 \\ -1 & 0 \end{bmatrix}$

(2) $[T] = \begin{bmatrix} -1 & 0 \\ 1 & 1 \end{bmatrix}$

(3) $[T] = \begin{bmatrix} 0 & -1 \\ 1 & 0 \end{bmatrix}$

(4) $[T] = \begin{bmatrix} 1 & 0 \\ 0 & 1 \end{bmatrix}$

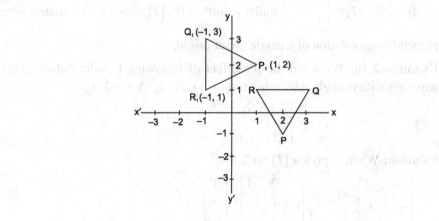

Fig. 2.10.

Triangle PQR will be represented as transformation matrix

$\begin{array}{c|cc} & & \\ P & 2 & -1 \\ Q & 3 & 1 \\ R & 1 & 1 \end{array}$ Multiplication of

$$[T] = \begin{bmatrix} P \\ Q \\ R \end{bmatrix} = \begin{bmatrix} 2 & -1 \\ 3 & 1 \\ 1 & 1 \end{bmatrix} \begin{bmatrix} 0 & 1 \\ -1 & 0 \end{bmatrix}$$

$$= \begin{bmatrix} 1 & 2 \\ -1 & 3 \end{bmatrix}$$

Thus, co-ordinates of transformed matrices of triangle are P_1 (1, 2), $Q(-1, 3)$, $R(-1, 1)$, which is shown in Fig. 2.10 Figure suggests that triangle is rotated anticlockwise 90° about origin. Since, for two-dimensional rotation Transformation matrix is represented as

$$[T] = \begin{bmatrix} \cos\theta & \sin\theta \\ -\sin\theta & \cos\theta \end{bmatrix}$$

Put $\theta = 90°, [T] = \begin{bmatrix} -1 & 0 \\ 0 & -1 \end{bmatrix}$

Similarly $\theta = 180° \ [T] = \begin{bmatrix} -1 & 0 \\ 0 & -1 \end{bmatrix}$

$\theta = 270° \ [T] = \begin{bmatrix} 0 & -1 \\ 1 & 0 \end{bmatrix}$ and $\theta = 360°$ or $0°$, $[T]$ = above four matrix gives perpendicular rotation of triangle about origin.

Example 2.10: What will be the effect of following transformation matrix applying with triangle ABC where $A(-3, 1)$, $B(-4, 1)$, $C(-2, 1)$.

$$[T] = \begin{bmatrix} -1 & 0 \\ 0 & -1 \end{bmatrix}$$

Solution: When applying $[T]$ with ABC

$$\begin{bmatrix} -3 & -1 \\ -4 & 1 \\ -2 & 1 \end{bmatrix} \begin{bmatrix} -1 & 0 \\ 0 & -1 \end{bmatrix} = \begin{bmatrix} 3 & 1 \\ 4 & -1 \\ 2 & -1 \end{bmatrix} = \begin{bmatrix} A' \\ B' \\ C' \end{bmatrix}$$

Thus, ordinates of transformation vertices of the triangle are A (3, 1), B (4, –1), C (2, – 1) which is shown in Fig. (2.11)

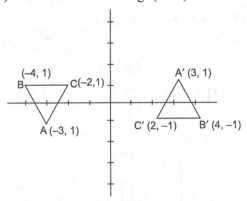

Fig. 2.11.

Figure suggest mirror image of original object (*i.e.*, triangle. In other words triangle is reflected about *x*-axis, $y = 0$

From above figure we notice that reflection is a 180° rotation. Two pure reflection transformation will give pure rotation about origin.

Example 2.11: What will be effect of following homogeneous transformation matrix applying on ABC where $A(3, 1)$, $B(4, 1)$ and $C(2, 1)$

(*a*) $T = \begin{bmatrix} 2 & 0 \\ 0 & 2 \end{bmatrix}$

(*b*) $T = \begin{bmatrix} 1 & 0 \\ 0 & 3 \end{bmatrix}$

Solution:

$$\begin{bmatrix} A \\ B \\ C \end{bmatrix} [T] = \begin{bmatrix} 3 & -1 \\ 4 & 1 \\ 2 & 1 \end{bmatrix} \begin{bmatrix} 2 & 0 \\ 0 & 2 \end{bmatrix} = \begin{bmatrix} 6 & -2 \\ 8 & 2 \\ 4 & 2 \end{bmatrix}$$

Changed co-ordinate point *A, B, C* are $(6, -2)$ $(8, 2)$ $(4, 2)$ respectively. From Figure 2.12, it is scaled by factor 2 on each coordinates. In other words it is uniform scaling in each co-ording by increase of factor 2. Similarly

$$\begin{bmatrix} A \\ B \\ C \end{bmatrix} [T] = \begin{bmatrix} 3 & -1 \\ 4 & 1 \\ 2 & 1 \end{bmatrix} \begin{bmatrix} 1 & 0 \\ 0 & 3 \end{bmatrix} = \begin{bmatrix} 3 & -3 \\ 4 & 3 \\ 2 & 3 \end{bmatrix} = \begin{bmatrix} A_1 \\ B_1 \\ C_1 \end{bmatrix}$$

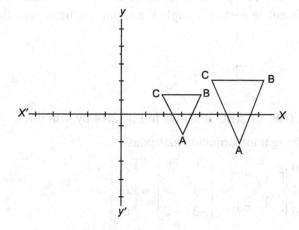

Fig. 2.12 Scale effect unit.

Changed co-ordinate points are A_1 $(3\ -3)$, B_1 $(4, 3)$ and C_1 $(2, 3)$. From Fig. 2.13 scale is done on only *y* direction *i.e.* non-uniform expansion is done.

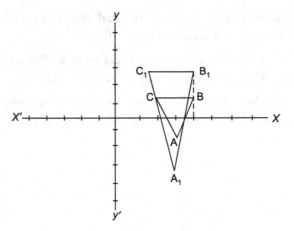

Fig. 2.13 Scale effect.

From above example, it is clear that if transformation matrix is represented as:

$$[T] = \begin{bmatrix} a & b \\ c & d \end{bmatrix}$$
where $b = c = 0$

Then

(*a*) $a = d$ produce uniform scaling.

(*b*) $a \# d$ produce non-uniform scaling.

Where if $a = d > 1$ then uniform expansion occurs and

if $a = d < 1$ then uniform compression occurs.

Example 2.12: The position vector of triangle *ABC* are   (1, 0), (0, 1) and (−1, 0). Calculate area of triangle after applying transformation matrix given below.

$$[T] = \begin{bmatrix} 3 & 2 \\ -1 & 2 \end{bmatrix}$$

Solution: Triangle ABC is shown in Fig. 2.14 by firm line

After applying transformation matrix as

$$\begin{bmatrix} 1 & 0 \\ 0 & 1 \\ -1 & 0 \end{bmatrix} \begin{bmatrix} 3 & 2 \\ -1 & 2 \end{bmatrix} = \begin{bmatrix} 3 & 2 \\ -1 & 2 \\ -3 & -2 \end{bmatrix} = \begin{bmatrix} A_1 \\ B_1 \\ C_1 \end{bmatrix}$$

New co-ordinate of triangle will be $A_1(3, 2)$, $B_1(-1, 2)$, $C_1(-3, 2)$ which is shown in Fig. 2.14 by dotted lines *T* then area of new triangle will be

$$\text{Area} = \frac{1}{2} \text{ base} \times \text{height} = (4 \times 4) = 16$$

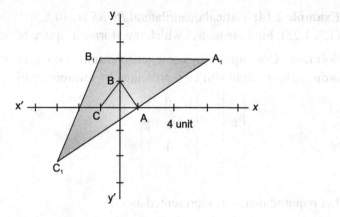

Fig. 2.14 Scale effect.

Example 2.13: The position vector of triangle ABC are $A(1, 1)$, $B(3, 3)$ and $C(2, 4)$.

Solution: Let arm AB and AC of triangle ABC is scaled up by factor 1.7 such that point A remain fixed. Find new co-ordinates of point B and C using $2D$ transformation.

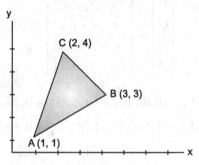

Fig. 2.15

When co-ordinates. If we want to make point A fixed we will shift it to origin. So now co-ordinates in $2D$ will be

$A (0, 0)$, $B (2, 2)$, $C (1, 3)$

after shifting A to origin. Now triangle ABC applying transformation by 1.7, we will get new co-ordinate :

$A \to (0, 0)$

$B \to (2 \times 1.7 \quad 2 \times 1.7) \to (3. 4 \; 3.4)$

$C \to (1 \times 1.7 \quad 3 \times 1.7) \to (1.7 \; 5.1)$

Now we will again shift A_1 back to $(1, 1)$ to get actual co-ordinates as

B_1 (4.4, 4.4) and C_2(2.7, 6.1)

Here new co-ordinates are A_2 $(1,1)$, B_2 $(4.4, 4.4)$, C_2 $(2.7, 6.1)$

Example 2.14: Vertical quadrilateral *PQRS* are (0.5, 0.75), (1, 2), (2, 2.5) and (1.5, 1.25). Find the matrix which transforms a square of unit dimension.

Solution: Unit square in homogeneous transformation form when one co-ordinate is at origin will be represented by formula matrix

$$\begin{bmatrix} A \\ B \\ C \\ D \end{bmatrix} = \begin{bmatrix} 0 & 0 & 1 \\ 1 & 0 & 1 \\ 1 & 1 & 1 \\ 0 & 1 & 1 \end{bmatrix}$$

Let required matrix is represented as

$$[T] = \begin{bmatrix} a & b & p \\ c & d & q \\ t_x & t_y & s \end{bmatrix}$$

Then [T], [A]= [0, 0, 1][a, b, b]

$$\therefore \quad [T]\begin{bmatrix} A \\ B \\ C \\ D \end{bmatrix} = \begin{bmatrix} P \\ Q \\ R \\ S \end{bmatrix} = \begin{bmatrix} 0.5 & 0.75 & 1 \\ 1 & 2 & 1 \\ 2 & 2.5 & 1 \\ 1.5 & 1.25 & 1 \end{bmatrix}$$

$$\Rightarrow \begin{bmatrix} 0a+0.c+1.t_x & 0.b+0.d+1.t_y & 0.p+0.q+1.s \\ 1.a+0.c+1.t_x & 1.b+0.d+1.t_y & 1.p+0.q+1.s \\ 1.a+1.c+1.t_x & 1.b+0.d+1.t_y & 1.p+1.q+1.s \\ 0.a+1.c+1.t_x & 0.b+1.d+1.t_y & 0.p+1.q+1.s \end{bmatrix} = \begin{bmatrix} 0.5 & 0.75 & 1 \\ 1 & 2 & 1 \\ 2 & 2.5 & 1 \\ 1.5 & 1.25 & 1 \end{bmatrix}$$

$\therefore \quad t_x = 0.5, \, t_y = 0.75, \, s = 1, \, a = 0.5, \, b = 1.25, \, p = 0, \, c = 1, \, d = 0.5, \, q = 0$

Hence, transformation matrix will be

$$\begin{bmatrix} 0.5 & 1.25 & 0 \\ 1 & 0.5 & 0 \\ 0.5 & 0.75 & 1 \end{bmatrix}$$

Example 2.15: Co-ordinate of rectangle *PQRS* are $P(50, 50)$, $Q(100, 50)$, $R(100, 80)$ and $S(50, 80)$. Find new co-ordinate of rectangle PQRS if scaling factor $S_x = 0.5$ and $S_y = 0.6$.

Solution : Transformation matrix when axis.

Scaling factor is given can be respective

$$[T] = \begin{bmatrix} S_x & 0 \\ 0 & S_y \end{bmatrix} = \begin{bmatrix} 0.5 & 0 \\ 0 & 0.6 \end{bmatrix}.$$

This new co-ordinate will be calculated as

$$\begin{bmatrix} P \\ Q \\ R \\ S \end{bmatrix}[T] = \begin{bmatrix} 50 & 50 \\ 100 & 50 \\ 100 & 50 \\ 50 & 80 \end{bmatrix}\begin{bmatrix} 0.5 & 0 \\ 0 & 0.6 \end{bmatrix}$$

$$= \begin{bmatrix} 50.0.5+50.0 & 50.0+50.06 \\ 100.0.5+50.0 & 100.0+50.0 \\ 100.0.5+50.0 & 100\,0+50.0 \\ 50.05+80.0 & 50.0+80.0 \end{bmatrix} = \begin{bmatrix} 25 & 30 \\ 50 & 30 \\ 50 & 30 \\ 25 & 48 \end{bmatrix} = \begin{bmatrix} P_1 \\ Q_1 \\ R_1 \\ S_1 \end{bmatrix}$$

Hence, new co-ordinate of rectangle $PQRS$ will be $P(25, 30)$, $Q(50, 30)$, $R(50, 30)$ and $S(25, 48)$

Example 2.16: What will be the effect of following transformation matrix after apply since AB where coordinate of $A(1, 3)$, $B(4,1)$

$$[T] = \begin{bmatrix} 1 & 0 & 1 \\ 0 & 1 & 1 \\ 0 & 0 & 1 \end{bmatrix}$$

Solution: Transformation matrix give and is in homogeneous co-ordinates system for term of homogeneous co-ordinate system for point A and B can be represented by $A \rightarrow [1\ 3\ 1]$ and $B \rightarrow [4\ 1\ 1]$ where A and B is located into the $h = 1$ physical plane, therefore

$$\begin{bmatrix} A \\ B \end{bmatrix}[T] = \begin{bmatrix} 1 & 3 & 1 \\ 4 & 1 & 1 \end{bmatrix}\begin{bmatrix} 1 & 0 & 1 \\ 0 & 1 & 1 \\ 0 & 0 & 1 \end{bmatrix}$$

$$= \begin{bmatrix} 1 & 3 & 5 \\ 4 & 1 & 6 \end{bmatrix} = \begin{bmatrix} A_1 \\ B_1 \end{bmatrix}$$

Here new co-ordinate of straight line AB are $A_1 \rightarrow [1\ 3\ 5]$ and $B_1 \rightarrow [4\ 1\ 6]$. This new co-ordinate are not located onto the $h = 1$ physical plane but located onto the $h \neq 1$ physical plane. If we want only $h = 1$ physical plane, we have to project back onto $h = 1$ physical plane by dividing through the homogeneous co-ordinate factor then new co-ordinate will be $A_2(1/5, 3/5, 1)$ and $B_2(4/6,\ 1/6, 1)$. This indicate that transformation ....

Example 2.17: What will be the new co-ordinate, of the unit cube having one of its corner is at origin and three edges are alone the three principal axis as shown in Fig. 2.16 after sealing by 1/2.

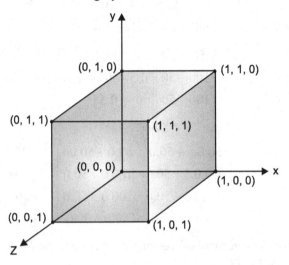

Fig. 2.16

Solution: Unit cube given in Fig. 3.19 can be represented in homogeneous position vector as

$$\begin{bmatrix} 0 & 0 & 0 & 1 \\ 1 & 0 & 0 & 1 \\ 1 & 1 & 0 & 1 \\ 0 & 1 & 0 & 1 \\ 0 & 0 & 1 & 1 \\ 1 & 0 & 1 & 1 \\ 1 & 1 & 1 & 1 \\ 0 & 1 & 1 & 1 \end{bmatrix} = [\vec{A}]$$

Following transformation matrix can be

$$[T] = \begin{bmatrix} 0 & 0 & 0 & 0 \\ 0 & 1 & 0 & 0 \\ 0 & 0 & 1 & 0 \\ 0 & 0 & 0 & \dfrac{1}{2} \end{bmatrix}$$

Here overall scaling factor $s = 1/2 = 0.5 < 1$

Then $\quad\quad [A][T] = \begin{bmatrix} 0 & 0 & 0 & 0.5 \\ 1 & 0 & 0 & 0.5 \\ 1 & 1 & 0 & 0.5 \\ 0 & 1 & 0 & 0.5 \\ 0 & 0 & 1 & 0.5 \\ 1 & 0 & 1 & 0.5 \\ 1 & 1 & 1 & 0.5 \\ 1 & 1 & 1 & 0.5 \end{bmatrix}$

Above new coordinate indicate that new position is not at $h = 1$ physical plane *i.e.*, $h \neq 1$. Thus so obtain the ordinary or physical coordinate, each position vectors in above matrix must be divided by h *i.e.*, 0.5. thus new result will be.

$$\begin{bmatrix} 0 & 0 & 0 & 1 \\ 2 & 0 & 0 & 1 \\ 2 & 2 & 0 & 1 \\ 0 & 2 & 0 & 1 \\ 0 & 0 & 2 & 1 \\ 2 & 0 & 2 & 1 \\ 2 & 2 & 2 & 1 \\ 0 & 2 & 2 & 1 \end{bmatrix}$$

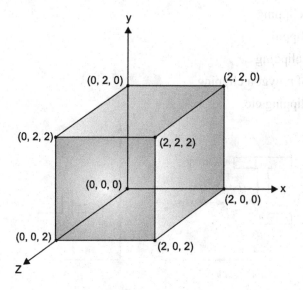

Fig. 2.17 Cubic Daible Size

2.8 WINDOWING AND CLIPPING

In real life we view the outside world through a small window on wall. Similarly graphics may use a window to select portions of the drawing objects located on the screen. Windows may be rectangular or square in shape depending on area to be selected. The concept of "window" is used for clipping operations in computer graphics.

Clipping operation plays a critical role for displaying graphical images in computer graphics. The process of determining the visible portion of a drawing within a window is called clipping. The objective of clipping operation is to select lines or line fragments that lie within the display window and discard the remaining portion. In clipping each displayed object is tested to check whether or not it lies fully outside or inside the window or crosses a window boundary.

After clipping, portion outside the boundary are not considered but portions which lie inside are considered to display the images as shown in [Figs. 2.18 (a), 2.18(b), 2.18(c)]. The regular or shaped area used as the reference for clipping an object is called a clip window. From [Fig. 2.18(a), 2.18(b) and 2.18(c)], we see that all the regions outside the window are clipped (only for display purpose). Clipping may find its use in zooming and panning operations of an image.

The following variety of clipping algorithms is explained in the subsequent sections:

1. Point clipping
2. Line clipping
3. Curve clipping
4. Area of polygon clipping
5. Text clipping etc.

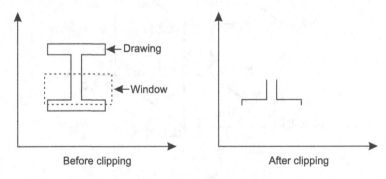

Before clipping   After clipping

Fig. 2.18(a) Clipping of sectioning circle (Curve clipping)

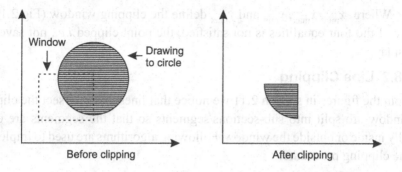

Fig. 2.18(b) Clipping of sectioning circle (Curve clipping)

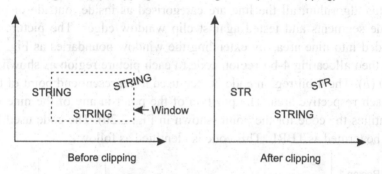

Fig. 2.18(c) Clipping of text

For 2D clipping, various algorithms are used and it can be extended for 3D clipping. The line clipping techniques are standard components for graphical packages. The way to handle curved objects is to approximate them with standard line segments and applying the line clipping procedure. For curved objects' clipping many software package are available.

2.8.1 Point Clipping

The window for clipping is assumed to be of rectangular shape in regular position. We want to save a point P_0 $(x_0\ y_0)$ for display purpose. Then the following inequalities conditions must be satisfied.

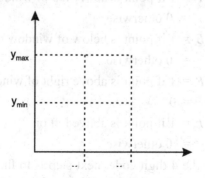

Fig. 2.19 Point Clipping.

Where x_{min}, x_{max}, y_{min} and y_{max} define the clipping window (Fig 2.19). If any of the four equalities is not satisfied, the point clipped *i.e.*, not saved for display.

2.8.2 Line Clipping

From the figures in section 2.11 we notice that lines that intersect the clipping window are split into sub-sections/segments so that the segments are either fully inside or outside the window. Following algorithms are used to implement line clipping procedure.

2.8.2.1 Cohen Sutherland Clipping Algorithms

In this algorithm, all the line are categorised as inside, outside or partially inside segments and tested against clip window edges. The picture area is divided into nine areas by extending the window boundaries as Fig. 2.20(*a*) and then allocating 4-bit region code to each picture region as shown in Fig. 2.20 (*b*). The 4-bit region code is then used to represent end point of the line in each respective area. The position of the point in any of the nine regions identifies the code for the point (shown in Fig. 2.20). The code used for this can be termed as TBRL. This code is identified as follows:

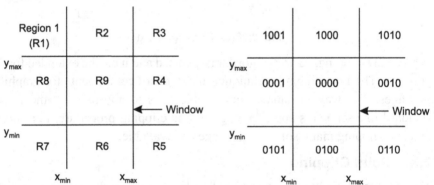

Fig. 2.20 (*a*) Region representation for clipping   **Fig. 2.20.** (*b*) Region with code

$T = 1$ if point is above top of window or

$\quad = 0$ otherwise

$B = 1$ if point is below of window or,

$\quad = 0$ otherwise

$R = 1$ if point is above right of window or,

$\quad = 0$

$L = 1$ if point is above left or

$\quad = 0$ otherwise

After assigning the 4 digit code, next step is to find out whether the line is fully in or out or partially out of the window by the following conditions.

1. The line is inside the window if the both end points are equal to 0000.

2. The line is outside the window if both end points are not equal to 0000.

For those line which are partly inside the window, they are split at the window edge and discard the line segment outside the clip window. On example of line clipping algorithm is shown in [Fig. 2.20(c)].

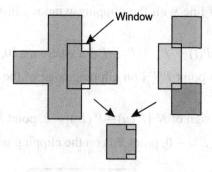

Window

Fig. 2.20(c) Clipping result in two ways.

But from Fig. 2.20, we notice that the different geometrics have identical display by Cohen-Sutherland line clipping method. This is the drawback of above method. This ambiguity will be resolved by the use of polygon clipping algorithm designed by Sutherland. In perspective projection the dimension of the projected object is determined by the distance between the object and the projection plane or view plane. - Hodgman and Weiler-Atherton.

2.8.2.2 Cyrus Beck Line Clipping Algorithms

Cyrus Beck algorithm is much faster algorithm that Sutherland algorithm as it avoids the repetitive looping needed to perform multiple clipping of rectangle edges. Cyrus Beck algorithm is based on the following formulation of the intersection between two lines. In Fig. 2.21, the Cyrus Beck algorithm clips the line P_0P_1. Consider an edge E_i of a clipped window with an outward normal NP.

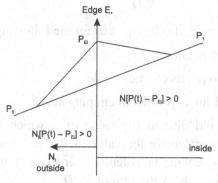

Fig. 2.21 Cyrus beck algorithm clips.

Now parametric equation of line is given by

$$y = y_0 + u(y_1 - y_0)$$
$$x = x_0 + u(x_1 - x_0)$$

In this, we want to calculate parameter u for each point of intersection of the line with the clipped boundary. The value of u determines the point of intersection of line with the clipping window. In this, line is represented parameterically as

$$P(t) = P_0 + (P_1 - P_0)u \text{ where } u \in [0, 1]$$

Consider any point $P[E_i]$ on clipping edge of the window and normal N_i to the edge.

Consider the sign of $N_i[P(u) - P(E_i)] > 0$, point P is outside the clipping

$N_i[P(u) - P(E_i)] = 0$, point P is on the clipping window

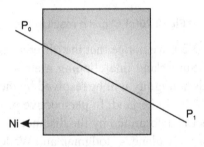

P_0

P_1

Ni

Fig. 2.22

To find the value of u for points intersection

$$N_i[P_0 + (P_1 - P_0)u - P(E_i)] = 0$$

Put $P_1 - P_0 = D$

$$N_i P_0 + N_i Du - P(E_i).N_i = 0$$

$\therefore$ $$u = \frac{N_i[P(E_i) - P_0]}{N_i D}$$

Algorithm should also be checked for the following points:

1. $N_i \neq 0$ (Not possible)

2. $D \neq 0$ (Two points can't coincide)

3. $N_i D \neq 0$ (Line is parallel to clipping edge)

Now we would discard the value of u which are outside the region $(0, 1)$. We would categorize the value of u as u_e or u_i. According to this, if line is potentially leaving or potentially entering. For potentially leaving or potentially entering, check the sign of $N_i.D$.

If $N_i D < 0$, the potentially entering.

If $N_i D > 0$, the potentially leaving.

The the clipped line will be between u_e and u_l with this value of u_e and u_l, appropriate intersection value can be calculated. Otherwise line is rejected. This line between $P(u_e)$ and $P(u_l)$ is displayed.

2.8.3 Polygon Clipping

2.8.3.1 Sutherland-Holgman Polygon Clipping Algorithm

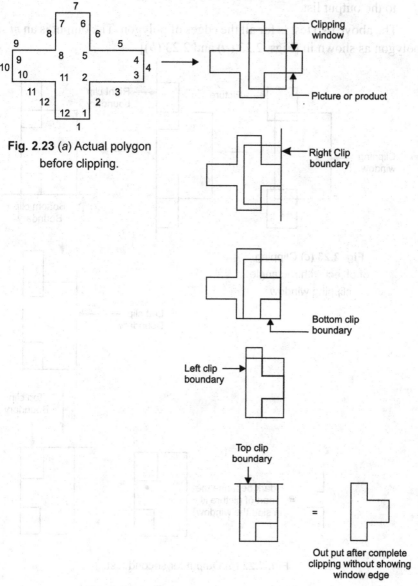

Fig. 2.23 (a) Actual polygon before clipping.

Fig. 2.23 (b) Output after clipping for first test.

An n sided polygon is represented by n vertices as shown in [Fig. 2.23(a)]. This idea is used in polygon clipping. All the edges of the polygon are examined with respect to each of the clip window. Depending on the test results, an edge ew, may be added, and existing edges must be discarded, retained or divided. For every edge of the polygon two tests are conducted.

1. If the edges of the polygon intersect the clipping window edge, the antecedent point is inserted to the output list.

2. If the subsequent vertex is outside the window it is discarded or else added to the output list.

The above two test is for all the edges of polygon. The output is an m sided polygon as shown in [Figs. 2.23 (a) and 2.23 (b)].

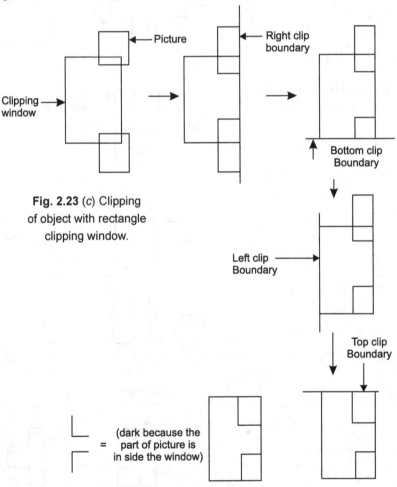

Fig. 2.23 (c) Clipping of object with rectangle clipping window.

Fig. 2.22 (d) Output for second test.

From Fig. 2.23(*c*) and 2.23(*d*) we see that the different geometry of products picture we have same clipping produced or output from above clipping algorithm. We see that this algorithm is worked only for convex clipping regions. Further this can be easily extended to 3*D*.

2.8.3.2 Liang-barsky Algorithm

Cyrus and Beck developed a comparatively efficient algorithm than the Cohen-Sutherland algorithm (which consists of four digit binary code). Later Liang and Barsky independently devised an even faster parametric line-clipping algorithm. In this technique, the clip window is assumed to be rectangular in standard position, a point $P = (m, n)$ is considered to be displayed, if the following equations are satisfied.

$$m\,\omega_{min} \leq m \leq m\,\omega_{max}$$

$$n\,\omega_{min} \leq n \leq \omega_{max}$$

where the co-ordinate boundaries are $n\,\omega_{max}$, $m\omega_{max}$, $n\omega_{min}$ and $m\omega_{min}$. The point is clipped if at least one inequality fails. .

Now, the parametric formula for a line with endpoints (m_1, n_1) and (m_2, n_2) in which one or both endpoints fall outside the clipping boundary, is given as follows:

$$m = m_1 + p\,(m_2 - m_1)$$

$$n = n_1 + p\,(n_2 - n_1),\ 0 < P < 1 \qquad ...(1)$$

(2) can be used to establish the value of parameter P with the co-ordinates of the boundary defining the clipping window.

$$m = m_1 + p\,(m_2 - m_1)$$

$$n = n_1 + p\,(n_2 - n_1),\ ) < P < 1 \qquad ...(2)$$

Equation (2) can be used to determine value of parameter P with the clipping boundary co-ordinates.

We can rewrite the above eqn. (2) as.

$$m = m_1 + p\,\Delta m$$

$$n = n_1 + P\,\Delta n,\ 0 < p < 1 \qquad ...(3)$$

$$\Delta m = m_2 - m_1$$

$$\Delta n = n_2 - n_1$$

using equation (3) in the quation (1) we have

$$m\omega_{min} < m_1 + p\,\Delta m \leq n\,\omega_{max}$$

$$n\,\omega_{min} < n_1 + p\,\Delta n \leq n\,\omega_{max} \qquad ...(4)$$

Now, we can express the above four inequalities as

$$Z_K P \le U_K, \quad K = 1, 2, 3, 4, \qquad \qquad \dots (5)$$

where the parameters Z and U are defined as :

$$Z_1 = -\Delta_m, \; U_1 = m_1 - m\,\omega_{min}$$
$$Z_2 = \Delta_m, \; U_2 = m\,\omega_{max} - m_1$$
$$Z_3 = -\Delta_n, \; U_3 = n_1 - n\omega_{min}$$
$$Z_4 = \Delta_n, \; U_4 = n\omega_{max} - n_1$$

Observing the following facts:

- If $Z_K = 0$, the line is parallel to the boundary.

$$\begin{cases} \text{If } U_K < 0, \text{the line is outside and can be eliminated} \\ \text{If } U_K \ge 0, \text{the line is inside and needs further consideration} \end{cases}$$

- If $Z_K > 0$, the line progresses from outside towards inside, of the corresponding boundary line.
- When $Z_K \ne 0$, the value of P that corresponds to the intersection point is U_K / Z_K.

Now, we can state the Liang-Barsky algorithm as.

1. If $Z_K = 0$ and $U_K < 0$ for K, stop and reject the line, else proceed.
2. For all K such that $Z_K < 0$, calculate $r_K = U_K/Z_K$. Let maximum of the set containing be d_1 and all calculated r values including 0.
3. For all K such that $Z_K > 0$ calculate $r_K = U_K/Z_K$. Let minimum of the set containing l be d_2 and calculated r values.
4. If $d_1 > d_2$, the line is outside the boundary of the clipping window, reject it, else use d_1 and d_2 to estimate the clipped line end points.

In general, the Liang Barsky algorithm in more efficient as it reduces the calculations: only one division is needed by the updated parameters d_1 and d_2. This algorithm can also be applied to 3D clipping.

2.8.3.3 Weiler-Atherton Algorithm for Polygon Clipping

A polygon is called a convex polygon, if for any two interior points in the polygon, the line connecting those lies fully inside the polygon. A non-convex polygon is called a concave polygon. Weiler-Atherton Algorithm deals with the concave polygon. This clipping method was proposed as a method for recognizing surfaces that are visible and so it is appropriate for any random polygon-clipping regions.

In this algorithm the window boundaries are sometimes traced instead of progressing along the polygon edges as vertices are processed. Let the clipping window be initially called the clip polygon and the polygon to be clipped as the reject polygon. Staring with an arbitrary vertex of the subject polygon, trace around its path either in the clockwise course of direction or anticlockwise direction until the clipping polygon is crossed. Here, for clockwise movement for tracing of polygon vertices, we start as:

- If the edge enters the clip polygon, record the intersection point and continue to trace the subject polygon.

- If the edges leave the clip polygon, record the intersection point and make a right turn to follow the clip polygon in the same manner.

Whenever, our path of traversal forms a sub-polygon we place the sub-polygon as part of the display result. We then continue to trace the rest of the original subject polygon from a recorded interaction point that marks the beginning of a not-yet-traced edge or portion of an edge. The algorithm terminates when the entire border of the original subject polygon has been traced exactly once.

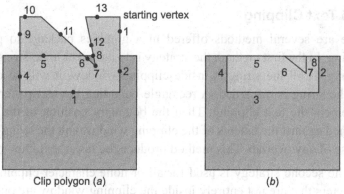

Clip polygon (a)   (b)

Fig. 2.24 Polygon clipping.

For example, in above Fig 2.24 (a) the edges are traced in block wire direction. We select an starting vertex and continue along the same edge (from 1 to 2) of the subject polygon as it enters the clip polygon. As we move along the edge that is leaving the clip polygon we make a right turn-(from 4 to 5) into the clip polygon, which is now considered the subject polygon. Following the same way leads to next right turn (from 5 to 6) onto the current clip polygon, which is really the original subject polygons. We proceed with the next step in the (from 7 to 8) same way, now we a have a sub polygon for output in [Fig. 2.24(b)]. Now we move to our traversal of the original subject polygon from the recorded intersection point where we first changed our course. Traveled from 9 to 10 to 11 produces no result. Now skipping the already traversed 6 and 7, continue with 12 and 13 and came to an end. The [Fig. 2.8 (b)] is the final result.

2.8.4 Curve Clipping

Clipping of curve objects such as circle and ellipse etc., having its area filled with colour, can be done with methods similar to polygon clipping. Curve clipping procedure involves non linear boundaries like lines and polygons.

The rectangular clipping window for a curve objects such as circle etc. can be used to analyze the overlapping or bounding region (rectangle) of the object. If the surrounding rectangle completely bounds the curved object, it will be displayed entirely or if it is fully outside the clipping window, the curved object will be completely discarded. In both the above cases, no further computation is necessary. However, if the curved object it partly inside the clipping window, the clipping operation on the curved object will be executed in steps. For example; if a circle is shown in Fig. 2.24(*b*) is partially inside the clipping window, the extends of individual quadrants and then octants for initial analysis to determine outside or inside parts before calculating curve window intersections.

2.8.5 Text Clipping

There are several methods offered in a graphics package to provide text clipping. In the first method, the strategy is to use all or none-string (character) clipping. If all the string is inside clipping window, it will be displayed, if not, the string is discarded. A rectangle bounding the text pattern is used to implement the text clipping. Then the boundary position of the rectangle is matched against the extents of the clipping window and the string is discarded in case of any overlap. This method produce the faster text clipping.

The second strategy is used for all or none character-clipping. Here, the characters that are not entirely inside the clipping window are only discarded as shown in [Fig. 2.18 (*c*)] In this case; the extents of individual characters are tallied against the clipping window. Otherwise if any character lies over or outside the boundary of a clipping window, the character is clipped.

□□□

3

3D Object Representation and Viewing

3.1 INTRODUCTION

For three-dimensional graphics applications, it is important to identify how views are to be generated, since the display content of a 3D object is dependent on the position of the viewer (front, rear, above, beneath or even inside the object). Moreover, the 3D depiction of objects should be projected onto a flat viewing plane (2D) of the output device. The boundaries of the viewing window encompass a volume of space and the shape of the object is determined by the sort of projection we select. In this chapter, we explore the various operations needed to depict a realistic 3D object onto the output device.

3.2 HIDDEN LINES AND SURFACES

3.2.1 Introduction of Hidden Surface Removal

One of the major issues in computer graphics is to generate visually realistic 3-D objects. When a collection of 3-D surfaces is projected onto a 2-D screen, it is important to discover the visible surface and the hidden surfaces. The visual occlusion of any 3-D object may occur due to the surrounding objects or by a part of its own body. If any part of a surface of a 3-D object is not visible from the present viewing plane is not removed, it creates ambiguity in the display of the object. Visible Surface Detection or hidden surface removal is the procedure that removes any such lines or surfaces which are not to be displayed in the 3-D view. A method may be designed to draw the objects beginning with the objects lying furthest from the view plane to the nearest one. An important part in the development of realistic graphical displays is recognizing those parts of a picture that are hidden from a selected viewing point. There are several techniques we can adapt to resolve this problem, and many algorithms have been designed for proficient recognition of hidden objects for various types of applications. Some techniques need more memory, a few engage in increased processing time, and some pertain to particular types of objects. Selecting a specific method for a specific application can rely on various aspects like type of objects to be displayed, the intricacy involved in the scene; images to be displayed are static or animated and available equipments. These algorithms are referred to as hidden-surface elimination methods. These methods are also called as visible-surface detection techniques. However, there can be a slight distinction between selecting a visible surface and eliminating hidden surface. For example in case of a wireframe display, the hidden line/surface may not be completely eliminated but displayed by dashed lines. In this chapter, we study some frequently used methods for removal of hidden surfaces in a 3D scene.

3.2.2 Classification of Hidden Surface Removal Algorithms

Hidden Surface Removal techniques are broadly categorized as object-space methods and image-space methods based on whether they operate directly on the objects or on their projected images.

An object-space method contrasts objects and parts of objects to each other within the picture description to identify the hidden surfaces or lines. On the contrary in case of an image-space algorithm, visibility is determined at each pixel position on the projection plane. Generally visible-surface algorithms are based on image-space methods. However, in some cases object space methods may also be used to locate visible surfaces. Line generation algorithms, on the other hand, generally use object-space methods to determine visible lines in wireframe displays, but many image-space algorithms can be modified easily for visible-line identification.

Though there are major diversities in the fundamental approach adapted by the different hidden surface removal algorithms, most of them use ordering and coherence methods to enhance performance. Ordering is used to aid depth based assessment by sorting the individual surfaces in a scene according to their distance from the view plane. Coherence methods are used to handle symmetry in a scene. An individual scan-line mostly contains intervals of non-altering pixel intensities, and scan-line patterns usually do not change between adjacent lines. Motion picture frames contain alterations only in the neighbourhood of moving objects.

3.2.2.1 Object-space Methods (Continuous)

The object-space methods compare parts of objects with each other to establish which surfaces should be labelled as visible. It arranges the facets being drawn, such that it offers an accurate impression of depth variations and locations.

3.2.2.2 Image Space Methods (Discrete)

The image space methods decide the visibility of each pixel position on the projection plane. However, screen resolution can be a limitation for these methods.

There are quite a few coherence properties which are used for Visible Surface Detection algorithms which ensure faster computation.

3.2.2.3 Some Important Coherence Properties

In this segment different categories of coherence are discussed. Some of these varieties of coherence are not mutually exclusive and they can be used interchangeably.

(*i*) *Span Coherence*: Coherence may be present among successive scan-lines and may exist within the same scan-line. Spans are referred as section of a scan-line having some specific property. All scan-line based algorithms (*e.g.,* polygon filling, hidden surface removal) are based on the concept of span coherence, which is specified amid a single span and also amid adjacent spans.

(*ii*) *Object Coherence*: Object coherence explores the association among parts of the same object or even between different objects. Adjacent space is usually covered by the same object. Based on these associations, operations like clipping, comparison, sorting, or intersection can be executed at the object level to decrease the intricacy and degree of computations on low-level geometry.

(*iii*) *Ray Coherence*: Rendering a picture has been often performed by extensive rays tracing through an object environment. In this technique, for each pixel of an image, a ray is traced from the observer's location into object space to ascertain the crossing point of the first visible object. Shadow calculation is completed by tracing rays from the intersection point to the numerous sources of light. This procedure is called ray coherence. Ray tracing is computationally expensive and complex.

(*iv*) *Edge Coherence*: Edge coherence specifies that if an edge crosses behind a visible facet, the visibility will change.

(*v*) *Face Coherence*: For face coherence, the even deviation across a face should be incrementally modified.

(*vi*) *Scanline Coherence*: The notion that few changes occur in between successive scan-lines and nearly the same polygons are visible on consecutive scan-lines, is referred as scan-line coherence. Therefore, a processing of scan-line can be done by only revising the information of the preceding scan-line.

(*vii*) *Implied Edge Coherence*: Implied edge coherence refers to the idea that line of intersection of a planar face piercing another line, can be acquired from the two intersection points.

(*viii*) *Depth Coherence*: The depth to the observer at some surface point always varies progressively. This theory is expressed by depth coherence. Usually the adjacent portions of a surface are close in distance. Therefore, the depth at some surface point can be effectively calculated by incrementing the preceding depth information of an adjacent surface point.

(*ix*) *Area Coherence*: The concept of area coherence begins with image coherence and utilizes the information of nearby pixels of a raster image having similar intensity values or colour.

(*x*) *Frame Coherence*: Frame coherence represents the concept that consecutive frames of a video or an animation are probably very similar when the time difference is small.

(*xi*) *Spatial Coherence*: Spatial coherence portrays spatial uniformity. These are a result of progressive variation in the spatial organization of objects or surfaces.

(*xi*) *Temporal Coherence*: Temporal coherence represents the event of gradual changes in surroundings over a period of time, like movement of an object (object space temporal coherence). Computation of animation sequences uses temporal coherence.

3.2.3 Hidden Surface Removal Algorithms

Several approaches have been developed for hidden surface removal of 3-D objects in a scene.

3.2.3.1 Back-Face Detection (Object space algorithm)

Back face detection method is based on object-space method. It determines the back faces of an object using the "inside-outside" surface examination. A point $P_0(x, y, z)$ is said to be "inside" a polygon surface (defined by parameters A, B, C, and D), if the point is on the line of sight to the surface (the observer is assumed to be inside that face and is unable to view the front of the object).

The evaluation can be simplified by using the normal vector N (defined by the component A, B, C) to a polygon surface. In general, if P is a vector pointing towards the observer's (or "camera") position (figure 3.1),then the polygon is a back face if

$$P.N > 0.$$

Let P is expressed as $(0, 0, P_z)$ and $N = A_i + B_j + C_k$.

Then $\qquad\qquad P.N = P_z.C;$

Let P_z be along +ve z-axis.

The sign of the component C of the normal vector N is essential for this evaluation.

In a right-handed co-ordinate system with the observer pointing to the –ve z-axis, the polygon is on the back side of the visible surface, if $C < 0$. Also, a face is not visible if $C = 0$, since the viewing direction of the observer is browsing that polygon. Hence, a polygon is categorized as a "back face" if the z component value is less than or equal to 0.

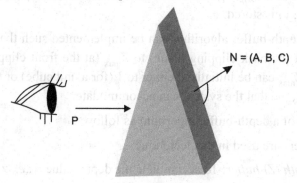

N = (A, B, C)

P

Fig. 3.1 Back face detection.

Same concept may be used for a left-handed viewing system. In left handed viewing system, the normal vectors of back faces are directed away from the observer location and are recognized by $C >= 0$ when the viewing direction is along the positive z-axis. By probing the parameter C for all the planes bounding an object, all the back faces can be determined.

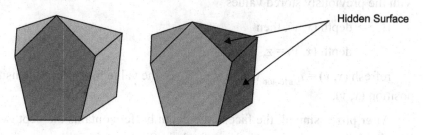

Hidden Surface

Fig. 3.2 Hidden surface detection.

3.2.3.2 Depth-Buffer Method

Depth-buffer is a frequently used image-space method for removing hidden surfaces. The method also known as the z-buffer method, evaluates relative surface depths at each pixel (on the projection plane) position from the view plane along the z-axis of a view co-ordinate system. The method is mostly applied to polygon surfaces, processing one pixel at a time throughout the surface. However, non-planar surfaces can also be processed by depth-buffer method. The descriptions of objects are transformed to projection co-ordinates and each (x, y, z) point on a polygon surface corresponds to the orthographic projection point (x, y) on the view plane. Therefore, object depths can be evaluated by monitoring each pixel position (x, y) on the view plane and comparing its z values. Figure 3.3 shows three surfaces at varying distances along the orthographic projection line from point (x, y) in a view plane considered as the $x_p y_p$ plane. Surface S_1, is nearest at this point, so the intensity of S_1 at (x, y) is stored.

The depth-buffer algorithm can be implemented such that z values range from 0 (at the back clipping plane) to Z_{max} (at the front clipping plane). The value of Z_{max} can be initialized either to 1 (for a unit cube) or to the maximum possible value that the system can accommodate.

The steps of a depth-buffer algorithm as follows:

Two buffers are used in this technique.

(*i*) *Depth (Z) buffer*: To accumulate the depth values (*i.e.,* z-component) for each (x, y) position, in every surfaces.

(*ii*) *Refresh Buffer*: To store the intensity value at each position (x, y).

Initially set the values of depth buffer and refresh buffer for all pixel positions (x, y) as depth $(x, y) = 0$, refresh $(x, y) = I_{bgcolor}$ where $I_{bgcolor}$ is the value for background intensity for position (x, y).

For each point on each polygon facet, the z value is computed and compared with the previously stored values.

If $z >$ depth (x, y), then

depth $(x, y) = z,$

refresh $(x, y) = I_{surfcolor}$ where $I_{surfcolor}$ is the value for surface intensity for position (x, y).

After processing all the facets, the depth buffer contains the depth values for all visible surfaces and the refresh buffer contains the corresponding intensities.

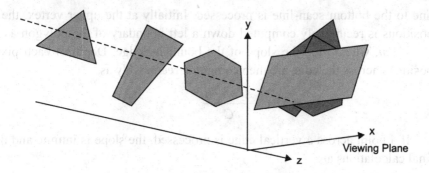

Fig. 3.3 Depth Buffer to remove hidden surfaces.

Depth values for a surface position (x, y) are computed from the plane equation for each surface:

$$Ax + By + C_z + D = 0$$

$$\text{depth } (x, y): z = \frac{-Ax - By - D}{C}$$

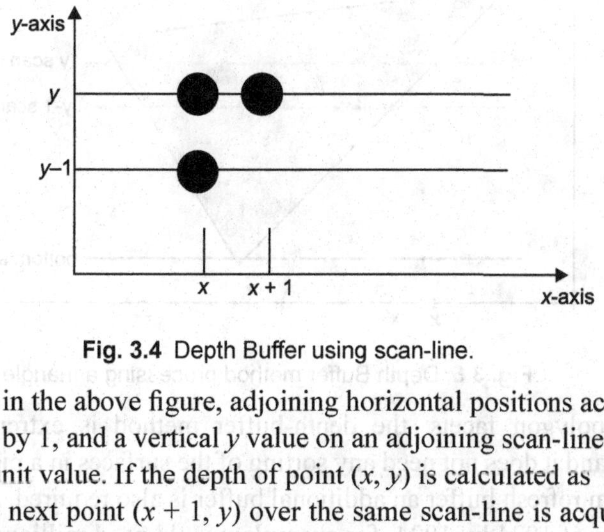

Fig. 3.4 Depth Buffer using scan-line.

As shown in the above figure, adjoining horizontal positions across every scan-line vary by 1, and a vertical y value on an adjoining scan-line also has a difference of unit value. If the depth of point (x, y) is calculated as z, then the depth z' of the next point $(x + 1, y)$ over the same scan-line is acquired from equation of (x, y) as :

$$\text{depth } (x + 1, y): z' = \frac{-A(x+1) - By - D}{C} = \frac{z - A}{C}$$

The value of $-A/C$ is constant for each surface, so subsequent depth values across a scan-line are acquired from previous depth information with a unit addition. For each scan-line, the depth on a left edge of the surface that crosses that scan-line is computed. Depth values at each position in a row across the scan-line are then identified by the preceding equations. The bounds of y-co-ordinates of each polygon are procured and the facet from the upper scan-line to the bottom scan-line is processed. Initially at the upper vertex, the x positions is recursively computed down a left boundary of the polygon as $x' = x - 1/m$, where m is the slope of the boundary edge. Depth of each pixel positions across the edge are then computed recursively as

$$z' = z + \frac{A/m + B}{C}$$

If a point across a vertical edge is processed, the slope is infinite and the final calculations are

$$\text{depth } (x, y-1): \quad z' = \frac{-Ax - B(y-1) - D}{C} = z + \frac{B}{C}$$

An alternate technique is to use a midpoint method or Bresenham algorithm for computing x co-ordinates on left edges for every scan-line. The method can also be used for curved surfaces by evaluating the depth and intensity values at every surface projection point.

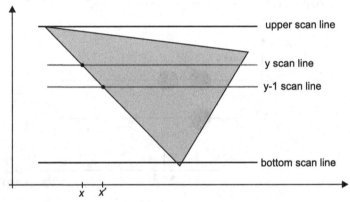

Fig. 3.5 Depth Buffer method processing a triangle.

For polygon facets, the depth-buffer method is extremely simple to execute, and it does not need any sorting of the surfaces in a picture. However, apart from refresh buffer an additional buffer is also required. A system with a resolution of 1024 by 1024, for example, would need millions of locations in the depth buffer, with each location having adequate bits to signify the number of required depth increments. To reduce the storage needs, the entire scene is partitioned and each part is processed at a time, using a relatively smaller depth buffer. After each part is processed, the buffer is reused for the subsequent part.

3.2.3.3 A-Buffer Method

The A-buffer approach is an expansion of the depth-buffer method. The A-buffer method is based on the visibility recognition method for the rendering system "REYES" (Renders Everything You Ever Saw). The A-buffer expands the notion of depth buffer scheme to incorporate transparencies. One prime component in the A-buffer is the accumulation buffer.

Algorithm

Step 1:   Each point in the A- Buffer has two fields

Depth Field: Saves a positive or negative real value

Intensity Field: Saves intensity (value or pointer) of surface

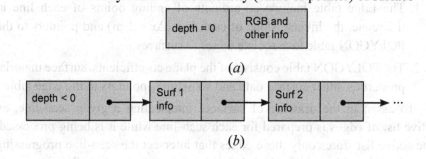

(a)

(b)

Step 2:   If depth $> = 0$, then the depth field saves the depth of the pixel position as before.

Step 3:   If depth < 0 then the data field saves a pointer to a linked list containing surface data.

Step 4:   The surface information in the A-buffer scheme contains the following parameters:

(*i*)   RGB intensity components,

(*ii*)   Opacity parameter,

(*iii*)   Depth,

(*iv*)   Surface identifier,

(*v*)   Percent of area coverage,

(*vi*)   Other surface rendering parameters.

The algorithm executes in a similar way as depth buffer method. However, the depth and opacity values are both used to identify the ultimate colour of a pixel.

Fig. 3.6 A –buffer method to illustrate the consequence of transparency.

3.2.3.4 Scan-Line Method

Another image space based method for identifying visible surfaces is the Scan-line method. It computes and contrasts the depth values along all the scan-lines in an image. Computations of depth values are performed across each scan-line, to find out the nearest surface to the view plane at each position.

For Scan-Line, two tables are used:

1. The Edge table include co-ordinate of ending points of each line in the scene, the inverse slope of each line ($\Delta x = 1/m$) and pointers to the POLYGON table to associate edges to surfaces.

2. The POLYGON table consists of the plane co-efficients, surface material properties, other surface data and sometimes pointers to the edge table.

To assist in the drawing of surfaces intersecting a given scan-line, an active list of edges is prepared for each scan-line while it is being processed. The active list stores only those edges that intersect the scan-line progressing towards the positive x direction. A flag is also set for each surface to specify whether a point on a scan-line is inside or outside the surface. Pixel positions on each scan-line are examined from left to right. At the left crossing point of the surface and scan-line, the surface flag is set as true. At the right crossing point the flag is set as false. If no flags are true then nothing is drawn If one flag is true then the colour of that polygon is used. If more than one flag is true then the uppermost polygon must be determined.

Algorithm

Step 1:   For each scan-line do,

Step 2:   For each pixel position (x, y) on the scan-line,

Step 3:   Set z_buffer $(x) = 0$,

Step 4:   Set image_buffer (x, y) = background_colour

Step 5:   End For

Step 6:   For each surface in the image do,

Step 7:   For each pixel (x, y) on the scan-line that is enclosed by the surface do,

Step 8:   Evaluate the depth of the surface at pixel position (x, y),

Step 9:   If depth $< z$_buffer (x) then,

Step 10: Set z_buffer (x) = depth,

Step 11: Set image_buffer (x, y) = colour of the polygon,

Step 12: End For,

Step 13: End For.

The figure 3.7 demonstrates the scan-line method for identifying visible portions of objects for every pixel positions on the line. Initially the image buffer is filled with background intensity value. The active list for line number 1 stores data from the edge table regarding AD, BC, EH, and FG. The flag for surface S_1 is only true for the section between edges AB and BC on the scan-line. Hence, depth calculation is not needed, and intensity information for surface S_1, is accumulated into the refresh buffer from the polygon table. Similarly, for the section between edges EH and FG, the flag for surface S_2 is only set true. The intensity of remaining areas are set to the background intensity as no other points on the scan-line 1 cross any surfaces..

In figure 3.7, the active edge list for scan-lines 2 and 3, includes AD, EH, BC, and FG edges. The flag for surface S_1 is set true along 2nd scan-line from edge AD to edge EH. However, both the surface flags are on between edges EH and BC and the depth of S_1 is supposedly less than that of S_2, so intensities for surface S_1 are accumulated into the refresh buffer until edge BC is reached. Then the flag for S_1 is set false, and intensities for S_2 are loaded until edge FG is crossed.

The benefit of scan-coherence across the scan-lines might be utilized as the method proceeds from one scan-line to the other. For scan-line 3 no changes occur in crossing of edges, so, depth calculations between edges EH and BC is not processed. Now, the intensity for surface S_1 are entered into the refresh buffer until edge BC is reached. Then the flag for surface S_1 is set false and intensities for surface S_2 are loaded until edge FG is passed.

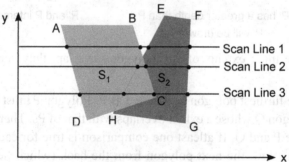

Fig. 3.7 Scan-line methods.

The prime advantage of this technique is that the number of comparisons between edges is lowered due to sorting of vertices along the normal of the scanning plane. Another benefit is that the points (on the edges) passing through the current scan-line are only stored in active memory and each vertex are read only once.

This method can be integrated with other techniques, such as the Phong reflection model (discussed in the next section) or the Z-buffer technique.

3.2.3.5 Depth Sorting Method

The depth sorting scheme is used to draw objects from rear to front into the frame buffer. The objects closer to viewer are drawn over the objects that are further away. Sorting functions are executed in both object and image space. The algorithm is also called the painter's algorithm because it replicates the working of a painter who draws the background before the foreground.

Algorithm

Step 1: All surfaces are sorted based on their relative distances from the observer.

Step 2: The objects are rendered into the image buffer one by one starting from the farthest surface.

Step 3: Surfaces far away from observer are replaced by the one closer.

Step 4: After rendering all the surfaces in the scene, the image buffer stores the final image.

There are certain issues related to simple Painter's algorithm:

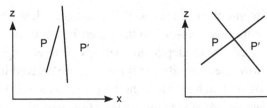

P' has a greater depth than P·   P' and P intersect
P' will be drawn first.

In case the z extents of any polygons overlap, they should be properly compared.

Let the furthest polygon be denoted as P. Polygon P must be tested against every polygon Q whose z extent overlaps with that of Ps. There are 5 test cases to compare P and Q. If atleast one comparison is true for each of the Qs then P is drawn. Now, the next polygon from the back (which lies ahead of P) is chosen as the new P.

The 5 test cases are as follows:

1. Check for no overlap in P and Q's x-extents.

2. Check for no overlap in P and Q's y-extents.

3. Check if P is totally on the other side of Q's plane from the viewport.

4. Check if Q is totally on the same side of P's plane as the viewport.

5. Check for no overlap in the projections of P and Q onto the (x, y) plane.

If all 5 tests fail, swapping of P and Q is opted. Tests 1, 2, and 5 do not distinguish between P and Q but 3 and 4 do. So 3 and 4 are re-written.

Point 3 is updated as check if Q is totally on the opposite side of P's plane from the viewport.

Point 4 is updated as check if P is totally on the same side of Q's plane as the viewport.

If any of 2 tests are successful, then Q and P are switched and the new P (previously Q) is compared with all the polygons whose z extent overlaps it's z extent.

If both these tests be unsuccessful then either Q or P is divided into 2 polygons utilizing the plane of the other. These split polygons are then sorted in the list and the subsequent steps are executed.

In the Fig. 3.8, the surface S is farthest away from the observer. The z extent of S is compared with that of the other surfaces in the scene to find out whether there exits any overlaps. If no z extent overlaps occur, S is scan converted. This procedure is repeated for all the surfaces in the scene. In case an overlap in depth is perceived, the above mentioned 5 tests are to be used.

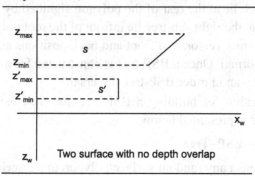

Fig. 3.8 Depth sorting.

3.2.3.6 BSP-Tree Method

A binary space partitioning tree (BSP-tree) is a binary tree whose nodes are constituted of polygons. Binary space partitioning, or BSP, segregates the space into distinct parts by building a tree representing that space. It is used to sort the polygons. The algorithm accepts polygons and partitions them into two groups by selecting a splitting plane (splitting plane is usually considered from the set of polygons) and bifurcates the scene into two spaces. It evaluates the side of the plane each polygon resides, or the polygon may also reside on the plane. If a polygon crosses the splitting plane it must be partitioned into two separate polygons, one on both side of the plane. The tree is built by choosing a partitioning plane and dividing the remaining polygons into two or three lists: Front, Back and on lists – done by evaluating the normal vector of the plane with against each polygon.

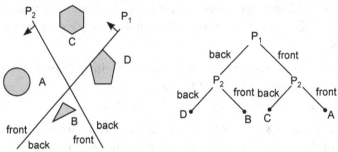

Fig. 3.9 A region partitioned by P_1 and P_2 to generate a BSP tree representation.

For each node in a BSP-tree the nodes in the left sub-tree represents the polygons which lie at the rear of the polygon signified by the root node while the polygons in the right sub-tree lie infront of the root polygon. Each polygon has a fixed normal vector, and front and back positions are measured relative to this fixed normal. Once a BSP-tree is constructed for a scene, the polygons are rendered by an in order BSP-tree traversal.

The algorithm for building a BSP-tree and then using the BSP-tree to render a scene is presented below:

Algorithm for BSP–Tree

Step 1:   Select any random surface/polygon in the scene as the root.

Step 2:   Partition the rest of the polygons in the scene either as a node in the left sub-tree (if lies at the back of the root) or as a right sub-tree node (if lies at the front of the root).

Step 3:   Divide all the surfaces that lie on both sides of the root polygon.

Step 4:   Construct the left and right sub-trees recursively.

3.2.3.7 Area-Subdivision Method

The area-subdivision method uses the notion of area coherence in a picture by determining the view areas formed by only one surface. The technique is implemented by partitioning the complete viewing area into smaller rectangles such that each rectangle is either the projection of fraction of only one visible surface or none. This process is continued until the fractions are recognized as a part of only one surface or they are diminished to one pixel.

   This process begins by successively partitioning the area into four identical parts at each step. A surface can be associated with a specified area boundary in four probable ways:

Algorithm

Step 1:   Every surface existing in the scene is categorized, based on the following conditions:

Surrounding surface–one surface encircles the area completely.

Overlapping surface–only one surface is partially inside and partially outside the area.

Outside surface–only one surface is completely outside the area.

Inside surface–only one surface is entirely inside the area.

The bounding rectangles of surface can enhance the processing speed of identifying the categories of the respective surfaces.

Step 2:   If any of the subsequent condition is true, then, further partitioning of this area is not required

(*i*)   All facets are outside the area.

(*ii*)   A single surface is present either inside or overlapping or surrounding the area.

(*iii*)   An adjacent surface conceals all other surfaces inside the boundaries of an area.

For the (*ii*) and (*iii*) point in step 2, the colour of the area is determined by the colour of the said area.

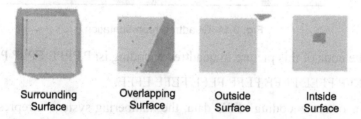

Surrounding   Overlapping   Outside   Intside
Surface   Surface   Surface   Surface

Fig. 3.10 Polygon surfaces and the corresponding rectangular area in
Area subdivision method.

3.2.3.8 Octree

An octree is a tree based data structure, where each internal node has exactly eight children. Generally, octrees are used to partition a 3D space by recursively sub-dividing it into eight octants. Octrees are the 3D version of quadtrees. The name is formed from oct + tree, though it is normally written "octree". Octrees are frequently used by 3D graphics and 3D game engines.

In a point region octree, the node saves a unique 3D point, which is the "centre" of the sub-division for that node; the point signifies one of the corners for each of the eight children. In a matrix based octree, the sub-division point by default represents the centre of the space denoted by the node.

Octrees reduce storage needs for 3D objects, since octrees are hierarchical tree structures describing each area of 3D space as nodes, when compared with the basic voxel representation. It also offers a suitable representation for storing information about objects' interior. Octree representation method is an expansion of the quadtree representation of 2D images:

Quadtree structure for the 2D object is represented as:

F = full, E = empty and P = partially full.

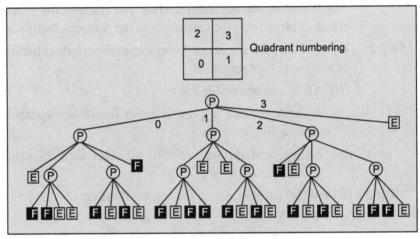

Fig. 3.11 Quadtree representation.

The code of this picture in quadtree encoding is: P PPPE EPPF PEEP FEPP FFEE FEFE FEFF FEFE FEFE EFFE.

For octree encoding of 3D data, the numbering system is represented as follows:

In these techniques, nodes of an octree are projected onto the view plane in a front-to-rear order. Any facets at the backside of the front octants (0,1,2,3) or in the back octants (4,5,6,7) may be hidden by the front facets.

The numbering scheme (0,1,2,3,4,5,6,7), denotes nodes representing octants 4,5,6,7 for the entire region are visited after the nodes representing octants 0,1,2,3. Similarly, the nodes for the four rear sub-octants are traversed after the nodes for the front four sub-octants of octant 0. When a colour is

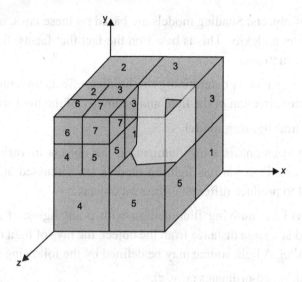

Fig. 3.12 Octree representation.

encountered in an octree node, the analogous pixel in the frame buffer is rendered only if no prior colour has been accumulated for the same pixel position. In general, both a front and a rear octant must be considered in computing the correct colour values for a quadrant. But the following points should be noted.

- If the front octant is consistently filled with some colour, the back octant is not processed.
- If the front is vacant, it is essential only to handle the rear octant.
- If the front octant has assorted or non-homogeneous regions, it has to be partitioned and the sub-octants are processed recursively.

3.3 ILLUMINATION MODEL AND ALGORITHM

3.3.1 Introduction

To obtain more realistic graphical objects, the optical properties of the objects (colour, reflectance, opacity, surface texture, etc.) and the location and intensity of the light sources should be considered. The physics of light is an intricate topic. Light is a narrow band of electromagnetic frequencies with wavelength ranging from 400 to 700 nm. The presence of light is perceived when the electromagnetic energy of the wavelength falls on the retina of the eye. The colours are professed according to the wavelength of the light. The term "illumination" is defined as the flow of luminous flux from light sources amid different points through direct and indirect paths. The computation of the luminous intensity (outgoing light) at a particular 3D point is defined as lighting of objects. Shading models are based on these laws, in varying levels of realism/complexity. This is based on the fact that facets, for the most part, are approximations.

The three factors determining the lighting effects are composition of the light source, direction of the light and geometry of the light source.

Lighting and lighting model

This section emphasises on illuminating the objects in various scenes with light sources. First various lighting models are discussed and then they are combined to produce different effects on objects.

We will be studying illumination with point lights. If a point light is positioned at a large distance from the object, the rays of light may be assumed to be parallel. A light source may be defined by the following six parameters:

- Position co-ordinates (x, y, z),
- Intensity I,
- Direction of emission,
- Angles of emission, φ and θ.

When ray of light hits a surface, several things can happen:

1. Reflection occurs when the entire light hitting the surface is returned by the object.
2. Refraction occurs when certain portion of the light incident on the surface penetrates the object.

Reflection may be diffused where the reflected rays travel in all possible directions, or may be specular, where reflected rays go only in one direction. Snell law governs it. The angle of incidence (α_1) is equal to the angle of reflection (α_2).

In case of diffused refraction–Light is transmitted in all directions inside the object and in specular refraction–Light is transmitted in only one direction.

3.3.2 The Basic Lighting Model

The equation defining the Basic lighting model is:

Surface_Colour = emissive + ambient + diffuse + specular

3.3.2.1 Emissive Lighting

The emissive lighting represents light emitted by a surface. This light does not depend on any other light sources. The emissive object in a dark room appears to be as the colour of light it emits. Figure 3.13 depicts the emissive term conceptually, and Figure 3.14 shows a rendering of an emissive object. The rendering is identical all over the object. Unfortunately, an object's emissive glow does not illuminate other neighbouring objects in the scene.

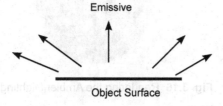

Fig. 3.13 The Emissive lighting.

Fig. 3.14 Rendering the Emissive lighting.

The emissive term is represented as follows:

$$I_e = K_e$$

where K_e is the material's emissive colour.

3.3.2.2 Ambient Lighting

The ambient lighting accounts for the light that has reflected extensively such that it appears to come from all over the scene and cannot be perceived from any specific direction; rather, it appears to come from all directions. Because of this, the ambient lighting term does not depend on the light source position. Figure 3.15 illustrates this theory, and Figure 3.16 shows rendering of an object receiving ambient light only. The ambient term is based on material's ambient reflectance, and the colour of the ambient light that hits the surface.

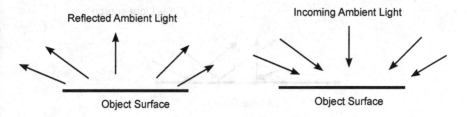

Fig. 3.15 The Ambient lighting.

Fig. 3.16 Rendering the Ambient lighting.

The equation used for the ambient term is as follows:

$$I_{amb} = K_a I_a$$

where: K_a is the material's ambient reflectance and I_a is the intensity of the ambient light.

3.3.2.3 Diffused Reflection

Diffuse reflections are even over each surface in a portrait, irrespective of the observer's direction. The diffuse reflectivity or diffuse-reflection co-efficient K_d, of each surface determines the fraction of the incident light that will be diffusely reflected. Parameter K_d is allotted a fixed value ranging from 0 to 1, according to the desired reflecting properties to be set for any surface. The value of K_d is set close to 1 for a highly reflective surface. High value of K_d generates a bright surface by setting the intensity of the reflected ray being close to that of incident light. The parameter K_d of a surface is set to a value near 0 to simulate the effect of almost complete absorption of the incident light. Although, K_d is a function of the colour of the surface, but it is assumed to be a constant. The intensity of the diffuse reflection at any point for a surface under ambient lighting, is expressed as

$$I_{ambdiff} = K_d I_a$$

The diffuse term is applicable for directed rays reflected off a facet evenly in all directions. When incoming light rays hit the rough surface of any material, the rays gets reflected in all directions, as shown in Figure 3.17.

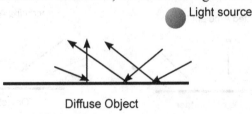

Light source

Diffuse Object

Fig. 3.17 Diffuse Light Scattering.

The amount of reflected beam is proportional to the angle of incidence of the light hitting the surface. Dull surfaces, such as a rugged surface are referred as diffuse object. Figure 3.18 shows a rendering of a diffuse object and the diffusion of light is independent of the view point.

Fig. 3.18 Rendering the diffuse lighting.

Lambert's Cosine Law

Lambert's cosine law guides the reflection of ideal diffuse reflectors (also referred Lambertian reflectors).

Lambert's law states that "the reflected light from a small surface area in a specific direction is proportional to cosine of the angle between that direction and the surface normal".

Lambert's law approximates the amount the incoming ray to be reflected in any specific direction and is constant in this model. The intensity of the reflected ray is dependent on the orientation of the light source with respect to the surface, and this property is guided by Lambert's law. The diffuse reflection equation for a point on the surface, where I_1, is the intensity of the point light source, is as follows

$$I_d = I_1 K_d \cos(\theta) \text{ where } 0 \le K_d \le 1 \text{ and } 0 \le \theta \le p/2$$

The Lambertian illumination model is expressed as

$$I_L = I_1 K_d \cos(\theta) + I_a K_a$$

From figure 3.19

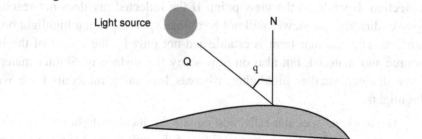

Fig. 3.19

Figure 3.19 Angle of incidence θ between light source vector Q and the unit surface normal N.

$$I_L = I_i K_d (N \bullet Q) + I_a K_a$$

3.3.2.4 The Specular Reflection

The specular reflection signifies scattered light from a facet primarily around the direction of the mirror. The term specular refection is most predominant on shiny and smooth objects, such as polished metals. Figure 3.20 illustrates the notion of specular reflection and rendering of an object using specular reflection is shown in Figure 3.21.

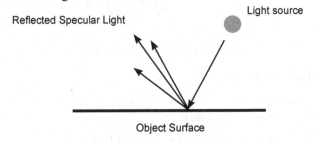

Fig. 3.20 The Specular Reflection.

Fig. 3.21 Rendering the Specular Reflection.

Unlike the ambient, emissive and diffuse forms of lighting, the specular reflection depends on the view point. If the reflected ray does not reach the viewer directly, the viewer will not be able to spot a specular highlight on the surface. The specular term is established not only by the colour of the light source and material, but also on how shiny the surface is. Shinier materials have distinct, smaller highlights, whereas less shiny materials have wider highlights.

The angle of specular-reflection equals the incident light angle, with the two angles calculated on opposite sides of the unit normal surface vector N. Let Q represent the unit vector pointed towards light source; R denotes the unit vector in the direction of ideal specular reflection; and V is the unit vector aligned to the observer's direction from the surface position and angle Φ is the viewing angle with respect to the specular-reflection direction. In this case- we can see the reflection if V and R coincide ($\Phi = 0$).

The shininess of any material surface is determined by ηs, the specular reflection parameter. A practical model for computing the specular-reflection is proposed by Phong BuiTuong and referred as the Phong model, or the Phong specular-reflection model. It fixes the intensity of specular reflection relative to $\cos^{\eta s} f$. The angle Φ may have values ranging from 0 to 90 degrees.

The mathematical formulation used for the specular reflection is given as:

$$Ispec = K_s I_1 \cos^{\eta s} f$$
$$= K_s I_1 (V \bullet R) \cos^{\eta s} f$$

where K_s is the material's specular color and the value of $\cos \Phi$ can be calculated with the dot product $V \bullet R$.

A simpler version of Phong model may be obtained by using H, the halfway vector between L and V to compute the range of specular reflections. If $V.R$ in the Phong model is replaced by $N.H$, this merely substitutes the observed $\cos\Phi$ calculation with the observed $\cos \alpha$ calculation

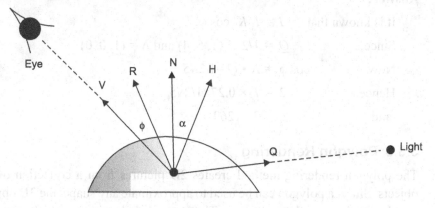

Fig. 3.22 Calculating the Specular Reflection

$$I_{spec} = K_s I_1 (N.H)^{\eta s}$$

Adding the reflections with multiple light sources

The ambient, diffuse, and specular lighting can be mixed to generate the final form of lighting object, as shown in Figure 3.23. In the figure, the emissive form of lighting is purposely removed since it contributes only for producing special effects and is hardly used for normal lighting.

$$I_{pr} = I_{amb} + I_d + I_{spec}$$
$$= I_1 K_d (N \bullet Q) + I_a Ka + K_s I_1 (N \bullet H)^{\eta s}$$

Now let us consider the combined illumination for multiple light sources. Let there be p light sources.

$$I_{pr} = I_a K_a + \sum_{i=1}^{p} I_{li}[K_d(N \cdot Q) + K_a(N \cdot H)^{\eta_s}]$$

Fig. 3.23 Phong Reflection.

Problem: A surface is represented by three points $P(1,0,1)$, $Q(1,1,1)$ and $R(1,0,0)$. A light source is situated far way from this surface in the direction $1/2\sqrt{5}$ $(1, 5, 4)$. If the shaded intensity for the facet is fixed at 2, find out the intensity of the light necessary at the source. There is no specular reflection and the diffuse reflectivity of the surface is 0.27.

Answer:

It is known that $I = I_s K_d \cos \varphi$,

Since, $Q = 1/2\sqrt{5}$ $(1, 5, 4)$ and $N = (1, 0, 0)$

Now, $\cos \varphi = N \bullet Q = 1/2\sqrt{5}$

Hence, $2 = I_s \times 0.27 \times 1/2\sqrt{5}$

and $I_s = 33.1269$.

3.3.3 Polygon Rendering

The polygon rendering method creates 2D pictures from a collection of 3D objects. Since, a polygon can be used to approximate any shape, the 3D objects are depicted using flat polygons. The group of algorithms which generate the 2D image are collectively referred as a rendering pipeline. A polygon rendering pipeline is used by most 3D computer graphics applications to produce images. Each polygon can either be rendered with the same intensity all throughout, or the intensity can be evaluated at each point of the polygon using an interpolation method.

Objects are assembled into a picture, alongwith the illuminating sources, and an imaginary observer or camera. Once, a scene has been generated, it is provided as an input to the rendering pipeline, and the ouput is a 2D image from the view of the imaginary observer.

The various Polygon Rendering Methods are :

(*i*) Constant intensity rendering also called "flat shading".

(*ii*) Intensity interpolation rendering referred as "Gouraud shading".

(*iii*) Normal vector interpolation rendering referred as "Phong shading".

3.3.3.1 Constant-Intensity Shading

A simple and fast scheme for colouring a 3-D object with polygon surfaces is constant-intensity shading, also called flat shading. For each polygon, a particular intensity is computed and then all the surfaces of the polygon are rendered with the particular intensity. Fast shading may be used for rapidly portraying the generic facet of a curved facet object, as in Fig. 3.24.

The constant shading of a polygon surface is accurate if all the following assumptions are true:

(*i*) The object is not actually a curved facet object but is a polyhedron.

(*ii*) All light sources enlightening the object are placed far from the surface so that the attenuation function and the vectors Q and N are same all throughout the surface.

(*iii*) The observer's point is adequately far from the surface so that $V. R$ remains same for every point over the surface.

However, when all the above mentioned conditions are not true, it is still possible to render a polygon effectively with constant shading by using small polygon facets and computing the intensity for each such facet.

Fig. 3.24 Constant Shading.

3.3.3.2 Gouraud Shading

The intensity-interpolation method for shading proposed by Gouraud is commonly referred as Gouraud shading. The technique is used to render a surface by simply interpolating the intensities throughout the surface. Intensity information for each polygon is compared with the intensity information of neighbouring polygons having common edges. This enables the Gouraud shading method eliminate the intensity irregularities that take place in constant shading.

The Gouraud shading steps are as follows:

   (*i*) For each polygon vertex, compute the average unit normal vector.

  (*ii*) The vertex intensity is computed using an illumination model.

 (*iii*) The vertex intensities are then linearly interpolated over the polygon surface.

By calculating the average of the surface normals of all polygons sharing a vertex, a normal vector for the shared vertex is obtained, as shown in Fig. 3.25. This is continued for all shared vertices.

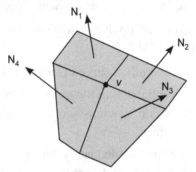

Fig. 3.25 Calculation of normal at vertex v.

For any vertex *v*, the unit vertex normal N_v is calculated using the following equation:

$$Nv = \frac{\sum_{i=1}^{p} N_i}{\left| \sum_{i=1}^{p} N_i \right|}$$

Once the normal at each vertex is available, the intensity at all the vertices can be computed using any illumination model.

In the subsequent step the intensities along the edges of the polygon is interpolated. Then the intensity at the crossing point of a polygon edge with a scan-line is linearly interpolated using the intensities at the edge endpoints. This is repeated for all scan-lines.

Let there be a polygon whose edge with endpoint vertices at positions 1 and 2 is intersected by the scan-line at point 5 (as in Figure 3.26). The intensity at vertex 1 and 2 are I_1 and I_2 respectively. A speedy method for obtaining the intensity at point 5 is to interpolate the intensities I_1, and I_2, using simply the concept of vertical displacement of the scan-line.

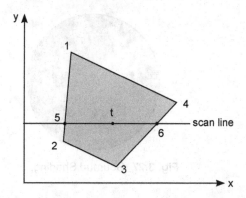

Fig. 3.26 Intensity interpolation in Gouraud shading.

$$I_5 = \frac{y_5 - y_2}{y_1 - y_2} I_1 + \frac{y_1 - y_5}{y_1 - y_2} I_2$$

Note: The impact of the intensity at the point 2 *i.e.*, I_2 is more on I_5 (intensity at point 5) than I_1; since 5 is closer to 2, or in other words

$$\frac{y_5 - y_2}{y_1 - y_2} < \frac{y_1 - y_5}{y_1 - y_2}$$

Hence, the impact of I_2 is greater on I_5 than I_1 and is measured by the ratio of distance of point 5 w.r.t. point 1 and 2.

Similarly, the intensities at vertices 3 and 4 are interpolated to obtain the intensity at point 6.

$$I_6 = \frac{y_6 - y_3}{y_4 - y_3} I_4 + \frac{y_4 - y_6}{y_4 - y_3} I_3$$

Once the intensities at these end points are evaluated along a scan-line, a point situated on the scan-line (such as point *t* in Figure 3.26) is interpolated from the intensities at points 5 and 6 as

$$I_t = \frac{x_t - x_5}{x_6 - x_5} I_6 + \frac{x_6 - x_t}{x_6 - x_5} I_5$$

Similar calculations are used to compute intensities at successive horizontal pixel positions along every scan-line.

At the time of rendering polygon surfaces, the intensity of each colour component is computed for every vertex. A hidden-surface algorithm and Gouraud shading can be coupled to render all visible polygons along any scan-line.

The intensity discontinuities caused by constant-shading model can be eliminated by Gouraud shading (Fig. 3.27).

Fig. 3.27 Gouraud Shading.

Demerits

The highlights on the polygon surface occasionally shows inconsistent shapes, and the method of linear intensity interpolation may result in dark or bright intensity stripes/bands. These bands are called Mach bands. The Mach bands can be minimized by further partitioning the surface into several polygon faces or by using as Phong shading.

3.3.3.3 Phong Shading

A more precise technique for polygon surface rendering is Phong shading. In this method, the normal vectors are interpolated, and the illumination at each surface point is computed. This method, proposed by Phong Bui Tuong is also referred as normal-vector interpolation shading. It presents more pragmatic highlights on a facet and reduces the Mach-band effect to a large extent.

The steps of Phong shading technique is as follows:

1. For all vertices of the polygon, compute the average unit normal vector.

2. For all the vertices over the surface of the polygon, linearly interpolate the normals.

3. To evaluate the intensities of the projected pixel for each surface point, an illumination model is applied along each scan-line.

The interpolation of surface normals between two vertices across a polygon edge is demonstrated in Fig. 3.28. The normal vector N_5 for the scan-line crossing point along the edge between vertices 1 and 2 can be calculated by interpolating vertically between endpoint edge normals.

From figure 3.28 the equation of interpolation of surface normals along a polygon edge for Phong shading is given as

$$N_5 = \frac{y_6 - y_2}{y_1 - y_2} N_1 + \frac{y_1 - y_6}{y_1 - y_2} N_2$$

$$N_6 = \frac{y_6 - y_2}{y_1 - y_2} N_1 + \frac{y_1 - y_6}{y_1 - y_2} N_2$$

$$N_t = \frac{x_t - x_5}{x_6 - x_5} N_6 + \frac{x_6 - x_t}{x_6 - x_5} N_5$$

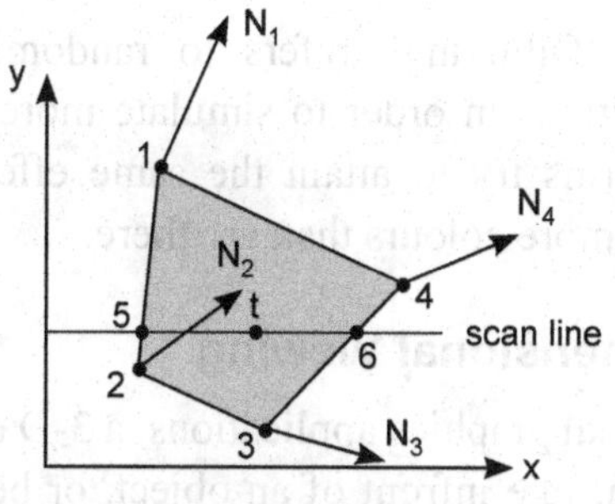

Fig. 3.26 Surface normal interpolation in Phong shading.

Normal between two adjacent scan-lines and along every scan-line can be calculated by incremental methods. The illumination model is used at each pixel position along a scan-line, to establish the surface intensity at that point. Evaluation of intensity components at each point along the scan-line, using an approximated normal vector actually generates more accurate results than the Gouraud shading.

However, Phong shading involves comparatively more calculations.

Fig. 3.29 Phong Shading.

Gouraud Shading	Phong Shading
Vertex wise illumination calculation	Instead of interpolation, Illumination is considered for each pixel inside the polygon
Normal is needed for each vertex	Normal is required for all the pixels
Vertex wise normal can be computed by interpolating the normal of the neighbouring face	Need to plot the normal back to world or eye space
Drawback: Inaccurate lighting inside the polygon.	Drawback: Slow, Complex calculation

Note: "Halftoning" is a term used in the print industry to describe how to imitate varying tones with significantly fewer inks. In halftoning a fixed pattern of dots vary in size in order to create the illusion of continuous tone.

Another term "Dithering" refers to randomization of colour values or intensity or positions in order to simulate more tones than are available. Essentially both terms try to attain the same effect, to make the observer believe into seeing more colours than are there.

3.3.4 Three-Dimensional Viewing

For three-dimensional graphics applications, a 3-D object can be viewed from any spatial position, like infront of an object, or behind the object, or in the middle of a group of objects, and even inside an object. In addition, three-dimensional depictions of objects must be projected onto the output device (2-D). And the clipping boundaries now surround a volume of space, whose outline depends on the type of chosen projection.

3.3.4.1 Viewing Pipeline

Modelling and Viewing Transformation can be achieved by 3D transformations. In graphics packages, the viewing-co-ordinate system is utilized as an indication for specifying the observer's position and the projection plane's location. Projection operations transform the world viewing-co-ordinate (3D) to co-ordinates on the projection plane (2D).

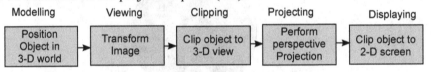

Fig. 3.30 General 3-D transformation pipelines, from modelling co-ordinates to final device co-ordinates.

Once the scene has been designed (as in figure 3.30), world-co-ordinate points are transformed to viewing co-ordinates. The viewing-co-ordinate system is used in graphics packages as a reference for specifying the viewing position of the observer and the location of the projection plane. Next, projection operations are executed to transform the viewing-co-ordinate depiction of the scene to the projection plane co-ordinates, which is in turn plotted to the output device.

3.3.4.1.1 Viewing Co-ordinates

A Viewing co-ordinates system or view reference co-ordinate system $[x_v, y_v, z_v]$, describes 3D objects with respect to an observer as shown in Figure 3.31. The following steps are implemented to specify a viewing co-ordinate.

(*i*) A projection plane, or view plane, is then established in alignment with (x_v, y_v) and perpendicular to the viewing z_v.

(*ii*) The world-co-ordinate positions in the picture are converted to viewing co-ordinates and subsequently the co-ordinates of the viewing system are projected onto the view plane.

(*iii*) To constitute the viewing-co-ordinate reference frame, a world co-ordinate position called the view reference point (eye or camera position) $P_0(x_0, y_0, z_0)$ is selected. This point is the origin of the viewing-co-ordinate system.

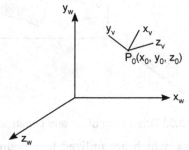

Fig. 3.31 A right-handed viewing co-ordinate system

(*iv*) Next, by specifying the view-plane normal vector N, the orientation of the view plane and the positive direction for the z_v is selected.

(*v*) A point in the world-co-ordinate position P is selected and this point establishes the direction for N relative either to the world origin or to the viewing-co-ordinate origin P_0. N is basically specified as a world-co-ordinate vector (shown in figure 3.32).

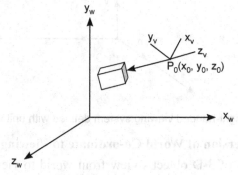

Fig. 3.32 Orientation of the vector N with look-at point P.

(*vi*) A vector V referred as the view-up vector is selected for up direction of the view. This is used to set up the positive direction for the y_v axis (Fig. 3.33).

(*vii*) The direction of the x_v axis is represented using a 3rd vector U which is computed using N and V. U is right-angled to both N and V (Fig. 3.33). Now, the orientation of V can be redirected as perpendicular to both N and U, to set up the y_v direction.

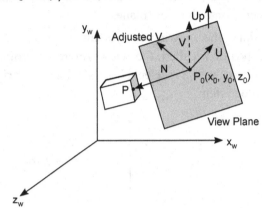

Fig. 3.33 Orientation of V and U with view plane

Unit axis vectors, which are utilized to procure the constituents of the world-to-viewing-co-ordinate transformation matrix are also needed for the transformation of World to Viewing Co-ordinates. The viewing system is often referred as a "uvn system" (Fig. 3.34).

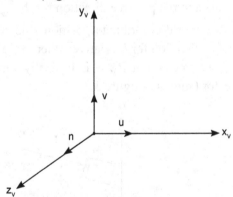

Fig. 3.34 A right-handed viewing system defined with unit vectors u, v, and n.

3.3.4.1.2 Conversion of World Co-ordinate to Viewing Co-ordinate

The conversion of 3-D object's view from world to viewing co-ordinates is same as using translation and rotation to place the viewing reference frame onto the world frame. Initially, the view reference point is transformed to the origin of the world-co-ordinate system using translation. Then rotation operation is applied to x_v, y_v, and z_v axes to align it with the world co-ordinate axes, respectively (shown in Fig. 3.35).

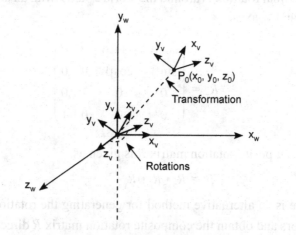

Fig. 3.35 Aligning a viewing co-ordinate system along the world
co-ordinate axes using transformations.

If the reference point of the view is set at world co-ordinate P_0 (x_0, y_0, z_0), this point is translated to the world origin (as shown in Fig. 3.35) with the matrix transformation T which is represented as follows:

$$T = \begin{pmatrix} 1 & 0 & 0 & -x_0 \\ 0 & 1 & 0 & -y_0 \\ 0 & 0 & 1 & -z_0 \\ 0 & 0 & 0 & 1 \end{pmatrix}$$

The series of rotation operations may require three co-ordinate-axis rotations, depending on the direction of N.

(*i*) First the rotation takes place around x_w-axis with an angle q to bring z_v into the x_w-z_w plane.

$$R_x = \begin{pmatrix} 1 & 0 & 0 & 0 \\ 0 & \cos\theta & -\sin\theta & 0 \\ 0 & \sin\theta & \cos\theta & 0 \\ 0 & 0 & 0 & 1 \end{pmatrix}$$

(*ii*) Next the rotation takes place around the world y_w axis with an angle α to align the z_w and z_v axes.

$$R_y = \begin{pmatrix} \cos\alpha & 0 & \sin\alpha & 0 \\ 0 & 1 & 0 & 0 \\ -\sin\alpha & 0 & \cos\alpha & 0 \\ 0 & 0 & 0 & 1 \end{pmatrix}$$

(*iii*) The final rotation is around the world z_w axis with an angle β to align the y_w and y_v axes.

$$R_z = \begin{pmatrix} \cos\beta & -\sin\beta & 0 & 0 \\ \sin\beta & \cos\beta & 0 & 0 \\ 0 & 0 & 1 & 0 \\ 0 & 0 & 0 & 1 \end{pmatrix}$$

The composite rotation matrix R is given as:

$$R = R_z \bullet R_y \bullet R_x$$

There is an alternative method for generating the rotation matrix through *uvn* vectors and obtain the composite rotation matrix R directly as follows.

$$R_z = \begin{pmatrix} u_1 & u_1 & u_3 & 0 \\ v_1 & v_2 & v_3 & 0 \\ n_1 & n_2 & n_3 & 0 \\ 0 & 0 & 0 & 1 \end{pmatrix}$$

Where u, v, n are calculated using N and V as follows

$$n = \frac{N}{|N|} = (n_1, n_2, n_3)$$

$$u = \frac{V \times N}{|V \times N|} = (u_1, u_2, u_3)$$

$$v = n \times u = (v_1, v_2, v_3)$$

For both the techniques the composite matrix for the viewing transformation is presented as

$$\text{Trans}_{w,v} = R \bullet T$$

3.3.4.1.3 View Volumes and General Projections

The amount of a scene captured by a camera is determined by its lens. In computer graphics, the dimension of the view window controls the amount of scene that will be displayed. A view window or projection window in the view plane is a rectangular view for 3-D viewing. The view window's edges are parallel to the x_v and y_v viewing axes and the view window is defined by its extreme points (shown in Fig. 3.36). A view window may be positioned anywhere on the view plane.

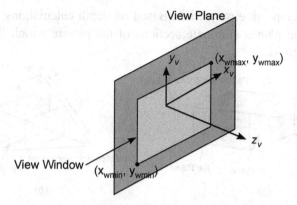

Fig. 3.36 View window boundary specification on view plane.

The term "view volume" basically identifies the objects which will appear in the generated display. The size and shape of view volume is determined by the size of view window and the type of projection used. Objects lying outside the view volume will not be included in the display scene. Regardless, four surfaces of the volume are planes located inside the window boundary. In case of a parallel projection, the view volume's surfaces turn into an infinite parallelepiped and in case of perspective projection, the view volume is a pyramid with apex at the projection reference point (Fig. 3.37).

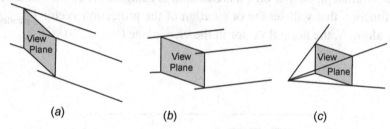

(a)   (b)   (c)

Fig. 3.37 Sample projection view volume for different projections (a) Orthographic projection, (b) Oblique projection, (c) Perspective projection.

The boundary of the volume must be restricted in the z_v direction for achieving a bounded view volume. This is established by two z-boundary planes known as the near plane and the far plane, or sometimes also referred as the front plane and back plane, of the viewing volume. At the specific points z_{near} and z_{far}, both the planes are parallel to the view plane. The two planes must reside on the same part of the reference point of projection, and the near plane should reside closer to the projection point than the far plane. The view volume is surrounded by six planes including the front and back planes as shown in Fig. 3.38. In case of an orthographic parallel projection, the six planes form a rectangular parallelepiped, and an oblique parallelepiped view volume is formed for an oblique parallel projection. A frustum is formed when the front and back clipping planes trim the infinite pyramidal view volume in case of a perspective projection. Based on depth calculations, the front and back clipping planes eliminate sections of the picture which lie beyond the viewing portions.

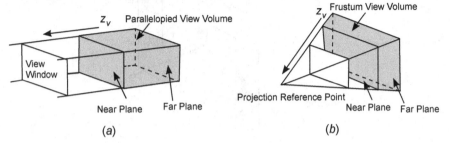

(a)   (b)

Fig. 3.38 View volumes bounded by top, bottom, two sides and near and far planes. (a) Parallel Projection (b) Perspective Projection.

3.3.4.1.4   General Parallel Projection Transformations

A vector from the reference point of projection to the centre of the view window is used to specify the direction of a parallel projection. The contour of a finite view volume for a specified projection vector depends on that of the view plane's projection window. An oblique projection transformation can be achieved by means of a shear function that transforms the view volume to a regular parallelepiped. For this, it is essential to compute the components of the shear function that will set the orientation of the projection vector $V_{parallel}(x_p, y_p, z_p)$ along N, the normal vector in the view plane (Fig. 3.39).

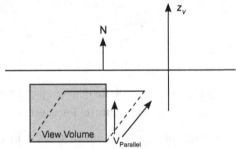

Fig. 3.39 Alignment of $V_{parallel}$ with N

The generic transformation matrix of $V_{parallel}$ is given as

$$
T_{obl} = \begin{pmatrix} 1 & 1 & L_1\cos\beta & 0 \\ 0 & 1 & L_1\sin\beta & 0 \\ 0 & 0 & 0 & 0 \\ 0 & 0 & 0 & 1 \end{pmatrix} = \begin{pmatrix} 1 & 1 & -\dfrac{x_p}{z_p} & 0 \\ 0 & 1 & \dfrac{y_p}{z_p} & 0 \\ 0 & 0 & 0 & 0 \\ 0 & 0 & 0 & 1 \end{pmatrix}
$$

3.3.4.1.5 General Perspective Projection Transformation

In case of perspective projection, the centre of projection may be located at any point in the viewing system, apart from view plane or amid the near and far clipping planes.

The subsequent steps are to be executed for perspective projection of view volume (Fig. 3.40).

1. Align the view volume so that the view plane is perpendicular to the centre line of the frustum by shear transformation (which is combination of rotation and translation).

2. Scale the view volume with a scaling factor that depends on $1 / z$. This is equivalent to perspective projection.

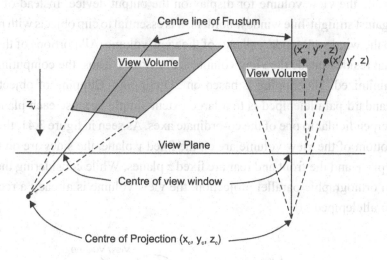

Fig. 3.40 Perspective View Volume Projection.

The transformation matrix is given as follows:

$$
T_{\text{persview}} =
\begin{pmatrix}
1 & 0 & \dfrac{-x_c}{z_c - z} & x_c z \\[2ex]
0 & 1 & \dfrac{-y_c}{z_c - z} & y_c z \\[2ex]
0 & 0 & 1 & 0 \\[2ex]
0 & 0 & \dfrac{-1}{z_c - z} & \dfrac{z_c}{z_c - z}
\end{pmatrix}
$$

$$= \begin{pmatrix} 1 & 0 & -\dfrac{x_c-(x_{w\min}+x_{w\max})/2}{z_c} & x_c-(x_{w\min}+x_{w\max})/2 \\ 0 & 1 & -\dfrac{y_c-(y_{w\min}+y_{w\max})/2}{z_c} & y_c-(y_{w\min}+y_{w\max})/2 \\ 0 & 0 & 1 & 0 \\ 0 & 0 & 0 & 1 \end{pmatrix}$$

3.3.5 Clipping

The idea behind 3D clipping is to determine and keep all surface segments inside the view volume for display on the output device. Instead of clipping against straight-line window borders, it is essential to clip objects with reference to the window boundary planes of the view volume. All portions of the objects that reside outside the view volume are removed. Thus, the computing time is minimized. 3D clipping is based on 2D clipping. Clipping of objects with a standard parallelepiped is to a large extent simple because each plane is now perpendicular to one of the co-ordinate axes. As seen in figure 3.41, the top and bottom of the view volume are on the fixed y plane, the sides are on the fixed x plane and the front and rear are fixed z planes. While considering the case of an orthographic parallel projection, the view volume is already a rectangular parallelepiped.

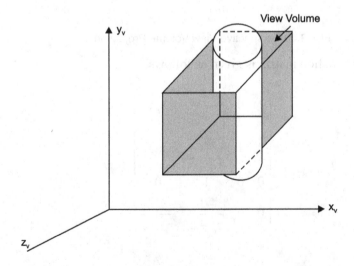

Fig. 3.41 Clipping of a Cylinder by a Parallelepiped view Volume.

3.3.5.1 3-D Object Clipping

For lines and polygon surfaces in a 3-D scene, the clipping procedure is implemented in the same way as 2-D clipping, but only with respect to clipping planes. The equations of curved surfaces are used for identifying the intersection lines with the parallelepiped planes. The 2-D theory of region codes are extended for 3-D by considering positions in left, right, below, above, front or back of the view volume. For 2-D clipping, 4 bits binary region code is used to identify the position of a line endpoint relative to the viewport boundaries. For 3-D clipping, 6 bits binary codes will be used. Each point in the 3-D scene is assigned 6 bit region code that identifies the relative location of the point with respect to the view volume. The bit code is defined as Fig. 3.42.

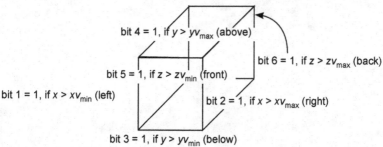

Fig. 3.42 6 bits Binary Region Code for 3-D clipping.

A point with code 010010 lies to the right and infront of the view volume. A point with code 000000 resides inside the view volume and should be displayed.

◻◻◻

Curve and Surface

4.0 INTRODUCTION

If one have two points in the plane and two directions associated with that points are known. Then any one can generate a curve that passes through the points with a pencil and paper who is familiar with parametric forms as shown in Fig. 4.0.

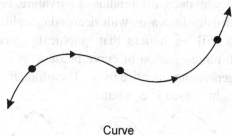

Curve

Fig. 4.0 Curve Passing Through Points.

There is need to represent and curves and surfaces suitability in geometric modelling. This need arises in two cases, first in modelling for improvement of existing objects (such as car body, a airplane, mountain etc.) and in second case, modelling from scratch where no pre-existing physical object is available. In the first case, a mathematical description of the object may or may not be available. If the mathematical description of object is available, one can represent the objects in the form of curve of surface with the help of programs and graphic software available in CAD/CAM software.

When mathematical description of the object is not available, one can use co-ordinates of the infinitely points of the object to model, but this is not possible for a computer which has the finite storage. In this position, one can split the object into pieces of plane, sphere or other simple shapes that are easy to describe mathematically or easily available. It is noted that points on our model must be closed to corresponding points on the actual object.

In the second case, when the designer creates new object by imagination as per requirements. Then geometry of each elements of product must be mathematically described so that its equivalent graphical forms must come on CRT monitor by the use of some programs and graphic software. The treatment of curve and surfaces in computer graphics and CAD/CAM is different than that in analytic geometry or approximation theory because some of the curve equation is not efficient to use in computer graphics and CAD/CAM software due to either computation or programming problems.

4.1 CURVES AND SURFACES REPRESENTATION

Curve and surface can be represented either by graphically or mathematically. Graphically curve may be represented by collection of property spaced points. When collection of points is done by short straight lines, it will produce on adequate visual representation of curve. Figure 4.1 shows the two alternative point representations for the same plane curve in [Fig. 4.1(*a*)], points along the curve are equally spaced along the curve length and in [Fig. 4.2(*b*)], points density increases with decreasing radius of curvature. Form [Fig. 4.1(*a*)] [and 4.2(*b*)], points density increases with decreasing radius of curvature. From [Fig. 4.1(*a*) and (*b*)] we notices that graphically second alternative yield better or smooth representation of curve because its shorter straight lines is responsible for generating smooth curves. Therefore, for generation of smooth curve, short straight is used in computer.

(a)   (b)

Fig. 4.1 Two ways graphical presentation of curves

Mathematically, a curve and surface may be represented by either a non-parametric form or by parametric form.

4.1.1 Non-parametric form for Representation of Curve

Non-parametric form means points or lines or curves or surfaces etc. are defined by co-ordinate value (*i.e.* position of points only). A non-parametric form is either explicit or implicit. Explicit means one value is clearly depended upon some factor of other value and their *vice versa* is called implicit. In other words, explicit equation is precisely and clearly expressed or readily observable but implicit is not directly expressed, it is inherent in the nature of something. For a curve, an explicit form is represented as:

$$Y = f(x) \hspace{4cm} ... (1)$$

In this case, for each value of x, only one y value is obtained. To understand the advantages and disadvantages of explicit and implicit form for representation of any objects, it is prudent to take basic well known objects such as straight line and circle. Similar to equation (1), equation of straight line [(shown in Fig. 4.2(a)] is represented as

$$y = mx + c \qquad \qquad \dots (2)$$

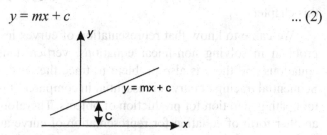

Fig. 4.2 (a) Straight Line Representation.

Where $m = \tan = dy/dx$ (slope) and c is intercept. As per Eqn. (2) when slope $\theta = 0°$, m $= \tan 0°$, then $y = c$, which represents horizontal lines. Similarly, when slope $\theta = 90°$, $m = \tan 90°$. $y = \infty x + c$, for finite value of y, $x = 0$, which represents vertical line. This suggests that when we go from horizontal to vertical line, slope becomes infinite or very large. With large value (*i.e.* infinite), solving the problem manually as well by computer is very difficult. This is the one drawback of explicit form of equation in geometric modelling. If a curve has nearly vertical tangents, one may experience overflow or rounding error problems due to large value when solving or computing the function values in equation. For these reason the use of explicit form in computer graphics and computer aided geometric design is very limited. Above explanations suggested that the explicit from is satisfactory when the function is single valued and the curve has no vertical tangents. Due to this, closed or multiple values curves such as circles, ellipse, parabola etc., are generally not be represented by explicit form. To represent these, one can use non-parametric implicit form which is represented as

$$f(x, y) = 0 \qquad \qquad \dots(3)$$

Equation (3) which is in implicit form can avoid the difficulties raised by vertical tangent and by closed or multiple values inherent in equation of explicit form. For example, a equation of a unit circle in implicit form is represented by $x^2 + y^2 - 1 = 0$, when its centre is at origin. If we require an explicit equation of the same circle, then it must be divided into two segments with for the upper half and for the lower half. But this kind of segmentation of the one circle creates a nuisance for computer programs because computer programs demands well defined sequential set of instructions. In this case, program may be written in two segments. For creating circle in computer, implicit form can avoid segmentation. But one drawback in implicit form is that it demands solution of the non-linear equations for each point and thus complex numerical procedure and analysis have to be employed.

Further to above, from equ. 1 and 2, we notice that both explicit forms are axis dependent. It means, the choice of co-ordinate system affects the ease of use, accuracy and quality of curve which is clearly explained in section 4.4 of this chapter.

We came to know that representation of curves in implicit/explicit gives problem in solving non-linear equations, vertical tangents, axis dependent equations and there is also problem to trace the curve in sequential manner. Sequential tracing of curves is essential in computer graphics and NC machine tool path generation for production of objects. Therefore, there is need to look another form of equation for representation of curve and surface. Parametric form to represent the curves and surfaces shall be the option to tackle above said problems which is discussed in the next section.

4.1.2 Parametric Form for Representation of Curve

Parametric form uses auxiliary parameter to represent the position of a point. For example, a unit circle with centre at origin in parametric form ...4(a) may be represented by single angle parameter u for $0 \leq u \leq 2\pi$ where

$$x(u) = \cos u \text{ and } y(u) = \sin u \qquad \qquad ...4(a)$$

Here we see that in parametric form (4a) each co-ordinate of a point on a curve is represented as a function of a single parameter. The position vector of a point on the curve is fixed by the value of the parameter. For a two dimensional curve with u as a parameter, the Cartesian co-ordinate of point P on the curve can be represented as

$$x = x(u), \quad y = y(u) \qquad \qquad ...(4b)$$

And for three dimensional curves with u as a parameter, curve will be represented as

$$x = x(u), y = y(u), \quad z = z(u) \qquad \qquad ...(4c)$$

Equation 4(b) and (c) indicate that parametric curve is axis independent where the position vector of point P represented as

$$\vec{P}(u) = [x(u) \, y(u)] \qquad \qquad ...(5)$$

And its derivative or tangent vector at point P is represented as

$$\vec{\dot{P}}(u) = \frac{\vec{P}(u)}{du} = \vec{t} = [x'(u) \, y'(u)] = \left[\frac{\partial x}{\partial u}, \frac{\partial y}{\partial u}\right] \qquad ...(6)$$

And its slope of the curve is represented as

$$\frac{dy}{dx} = \frac{dy/du}{dx/du} = \frac{y'(u)}{x'(u)} \qquad \qquad ...(7)$$

Note that when $x'(u) = 0$, the slope of curve is infinite as per equation (7). Infinite slope gives computational difficulties infinite capacity of computer. Computational difficulties are avoided by using the parametric derivative given in equation (6). As per equation (6), if $x'(u) = 0$, $\vec{t}$ has some valve which may be useful for generating curve. This is the reason in geometric modelling position vector of points and its tangent vector is taken as useful inputs in place of slope for generating curve. Thus from above discussion, it is clear that parametric form equation (5) and (6) can avoid problem of infinite slope exist an implicit and explicit form. Furthermore, the parametric method gives itself a piecewise description of curves and surfaces, which is a basis technique to define the free form or complex shapes. Due to these advantages, parametric curve are most commonly used for geometric modelling in CAD for designing. Moreover, it is convenient to normalize the parameter range for the curve segment of interest to $0 \leq u \leq 1$.

4.1.3 Advantages of Parametric over Non-parametric

Parametric equation gives many advantages over non-parametric forms are given below:

1. It provides more degree of freedom for controlling the shape of curves and surfaces. For example, a two-dimensional cubic curve in explicit form can be represented as

$$y = a + bx + cx^2 + dx^3 \qquad ...(8)$$

Above equation have four co-efficients that one change to control the curve. A similar two-dimensional cubic curve in parametric form can be represented as

$$x = a_x + b_x u + c_x u^2 + d_x u^3 \qquad ...(9a)$$
$$y = a_y + b_y u + c_y u^2 + d_y u^3 \qquad ...(9b)$$

Above parametric equation 9(a) and (b) has eight co-efficients available to control the shape of the curve rather than four control points in equation 8.

2. Transformations of geometric elements such as translation, rotation, reflection, projection and scaling can be performed directly on parametric equations.

3. It can easily handle infinite slopes without disturbance of computational procedure in computer.

4. It separates completely the roles of the dependent and independent variables and allows any number of variables.

5. Parametric or Geometric elements are easy to express in the form of vectors and metrics. This form allows us to use relatively simple computation techniques.

6. It provides easy programming for complex objects which is economized for designing.

7. Parametric value may be in terms of position value or dimension (*i.e.,* length) value or radius value or angle value as per demand and requirement.

Due to above advantages, later section is focussed on parameterization of unit circle, unit sphere and space curves and representation in parametric form of different objects including spline, Bezier and B-spline curves etc. Generally Auto CAD used nonparametric form and CAD software like Catia, Unigraphics, Pro-E used parametric form. In AutoCAD, when we change dimension of length, its dimensions value will change but length will remain same but in CAD, length will change with change of its dimensions

4.2 PARAMETERIZATION OF A UNIT CIRCLE

Unit circle in the first quadrant in explicit form can be represented as

$$0 \le x \le 1 \qquad\qquad ... (10)$$

One way of generation of curve by above equation is shown in [Fig. 4.3(*a*)], when putting equal increment at *x*. In [Fig. 4.3(*a*)] we see that arc lengths along the curve are unequal and looking like a sequence of unequal straight lines, which gives poor visual representation of the circle in graphics display. It is also found that calculation of the square root is computationally expensive due to large program needed for square root during processing by computer.

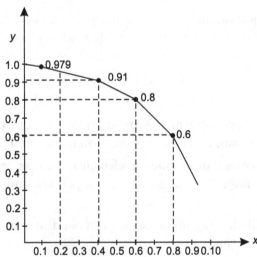

Fig. 4.3 (*a*) Curve from for $0 \le x \le 1$ y = $+ \sqrt{1 - x^2}$ for $0 \le x \le 1$.

To minimize above problem, one can represent above unit circle in parametric form. For this, one can assign co-ordinates as given below

$$x = \cos u, y = \sin u \qquad\qquad \text{for } 0 \le u \le \pi/2$$

where u is geometric angle parameter.

Let any point P on the arc of unit circle in first quadrant, then curve generated by point P is represented in standard parametric form as given below:

$$\vec{P}(u) = [x, y] = (\cos u \sin u] \qquad \qquad ...(11)$$

Curve represented by equation 11 in graphical form is shown in Fig 4.3(b) for parameter $0 \leq u \leq \pi/2$. Here we see that equal of increments of angle parameter u is producing equal arc length along the circumstance of quarter of circle and their visual representation is good as compare to curve generated in [Fig. 4.3(a)] $i.e.$ curve generated by explicit equation 10.

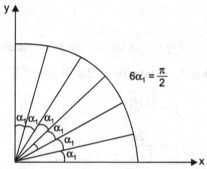

Fig. 4.3 (b) curve from [x, y] = [cos u sin u].

However, computation of the trigonometric function is also expressive, while processing in computer, thus there is need of another form of parametric equation without affecting the value of same unit circle. Following method can be used for graphical display and tool path to CNC. This could be achieved by approximation of a circle with a straight line PQ in such a way that Q is fixed and point P is used to generate circular sequence of points for circle. Let PQ makes angle α from diameter line Qx at a moment during path generation of unit circle. Then

$$\tan \alpha = \frac{y}{x+1}$$

Where co-ordinates of point P is (x, y)

Let $\tan \alpha = u$ $i.e.$, angle parameter for $0 \leq u \leq 1$

it means α, has some geometry meaning for generation of unit circle path

Then $\qquad \qquad y = (x + 1)\,u \qquad \qquad ...(12)$

Since equation of unit circle is represented as

$$x = \sqrt{1 - y^2} \qquad \qquad ...(13)$$

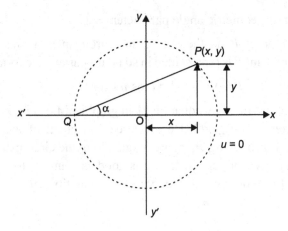

Fig 4.3 (*c*) Approximation of unit circle

Putting equation 13 in equation 12 will give

$$y = \left[(\sqrt{1-y^2}+1)u \right]$$

$$y = \frac{2u}{1+u^2} \qquad \qquad \dots (14)$$

Similarly from equation (13)

$$x = \frac{1-u^2}{1+u^2} \qquad \qquad \dots (15)$$

Then positional vector of any point P on circle in parametric form will be represented as

$$\vec{P}(u) = \left[\frac{1-u^2}{1-u^2}, \frac{2u}{1-u^2} \right] \qquad \qquad \dots (16)$$

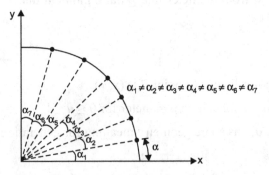

Fig. 4.3 (*d*) Curve for $x = \dfrac{1-u^2}{1+u^2}, y = \dfrac{2u}{1+u^2}$.

The curve generated from above equation (13) in the first quadrant is shown in [Fig. 4.3(*d*)], which shows that unequal arc (*i.e.,* perimeter) lengths along the circumference. Visual representation of circle generated by equation 16 [Fig. 4.3(*d*)] is better than the visual representation of circle generated by equation 10 [Fig. 4.3(*a*)] but not as good as visual representation of circle generated by standard parametric equation 11 [Fig. 4.3(b)]. However equation 16 is computationally less expensive than 11, therefore, equation 16 can also be taken as standard parametric equation for generation of unit circle in CAD as compromise. Thus, both forms (equation 11 and 16) of representation have their own advantage.

Similarly one can represent in parametric form of circle with radius *r* by

$$x = \cos (u) \text{ and}$$

$$y = r \sin u \text{ for } 0 \leq u \leq 2\pi$$

By restricting the range of parameter *u*, one can generate circular arcs. For $0 \leq u \leq \pi/2$, one can generate quarter circle in the first quadrant and for $0 \leq u \leq 3\pi/2$ one can generate the quarter circle in the third quadrant.

4.3 PARAMETERIZATION OF A UNIT SPHERE

Sphere is 3D objects bounded by surfaces. The non-parametric form of unit sphere (radius = 1) is represented by either

Explicite form: $x^2 + y^2 + z = 1$

or   Implicit form: $x^2 + y^2 + z^2 - 1 = 0$

Here, co-ordinate of points of sphere are axis dependent and also depends on other co-ordinates. To make independent form each other for convenience in computer graphics package, one can convert above equations in parametric form by the following way (Fig. 4.4).

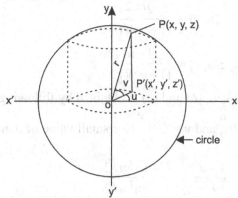

Fig 4.4 Surface Generation of Unit Sphere.

As we know that in Cartesian space, a point is defined by distances from the origin along the three mutually perpendicular axes *x*, *y* and *z* and in vector algebra, a point is often define by a position vector. Let r is displacement with the initial point at the origin. Then the path of a moving point can be described by the position vector at successive values by taking angle parameter u and v in case of surface (Fig. 4.4). Position vector r at a point P for surface generation is a function of u and v is expressed as

$$\vec{r}\ (u, v) = [x\ (u, v), y\ (u, v), z\ (u, v)]$$

Here, angle parameter u and v is also called longitude and latitude respectively.

From Fig 4.4.

Let $OP = 1$(radius of unit sphere)

$OP' = 1 \cos v$ and

$P' = 1 \sin v$

$x = OP' \cos u = \cos v \cos u,$

$y = OP' \sin u = \cos v \sin u$ and

$z = OP \sin v = \sin v$

$$\vec{r}\ (u, v) = [\cos v \cos u, \cos v \sin u, \sin v] \qquad \qquad \text{... (17)}$$

For $0 \le u \le 2\pi$ and $-\dfrac{\pi}{2} \le v \le \dfrac{\pi}{2}$

The equation 17 is very important equation of unit sphere in parametric form which is also represented by following rational parametric form given by modur (1986) as

$$x(u, v) = \frac{(1-u^2)(1-v^2)}{(1+u^2)(1+v^2)} \qquad \qquad \text{... (18}a\text{)}$$

$$y(u, v) = \frac{2(1-v^2)}{(1+u^2)(1+v^2)} \qquad \qquad \text{... (18}b\text{)}$$

and $$z(u, v) = \frac{(1-u^2)2v}{(1+u^2)(1+v^2)} \qquad \qquad \text{... (18}c\text{)}$$

Equations 18(a), (b) and (c) is obtained by following way

Let $u = \tan\dfrac{u}{2}$ and $v = \tan\dfrac{v}{2}$ (for small value of u and v such a $0 \le u \le 1$ and $0 \le v \le 1$)

Then $\dfrac{1-u^2}{1+u^2} = \dfrac{1-\tan^2 u/2}{1-\tan^2 u/2}$

$$= \frac{\cos^2 u/2 - \sin^2 y/2}{\cos^2 y/2 + \cos^2 u/2} = \frac{\cos\left(\dfrac{u}{2}+\dfrac{u}{2}\right)}{\cos\left(\dfrac{u}{2}-\dfrac{u}{2}\right)} = \cos u$$

Similarly,

$$\frac{1 - v^2}{1 - v^2} = \cos v \text{ and}$$

and

$$\frac{2u}{1 - u^2} = \sin v$$

Therefore,

$$\vec{r}(u, v) = [x(u, v), u(u, v), z(u, v)]$$

$$= [\cos v \cos u, \cos v \sin u, \sin v] \qquad ...(19)$$

Equation 19 is the Modur equation for parametric representation of unit sphere surface.

4.4 PARAMETERIZATION OF CIRCULAR HELIX AND CYLINDER

3D space curves can be either represented by non-parametrically or parametrically. A non-parametric (explicit) representation is

$$x = x, y = f(x), z = g(x) \qquad ...(20)$$

Non-parametric (implicit) representation of the curve can be represented by following equations 21 and 22. When the curve is generated by intersection of two surfaces as shown in [Fig 4.5(a)], which can be represented by equation given below

$$f(x, y, z) = 0 \qquad ...\text{surface (21)}$$

$$g(x, y, z) = 0 \qquad ...\text{surface (22)}$$

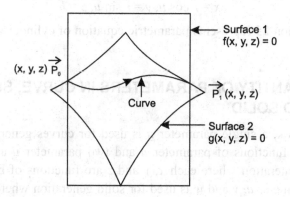

Fig. 4.5 Space curve Generation from Intersection of Surfaces.

In general, parametric space curve is expressed as

$$x = x(u), y = y(u), z = z(u) \qquad ...(23)$$

Where the parameter u varies over a range of $u_1 \leq u \leq u_2$ and x, y, z are the co-ordinate values of any point on the curve segment on parameter u. Thus, parametric equation completely separated the rates of dependent and independent variables. Some useful parametric space curves have known analytical solutions. Circular helix equation in parametric form is given by

$$x = r \cos u, y = r \sin u, z = bu \qquad \qquad ... (24)$$

Where r is the radius for $r \neq 0$, $b \neq 0$ and u is the angel parameter in radian for $\infty < u < \infty$.

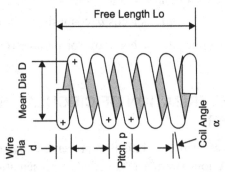

Fig. 4.5 (*b*) Helix with Pitch.

The effect of the equation $z = bu$ is to move the points of the curve infinitely in the z-direction. After each 2π radians interval in the parameter u, the variables x and y returns to their initial values but z increases or decreases by $2 \pi |b|$, depending upon the sine of b. This change in z is called the pitch of the helix. An example of circular helix with pitch is shown in [Fig. 4.5(*b*)]. Other examples of parametric equations are

$$x = r \cos u, y = r \sin u, z = h \qquad \qquad ... (25)$$

Equation 25 represents parametric equation of cylinder with radius r and height h.

4.5 QUANTITY OF PARAMETERS IN CURVE, SURFACE AND SOLID

In this book, a single parameter u is used for curves generation where x, y and z are functions of parameter u and two parameter u and v is used for surface generation where each x, y and z are functions of both u and v and three parameter u, v and w is used for solid generation where each x, y and z are functions of u, v and w. A parametric curve, surface and solid are shown in Fig 4.6, which shows how such entities are often displayed using CAD system. For example, the surface is displayed by means of a mesh of curves drawn on the surface of equal increment of the defining parameters u and v. (*i.e.*, at constant u and varying v and *vice versa*). There is a parameter u, associated with the curve, and whose value increases as the curve is traversed from one end to the other. The position of any point on the curve is given by the vector expression.

$$\vec{r} = \vec{r}\ (u)$$

Where $x = x(u), y = y(u), z = z(u)$

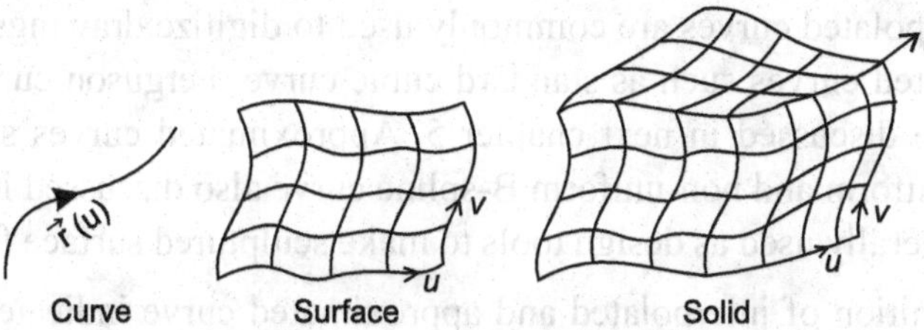

Curve Surface Solid

Fig. 4.6 Parametric Curve, Surface and Solid.

4.5.1 Interpolated and Approximated Curves

A curve can be generated by giving a set of co-ordinate positions, called control points. If co-ordinates of the control points are known then curve can be generated by fitting piecewise parametric polynomial sections of curve continually in one of the two ways.

If piecewise parametric polynomial sections are fitted in such a way that the curve is passing through the each control points [as shown in Fig. 4.7 (*a*)]. Then the resulting curve is said interpolated curve.

If piecewise parametric polynomial sections are fitted in such a way that the curve is generated without necessary passing through any control points as shown in Fig. 4.7(*b*), then the resulting curve is said approximated curve.

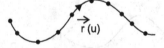

Fig. 4.7(*a*) Interpolated Curve.

Fig. 4.7(*b*) Approximated Curve.

Lagrange polynomial of degree n passing through $n+1$ data points is a popular method for generation of interpolated curve. However, Lagrange polynomial is not suitable in curve modelling because of the following reasons (*a*) Large computations required due to higher order and more data points.

(*b*) When the data points are too large there may be chances of oscillations between data points.

Above problems can be avoided by using small order curve such as cubic curves and its blending functions. These curves can be used to make large curve by using fitting techniques if required.

Interpolated curves are commonly used to digitize drawings. Some of the interpolated curves such as standard cubic curve, Ferguson curve and Spline curve are discussed in next chapter 5. Approximated curves such as Bazier curve, uniform and non-uniform B-spline curve also discussed in next chapter 5 are generally used as design tools to make sculptured surface for the objects.

Definition of interpolated and approximated curve indicates that a curve can be generated, modified and manipulated with operations on the control points. In addition to this, the curve can also be translated, rotated or scaled with transformations applied to the control points for changing curve shapes which were discussed in chapter 2. AutoCAD and CAD packages can also insert extra control points to aid a designer in adjusting the curve shapes whenever required.

4.6 CONVEX HULL AND ITS SIGNIFICANCE

Convex hull is the convex polygon boundary used to enclose a set of control points of the any curves or surfaces or solids. Convex polygon boundary is similar to path/boundary of a rubber band stretched around the position of the control points so that each control point is either on the perimeter of the hull boundary or inside the hull boundary of rubber band as shown in Fig. 4.8.

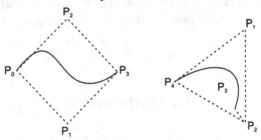

Fig 4.8 Convex Hull Property.

Significance of convex hull is that it is used to measure deviation of a curves or surfaces or solids from the polygon region which is bounded their control points because when these curves or surfaces or solids is bounded by the convex hull, then it is forced to follow the control points without erratic oscillations. Also, any objects (such as curves or surfaces or solids) region inside the convex hull can be used as a clipping region whenever required.

4.7 REPRESENTATION OF DIFFERENT OBJECTS IN PARAMETRIC FORM

(a) Straight line in $x\,y$ plane [(Fig. 4.9a)]

$$x = x_1 + (x_2 - x_1)\,u,\ \ y = y_1 + (y_2 - y_1)\,u \text{ for } 0 \le u \le 1$$

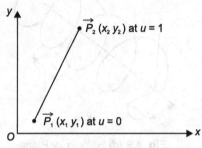

Fig. 4.9 (a) Straight line in xy plane.

(b) Straight line in space [Fig. 4.9(b)]

$$x = x_1 + (x_2 - x_1)u,\ \ y = y_1 + (y_2 - y_1)\,u \text{ and } z = z_1 + (z_2 - z_1)\,u$$

$$\text{for } 0 \le u \le 1$$

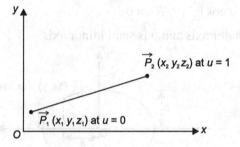

Fig. 4.9 (b) Straight line in xyz plane or in Space.

(c) **Circle in xy plane** [Fig.4.9(c)]

$$x = x_1 + r \cos \theta,\, y = y_1 + r \sin \theta \ \text{ for } 0 \le u \le 1 \text{ and}$$

$$x = x_1 + r \cos (2\pi u),\, y = y_1 + \sin (2\pi u) \ \text{ for } 0 \le u \le 1$$

(d) **Circular Arc in xy plane** [Fig. 4.9(c)]

$$x = x_1 + r \cos \theta,\, y = y_1 + r \sin \theta \quad \text{ for } -\pi/2 \le \theta \le 0$$

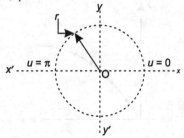

Fig. 4.9 (c) Circle and Circular Arc in xy Plane.

(e) Circular helix in *xy* plane [Fig. 4.9(*d*)]

$x = x_1 + r \cos \theta \ (2\pi u), \ y = y_1 + r \sin \theta \ (2\pi u), \ z = hu$ for $2\pi \leq \theta \leq 0$

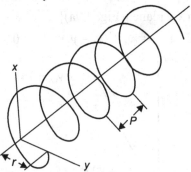

Fig. 4.9 (*d*) Helix in *xy* Plane

(f) Ellipse in *xy* plane [Fig. 4.9(*e*)]

$$\frac{x^2}{a^2} + \frac{y^2}{b^2} = 1$$

where $x = a \cos \theta, \ y = b \sin \theta$ for $0 \leq \theta \leq 2\pi$

a is semi major axis and *b* is semi minor axis

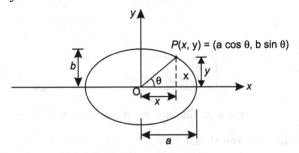

Fig. 4.9 (*e*) Ellipse in *xy* plane.

(g) Parabola ($y^2 = 4ax$) (Fig. 4.9f)

$$x = au^2, y = 2au^2 \ \text{for } 0 \leq u \leq 1$$

where *u* is the angle parameter

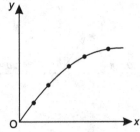

Fig. 4.9 (*f*) Parabola in *xy* Plane.

(*h*) Hyperbola [Fig. 4.9(*g*)]

$$\frac{x^2}{a^2} - \frac{x^2}{b^2} = 1$$

Where $x = a \sec \theta$, $y = b \tan \theta$ for $0 \le \theta \le 2\pi$

$x = a \cos h\,(\theta)$, $y = b \sin h\,(\theta)$

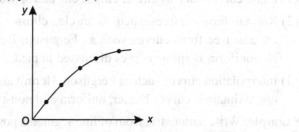

Fig. 4.9 (*g*) Ellipse in *xy* Plane.

(*i*) Free form curves such as

    (*a*) Spline or Furgusion or Herrmit curve which are Interpolated curves. These will discuss in the later section.

    (*b*) Bezier curve, *B*-spline curve, NURBS curve which are approximation curves.

Above free form curve can be written in following parametric form for cubic order

Algebric form

$$x = a_{0x} + a_{1x}u + a_{2x}u^2 + a_{3x}u^3$$
$$y = a_{0y} + a_{1y}u + a_{2y}u^2 + a_{3y}u^3$$
$$x = a_{0z} + a_{1z}u + a_{2z}u^2 + a_{3z}u^3 \qquad \text{for } 0 \le u \le 1$$

Here 12 unknown algebraic co-efficients.

Vector forms

$$\vec{P}(u) = \vec{a_0} + \vec{a_1}u + \vec{a_2}u^2 + \vec{a_3}u^3$$

Geometric form when curves described by end point and tangent vectors such as starting points $\vec{P_1}$ (x, y, z) end points $\vec{P_2}$ (x_2, y_2, z_2) starting tangent vectors $\vec{t_1}$ (x_1, y_1, z_1) and end tangent vector $\vec{t_2}$ (x_2, y_2, z_2) for $0 \le u \le 1$ then expected curve will be shown in [Fig. 4.9 (*i*)]

Fig. 4.9(*i*) Curve in geometric form

Four point form such as starting points (x, y, z) end points (x_2, y_2, z_2) and two intermediate points $(x_{1/3}, y_{1/3}, z_{1/3})$ and $(x_{2/3}, y_{2/3}, z_{2/3})$ for $0 \le u < 1$.

4.8 TYPES OF CURVES

From above discussion, curves may be of following types

(1) Plane curves such as circle, ellipse etc. and space curves such as helix etc.

(2) Known forms curves such as circle, ellipse, parabola and hyperbola etc and free from curves such as Ferguson, Bezier curve, Uniform and Nonuniform B-spline curves discussed in next chapter 5.

(3) Interpolation curves such as Ferguson, Hermit and Ferguson curve etc and approximation curves Bezier, uniform and non-uniform B-spline curve.

Example: Write parametric from of line segments position vector of points are $\overrightarrow{P_0}$ [2 3] and $\overrightarrow{P_1}$ [4 6]. Also find slope and tangent vector of the line segment.

Solution: For line $\overrightarrow{P_1 P_0}$, Parametric form is represented as

$$= [2\ 3] + \{[4\ 6] - [2\ 3]\}u \qquad\qquad 0 \le u \le 1$$

$$= [2\ 3] + [2\ 3]u \qquad\qquad 0 \le u \le 1$$

where
$$x(u) = x_0 + (x_1 - x_0)u$$
$$= 2 + (4 - 2)u = 2 + 2u$$
$$y(u) = y_0 + (y_1 - y_0)\, u$$
$$= 3 + (6 - 3)u = 3 + 3u$$

And its tangent vector

$$\overrightarrow{t} = \frac{d\,\overrightarrow{p(u)}}{du} = [x'(u)\ y'u] = [2\ 3]$$

$$= 2i + 3j$$

Where, i, j are unit vectors in the x, y directions respectively and the slope of the line segment is

$$\frac{dy}{dx} = \frac{dy/dy}{dx/du} = \frac{y'(u)}{x'(u)} = \frac{2}{3}$$

□□□

5

Geometric Modelling
of Curves

5.0 GEOMETRIC MODELLING

The term geometric modelling is the activity of generating mathematical equations of the curves. Once a geometric model is generated, suitable algorithm is constructed then it is converted into the program with the help of programming languages. These programs are called software which is tool to run the computer system for generation of curves. For geometric modelling, we will use positional, tangent and twist vectors, matrix, determinant, polynomial equations etc. There advantages are discussed in later section.

A useful curve in engineering is modeled as a composite curve composed of a number of curve segments, possibly of different types. For each curve segments a set of mathematical functions is used which is the relationship among the co-ordinate variables (x, y, z) for each point of the curve. Any kind of mathematical functions can be used do generate a curve model. However, in practice, polynomial curve models are widely used because they are easier do work with and yet the flexible enough to represent most of the curves. Curves can be represented either in implicit or in explicit or in parametric form. Each form has certain advantages and disadvantages for different application are also discussed here, but we found that parametric form with suitable order gives better results in computer graphics and CAD application. Higher order polynomial equations gives better accuracy and quality for free-form curves.

5.1 REPRESENTATION OF POLYNOMIAL CURVE

There are various form to represent polynomial curve model some of them are given below.

5.1.1 Non-Parametric Form

This form is also called analytic curve model. It can be implicit or explicit curve model such as

(*a*) **Implicit polynomial curve model**

$$g(x, y) = \sum_{i=0}^{m} \sum_{j=0}^{n} c_{ij} x^i y^j \text{ for 2D curves and}$$

$$g(x, y, z) = \Sigma_{i=0}^{m} \Sigma_{j=0}^{n} \Sigma_{k=0}^{0} c_{ijk} x^i y^y z^k \text{ for 3D curves}$$

(*b*) **Explicit polynomial curve model**

$$y = f(x) = a_0 + a_1 x + a_2 x^2 + a_3 x^3 + \qquad \ldots(i)$$

$$r = h(\theta) = \alpha + \beta\theta + \gamma\theta^2 + \qquad \ldots(ii)$$

where $x = r \cos \theta$ and

$y = r \sin \theta$

Above equations (*i*) and (*ii*) are for two dimensional (2D) Cartesian and polar co-ordinates respectively.

5.1.2 Parametric Form

Any curve can be represented in implicit form and this form can be represented in other form for easy to work and understand by computer system by assigning some parameter, called parametric form. In parametric form, polynomial curve model can be written in vector-valued form as equation (*iii*)

$$\vec{r}(u) = [x(u), y(u), z(u)]$$

$$= a_0 + a_1 u + a_2 u^2 + a_3 u^3 + \qquad \ldots(iii)$$

where *u* is the parameter varies from $u_1 \leq u \leq u_1$. Thus, it is possible to convert one form to another form. The process of converting an implicit form to parametric form is called parameterization and the reverse process is called implicitization. The major disadvantages of implicit representation is that it is difficult to trace the curve in a sequential manner but sequential tracing of a curve is essential in NC machining. Thus, in geometric modelling, parametrically represented curve is widely used for all order curves even for generation of conic sections because equations in parametric form can be used to trace the path in sequence during machining.

5.2 MODELLING OF CURVE SEGMENT

A useful curve in engineering is modelled as a composite curve composed of a number of curve segments. Therefore, during modelling of a composite curve *f*(*x*) by using curve segments, we try to represent the composite curve as a sum of smaller curve segments $\phi_i(x)$ called basis or blending functions (blending function is popularly known for defining small curves) as given below

$$f(x) = \sum_{i=0}^{n} a_i f_i(x) \qquad ...(5.1)$$

Blending functions can also be used for construction of a smooth transition between neighbouring curves and surfaces because there is possibility to construct small curves in size as possible for connecting two curves or surfaces for giving smoothness. This process is called rounding or filleting among design engineers. Blending functions are also popular among design engineering because blending function can be developed so small that it can be easy to work and computation and finally it can be display in computer graphics also. For this reason, blending functions are a better choice to generate polynomial curve models of any order.

In Cartesian space, a polynomial composite curve of degree n can be represented in following form

$$f(x) = a_0 + a_1 x + a_2 x^2 + ... + a_{n-1} x_{n-1} + a_n x^n \qquad ...(5.2)$$

Above composite polynomial curve equation $f(x)$ of degree n may be a continuous piecewise polynomial equation $f(x)$ of degree n which is a set of k polynomial equations $\phi_i(x)$, each of degree n and $k + 1$ knots (nodes) where $t_0, t_1, ..., t_k$ are the parametric values of each piecewise curve segments respectively. Then composite curve equation in terms of blending functions is represented as given below

$$f(x) = \sum_{i=0}^{n} a_i f_i(x) \qquad \text{for } t_i \leq x \leq t_i + 1 \qquad ...(5.3)$$
$$\text{and } i = 0, ... k - 1$$

Note that this definition requires the polynomials piecewise curve segments to match together at the knots (The knot points is the joint point between curve segments), that is $\phi_{i-1}(t_i) = \phi_i(t_i)$, $t = 1 .... (k-1)$. This requirement imposes no restrictions on how smoothly the polynomial segments of curve $\phi_i(x)$ fit together at knots. For example, there can be sharp corners or contours at the knots in composite curve as shown is Fig 5.1(a)

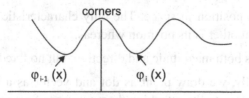

Fig. 5.1 (a) Composite curve with sharp corners or contours made by two small curve segments.

To avoid above problems we take other methods like continuity equations to fit smoothly, which will be discussed in chapter 6.

Polynomial equations of high degree are not very useful for curve designing because of their oscillatory nature. For designing curve, the cubic (degree 3) segments are generally used due to following reasons.

One is that the piecewise cubic curve is closely similar to the way a drafter uses a mechanical spline for a long time. Second, reason is that cubic is the smallest degree for describing pleasing shapes. Third but most important is that the minimum order/degree needed to represent three dimensional curve generations is three which can be fullfil by cubic polynomial equation. Less than three degree polynomial such as if $n = 1$, the n-polynomial equation will convert into straight line equation, and if $n = 2$, the n-polynomial equation will gives quadratic equation. These straight line and quadratic equations will give too little flexibility in controlling the shape of the curve. Similarly, higher degree polynomial composite curves (such as $n = 4$ called quartic, $n = 5$ pentic, etc.) can produce unwanted wiggles and contours and also require more computation because of more unknown co-efficients data available in high degree equations. These are the reasons, in this chapter and later chapters, vector valued cubic parametric polynomial equations are used. Despite this, higher degree curves are used in design of complex parts for cars, planes, ship's, bottles, mobiles and computers etc. in which higher degree derivatives must be controlled to create complex and smooth surfaces that are aerodynamically efficient which is beyond this level to discuss.

5.3 VECTOR VALUED PARAMETRIC POLYNOMIAL CURVE

To describe any curve of any objects placed in space in terms of vector valued parametric polynomial equation, position of all points and its vector value must be known where curve is to be pass. Therefore, the point and their vector are the fundamental 3 dimensional element for all operations in computer graphic and CAD. The point and vector are often confused when studying and students are frequently taught that points and vectors are "essentially" the same. However, they are very different explained here.

A point has position in space. The only characteristic that distinguishes one point from another is its position whereas.

A vector has both magnitude and direction, but no fixed position in space.

Geometrically, we draw point as dot and vector as a line segment with arrows. We draw vector by attaching them to a specific point, but it should be emphasized that any vector is position less. Mathematically points is denoted by capitalized bold letters such as R and S and vector is denoted by lower case letters with an arrow above such as $\vec{r}$ and $\vec{s}$. In general, the points are thought to play a primary role in the space while the vectors are utilized to move about in the space from one point to other.

In Cartesian space, a point is defined by distances from the origin along the three mutually perpendicular axes x, y, and z. In vector algebra, a point is often defined by a position vector $\vec{r}$ (say) which is the displacement with the initial point at the origin. The path of moving point $i.e.$, displacement is then described by the position vectors at successive values at the parameter say u. A parameter is a numerical or other measurable factor forming one of a set that defines a system or sets the conditions of its operation. Hence, the position vector $\vec{r}$ is a function of parameter u $i.e.$ $\vec{r} = \vec{r}\ (u)$. This suggests that vectors carries some inherent geometric meaning such as length and direction. In this book, symbol $\vec{r}(u)$ is taken for representation of the vector-valued parametric polynomial equation for all curve models (It may be equation for curve segments, composite curves and any other known curve models). Then the equation of cubic curve segments in vector-valued parametric form can be represented as

$$\vec{r}\ (u) = [x(u)\ y(u)\ z(u)] \qquad \text{for } u_1 \le u \le u_2 \qquad ...(5.4)$$

where

$$\left.\begin{array}{l} x(u) = a_x + b_x u + c_x u^2 + d_x u^3 \\ y(u) = a_y + b_y u + c_y u^2 + d_y u^3 \\ z(u) = a_z + b_z u + c_z u^2 + d_z u^3 \end{array}\right\} \qquad ...(5.5)$$

where a_x, b_x, c_x, d_x etc. are algebraic co-efficients.

Equation (5.4) and (5.5) represents the cubic equation in algebraic form. This curve equations will give infinite length if parameter u is not restricted in any specific interval, in other words, if u varies from $-\infty$ to $+\infty$. It is not possible to draw infinite length curve either in sheet or in monitor of computer system. So, there is need to restrict the parameter u within close interval a to b for creating finite length. To get smooth curve, its segment curves must be in small interval such as $u(0, 1)$ interval. In other words, parameter must be normalized. To normalize the parametric interval, we take value of u between 0 and 1 $i.e.$, $u \le (0, 1)$ or $0 \le u \le 1$ which is independent variable.

Equation (5.5) shows 12 algebraic constant or co-efficients which values must be known to generate parametric cubic curve shape, size, and its position in space. The two curves of the same shape have different algebraic co-efficients if they occupy a different position in space. Characteristics of the curve can be modified by applying transformation techniques. Equation (5.5) can be write in more compact form *i.e.*, vector valued form. Vector valued equation are not only less cumbersome to read and write, but they are also capable of denoting an arbitrary number of dimension. In other words, vector valued equation can handle several component equation at once. Thus, in vector valued notation, equation (5.5) is represented as equation (5.6) given below

$$\vec{r}(u) = \left[x(u) \ y(u) \ z(u) \right], \text{parameter} : 0 \le u \le 1$$

$$\vec{r}(u) = \vec{a} + \vec{b}(u) + \vec{c}u^2 + \vec{d}u^3$$

$$\vec{r}(u) = \begin{bmatrix} 1 & u & u^2 & u^3 \end{bmatrix} \begin{bmatrix} \vec{a} \\ \vec{b} \\ \vec{c} \\ \vec{d} \end{bmatrix}$$

$$\vec{r}(u) = U \cdot A$$

...(5.6)

Equation (5.6) is generalized parametric vector valued cubic curve equation in matrix form where $\vec{r}(u)$ is the position vector of any point on the curve segment and $\vec{a}, \vec{b}, \vec{c}$ and $\vec{d}$ is the vector equivalents of the scalar algebraic co-efficients (*i.e.* a_x, b_x, c_x, d_x etc).

During modelling, it is found that the algebraic co-efficients are not always the most convenient way of controlling the shape of the curve in typical modelling situation nor do they contribute much to attain an intuitive sense of a curve. Therefore there is need to convert algebraic co-efficients into suitable form. The geometric form seems to fulfill these needs. In geometric form, end condition of the curve is defined by its co-ordinate and their tangent and for curve fitting, end condition at meeting point is defined by curvature. Similarly, in geometric form, end condition of the surfaces is defined by corner points co-ordinate, tangent and twist vectors and end condition of the solid is defined by corner points, tangent vectors, twist vectors, and mixed partial derivatives.

5.4 PROPERTIES OF A VECTOR-VALUED PARAMETRIC CURVE

(*i*) Tangent vectors and arc length of curve segments

As discussed in Equation (5.4), Vector valued parametric curve segments for 3D points is represented as

$$\vec{r}(u) = [x(u) \ \ y(u) \ \ z(u)]$$

Then, its derivative with respect to parameter u will be

$$\dot{\vec{r}}(u) = \frac{d\vec{r}(u)}{du} \qquad \qquad ...(5.7)$$

$$= \left[\frac{dx(u)}{du}, \frac{dy(u)}{du}, \frac{dz(u)}{du} \right]$$

$$= \left[x'(u) \quad y'(u) \quad z'(u) \right] \qquad ...(5.8)$$

and magnitude of the derivative vector $\dot{\vec{r}}(u)$ is called flow rate of the curve which is given below.

Flow rate of the curve $= |\dot{\vec{r}}(u)|$

Flow rate of the curve $|\dot{\vec{r}}(u)|$ is also called tangent vector of any point on the curve segment and represented as $\vec{t}$. *i.e.*

$$\vec{t} = \left| \dot{\vec{r}}(u) \right| = \frac{d\vec{r}(u)}{du}$$

In any curve segments, if P_0 is starting and P_1 is end point, then arc length halves of the curve segment is represented as

$$s = \int_0^s \left| \dot{\vec{r}}(u) \right| du = \left| [\vec{P}_1 - \vec{P}_0] \right| \qquad ... (5.9)$$

(*ii*) Curvature of the curve segments

The unit tangent vector can be represented as

$$\hat{\dot{t}} = \frac{\dot{\vec{r}}(u)}{\left| \dot{\vec{r}}(u) \right|} \qquad \qquad ...(5.10)$$

$$= T \text{ (Let)}$$

Then curvature at the curve will be defined as

$$k = \left| \frac{dT}{ds} \right| \qquad \qquad ...(5.11)$$

$$kN = \frac{dT}{ds} \quad \text{where} \quad N = \frac{dT}{dS} \bigg/ \left| \frac{dT}{dS} \right|$$

Here N is called principal normal vector. Since T is the unit vector (*i.e.*, $T.T. = 1$), then

N should be perpendicular to T as shown in Fig 5.1(b).

The plane defined by two vectors T and N is called osculating plane and a third vector perpendicular to both vector T and N is called binomial vector that is represented as $B = T \times N$

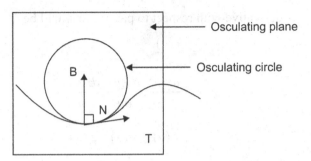

Fig 5.1 (*b*) Osculating plane with *T*, *N* and osculating circle

Again using equation (5.7)

$$\dot{\vec{r}}(u) = \frac{\overrightarrow{dr(u)}}{du}$$

Above equation can be split as

$$\dot{\vec{r}}(u) = \frac{\overrightarrow{dr(u)}}{ds} \cdot \frac{ds}{du} = T.\dot{s}. \qquad\qquad ...(5.11a)$$

Here *T* is unit tangent vector and $\dfrac{d\vec{r}(u)}{ds} = T$ is the Serret Frenet equation for space curve value put in from equation 5.11(*a*).

$$\ddot{\vec{r}}(u) = \frac{d\vec{r}(u)}{du}$$

$$= \frac{d}{du}[T.\dot{s}]$$

$$= \dot{s}\left(\frac{dT}{du}\right) + T\left(\frac{d\dot{s}}{du}\right)$$

$$= \dot{s}\left[\frac{dT}{ds} \cdot \frac{ds}{du}\right] + \ddot{s}T$$

$$= \dot{s}^{2}\frac{dT}{ds} + \ddot{s}T$$

$$= \dot{s}^{2}kN + \ddot{s}T \qquad\qquad ...(5.11b)$$

Then vector products of Eqs. (5.11*a*) and (5.11*b*) gives

$$\dot{\vec{r}}(u) \times \ddot{\vec{r}}(u) = \dot{s}T \times [\dot{s}^{2}kN + \ddot{s}T]$$

$\ddot{s}$ is very less *i.e.*, $\ddot{s} \approx 0$

$$\therefore \qquad \dot{\vec{r}}(u) \times \ddot{\vec{r}}(u) = \dot{s}T \times \dot{s}^{2}kN$$

$$= \dot{s}^{3}k(T \times N)$$

$$= \dot{s}^{3}k\beta$$

From Eq. (5.9)

$$\dot{s} = \frac{ds}{du} = |\dot{\vec{r}}(u)|$$

$$\therefore \qquad \dot{\vec{r}}(u) \times \ddot{\vec{r}}(u) = |\dot{\vec{r}}(u)|^3 k\beta$$

Above equation can be rewritten as

$$= k\beta = \frac{\dot{\vec{r}}(u) \times \ddot{\vec{r}}(u)}{|\dot{\vec{r}}(u)|^3} \qquad \qquad ...(5.12)$$

Where k is the curvature of the curve segments at any points it is noted that the radius of curvature for the curve at any point Q will be equal to the radius of osculating circle, and it will be given by following equation (Roh),

$$\rho = \frac{1}{k} \qquad \qquad ...(5.13)$$

(*iii*) Some other useful properties is given below to simply the vector equations

$$\vec{a} \times \vec{b} = \begin{vmatrix} i & j & k \\ x_1, y_1, z_1 \\ x_2 y_2 z_2 \end{vmatrix} \text{ and}$$

$$\vec{a} \cdot \vec{b} = x_1 x_2 + y_1 y_2 + z_1 z_2$$

where
$$\vec{a} = x_2\hat{i} + y_1\hat{j} + z_1\hat{k}$$
$$\vec{b} = x_2\hat{i} + y_2\hat{j} + z_2\hat{k}$$

Above properties (*i*), (*ii*) and (*iii*) are useful in generation of curve and surface. Generation of following parametric cubic curve models are discussed here one by one that are widely used in engineering practices and by the beginners.

(*a*) Standard polynomial curve model

(*b*) Fergusion curve or cubic spline model

(*c*) Bazier curve model.

(*d*) Uniform B-spline curve model and

(*e*) Non uniform B-spline curve model.

5.5 STANDARD POLYNOMIAL CURVE MODEL

A space curves is a line which gradually deviates from being straight for some or all of its length. That curve, in mathematics is defined as a path of a continuously moving point. Such a path is usually generated by an equation.

In Cartesian co-ordinates, point P_1 of the curve is defined by its co-ordinates x, y, and z. For any point on curve segment, curve equation in parametric form is represented as

$$\vec{r}(u) = [x(u)\ y(u)\ z(u)] \qquad \ldots (5.14)$$

Where u is the parameter for $u_1 \leq u \leq u_2$

In compact form, above curve equation is represented as

$$\vec{r}(u) = \sum_{i=0}^{n} \vec{a}_i \cdot u^i \text{ for } i = 0, 1, 2, \ldots \ldots \qquad \ldots (5.15)$$

The constant co-efficients a_i are determined by specifying boundary conditions for polynomials curves and

$$x(u) = \sum_{i=0}^{n} a_{ix} u^i \qquad \text{where} \qquad u = \frac{x - x_0}{x_1 - x_0}$$

$$= a_{0x} + b_{1x}\, u + c_{2x} u^2 + d_{3x} u^3 + \ldots\ldots\ldots + a_{nx} u^n$$

$$y(u) = \sum_{i=0}^{n} a_{iy} u^i$$

$$= a_{0y} + b_{1y}\, u + \ldots\ldots\ldots + a_{ny}\, u^n \text{ and}$$

$$y(u) = \sum_{i=0}^{n} a_{iz} u^i$$

$$= a_{0z} + b_{1z}\, u + \ldots\ldots\ldots + a_{nz}\, u^n$$

In compact form for simplicity, Eq. (5.15) can be written as

$$\vec{r}(u) = \vec{a} + \vec{b}u + \vec{c}u^2 + \vec{d}u^3 + \ldots\ldots + \vec{d}_n u^n \qquad \ldots (5.16)$$

For $u_1 \leq u \leq u_2$

Equation (5.16) is called standard polynomial parametric equation for curve segments. This equation can be used to fit $(n + 1)$ data points for n order curve. Curve of higher degree is used for generating very smooth and complex curve in CAD/CAM system but higher order curve and large interval of parameter takes more time to compute and generate curve.

$$x(u) = \sum_{i=0}^{n} a_{ix} u^i \qquad \text{where} \qquad u = \frac{x - x_0}{x_1 - x_0}$$

$$y(u) = \sum_{i=0}^{n} a_{iy} u^i$$

$$y(u) = \sum_{i=0}^{n} a_{iz} u^i$$

$$\vec{r}(u) = \vec{a} + \vec{b}u + \vec{c}u^2 + \vec{d}u^3 + \ldots\ldots + \vec{d}_n u^n$$

For generating smooth curve and for less computation, we generally restrict the interval of parameter between 0 and 1 and also let us take third order curve *i.e.*, cubic curve (as reason is discussed in previous sections 5.4), the cubic curve segment in parametric vector valued form is defined as

$$\vec{r}(u) = \vec{a} + \vec{b}(u) + \vec{c}\,u^2 + \vec{d}\,u^3 \qquad \qquad ...(5.17)$$

And in a power matrix form, it is represented as

$$\vec{r}(u) = \begin{bmatrix} 1 & u & u^2 & u^3 \end{bmatrix} \begin{bmatrix} \vec{a} \\ \vec{b} \\ \vec{c} \\ \vec{d} \end{bmatrix}$$

$$\vec{r}(u) = U.A \qquad \qquad ...(5.18)$$

where $U = \begin{bmatrix} 1 & u & u^2 & u^3 \end{bmatrix}$ and $A = \begin{bmatrix} \vec{a} \\ \vec{b} \\ \vec{c} \\ \vec{d} \end{bmatrix}$

Here U is called power-basis-vector and A is called co-efficient vector where $\vec{a}, \vec{b}, \vec{c}$ and $\vec{d}$ is the vector equivalents of the scalar algebraic co-efficients (*i.e.*, a_x, b_x, c_x, d_x etc). Equation (5.17 and 5.18) is called standard polynomial cubic parametric curve model/equation.

To locate a point on cubic curve segment unknown values $\vec{a}, \vec{b}, \vec{c}$ and $\vec{d}$ must be known. As discussed in section 5.4. The four data points of parametric curve can be determined by selecting either four points or three points and one tangent or two points and two tangent or one point and three tangent or all four tangent vectors.

5.5.1 Curve Generation Through Four Data Points

The standard polynomial cubic parametric curve equation (5.18) do not give much geometric meaning in its form thus, there is need to convert algebraic form to geometric form (*i.e*, in terms of positional vector points, tangents, curvatures, partial derivatives of points) for constructing a smooth curve. To generate a cubic curve segment, which is passing through four data points P_i ($i = 0, 1, 2, 3$), one way of fitting the four data points using cubic parametric curve model (5.17) is as follows:

Let $\vec{d}_i$ denote the chord length between two points $\vec{P}_i$ and $\vec{P}_{i+1}$ such that

$$\vec{d}_i = |\vec{P}_{i+1} - \vec{P}_i| \quad \text{for } i = 0, 1, 2, 3 \text{ and}$$

let parameter u at the data points $\vec{P}_i$'s are assigned as assuming chord length of each segment of curve is equal *i.e.*, $d_1 = d_2 = d_3$

at $\qquad \vec{P}_0,\, u_1 = 0 = \dfrac{0}{d_1 + d_2 + d_3}$

at $\qquad \vec{P}_1,\, u_2 = \dfrac{1}{3} = \dfrac{d_1}{d_1 + d_2 + d_3}$

at $\qquad \vec{P}_2,\, u_3 = \dfrac{2}{3} = \dfrac{d_1 + d_2}{d_1 + d_2 + d_3}$

at $\qquad \vec{P}_3,\, u_4 = \dfrac{3}{3} = 1 = \dfrac{d_1 + d_2 + d_3}{d_1 + d_2 + d_3}$

Above assignment is possible when $d_1 = d_2 = d_3$

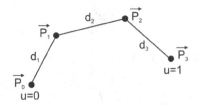

Fig. 5.2 Curve through four positional vector points.

Generated curve on the basis of above assigned value is shown in Fig 5.2. This curve has equal arc length between two consecutive data points as shown in Fig. (5.2.)

Similarly, for getting curve with unequal arc length, we have to set parameter *u* in equal spaced in this case also. From above said four points, curve is generated by interpolation called Lagrange Equation, which will not smooth (because of sharp corners).

For generation of curve with unequal length, we can use standard cubic parametric curve equation (5.17). To determine $\vec{a}, \vec{b}, \vec{c}$ and $\vec{d}$ which are the vector equivalents of the scalar algebraic co-efficients (*i.e.* a_x, b_x, c_x, d_x etc.) in geometric form *i.e.*, positional vector points, parameter and points can assigned as

at $\qquad u = 0, \quad \vec{P}_0 = \vec{r}\,(0) = \vec{a}$ $\qquad\qquad$ ... 5.19(*a*)

at $\qquad u = \dfrac{1}{3},\, \vec{P}_1 = \vec{r}\!\left(\dfrac{1}{3}\right) = \vec{a} + \vec{b}\dfrac{1}{3} + \vec{c}\dfrac{1}{9} + \vec{d}\dfrac{1}{27}$ $\qquad$ ... 5.19 (*b*)

at $\qquad u = \dfrac{2}{3},\, \vec{P}_2 = \vec{r}\!\left(\dfrac{2}{3}\right) = \vec{a} + \vec{b}\dfrac{2}{3} + \vec{c}\dfrac{4}{9} + \vec{d}\dfrac{8}{27}$ $\qquad$ ... 5.19 (*c*)

at $\qquad u = L,\, \vec{P}_3 = \vec{r}(1) = \vec{a} + \vec{b} + \vec{c} + \vec{d}$ $\qquad\qquad$ ... 5.19 (*d*)

Above four equations $\vec{a}$, $\vec{b}$, $\vec{c}$ can be rewritten in terms of four positional vector points $\vec{P}_0$, $\vec{P}_1$, $\vec{P}_2$ and $\vec{P}_3$ as

$$\therefore \qquad \vec{a} = P_0 \qquad \text{... 20}(a) \text{ \{from equation 5.19}(a)\}$$

$$\vec{a} + \frac{1}{3}\vec{b} + \frac{1}{9}\vec{c} + \frac{1}{27}\vec{d} = \vec{P}_1 \qquad \text{... 5.20}(b)$$

$$\vec{a} + \frac{2}{3}\vec{b} + \frac{4}{9}\vec{c} + \frac{8}{27}\vec{d} = \vec{P}_2 \qquad \text{... 5.20}(c)$$

$$\vec{a} + \vec{b} + \vec{c} + \vec{d} = \vec{P}_3 \qquad \text{... 5.20}(d)$$

Since, $(\vec{P}_1 - \vec{P}_0), (\vec{P}_2 - \vec{P}_1)$ and $(\vec{P}_3 - \vec{P}_2)$ are arc length that is equal to d_1, d_2 and d_3 respectively. Here, arc lengths are not equal $i.e.$, $d_1 \neq d_2 \neq d_3$

Then, $\qquad \vec{P}_1 - \vec{P}_0 = \vec{a} + \frac{1}{3}\vec{b} + \frac{1}{9}\vec{c} + \frac{1}{27}\vec{d} - \vec{a}$

$$\therefore \qquad \vec{P}_1 - \vec{P}_0 = \frac{1}{3}\vec{b} + \frac{1}{9}\vec{c} + \frac{1}{27}\vec{d} \qquad \text{... 5.21}(a)$$

Similarly,

$$\therefore \qquad \vec{P}_3 - \vec{P}_2 = \frac{2}{3}\vec{b} + \frac{4}{9}\vec{c} + \frac{8}{27}\vec{d} - \left[\frac{1}{3}\vec{b} + \frac{1}{9}\vec{c} + \frac{1}{27}\vec{d}\right]$$

$$= \frac{\vec{b}}{3} + \frac{3}{9}\vec{c} + \frac{7}{27}\vec{d} \qquad \text{...5.21}(b)$$

$$\vec{P}_2 - \vec{P}_1 = \vec{a} + \vec{b} + \vec{c} + \vec{d} - \left[\vec{a} + \frac{2}{3}\vec{b} + \frac{4}{9}\vec{c} + \frac{8}{27}\vec{d}\right]$$

$$= \frac{1}{3}\vec{b} + \frac{5}{9}\vec{c} + \frac{19}{27}\vec{d} \qquad \text{...5.21}(c)$$

From equation 5.21(a), 5.21(b) and 5.21(c), the values of $\vec{b}$, $\vec{c}$ and $\vec{d}$ are calculated as

$$\vec{b} = \frac{1}{2}[2\vec{P}_3 + 18\vec{P}_1 - 9\vec{P}_2 - 9\vec{P}_0]$$

$$\vec{c} = \frac{9}{2}[-\vec{P}_3 + 4\vec{P}_2 - 5\vec{P}_1 - 2\vec{P}_0]$$

$$\vec{d} = \frac{9}{2}[\vec{P}_3 - 3\vec{P}_2 + 3\vec{P}_1 - \vec{P}_0] = \frac{9}{2}[\vec{P}_3 - 3\vec{P}_2 + 3\vec{P}_1 - \vec{P}_0]$$

Putting values of $\vec{a}$, $\vec{b}$, $\vec{c}$ and $\vec{d}$ in equation (5.17) which is written below

$$\vec{r}(u) = \vec{a} + \vec{b}u + \vec{c}u^2 + \vec{d}u^3 \qquad \text{... (5.17)}$$

$$\vec{r}\,(u) = \vec{P_0} + \frac{1}{2}[2\vec{P_3} + 18\vec{P_1} - 9\vec{P_2} - 9\vec{P_0}]u + \frac{9}{2}[-\vec{P_3} + 4\vec{P_2} - 5\vec{P_1} - 2\vec{P_0}]u^2$$

$$+ \frac{9}{2}(\vec{P_3} - 3\vec{P_2} + 3\vec{P_2} - \vec{P_1})u^3$$

Thus,
$$\vec{r}\,(u) = \left[1 - \frac{9}{2}u + 9u^2 - \frac{9}{2}u^3\right]\vec{P_0} + \left[9u - \frac{45}{2}u^2 + \frac{27}{2}u^3\right]\vec{P_1}$$

$$+ \left[-\frac{9}{2}u + 18u^2 - \frac{27}{2}u^3\right]\vec{P_2} + \left[u - \frac{9u^2}{2} + \frac{9}{2}u^3\right]\vec{P_3}$$

$$\vec{r}\,(u) = \begin{bmatrix} 1 & u & u^2 & u^3 \end{bmatrix} \begin{bmatrix} 1 & 0 & 0 & 0 \\ \dfrac{-9}{2} & 9 & \dfrac{-9}{2} & 1 \\ 9 & \dfrac{-45}{2} & 18 & \dfrac{-9}{2} \\ \dfrac{-9}{2} & \dfrac{-27}{2} & \dfrac{-27}{2} & \dfrac{9}{2} \end{bmatrix} \begin{bmatrix} \vec{P_0} \\ \vec{P_1} \\ \vec{P_2} \\ \vec{P_3} \end{bmatrix} \quad ...(5.22)$$

Equation 5.22 represents cubic parametric curve model in geometric form passing through four data points by interpolation is also called Lagrane curve.

5.5.2 Cubic Spline Curve Model

In computer graphics and CAD application, spline curve was used first efficiently and even today for design of automobile bodies, aircrafts, spacecrafts surfaces, and ship building, etc.

Spline shape is originated from different ways. In drafting, flexible strip with desired orientation is assumed as spline. When several weights are placed along the length of the strip to hold it in a position on the drafting table, the path generated by flexible strip is assumed as spline curve shown in [Fig. 5.23 (a)]. Mathematically, spline curve is derived from thin elastic beam where beam is simply supported at specified point called supports as shown in [Fig. 5.3(b)] (for curve, support point can be called knots or ducks). The shape of the spline curve, corresponding to the deflection of the thin elastic beam due to self weight (let) y is obtained from Euler's equation (Derived and available in every books of strength of materials) given below. Euler's equation for the bending moment M_x along the length of the beam is given as

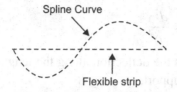

Fig 5.3. (*a*) Possible shape of the spline curve

$$M_x = EI\frac{1}{R_x} \qquad \qquad ...5.23(a)$$

$$= \begin{bmatrix} \text{Bending formula} \\ \dfrac{M_x}{I} = \dfrac{E}{R_x} = \dfrac{\sigma y}{y} \end{bmatrix} \qquad ...5.23(b)$$

Equation 5.23(*a*) is called Euler's equation and 5.23 is called bending formula

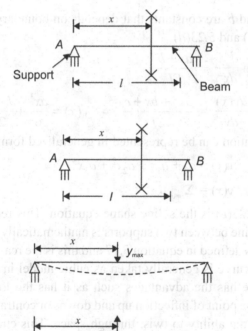

Fig. 5.3(*b*) Physical spline segment similar to pattern of beam deflection.

Where E is the young's modulus. I is an area moment of Inertia, R_x is the radius of curvature of the beam. For small deflection ($y \lll 1$), the radius of curvature is represented as

$$\frac{1}{R_x} = \frac{d^2 y}{dx^2}$$

where y represents the deflection along the length of the beam at distance x from lefthand side support.

Euler's equation 5.23(a) then becomes

$$\frac{d^2 y}{dx^2} = \frac{M_x}{EI}$$

$\therefore$ $\qquad\qquad M_x = EI \frac{d^2 y}{dx^2}$ ... 5.33(c)

For the case of simply supported beam, due to selfweight, bending moment will vary linearly near to straight line between supports as shown in [Fig. 5.3(b)], and let it can be represented as

$$M_x = ax + b \qquad\qquad ...5.23(d)$$

Where a and b are constants that depends on boundary conditions. From equation 5.23(c) and 5.23(d)

$$\frac{d^2 y}{dx^2} = \frac{ax + b}{EI}$$

$$\frac{dy(x)}{dx} = \frac{ax^2 + bx + c}{EI} \quad \Rightarrow \quad y(x) = \frac{ax^3}{6} + \frac{bx^2}{2} + c_1 x + c_2$$

Above equation can be represented in generalized form as

$$y(x) = a_0 + a_1 x + a_2 x^2 + a_3 x^3$$

$\therefore$ $\qquad\qquad y(x) = \Sigma_{i=0}^3 a_i x^i$ ...5.23(e)

Equation 5.23(e) is the spline shape equation. This result shows that the shape of the spline between two supports is mathematically described by cubic curve models as defined in equation 5.17 and this is the reason, a mathematical model for any curve is generally taken as cubic model in this book. Further, the cubic spline has the advantages such as it has the lowest degree curve which allows the point of inflection up and downs or contraflexure or inflexion and which has the ability to twist through space. This cubic spline was also modelled by scientist Fergusson by normalizing cubic spline to unity given in next section 5.7.

5.6 FERGUSSON CURVE MODEL

Scientist Fergusson in 1964 introduced a different way for creating a curve system by using standard parametric cubic curve equation (5.17). For this equation, four data points must be known due to cubic in nature. Fergusson is generated his cubic curve segments [Fig. 5.4 (a)] by using following four known values of the ends points where (a) curve is joining by two known end points $\vec{P}_0$ and $\vec{P}_1$ and (b) each end point have known tangents values $\vec{t}_0$ and $\vec{t}_1$ respectively

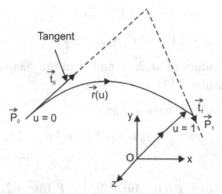

Tangent

5.4. (a) Fergusson curve segment

Where point $\vec{P}_0$ and $\vec{P}_1$ be the position vectors and $\vec{t}_0$ and $\vec{t}_1$ are the tangent vectors at the ends of the cubic curve segment.

Since standard polynomial cubic curve model Eq. 5.17 is as follows:

$$\vec{r}(u) = \vec{a} + \vec{b}u + \vec{c}u^2 + \vec{d}u^3 \qquad \text{for } 0 \le u \le 1$$

and its derivative with respect to u will be

$$\frac{\vec{r}(u)}{du} = \vec{b} + 2\vec{c}u + 3\vec{d}u^2$$

where $\dfrac{\vec{r}(u)}{du}$ = tangent vectors = $\dot{\vec{r}} = \vec{t}_i$ (slope)

To generate a Fergusson cubic curve segment passing through the four data points (in terms two position vectors at end and two tangent vector at ends), unknown co-efficients of Eq. (5.17) $\vec{a}, \vec{b}, \vec{c}$ and $\vec{d}$ must known. This can be determined by following procedure [refer Fig 5.4(a) also]

at $\quad u = 0, \quad \vec{P}_0 = \vec{r}(0) = \vec{a}$ $\hfill$ ...5.24(a)

at $\quad u = 1, \quad \vec{P}_1 = \vec{r}(1) = \vec{a} + \vec{b} + \vec{c} + \vec{d}$ $\hfill$ ...5.24(b)

at $\quad u = 0, \quad \vec{t}_0 = \dfrac{dr(u)}{du}\bigg|_{u=0} = \dot{\vec{r}}(u)_{u=0} = \vec{b}$ $\hfill$ ...5.24(c)

at $\quad u = 1, \quad \vec{t}_1 = \dfrac{dr(u)}{du}\bigg|_{u=1} = \dot{\vec{r}}(u)_{u=1} = \vec{b} + 2\vec{c} + 3\vec{d}$ $\hfill$ ...5.24(d)

Vector equivalents $\vec{a}, \vec{b}, \vec{c}$ and $\vec{d}$ of the scalar algebraic co-efficients $\vec{a}, \vec{b}$, $\vec{c}$ and $\vec{d}$ in terms geometric form (four data points $\vec{P}_0, \vec{P}_1, \vec{t}_0$ and $\vec{t}_1$) will be

$$\therefore \qquad \vec{a} = \vec{P}_0$$

$$\vec{b} = \vec{t}_0$$

$$\vec{c} = -3\vec{P}_0 + 3\vec{P}_1 - 2\vec{t}_0 - \vec{t}_1$$

and $\qquad \vec{d} = 2\vec{P}_0 - 2\vec{P}_1 + \vec{t}_0 + \vec{t}_1$

Putting above values of $\vec{a}, \vec{b}, \vec{c}$ and $\vec{d}$ in the standard cubic polynomial curve segment equation 5.17

$$\vec{r}(u) = \vec{a} + \vec{b}u + \vec{c}u^2 + \vec{d}u^3$$

$$= \vec{P}_0 + \vec{t}_0 u + [-3\vec{P}_0 + 3\vec{P}_1 - 2\vec{t}_0 - \vec{t}_1]u^2$$

$$+ [2\vec{P}_0 - 2\vec{P}_1 + \vec{t}_0 + \vec{t}_1]u^3$$

$$\vec{r}(u) = \vec{P}_0[1 - 3u^2 + 2u^3] + \vec{P}_1[3u^2 + 2u^3]$$

$$+ \vec{t}_0[u - 2u^2 + u^3] + \vec{t}_1[-u + u^3] \qquad ...(5.25)$$

The above Eq. (5.25) is more conveniently expressed in a matrix form (because its geometric operation, analysis and manipulation is simple in matrix form) as

$$\vec{r}(u) = [1 \ u \ u^2 \ u^3]\begin{bmatrix} 1 & 0 & 0 & 0 \\ 0 & 0 & 1 & 0 \\ -3 & 3 & -2 & -1 \\ 2 & -2 & 1 & 1 \end{bmatrix}\begin{bmatrix} \vec{P}_0 \\ \vec{P}_1 \\ \vec{t}_0 \\ \vec{t}_1 \end{bmatrix}$$

$$\vec{r}(u) = VCS \qquad\qquad ...(5.26)$$

Where $U = [1 \ u \ u^2 \ u^3]$, $C = \begin{bmatrix} 1 & 0 & 0 & 0 \\ 0 & 0 & 1 & 0 \\ -3 & 3 & -2 & -1 \\ 2 & -2 & 1 & 1 \end{bmatrix}$

The curve equation 5.26 is called Fergusson cubic curve model, which is in power basis form, where U is called power-basis-vector matrix for parameter similar to as defined in Eq. 5.18, C is called geometric co-efficient matrix or universal transformation matrix and

$$S = \begin{bmatrix} \vec{P}_0 \\ \vec{P}_1 \\ \vec{t}_0 \\ \vec{t}_1 \end{bmatrix}$$ is the matrix for conditions of end points.

Practically, it is not easy to specify the magnitude of the end tangents. It is a common practice to set the magnitude of end tangent vectors equal to the chord length, that is, $|\vec{t}_0| = |\vec{t}_1| = |\vec{P}_0 - \vec{P}_1|$.

This choice gives a reasonable shape of the curve.

Here, we notice that one can select two points and two tangents to represent Fergusson parametric cubic curve segment. Similarly, one can select four tangent vectors only or four positional vector points or three tangent vectors and one positional vector point or three positional vector points and one tangent vector. Since, Fergusson curve is generated by joining points, therefore it can also called interpolated curve. From standard cubic polynomial equation, we see that there are twelve degree of freedom because of 12 scalar algebraic co-efficients (*i.e.*, $a_x, b_x, c_x, d_x, a_y, b_y, c_y, d_y, a_z, b_z, c_z$, and d_z : four vector data point $\vec{a}, \vec{b}, \vec{c}$ and $\vec{d}$ has three Cartesian component *i.e.*, *x.y.z*) to to define fully and unambiguously the equation of the curve.

5.6.1 Hermite Blending (Lofting) Function

Fergusson parametric polynomial cubic curve mode 5.26 can be expressed in different ways as given below

$$\vec{r}(u) = UCS$$
$$= (1 - 3u^2 + 2u^3)\,\vec{P}_0 + (3u^2 - 2u^3)\,\vec{P}_1$$
$$+ (u - 2u^2 + u^3)\vec{t}_0 + (-u^2 + u^3)\vec{t}_1$$

Hermite nineteenth century French mathematician has represented above equation in following ways.

$$\vec{r}(u) = H_0^3(u)\,\vec{P}_0 + H_1^3(u)\,\vec{t}_0 + H_2^3(u)\,\vec{t}_1 + H_3^3(u)\,\vec{P}_1 \ldots(5.27)$$

where $H_0^3(u) = (1 - 3u^2 + 2u^3)$,

$H_1^3(u) = (u - 2u^2 + u^3)$,

$H_2^3(u) = (-u^2 + u^3)$ and

$H_3^3(u) = (3u^2 + 2u^3)$

Equation 5.27 is called Hermite cubic curve equation. Functions $H_i^3 (i = 0, 1, 2, 3)$ in equation (5.27) are called cubic Hermite blending (or lofting) functions. Blending function is the core by which curve can be generated and segmentation or curve splitting is defined as replacing one existing curve by one or more curve segments of the same curve type such that the slope at the composition curve is identical to that of the original curve. Triminaing can truncate or extend a curve. Thus, blending segmentation and trimming is a very useful feature for CAD/CAM.

Example 1. Calculate the parametric mid-point of the Hermite cubic curve that fits the points $\vec{P}_0 = [1\ 1]$, $\vec{P}_1 = [6, 5]$ tangent vectors are $\vec{t}_0 = [0\ 4]$ and $\vec{t}_1 = [4\ 0]$.

Solution: Putting the given values in Hermite cubic curve equation given below

$$\vec{r} = (1 - 3u^2 + 2u^3)\,\vec{P}_0 + (3u^2 - 2u^3)\,\vec{P}_1 +$$
$$(u - 2u^2 + u^3)\vec{t}_0 + (-u^2 + u^3)\vec{t}_1$$

$$\therefore \qquad \vec{r}(0.5) = [1\ 1]\,[1 - 3 \times (0.5)^2 + 2(0.5)^3]$$
$$+ (3\,(0.5)^2 - 2(0.5)^3[6\ 5]$$
$$+ [0.5 - 2 \times (0.5)^2 + (0.5)^3]\,[0\ 4]$$
$$+ [(0.5)^2 + (0.5)^3][4\ 0]$$
$$= [3\ 3.5]$$

Hence, x and y co-ordinates at midpoints are 3 and 3.5 respectively.

5.6.2 Benefit of Tangent Vectors

Using Standard polynomial cubic curve segment represented as given below:

$$\vec{r}\,(u) = [x(u)\ y(u)\ z(u)] = \vec{r} = [x(u)\ y(u)\ z(u)]$$
$$\vec{r}\,(u) = \vec{a} + \vec{b}\,u + \vec{c}\,u^2 + \vec{d}\,u^3 \quad \text{or} \quad 0 < u \le 1.$$

where
$$x(u) = a_x + b_x u + c_x u^2 + d_x u^3$$
$$y(u) = a_y + b_y u + c_y u^2 + d_y u^3$$
$$z(u) = a_z + b_z u + c_z u^2 + d_z u^3 \qquad \qquad ...5.28$$

(12 set of algebraic co-efficients)

To generate curve from Eq. 5.28, four data points must be known *i.e.*, $\vec{a}$, $\vec{b}$, $\vec{c}$ and $\vec{d}$. For determining $\vec{a}$, $\vec{b}$, $\vec{c}$ and $\vec{d}$, we can take various options *i.e.*, either four co-ordinates points or one point and three tangent vector or two tangent and two co-ordinate points or three points and one tangent. In all cases, we have 12 algebraic co-efficients *i.e.*, we have 12 degrees s of freedom to control the behaviour of curve.

In the case of Fergusson curve, only 10 out of 12 degree of freedom are implied where six are supplied by the two end points co-ordinates *i.e.*, $P_0\ (x_0, y_0, z_0)$ and $P_1(x_1, y_1, z_1)$, and four are supplied by the tangents *i.e.*, slopes (or direction cosines), two from each end. Because there are only two independence slopes (or direction cosines) at any point on a curve. The third direction cosine may be derived from any given two because the sum of the squares of the three direction cosines at a point equals one. Thus, two more degrees of freedom are available to control the behaviour of a curve.

In the Geometric forms, the slopes are represented by tangent vectors $\vec{t}_0$ and $\vec{t}_1$ where

$$\vec{t}_0 = \vec{t}_{0x}\hat{i} + \vec{t}_{0y}\hat{j} + \vec{t}_{0z}\hat{k} \qquad \text{at } u = 0 \text{ and} \qquad ...(5.28a)$$

$$\vec{t}_1 = \vec{t}_{1x}\hat{i} + \vec{t}_{1y}\hat{j} + \vec{t}_{1z}\hat{k} \qquad \text{at } u = 0 \text{ and} \qquad ...(5.28b)$$

and $\qquad \vec{t}_{0x} = x_0' = \dfrac{dx(u=0)}{du}$; $\quad \vec{t}_{0y} = y_0' = \dfrac{dy(u=0)}{du}$,

$$\vec{t}_{0z} = z_0' = \dfrac{dz(u=0)}{du}$$

Similarly, $\quad \vec{t}_{1x} = x_1' = \dfrac{dx(u=1)}{du}$; $\quad \vec{t}_{1y} = y_1' = \dfrac{dy(u=1)}{du}$,

$$\vec{t}_{1z} = z_1' = \dfrac{dz(u=1)}{du}$$

For all cases $\sqrt{t_x^2 + t_y^2 + t_z^2} = 1$ and

unit vector $\quad |\vec{t}| = \dfrac{\vec{t}}{|\vec{t}|}$ $\qquad\qquad\qquad\qquad ... (5.29)$

From above explanation, it is noted that tangent vector at ends is also a good option to generate curve segments.

5.7 BEZIER CURVE MODEL AND THEIR DIFFERENT SHAPES

A Bezier curve is a parametric curve of any degree as per requirement frequently used in computer graphics and CAD. Previous techniques (upto 1960s) used for curve generation were interpolation (*i.e.* curves passes through the given set of points). Interpolation techniques does not allow to change or control the shape of the curve. This disadvantage is eliminated by Pier Bezier, 1986 who was an engineer of French car company (Renault). Bezier curve is a free form curve made by approximation technique. They developed a method for modelling of free from curves and surfaces which has been used for panel body design for several cars, aircrafts wings, fuselages, ship hulls, glassware etc.

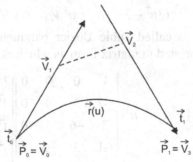

Fig. 5.4 Bezier curve.

There are many ways of defining a Bezier curve. In this section, Bezier curve is generated from Fergusson curve Eq. (5.25) by assigning their end points $\vec{P}_0$ and $\vec{P}_1$ and their tangent $\vec{t}_0$ and $\vec{t}_1$ in the following ways as shown in [Fig. 6.8(a)]

$$\vec{r}(u) = [1 - 3u + 2u^3]\,\vec{P}_0 + (3u^2 - 2u^3)\,\vec{P}_0$$
$$+ (u - 2u^2 + u^3)\vec{t}_0 + (-u^2 + u^3)\vec{t}_1 \quad \text{for } 0 \le u \le 1. \quad ...(5.25)$$

Let us consider the four input control points $\vec{V}_0\,[x_0\ y_0\ z_0]$, $\vec{V}_1\,[x_1\ y_1\ z_1]$, $\vec{V}_2\,[x_2\ y_2\ z_2]$ and $\vec{V}_3[x_3\ y_3\ z_3]$ which are setting in following ways

1. $\vec{V}_0$ is set at start point of the Ferguson curve segment which is *i.e.*,

$$\vec{V}_0 = \vec{P}_0$$

2. $\vec{V}_1$ is set at one third on starting tangent vector of Fergusson curve segment, *i.e.*,

$$\vec{V}_1 = \vec{V}_0 + \frac{\vec{t}_0}{3}$$

3. $\vec{V}_2$ is set at two third points on ending tangent vector of Fergusson curve segment *i.e.*,

$$\vec{V}_2 = \vec{V}_3 - \frac{\vec{t}_1}{3}$$

4. $\vec{V}_3$ is set at end point of the Fergusson curve segment which is $\vec{P}_0$, *i.e.*,) $\vec{V}_3 = \vec{P}_1$

It means, for Bezier curve generation, order of the points is very important. Let as express all Fergusson curve input vectors ($\vec{P}_0$, $\vec{P}_1$, $\vec{t}_0$ and $\vec{t}_1$) in terms of Bezier control points $\vec{V}_0$, $\vec{V}_1$, $\vec{V}_2$ and $\vec{V}_3$ as per assignments given above are :

$$\vec{P}_0 = \vec{V}_0,\ \vec{P}_1 = \vec{V}_3,\ \vec{t}_0 = 3\,(\vec{V}_1 - \vec{V}_0)\text{ and }\vec{t}_1 = 3(\vec{V}_3 - \vec{V}_2) \qquad ...(5.30)$$

Putting above relations in equation (5.25)

$$\vec{r}(u) = (1 - 3u + 2u^3)\vec{V}_0 + (3u^2 - 2u^3)\vec{V}_3 - (u - 2u^2 + u^3)$$
$$= 3(\vec{V}_1 - \vec{V}_0) + (-u^3 + u^3).3(\vec{V}_3 - \vec{V}_2)$$
$$\vec{r}(u) = (1 - 3u + 3u^2 - u^3)\vec{V}_0 + (3u - 6u^2 + 3u^3)\vec{V}_1 +$$
$$(3u^2 - 3u^3)\vec{V}_2 + u^3\,\vec{V}_3 \qquad ...(5.31)$$

Equation 5.31 is called cubic Bezier parametric curve equation. This equation can be reprinted in matrix form as which is said in power basis form

$$\vec{r}(u) = [1\ u\ u^2\ u^3]\begin{bmatrix} 1 & 0 & 0 & 0 \\ -3 & 3 & 0 & 0 \\ 3 & -6 & 3 & 0 \\ -1 & 3 & -3 & 1 \end{bmatrix}\begin{bmatrix} \vec{V}_0 \\ \vec{V}_1 \\ \vec{V}_2 \\ \vec{V}_3 \end{bmatrix} \qquad ...(5.32)$$

$$\vec{r}(u) = \text{UMR with } 0 \le u \le 1$$

The main advantages of power basis is computational efficiency during generating curve using computer system,

where $U = [1 \; u \; u^2 \; u^3]$,

$$M = \begin{bmatrix} 1 & 0 & 0 & 0 \\ -3 & 3 & 0 & 0 \\ 3 & -6 & 3 & 0 \\ -1 & 3 & -3 & 1 \end{bmatrix}$$

$$R = \begin{bmatrix} \vec{V}_0 \\ \vec{V}_1 \\ \vec{V}_2 \\ \vec{V}_3 \end{bmatrix}$$

A nice feature of Bezier curve is that the ability to modify their own shape of curve by changing the position of the control vertices as shown in [Fig. 6.8 (*a*), (*b*), (*c*), (*d*) and (*e*)].

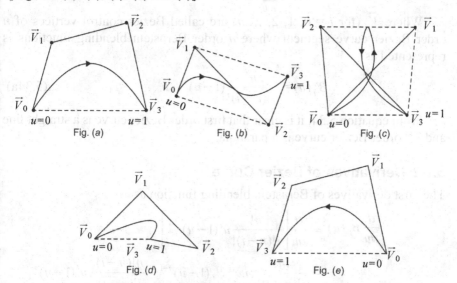

Fig. (*a*)   Fig. (*b*)   Fig. (*c*)

Fig. (*d*)   Fig. (*e*)

5.5 Different shaped Bezier curve.

These figures suggested that order of control vertices is very important in generating different shapes of the Bezier curve. A polygon obtained by joining successive control vertices is called characteristic polygon. Important properties of Bezier curve is that reversing the sequence of control points does not change the shape of the curve as shown in [Fig. 5.5 (*e*)] [reversing the Fig. (5.5(*a*)]. Above discussion indicate that Bezier curve is confined by convex polygon, this property is the convex hull property.

5.7.1 Bernstein Blending Function of Bezier Curve Model

As Fergusson curve is written in Hermit form (5.27), in a similar way, Bezier curve can be written in Bernstein form that is as

$$\vec{r}(u) = B_0^3(u)\vec{V}_0 + B_1^3(u)\vec{V}_1 + B_2^3(u)\vec{V}_2 + B_3^3(u)\vec{V}_3$$

Where

$$B_0^3(u) = 1 - 3u + 3u^2 - u^3 = (1 - u)^3$$

$$B_1^3(u) = 3u - 6u^2 + 3u^2$$

$$= 3u(1 - u^2)$$

$$B_2^3(u) = 3u^2(1 - u)$$

$$B_3^3(u) = u^3$$

$$\vec{r}(u) = B_{i=0}^3(u)\vec{V}_{i_i} \qquad\qquad ...(5.33)$$

(in compact form)

Where $B_i^3(u)$ are called cubic Bernstein polynomial blending functions. Similarly Bezier curve for degree-n for $(n+1)$ control points is represented

$$\vec{r}(u) = \sum_{i=0}^{n} B_1^n(u)\vec{V}_i \qquad\qquad \text{for } 0 \le u \le 1 \qquad ...(5.34)$$

Where $\vec{V}_i$ (for $i = 0, 1, 2, ...n$) are called Bezier control vertices of n order Bezier curve segment where n order Bernstein blending functions is represented as

$$B_i^n(u) = \frac{n!}{i!(n-i)!}(1-u)^{n-i}.u^i \qquad\qquad ...(5.34a)$$

From equation 5.34, it is clear that first order Bezier curve is a straight line and 2nd order Bezier curve is a parabola.

5.7.2 Derivatives of Bezier Curve

The first derivatives of Bernstein blending function as

$$\frac{d}{du}B_i^n(u) = \frac{d}{du}\left[\frac{n!}{i!(n-i)!}u^i(1-u)^{n-i}\right]$$

$$= \frac{in!}{i!(n-i)!}.i.u^{(i-1)}.(1-u)^{n-1} - \frac{n!(n-i)}{i!(n-i)}.u^i(1-u)^{n-i-1}$$

$$= n[B_{i-1}^{n-1}(u) - B_i^{n-1}(u)] \qquad \begin{bmatrix} 0! = 1 \\ u^i = 1, \text{ when } u \text{ and } i = 0 \end{bmatrix}$$

Thus, the derivative of Bezier curve of degree n will be represented as

$$\frac{d}{du}\vec{r}^n(u) = \frac{d}{du}\Sigma_{i=0}^n B_i^n(u)\vec{V}_i$$

$$\frac{d}{du}\vec{r}^{n}(u) = \sum_{i=0}^{n}. n\,[B_{i-1}^{n-1}(u) - B_{i}^{n-1}(u)]\,\vec{V}_i$$

$$= n\Sigma_{i=0}^{n}(\vec{V}_{i_{i+1}} - \vec{V}_{i_i})B_{i}^{n-1}(u) \qquad \qquad ...(5.35)$$

At $u = 0$ and at $u = 1$, we have

$$\vec{r}\ (u) = \vec{V}_0$$

$$\vec{r}\ (u) = \vec{V}_n$$

$$\vec{r}\ (u) = \frac{d}{du}\vec{r}(0) = n\,(\vec{V}_1 - \vec{V}_0) = \vec{t}_0 \ \ (\text{starting tangent})$$

$$\vec{r}\ (u) = \frac{d}{du}\vec{r}(1) = n(\vec{V}_n - \vec{V}_{n-1}) = \vec{t}_n \ \ (\text{ending tangent})$$

Thus, derivatives of Bezier curve at parameter (u: 0, 1) gives same end condition as Fergusson curve has.

Example 2: Define a quadratic Bezier curve at $0 \le u \le 1$.

Solution. Here we require only three control points let $\vec{V}_0$, $\vec{V}_1$ and $\vec{V}_2$. Using Bezier curve equation 5.31

$$\vec{r}\ (0) = V_0,\ \vec{r}\ (1) = \vec{V}_2$$

$$\dot{\vec{r}}\ (0) = 2(\vec{V}_1 - \vec{V}_2)$$

$$\dot{\vec{r}}\ (1) = 2(\vec{V}_2 - \vec{V}_1)$$

Quadratic polynomial curve segment can be written as

$$\vec{r}\ (u) = \vec{a} + \vec{b}\,u + \vec{b}\,u^2$$

Therefore,

$\therefore$

$$\vec{r}\ (0) = V_0 = \vec{a}$$

$$\vec{r}\ (1) = \vec{V}_2 = \vec{a} + \vec{b} + \vec{c}$$

$$\dot{\vec{r}}\ (0) = 2(\vec{V}_1 - \vec{V}_2) = \vec{b}$$

$$\dot{\vec{r}}\ (1) = 2(\vec{V}_2 - \vec{V}_1) = \vec{b} + 2\vec{c}$$

$\therefore$

$$\vec{a} = \vec{V}_0.\ \vec{b} = 2(\vec{V}_1 - \vec{V}_2),\ \vec{c} = \vec{V}_0 - 2\vec{V}_1 - \vec{V}_2$$

Substituting

$\therefore$

$$\vec{r}\ (u) = \vec{V}_0 + 2(\vec{V}_1 - \vec{V}_0)u + (\vec{V}_0 - 2\vec{V}_1 - \vec{V}_2)u^2$$

$$= (1 - u)u^2\,\vec{V}_0 + 2u(1-u)\vec{V}_1 + u^2\vec{V}_2$$

$$= [1\ u\ u^2]\begin{bmatrix} 1 & 0 & 0 \\ -2 & 2 & 0 \\ 1 & -2 & 1 \end{bmatrix}\begin{bmatrix} \vec{V}_1 \\ \vec{V}_2 \\ \vec{V}_3 \end{bmatrix} \qquad ...(5.36)$$

Equation 5.36 represents quadratic Bezier curve.

Example 3: Find co-ordinate points of Bezier curve at $u = 0.4$ and at $u = 0.6$ for four control vertices.

Solution :

$$\vec{r}\,(u) = [x(u) \ \ y(u)]$$

Where
$$x(u) = 1[1 - 3u + 3u^2 - u^3] + 3[3u - 6u^2 + 3u^3],$$
$$+ 5[3u^2 - 3u^3 + 7u^3]$$
$$y(u) = 1[1 - 3u + 3u^2 - u^3] + 6[3u - 6u^2 + 3u^3]$$
$$+ 7[3u^2 - 3u^3 +] + 2u^3$$

or

$$\vec{r}\,(u) = [1 \ 1][1 - 3u + 3u^2 - u^3] + [3 \ 6][3u - 6u^2 + 3u^3]$$
$$+ [5 \ 7][3u^2 - 3u^3] + [5 \ 7]u^3$$

Putting $u = 0.4$,
$$\vec{r}\,(0.4) = [3.4 \ \ 4.952]$$

Putting $u = 0.6$,
$$\vec{r}\,(0.6) = [4.6 \ \ 5.248]$$

Example 4: Vertices of Bezier polygon are $\vec{V}_0[1, 1]$, $\vec{V}_1[2, 3]$, $\vec{V}_2[4, 3]$ and $\vec{V}[3, 1]$. Find seven points on Beizer curve for parameter $0 \le u \le 1$.

Solution: Refer Fig. 5.6 showing four control points. To find seven points for generation of a Bezier curve, let us use standard Bezier curve segment which is in Bernitein form

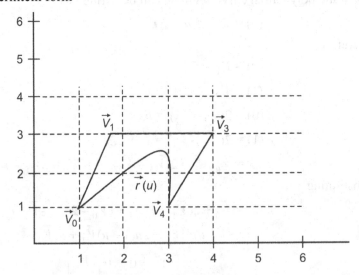

Fig. 5.6 Bezier Curve.

$$\vec{r}\,(u) = \sum_{i=0}^{n} B_i^n(u)\vec{V}_i$$

Where

$$B_i^n(u) = \frac{n!}{i!(n-i)!} u^i (1-u)^{n-i}$$

For four control vertices $\vec{V}_i$, $i = 0, 1, 2, 3$, n will be 3.

Hence, $B_0^3(u) = \dfrac{3!}{0!(3-0)!} u^0 (1-u)^{3-0} = (1-u)^3$

$\qquad\qquad = (1 - 3u + 3u^2 - u^3) \qquad \therefore \quad 0! = 1$

Similarly, $B_1^3(u) = 3u(1-u)^2 = 3u - 6u^2 + 3u^3$

$\qquad\quad B_2^3(u) = 3u^2 - 3u^3$ and

$\qquad\quad B_3^3(u) = u^3$

$\therefore \qquad \vec{r}(u) = (1 - 3u + 3u^2 - u^3)\vec{V}_0 + (1 - 3u + 3u^2 - u^3)\vec{V}_1$

$\qquad\qquad\qquad + (3u^2 - 3u^3)\vec{V}_2 + u^3 \vec{V}_3 \qquad\qquad ...(5.37)$

Let we are selecting at random seven points as

$u_1 = 0$, $u_2 = 0.15$, $u_3 = 0.35$, $u_4 = 0.5$, $u_5 = 0.65$, $u_6 = 0.85$ and $u_7 = 1$

Then each point on Beizer curve segment will be

$\qquad \vec{r}(u_1 = 0) = [1 \ 1] = \vec{V}_1$

$\qquad \vec{r}(0.15) = [1.5 \ 1.765]$

$\qquad \vec{r}(0.5) = [2.75 \ 2.5]$

$\qquad \vec{r}(0.65) = [3.122 \ 2.367]$

$\qquad \vec{r}(0.85) = [3.248 \ 1.765]$

$\qquad \vec{r}(1) = [3 \ 1] = \vec{V}_3$

Form above seven points, Bezier curve will be generated as shown in Fig. 5.6.

5.8 B-SPLINE CURVE MODEL (BASIS SPLINE CURVE MODEL)

Some complicated curves cannot be represented by a single Bezier curve or a single Fergusson curve model. Also, in some curve, local change in shape is required which is difficult in Bezier or Fergusson curve because in this curve, local changes propagates entire curve shapes i.e., global propagation starts. In other words, a change in one vertex of Bezier curve is felt through the entire curve. This eliminates the ability to produce a local change within curve. If we increase the degree of Bezier curve, it adds flexibility to the curve for shape design but increase the processing effort for curve evaluation and manipulation alongwith numerical noise in computation. For these reasons, designer often split the complex curve into small pieces in such a way that each pieces can be represented by a lower degree Bezier curve. This method of representation is called piecewise representation. A curve that is made of several small pieces of Bezier curves is called a composite Bezier curve. But there are primarily two disadvantages associated during generation of the composite Bezier curve.

1. Need of some order of continuity equations at the joining point while joining two piece of Bezier curves. Thus, for whole composite curves much more continuity equations required and second.

2. Due to above reason, a composite Bezier curve requires more control vertices than B-spline curve discussed here.

Above disadvantage can be eliminated by the B-Spline basis (or Basis-spline curve), which avoids above problems by using a special set of Blending functions that has only local influence and depends on only a few neighbouring control points. This Basis-spline curve is generally non-global. The no global behaviour of B-Spline curve is due to the fact that each vertex V_i is associated with a unique basic function. Thus, each vertex affects the shape of a curve only over a range of parameter values where its associated basis function is non-zero. The B-Spline basis also allows changing the degree of curve without changing the number of defining polygon vertices. In 1940, Schoenberg suggested first about B-Spline, but B-Spline was not populare in the industry until De Boor and Cox published their work in the early 1970s. There are two types of B-Spline curve used in industries.

(1) Uniform B-Spline

(2) Non-uniform B-Spline.

The uniform B-Spline curve [where chord-lengths $P_i - P_{i-1}$ are identical] is the modification of Fergusson and Bezier curve discussed in section 5.9.1. But non-uniform B-Spline is made by using recursive scale functions discussed in section 5.9.2.

5.8.1 Uniform B- Spline curve model

Uniform B-Spline curve is similar to Fergusson curve but the start and end points $\vec{P}_0$, $\vec{P}_1$ as well as the end tangents $\vec{t}_0$, $\vec{t}_1$ are defined in a different way within the convex hull of Bezier curve as shown in Fig. 5.7.

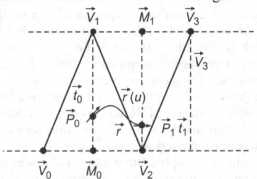

Fig. 5.7 Uniform B-Spline (Cubic) curve segment

As shown in figure, let us define in following ways

$$M_0 = \frac{\vec{V}_0 + \vec{V}_1}{2} \quad \text{[middle point of } \vec{V}_0 \text{ and } \vec{V}_2]$$

$$M_1 = \frac{\vec{V}_1 + \vec{V}_3}{2} \quad \text{[middle point of } \vec{V}_1 \text{ and } \vec{V}_3]$$

$$\vec{P}_0 = \vec{V}_1 + \frac{1}{3}(\overline{M}_0 - \vec{V}_1)$$

[one third position on the line joining $\vec{V}_1$ and $\overline{M}_0$]

$$= \frac{3\vec{V}_1 + M_0 - V_3}{3} = \frac{2\vec{V}_1 + M_0}{3}$$

$$= \frac{4\vec{V}_1 + V + V}{6} \quad \text{and}$$

$$\vec{P}_1 = \vec{V}_2 + \frac{1}{3}(\overline{M}_1 - \vec{V}_2)$$

[one third position on the line joining $\vec{V}_2$ and $\overline{M}_1$]

$$= \frac{2\vec{V}_2 + \overline{M}_1}{3}$$

$$= \frac{4\vec{V}_2 + (\vec{V}_1 + \vec{V}_3)}{6}$$

Using above definitions, different points are set in following ways for generating a cubic B-Spline curve segment $\vec{r}\,(u)$.

(a) It starts form $\vec{P}_0$ and ends at $\vec{P}_1$.

(b) The start tangent vector $\vec{t}_1$ is set at $\vec{P}_0$ such that $\vec{t}_0 = \overline{M}_1 - \vec{V}_0$.

$$\therefore \quad \vec{V}_2 = \frac{\vec{V}_0 + \vec{V}_2}{2} - \vec{V}_0 = \frac{\vec{V}_2 - \vec{V}_0}{2}$$

(c) The end tangent vector $\vec{t}_1$ set at $\vec{P}_1$ such that

$$\vec{t}_0 = \overline{M}_1 - \vec{V}_1.$$

$$= \frac{\vec{V}_3 - \vec{V}_1}{2}$$

Obviously curve generated by above settings is a Fergusson curve type. Thus, using standard Fergusson curve equation and putting all values $\vec{P}_0, \vec{P}_1$ to $\vec{t}_0$ and $\vec{t}_1$ in terms of Bezier control vertices $V_i = (0, 1, 2, 3)$

$$\vec{r}\,(u) = (1 - 3u^2 - 2u^3]\,\vec{P}_0 + [3u^2 - 2u^3]\,\vec{P}_1$$
$$+ (u - 2u^2 + u^3)\vec{t}_0 + (-u^2 + u^3)\vec{t}_1$$

$$= (1 - 3u^2 + 2u^3)\left(\frac{\vec{V}_0 + 4\vec{V}_1 + V_2}{6}\right) + (3u^2 - 2u^3)\left(\frac{\vec{V}_1 + 4V_2 + \vec{V}_3}{6}\right) +$$

$$(u - 2u^2 + u^3)\left(\frac{-\vec{V}_0 + V_2}{2}\right) + (-u^2 + u^3)\left(\frac{V_3 + \vec{V}_1}{2}\right)$$

$$= \frac{1}{6}[(1 - 3u + 3u^2 - u^3)\,\vec{V}_0 + (4 - 6u^2 + 3u^3)\vec{V}_1 +$$

$$[1 + 3u + 3u^2 - 3u^3]\,\vec{V}_2 + u^3\vec{V}_3 \qquad\qquad ...(5.38)$$

$$\vec{r}(u) = [1 \; u \; u^2 \; u^3]\frac{1}{6}\begin{bmatrix} 1 & 4 & 1 & 0 \\ -3 & 0 & 3 & 0 \\ 3 & -6 & 3 & 0 \\ -1 & 3 & -3 & 1 \end{bmatrix}\begin{bmatrix} \vec{V}_0 \\ \vec{V}_1 \\ \vec{V}_2 \\ \vec{V}_3 \end{bmatrix} \; 0 \le u \le 1$$

$$\vec{r}(u) = \text{U.N.R} \qquad\qquad ...(5.39)$$

$$\text{where } N = \frac{1}{6}\begin{bmatrix} 1 & 4 & 1 & 0 \\ -3 & 0 & 3 & 0 \\ 3 & -6 & 3 & 0 \\ -1 & 3 & -3 & 1 \end{bmatrix}, R = \begin{bmatrix} \vec{V}_0 \\ \vec{V}_1 \\ \vec{V}_2 \\ \vec{V}_3 \end{bmatrix}$$

Equation 5.38 is called uniform cubic B-Spline curve segment equation and equation 5.39 is matrix form (power form) of B-spline curve.

5.8.1.1 B-spline Blending Function

Similar, to Fergusson and Bezier curve, uniform B-spline curve can also be represented in a different way such as

$$\vec{r}(u) = \sum_{i=0}^{n} N_1^3(u)\,\vec{V}_i \qquad\qquad ... (5.40)$$

for $i = 0, 1, 2, 3$

Where $N_i^3(u)$ is called B-Spline cubic blending function and for $i = 0, 1, 2$ and 3 blending function will be

where $\quad N_0^3(u) = (1 - 3u + 3u^2 - u^3)/6$

$\qquad\quad N_1^3(u) = (4 - 6u + 3u^3)/6$

$\qquad\quad N_2^3(u) = (1 + 3u + 3u^2 - 3u^3)/6$

$\qquad\quad N_3^3(u) = u^3/6$

Similarly, for n degree B-Spline blending function is represented as

$$\vec{r}(u) = \sum_{i=0}^{n} N_i^n(u)\,\vec{V}_i \qquad\qquad ...(5.41)$$

It is to know that the notation $N_i^3(u)$ is also written in another form as $N_{(n+1),\,i}(u)$ in various literatures. Here it is noted that for n degree B-Spline function which is explained in later section for non-uniform B-Spline recursive function, can be converted for uniform B-Spline by putting suitable values.

5.8.2 Non-Uniform B-Spline Curve Model

Uniform B-Spline curve is generated by passing a sequence of $n+1$ data points. To pass through all the sequence of points the curve must satisfy as

$$\vec{r}(u_1) = \vec{V}_0, \ \vec{r}(u_2) = \vec{V}_1, \ \vec{r}(u_3) = \vec{V}_3 \ldots \ldots \ \vec{r}(u_n) = \vec{V}_n,$$

which is the case of interpolation. For large control points, interpolation does not give a smooth curve. Thus, one can approximate the curve but large control points require more computation. This problem can be solved by splines. A spline is a curve that is a piecewise n^{th} degree polynomial. This means that, on any interval (u_i, u_{i+1}), the curve must be equal to a polynomial of degree at most n. When the polynomials from intervals $(u_{i-1}, u_i$ and $u_i, u_{i+1})$ meet at the point u_i, they must have the same value at this point and their derivatives must be equal to ensure that the curve is smooth.

For generation of non-uniform B-Spline curve, Cox-de Boor gives an algorithm which finds the value of spline curve segment $\vec{r}(u)$ at a point u, for given u_0, $u_1, \ldots \ldots, u_n$ and for its control vertices $\vec{V}_0, \vec{V}_1, \ldots \ldots, \vec{V}_n$. The equation of the position vector of any points on NUB curve segment for sequence of 3D points V_i can be represented as

$$\vec{r}(t) = \Sigma_{i=0}^n N_i^n(t)\vec{V}_i \quad \text{for } t_i \le t \le t_{i+1} \qquad \ldots(5.41)$$

Equation 5.41 is called Non-niform B-spline curve equation, where $N_i^n(t)$ is the Cox-de Boor recursive Scale or blending function, defined with respect to a non-decreasing sequence of knot points t_i and $N_i^n(t)$ is represented as

$$N_i^n(t) = \frac{(t-t_i)}{(t_{i+n-1}+t_i)} N_i^{n-1}(t) + \frac{(t_{i+n}-t)}{(t_{i+n}-t_{i+1})} \cdot N_{i+1}^{n-1}(t) \quad \text{for } t_{min} \le t \le t_{max}$$

$$\ldots(5.42)$$

where $N_i^1(t) = 1 \quad \text{for } t_i \le t \le t_{i+1}$

$$= 0 \text{ other wise} \qquad [t \in t_{min}, t_{max}]$$

The above recursive function given in equation 5.42 is the standard method of defining a B-Spline basis function (of degree $n-1$). To understand geometric properties of the function, we need to evaluate it from the beginning.

Let $n = 2$ in equation (5.42), then the first iteration is carried out as follows:

$$N_i^2(t) = \frac{(t-t_i)}{(t_{i+1}+t_i)} N_i^1(t) + \frac{(t_{i+2}-t)}{(t_{i+2}-t_{i+1})} L_{i+1}^1(t)$$

$$= \frac{(t - t_i)}{(t_{i+1} - t_i)} \text{ for } t_i \le t \le t_{i+2}$$

$$= \frac{(t_{i+2} - t)}{(t_{i+2} - t_{i+1})} \text{ for } t_{i+1} \le t \le t_{i+2}$$

$$= 0 \text{ otherwise}$$

In order to simplify algebraic manipulations, a difference operator   is introduced *i.e.*,

$$\nabla_i = (t_{i+1} - t_i) \qquad \qquad ...(5.43)$$
$$\nabla_i^k = \nabla_i + ... + \nabla_{i+k-1}$$
$$= (t_{i+k} - t_i)$$

Putting $i = 1, 2, 3 \ ...$

Then

$$\nabla_i^2 = (t_{i+2} - t_i) = \nabla_i + \nabla_{i+1}$$
$$\nabla_i^3 = (t_{i+3} - t_{i+1}) = \nabla_i + \nabla_{i+1} + \nabla_{i+2}$$
$$\nabla_{i+1} = (t_{i+2} - t_{i+1})$$
$$\nabla_{i+1}^2 = (t_{i+3} - t_{i+1})$$

Similarly, $\nabla_{i+2} = (t_{i+3} - t_{i+2})$

Using above operator, we get

$$N_i^2(t) = \frac{(t - t_i)}{\nabla_i} N_i^1(t) + \frac{(t_{i+2} - t)}{\nabla_{i+1}} N_{i+1}^1(t)$$

$$= \frac{(t - t_i)}{\nabla_i} \quad \text{for } t_i \le t \le t_{i+1}$$

$$= \frac{t_{i+2} - t_i}{\nabla_{i+1}} \quad \text{for } t_{i+1} \le t \le t_{i+2}$$

$$= 0 \text{ otherwise}$$

Again using difference operator, the next iteration with $n = 3$ will be as

$$N_i^3(t) = \frac{(t - t_i)}{\nabla_i^2} N_i^2(t) = \frac{(t_{i+3} - t)}{\nabla_{i+1}^2} N_{i+1}^2(t)$$

$$N_i^3(t) = \frac{(t - t_1)}{\nabla_1^2} \left[\frac{(t - t_i)}{(t_{i+1} - t_i)} N_i^1(t) + \frac{(t_{i+2} - t)}{t_{i+2} - t_{i+1}} N_{i+1}^1(t) \right]$$

$$\frac{(t_{i+3} - t)}{\nabla_{i+1}^2} \left[\frac{(t - t_{i+1})}{(t_{i+2} - t_{i+1})} N_{i+1}^1(t) + \frac{(t_{i+3} - t)^2}{t_{i+3} - t_{i+2}} N_{i+2}^1(t) \right]$$

$$= \frac{(t - t_i)^2}{\nabla_i^2 \nabla_i} \cdot N_i^1(t) + \frac{(t - t_i)}{\nabla_i^2} \frac{(t_{i+2} - t)}{\nabla_{i+1}} N_{i+1}^1$$

$$+ \frac{(t_{i+3} - t_i)}{\nabla_{i+1}^2} \cdot \frac{(t - t_{i+1})}{\nabla_{i+1}} N_{i+1}^1(t) + \frac{(t_{i+3} - t)^2}{\nabla_{i+1}^2 \cdot \nabla_{i+2}} \cdot L_{i+2}^1(t)$$

$$= \frac{(t-t_i)^2}{\nabla_i^2 \nabla_i} N_i^1(t) + \left[\frac{(t-t_i)(t_{i+2}-t)}{\nabla_i^2 \nabla_{i+1}} + \frac{(t_{i+3}-t)(t-t_{i+1})}{\nabla_{i+1}^2 \nabla_{i+1}} N_{i+1}^1 \right] N_{i+1}^1(t)$$

$$+ \frac{(t_{i+3}-t)^3}{\nabla_{i+1}^2 \nabla_{i+2}} L_{i+2}^1(t)$$

$$= \frac{(t-t_i)^2}{\nabla_i^2 \nabla_i} \quad \text{for} \quad t_i \le t \le t_{i+1} \qquad \dots 5.43(a)$$

$$= \frac{(t-t_i)^2}{\nabla_i^2 \nabla_i} - \frac{\nabla_i^3 (t-t_{i+1})^2}{\nabla_{i+1}^2 \nabla_{i+1} \nabla_i} \quad \text{for} \quad t_{i+1} \le t \le t_{i+2}$$

$$\qquad \dots 5.43(b)$$

$$= \frac{(t_{i+3}-t)^3}{\nabla_{i+1}^2 \nabla_{i+2}} \quad \text{for} \quad t_{i+2} \le t \le t_{i+3} \qquad \dots 5.43(c)$$

$$= \text{otherwise}$$

We notice that above Cox-de Boor formula is a recursive nature because its basis function of a given order n depends on lower down to order one for a given basis function . This dependence creates a triangular pattern.

The function (5.43) is the B-Spline of degree 2 (order) (*i.e.*, degree n (order $n+1$). Functional shapes of non-uniform B-Spline of degree upto 3 (order 4) are plotted in [Fig 5.9(a)]

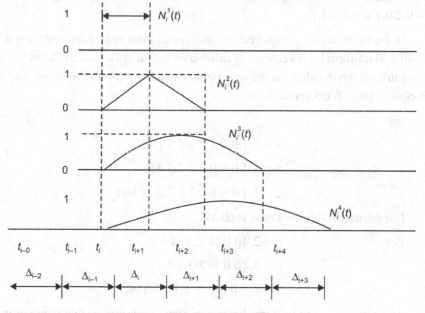

Fig. 5.9 (*a*) construction of non-uniform B-Spline function.

From [figure 5.9(b)], we notice that a B-Spline basis function has different forms on different intervals in the parameter space, this parametric space Δ is called knot values. The basis function in the kth interval is identified by the second subscript (k).

This is

$$N_{i,k}^n (t) = N_i^n(t) \text{ for } t_{i+k-1} \le t \le t_{i+k} \quad \text{and} \quad ...(5.44)$$
$$K = 1, 2, ... n$$

Here $N_{i,k}^n$ means i^{th} number of n order basis function at k^{th} interval. Equation (5.44) clearly indicates that the choice of knot points (called knot vectors) has a sufficient influence on the B-Spline basis function $N_{i,k}^n (t)$. The only requirement for a knot vector is that it satisfied the relation $t_{i+k-1} \le t_{i+k}$ $i.e$ it is monotonically increasing series of real numbers. Generally three types of knot vectors ($i.e.$, Δ) are used.

1. Uniform knot vectors

2. Open uniform knot vectors and

3. Non-uniform knot vectors.

In practice, uniform knot values (vectors) generally begins at zero and are incremented by 1 to some maximum value or are normalized in the range between 0 and 1 equal decimal intervals $e.g.$, [0.25, 0.5, 0.75, 1]. It means, knot values are evenly spaced in uniform knot vectors such as [0 1 2 3 4] , [– 0.2 0.1 0 0.1 0.2].

In the open uniform knot vectors, individual knot values are evenly spaced similar to uniform knot vectors but difference is that open uniform knot vectors has multiple knot values at the end points which equals to the order n of the B-Spline basis function such as

for

$$n = 2, [0\ 0\ 1\ 2\ 3\ 4\ 4]$$
$$n = 3, [0\ 0\ 0\ 1\ 2\ 3\ 3\ 3]$$
$$n = 4, [0\ 0\ 0\ 0\ 1\ 2\ 2\ 2\ 2] \text{ and}$$

For normalized increments such as

For
$$n = 2, [0\ 0\ ¼\ ½\ ¾\ 1\ 1]$$
$$n = 3, [0\ 0\ ½\ 2/3\ 1\ 1\ 1]$$
$$n = 4, [0\ 0\ 0\ ½\ 1\ 1\ 1\ 1] \text{ etc.}$$

The resulting open uniform basis function yields curves that behaves most nearly like Bezier curve.

Non-uniform knot vectors may have unevenly spaced internal knot values such as [0 0 0 1 1 2 2 2], [0 1 2 2 3 4] and [0 0.28 0.5 0.72] etc.

On the basis of the curve is passing the knots, there are two types of knots. First is periodic and second is non-periodic knots. In periodic knots, the curves does not passes through the first and last points as ensured by the Bezier curve as shown in the fig 5.7, whereas the non-periodic knots ensure that the first and last points passes through the curves .

According to the equation 5.44, the first interval of equation 5.44 can be re-written as follows:

$$N^3_{i,1}(t) = N^3_i(t) \quad \text{for} \quad t_i \le t \le t_{i+1}$$

$$= \frac{(t - t_i)^2}{\nabla^2_i \nabla_i}$$

Let us define the linear transformation of t in terms of u which is

$$u = \frac{t - t_i}{(t_{i+1} - t_i)} = \frac{t - t_i}{\nabla_i}$$

As shown in [figure 5.9(b)], only three B-Spline function at degree 3 are non-zero in the intervals $t_i \le t \le t_{i+1}$. They are $N^3_{i-2,3}(t)$, $N^3_{i-1,2}$ and $N^3_{i,1}(t)$. These B-Spline basis functions are easily obtained from equation (5.43 a, b, c) with index i shifted accordingly so that the range of the parameter t is always between t_i and t_{i+1}

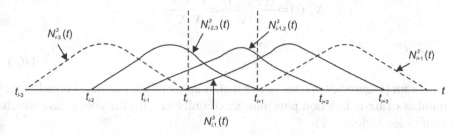

Fig. 5.9 (*b*) Construction at non-zero quadratic B-Spline basis function between t_i and t_{i+1}

$$\therefore \quad N^3_{i-2,3}(t) = \frac{(t_{i+1} - t)^2}{\nabla^2_{i-1} \nabla_i} = \frac{[(t_{i+1} - t_i)(t_i - t)]^2}{\nabla^2_{i-1} \nabla_i}$$

$$= \frac{(\nabla_i - u\nabla_i)^2}{\nabla^2_{i-1} \nabla_i}$$

$$= \frac{\nabla_i}{\nabla^2_{i-1}} - \frac{2u\nabla_i}{\nabla^2_{i-1}} + \frac{u^2\nabla_i}{\nabla^2_{i-1}}$$

$$= \frac{\nabla_i}{\nabla_{i-1}^2} - \frac{u(2\nabla_i)}{\nabla_{i-1}^2} + u^3 \cdot \frac{\nabla_i}{\nabla_{i-1}^2}$$

$$\text{for } 0 \le u \le 1 \qquad\qquad \dots 5.44(a)$$

Putting $i = i - 1$ in equation 5.43(b)

$$N_{i-1,2}^3(t) = \frac{(t - t_{i-1})^2}{\nabla_{i-1}^2 \nabla_{i-1}} - \frac{\nabla_{i-1}^3 (t - t_i)^2}{\nabla_i^2 \nabla_i \nabla_{i-1}},$$

$$= \frac{[(t - t_i) + (t_i - t_{i-1})]^2}{\nabla_{i-1}^2 \nabla_{i-1}} - \frac{\nabla_{i-1}^3 (t - t_i)^2}{\nabla_i^2 \nabla_i \nabla_{i-1}}$$

when $u = \dfrac{(t - t_i)}{\nabla_i}$, then

$$= \frac{(u\nabla_i + \nabla_{i-1})^2}{\nabla_{i-1}^2 \nabla_{i-1}} - \frac{\nabla_{i-1}^3 (u\nabla_i)^2}{\nabla_i^2 \nabla_i \nabla_{i-1}}$$

$$= \frac{u^2 \nabla_i^2}{\nabla_{i-1}^2 \nabla_{i-1}} + \frac{2u\nabla_i \cdot \nabla_{i-1}}{\nabla_{i-1}^2 \nabla_{i-1}} + \frac{\nabla_{i-1}^2}{\nabla_{i-1}^2 \nabla_{i-1}} - \frac{\nabla_{i-1}^3 u^2}{\nabla_i \nabla_{i-1}}$$

$$= \frac{\nabla_{i-1}}{\nabla_{i-1}^2} + u\left(\frac{2\nabla_i}{\nabla_{i-1}^2} \right) + u^2 \cdot \frac{\nabla_i}{\nabla_{i-1}} \left[\frac{\nabla_i}{\nabla_{i-1}^2} - \frac{\nabla_{i-1}^3}{\nabla_i^2} \right] \qquad \dots(5.44 - b)$$

$$\dots 5.44(b)$$

and

$$N_{i,1}^3(t) = \frac{(t - t_{i-1})^2}{\nabla_i^2 \nabla_i} = \frac{(u\nabla_i)^2}{\nabla_i^2 \nabla_i}$$

$$= \frac{u^2 \nabla_i^2}{\nabla_i^2 \nabla_i} \qquad\qquad \dots 5.44(c)$$

From [Figure 5.9 (b)] we notice that, number of knot values is equal to the number of basis function plus number of order i.e., for the above case which is of order 3 (degree 2)

Number of knot values = number of basis function for order.

$$= 3 + 3 = 6$$

Hence, the knot vector is $t_{i-2}, t_{i-1}, t_i, t_{i+1}, t_{i+2}, t_{i+3}$ for non-zero basis function. This means above basis functions will give quadratic NUB curve segment (of degree 2). Similarly, for four basis function of order 3 will require 7 knot values or vectors such as [0 1 2 3 4 5 6] etc., for $0 \le t \le 6$ and five 3rd order basis function requires 8 knot values such as [0 0 0 1 1 3 3 3] etc.

5.8.2.1 Quadratic Non-uniform B-Spline Curve Models

From the equation (5.41) NUB curve is represented as

$$\vec{r}(u) = \Sigma_{i=1}^3 N_i^n(t) \cdot \vec{V}_i \quad \text{for } t_i \le t \le t_{i+1}$$

For generating quadratic curve segment, let us use the quadratic basis function $N_i^3(t)$ defined in equation, then equation will be

$$\vec{r}(t) = \Sigma_{i=1}^3 N_i^3(t).\vec{V}_i \qquad \qquad ...(5.45)$$

Where $\vec{r}(t)$ is the position vector along the curve with as a functional parameter t. As shown in [Fig. 5.9 (b)], the blending function are non-zero only when $i(= i-2, i-1, i)$. Then let

$$\vec{V}_0 = \vec{V}_{i-2}$$
$$\vec{V}_1 = \vec{V}_{i-1}$$
$$\vec{V}_2 = \vec{V}_i$$

Then $\qquad \vec{r}(t) = \Sigma_{i=0}^3 N_i^3(t)\vec{V}_i$

$$= N_{i-2,3}^3(t)\vec{V}_{i-2} + N_{i-2,2}^3(t)\vec{V}_{i-1} + N_{i,1}^3(t)\vec{V}_i$$

Putting all values in 5.44 (a, b, c) and $\vec{V}_i$ in terms of parameter u will give

$$\vec{r}(u) = \left[\frac{\nabla_i}{\nabla_{i-1}^2} + \frac{2\nabla_i}{\nabla_{i-1}^2}u + \frac{\nabla_i}{\nabla_{i-1}^2}u^2\right]\vec{V}_0 +$$

$$\left[\frac{\nabla_{i-1}}{\nabla_{i-1}^2} + \frac{2\nabla_i}{\nabla_{i-1}^2}u + \frac{\nabla_i}{\nabla_{i-1}}\left\{\frac{\nabla_i}{\nabla_{i-1}^2} - \frac{\nabla_{i-1}^3}{\nabla_i^2}\right\}u^2\right]\vec{V}_1 + \left[\frac{\nabla_i^2}{\nabla_i^2\nabla_i}u^2\right]\vec{V}_2$$

$$\vec{r}(u) = N_0^3(u)\vec{V}_0 + N_1^3(u)\vec{V}_1 + N_2^3(u)\vec{V}_2 \text{ in blended form}$$

$$\vec{r}(u) = UN_q R \qquad \qquad ....(5.46)$$

where $\qquad u = [1 \quad u \quad u^2]$

where $\qquad R = [\vec{V}_0 \quad \vec{V}_1 \quad \vec{V}_2]$ and

$$N_q = \begin{bmatrix} \dfrac{\nabla_i}{\nabla_{i-2}^2} & \dfrac{\nabla_{i-1}}{\nabla_{i-1}^2} & 0 \\[3mm] \dfrac{-2\nabla_i}{\nabla_{i-1}^2} & \dfrac{2\nabla_i}{\nabla_{i-1}^2} & 0 \\[3mm] \dfrac{\nabla_i}{\nabla_{i-1}^2} & \dfrac{\nabla_i}{\nabla_{i-1}}\left\{\dfrac{\nabla_i}{\nabla_{i-1}^2} - \dfrac{\nabla_{i-2}^3}{\nabla_i^2}\right\} & \dfrac{\nabla_i}{\nabla_i^2} \end{bmatrix}$$

where $\nabla_i = (t_{i+1} - t_i)$, $\nabla_i^2 = \nabla_i + \nabla_{i+1}$ for $i = 0, 1 ...., (n-1)$

The curve segment equation (5.46) represents quadratic NUB curve segment. Above derivation suggested that the quadratic curve is supported by six knots t_{i-2} through t_{i+3} eventhough its parameter range is $t_i \le t \le t_{i+1}$.

$$\vec{r}(t) = N_{i-3}^4(t)\vec{V}_{i-3} + N_{i-2}^4(t)\vec{V}_{i-2} + N_{i-1}^4(t)\vec{V}_{i-1} + N_i^3(t)\vec{V}_i$$

Let $\vec{V}_{i-3} = \vec{V}_0$ (starting control points)

$$\vec{V}_{i-2} = \vec{V}_1$$

$$\vec{V}_{i-1} = \vec{V}_2$$

$$\vec{V}_i = \vec{V}_3 \text{ (end control points)}$$

Thus, $\vec{r}(t) = N^4_{i-3}(t)\vec{V}_0 + N^4_{i-2}(t)\vec{V}_1 + N^4_{i-1}(t)\vec{V}_2 + N^3_i(t)\vec{V}_3$

$$\vec{r}(t) = UN_C R \qquad\qquad .... (5.47)$$

Putting values of blending function in terms of V and u, we get

where $U = [1 \quad u \quad u^2 \quad u^3]$

$$R = \begin{bmatrix} \vec{V}_0 \\ \vec{V}_1 \\ \vec{V}_2 \\ \vec{V}_3 \end{bmatrix} = [\vec{V}_0 \ \vec{V}_1 \ \vec{V}_2 \ \vec{V}_3]$$

$$N_c = \begin{bmatrix} \dfrac{\nabla^2_i}{\nabla^2_{i-1}\nabla^3_{i-2}} & (1 - n_{11} - n_{13}) & \dfrac{(\nabla_{i-1})^2}{\nabla^3_{i-1}\nabla^2_{i-1}} & 0 \\[3mm] -3n_{11} & (3n_{11} - n_{23}) & \dfrac{\nabla^2_i}{\nabla^2_{i-1}\nabla^3_{i-2}} & 0 \\[3mm] 3n_{11} & -(3n_{11} + n_{33}) & \dfrac{\nabla^2_i}{\nabla^2_{i-1}\nabla^3_{i-2}} & 0 \\[3mm] -n_{11} & n_{11} - n_{43} - n_{44} & n_{43} & \dfrac{(\nabla_i)^2}{\nabla^3_i\nabla^2_i} \end{bmatrix}$$

where $n_{43} = -\left\{ \dfrac{1}{3}n_{33} + n_{44} + \dfrac{\nabla^4_i}{\nabla^2_i\nabla^3_{i-1}} \right\}$

$n_{i,j}$ = element in row i, column j

$$\nabla^k_i = \nabla_i + \nabla_{i+1} + ... + \nabla_{i+k-1}$$

For $i = 0, 1 ..... (n-1)$

The curve segment given by equation (5.47) is called cubic NUB cuve segment. However, the end knots t_{i-2} and t_{i+3} are redundant because this information is not used in computing the curve. This is the reason as quadratic NUB curve segment is completely defined by the three knot spans ∇_{i-1}, ∇_i and ∇_{i+1} the three control vertices $\vec{V}_0$, $\vec{V}_1$ and $\vec{V}_2$. From above discussion we see that the number of knots is always equal to number of points plus the order of the curve.

5.8.2.2 Cubic Non-uniform B-spline Curve Model

To generate cubic NUB curve model, equation (5.42) can be iterated one step further such as

$$N_i^4(t) = N_{i,4}^4(t) \quad \text{for} \quad t_{i+k-1} \leq t \leq t_{i+k} \quad \text{where } k = 1, 2, 3, 4$$

This equation is used for generating cubic curve of order four with similar approach we can get

$$N_{i,1}^4(t) = \frac{(t - t_i)^3}{\nabla_i^3 \nabla_i^2 \nabla_i}$$

$$N_{i,1}^4(t) = N_{i,1}^4(t) = \frac{\nabla_i^4 (t - t_{i+1})^3}{\nabla_{i+1}^3 \nabla_{i+1}^2 \nabla_{i+1} \nabla_i}$$

$$N_{i,3}^4(t) = N_{i,4}^4(t) = \frac{\nabla_i^4 (t_{i+3} - t)^3}{\nabla_{i+2} \nabla_{i+1}^3 \nabla_{i+1}^2 \nabla_i^3} \quad \text{and}$$

$$N_{i,4}^4(t) = N_{i,4}^4(t) = \frac{(t_{i+4} - t)^3}{\nabla_{i+3} \nabla_{i+2}^2 \nabla_{i+1}^3}$$

With the use of same steps as done in the quadratic case, a cubic NUB curve segment $\vec{r}(t)$ can be generated as

$$\vec{r}(t) = \sum_{i=0}^{4} N_i^4(t) v_i \quad \text{for} \quad t_i \leq t \leq t_{i+1}$$

In equation 5.47 when we put uniform knot values $i.e.$,

$$\nabla_i = 1 \quad \text{for} \quad \text{all } i,$$

Then, the NUB co-efficient matrix N_c in equation (5.47) becomes the co-efficient matrix N of the cubic uniform B –Spline curve which is

$$N_c = \begin{bmatrix} \dfrac{1}{6} & \dfrac{2}{3} & \dfrac{1}{6} & 0 \\[2mm] -\dfrac{1}{2} & 0 & \dfrac{1}{2} & 0 \\[2mm] \dfrac{1}{2} & -1 & \dfrac{1}{2} & 0 \\[2mm] -\dfrac{1}{6} & \dfrac{1}{2} & -\dfrac{1}{2} & \dfrac{1}{6} \end{bmatrix}$$

$$= \frac{1}{6} \begin{bmatrix} 1 & 4 & 1 & 0 \\ -3 & -0 & 3 & 0 \\ 3 & -6 & 3 & 0 \\ -1 & 3 & -3 & 1 \end{bmatrix}$$

$$= \frac{1}{6} N \text{ of uniform cubic B-spline curve.}$$

Let use define a knot sequence as

$$t_{i-2} = t_{i-1} = t_i = 0$$

$$t_{i+1} = t_{i+2} = t_{i+3} = 1$$

Then, the corresponding knot spans are given by

$$\nabla_i = 1 \text{ and}$$

$$\nabla_j = 0 \quad \text{for all } j \neq i$$

Above values makes the co-efficient matrix N_c in equation (5.47) to the coefficient matrix of cubic Bezier curve (equation). Thus, we can say that both Bezier and uniform B-Spline curve are special case of a NUB curve.

5.9 RATIONAL MODEL OF NUB CURVE

When we express any curve model in term of the ratio of two polynomial functions of curves then, it is called Rational curve model. In rational curve models, each control vertices $V_i = (x_i, y_i, z_i)$ is expressed in terms of normalized homogenous control points a

$$V_i^h = (x_i, y_i, z_i, 1) \quad \text{for} \quad i = 0, 1, 2, \dots\dots$$

Let H_i denote homogeneous control vertices such that

$$H_i = w_i V_i^h = (w_i x_i, w_i y_i, w_i z_i, w_i); \, w \neq 0 \qquad \dots(5.48)$$

Where $w_i v_i$ are weighted control points. Then

Then, the Cartesian co-ordinates of a homogeneous control vertex H_i are the same as those of a 3D control vertex $\vec{V}_i$ regardless of the value of the weight (as long as it is non-zero).

The advantage of weights w_i is that w_i proves additional flexibility for controlling shape of the objects. Conversion of Cartesian co-ordinates into homogeneous co-ordinates is widely used in co-ordinates transformation in the field of computer graphics and robotics. This section presents the rational extension of the non-uniform B- Spline curve which can be generalized for other curve like Bezier, B-Spline, etc. As already know that

$$\vec{r}(u) = [x(u), y(u), z(u)]$$

$$= \sum_{i=0}^{n} N_i^n(u)\vec{V}_i$$

By using homogeneous co-ordinates of control vertices in equation 5.48, the above *NUB* curve segment of degree n can be concisely expressed in a homogeneous form as

$$\vec{R}(u) = [X(u), Y(u), Z(u) \, h(u)]$$

$$= \sum_{i=0}^{n} N_i^n(u)\overrightarrow{H}_i \qquad \qquad ...(5.49)$$

The homogeneous NUB equation (5.49) is expressed in a component form as

$$\overrightarrow{R}(u) = [X(u),\ Y(u),\ Z(u)\ h(u)]$$

$$= \left[\sum_{i=0}^{n} N_i^n(u)w_i x_i,\ \sum_{i=0}^{n} N_i^n(u)w_i y_i,\ \sum_{i=0}^{n} N_i^n(u)w_i z_i,\ \sum_{i=0}^{n} N_i^n(u)w_i \right]$$

Where, the Cartesian co-ordinates are recovered as

$$x(u) = \frac{X(u)}{h(u)},\ y(u) = \frac{Y(u)}{h(u)},\ z(u) = \frac{Z(u)}{h(u)}$$

Which are more concisely expressed in a rational form as

$$\overrightarrow{r}(u) = [x(u),\ y(u),\ z(u)]$$

$$= \sum_{i=0}^{n} N_i^n(u)w_i v_i \bigg/ \sum_{i=0}^{n} N_i^n(u)w_i \qquad \qquad ...(5.50)$$

Where $V_i = (x_i,\ y_i,\ z_i)$, and Eqn. (5.50) is called Non Uniform Rational Bazier (NURB) curve model.

We see that same homogeneous expression eqn. (5.49) can be expressed in rational from (eqn. 5.50). The rational form provides more degree of freedom to define curve shape inside characteristic polygon. Thus, rational form gives convex hall property. In a similar way, we can express quadratic and cubic Bezier curve in rational form. From the equation (5.50), we see that the shape of non-uniform. Similarly, we can express quadratic and non-uniform Rational B-Spline (NURB curve) curve is controlled by knot spacing, control vertices, and weights. This is the reason NURB curve is very flexible. NURBS development began in nineteen fifties by engineer who were in need of a mathematically of exact representation of free from surfaces. When, using modern CAD/ CAM system, designers adopt more free-form or contoured geometric slopes for the design and modelling of complex parts such as parts of car bodies, ship hulls etc. Since, conventional CNC (Computer Numerial control) machines only provide linear (G01) and circular (G02, G03) interpolations, CAM systems have to create many linear and circular segments to approximate the contoured geometry under given to clearences before sending NC codes CNC machines. However, when the part accuracy becomes tighter, the conventional approach gives following problems.

1. Tighter to clearances gives shorter data segment.

2. There is feed rate fluctuation and velocity discontinuity during function of two connected line segments.

3. During high-speed machining, data transmission cannot catchup with the large amount of data transfer..

4. Excessive jerk, vibration and acceleration discontinuity, occurring at high which reduce the machining quality.

Above drawbacks shows that conventional approach to not able to satisfy the requirement of high speed and high accuracy machining needed in modern manufacturing   systems. In order to overcome above drawbacks, parametric curve and surfaces from early Bezier to more recent B-Spline and NURBS have been adopted by CAD/CAM and CNC systems now a days. Since NURBS can represent both analytic geometry and free form of the shape of the objects, it has emerged as the standard geometry representation too. Along with others advantages, NURB interpolation does not need to segment NURBS curve into linear and circular segments, thus NURBS curve can reduce the transmitted data between CAD/CAM and CNC system substantially. Various NURBS interpolation algorithms have also been proposed by various researchers to reduce federate fluctuation and to improve machining accuracy. Finally, NURBS are useful for a number of reasons and somerized as

(*a*) Offer one common mathematical form for both analytical (e.g. conics) and free form slapes.

(*b*) Offer flexibility to design a large variety of shapes.

(*c*) Reduce the memory consumption when storing shapes.

(*d*) Evaluated reasonably fast by numerically stable and accurate algorithm

(*e*) Invariant under offline.

(*g*) Generalization of non-rational B-Splines, non-rational and rational Bezier curves and surfaces.

UNSOLVED PROBLEM

1. Find parametric cubic curve for $u_1 = 0$, $u_2 = 1/4$, $u_3 = 3/4$, $u_4 = 1$.

2. Find parametric quintic curve for six data points with $u_1 = 0$, $u_2 = 0.2$, $u_3 = 0.4$, $u_4 = 0.6$, $u_5 = 0.8$, $u_6 = 1$.

3. Plot Fergusson curve for

(*a*) $\qquad |\vec{t}_0| = |\vec{t}_1| = 100$

(*b*) $\qquad |\vec{t}_0| = |\vec{t}_1| = 300$

(*c*) $\qquad |\vec{t}_0| = |\vec{t}_1| = 900$

(*d*) $\quad |\vec{t}_0| = 100$ and $|\vec{t}_1| = 900$

4. Find the algebraic co-efficients of a parametric curve whose co-ordinates at $u = 0$ are $[-1, -2, -1]$ and at $u = 1$ are $(6\ 3\ 6)$ and whose direction cosines are constant at all points on the curve determine all direction cosines.

5. Find algebraic co-efficients of a parametric curve laying in the $x = 8$ plane whose geometric characteristic at $u = 0$ $(8, 2, 2)$ and $\dfrac{dz}{dy} = 2$ at $= 0.5$ are $(8, 3, 3)$ and at $u = 1$ are $(5, 5, 1)$ and $\dfrac{dz}{dy} = -2$.

6. Prove that quintic Bezier curve is represented by following equation.

$$\vec{r}(u) = \begin{bmatrix} 1 & u & u^2 & u^3 & u^4 \end{bmatrix} \begin{bmatrix} 1 & -4 & 6 & -4 & 1 \\ -4 & 12 & -12 & 4 & 0 \\ 6 & -12 & 6 & 0 & 0 \\ -4 & -4 & 0 & 0 & 0 \\ 1 & 0 & 0 & 0 & 0 \end{bmatrix} \begin{bmatrix} \vec{V}_0 \\ \vec{V}_1 \\ \vec{V}_2 \\ \vec{V}_3 \\ \vec{V}_4 \end{bmatrix}$$

Hint: $\vec{r}(u) = \sum_{i=0}^{5} B_i^n(u)\,v_i$ where $i = 0, 1, 2, 3, 4, 5$

$$B_i^n(u) = \frac{n!}{(n-i)!\,i!}\,u^i\,(1-u)^{n-i}$$

7. Find out quartic Bezier curve segment corresponding to five Bezier polygon points.

Hint: $\vec{r}(u) = \sum_{i=0}^{n} B_i^n(u)v_i$, where $B_i^n(u) = \dfrac{n!}{(n-i)!\,i!}\,u^i\,(1-u)^{n-i}$

8. Find quadratic B-Spline curve equation for which

$$\vec{r}(u) = \begin{pmatrix} 1 & u & u^2 \end{pmatrix} \frac{1}{2} \begin{bmatrix} 1 & 1 & 0 \\ 2 & 2 & 0 \\ 1 & -2 & 0 \end{bmatrix} \begin{bmatrix} \vec{V}_0 \\ \vec{V}_1 \\ \vec{V}_2 \end{bmatrix}$$

9. Find quartic B-Spline curve

$$\vec{r}(u) = \begin{pmatrix} 1 & u & u^2 & u^3 & u^4 \end{pmatrix} \frac{1}{24} \begin{bmatrix} 1 & 11 & 11 & 1 & 0 \\ -4 & -12 & 12 & 4 & 0 \\ 6 & -6 & -6 & 6 & 0 \\ -4 & 12 & -12 & 4 & 0 \\ 1 & -4 & 6 & -4 & 1 \end{bmatrix} \begin{bmatrix} \vec{V}_0 \\ \vec{V}_1 \\ \vec{V}_2 \\ \vec{V}_3 \\ \vec{V}_4 \end{bmatrix}$$

10. Given $\vec{V}_0[1\ 1]\ \vec{V}_1[2\ 3]\ \vec{V}_4[5\ 4]$ and $\vec{V}_3[4\ 2]$ and the vertices of a Bezier polygon. Calculate second, third and fourth order B-Spline curve.

11. The polygon vertices are $V_0\ [0\ 0]\ V_1\ [3\ 9]\ V_2\ [6\ 3]\ V_3\ [9\ 6]$. Determine the fourth order periodic B-Spline curve defined by this polygon.

    Solution : For $k = 4$, $[0\ 1\ 2\ 3\ 4\ 5\ 6\ 7]$ with the parameter range $3 \le t \le 4$ is the knot vector for the periodic basis function.

12. Using non-uniform knot vector with knot values proportional to the chord distances between defining polygon vertices, determine the third order open spline curve defined by $V_0\ [0, 0],\ V_1\ [\ 2\ 6]\ V_2\ [4\ 3]\ V_3\ [6\ 6]$ $V_4\ [8\ 6]$

    Solution: First determine the chord length

    $$C_1 = |V_1 - V_0| = \sqrt{(x_2 - x_1)^2 + (y_2 - y_1)^2} = \sqrt{(2-0)^2} + (6-0)^2 = 6.32$$
    $$C_2 = |V_2 - V_1| = 3.606$$
    $$C_3 = |V_3 - V_2| = 3.606$$
    $$C_4 = |V_4 - V_3| = 2.0$$

    Total chord length is $\Sigma^4_{i=1}\ C_i = 15.537$

    Using Equation below for internal not vectors, it internal not values proportional to the chord distances between polygon vertices. Specifically, the knot vector is given by

    $$t_1 = 0.1 \le i \le n \ .... \ \{n = \text{order}\}$$

    $$t_{i+n} = \left[\left(\frac{i}{j-n+1}\right)C_{i+1} + \sum_{j=1}^{i} C_j\right](j-n+2) \bigg/ \sum_{i=1}^{j-1} C_i$$

    $$T = j - k + 2, \quad j \le i \le j + n$$

    $\therefore\ t_1 = 0,\quad t_2 = 0, t_3 = 0$ because three basis function

    and $\qquad\qquad\qquad t_6 = j - n + 1 = 5 - 3 + 1 = 3\ (5 \le i \le 8)$
    $$t_7 = 3, t_8 = 3$$

    And internal knots vectors

    $$t_{i+k} = t_{i+3} = x_4 = \left[\frac{i}{i-n+1}C_{i+1} + \sum_{i=1}^{i} C_j\right](j-n+1)/15.537$$

$$= \left[\frac{1}{5-3+1}C_2 + C_1\right]\frac{(5-3+1)}{15.537} = 1.453$$

$$t_{2+3} = t_5 = \frac{\left[\dfrac{2C_3}{3} + C_1 + C_2\right]}{15.537} = 2.382$$

The knot vector is thus,

$$[t] = [0\ 0\ 0\ 1.45\ 2.382\ 3\ 3\ 3]$$

The parameter range is $0 \le t \le 3$.

Composite Curve Fitting: Geometric Modelling

6.0 INTRODUCTION

A smooth composite parametric curve $\vec{r}\,(u)$ can be generated by passing a sequence of a data points (P_i, $i = 0, 1, ..., n$). Data points may be 2D or 3D as per requirements. Any of the curve models like Fergusson, Bezier and B-spline can be used infitting a curve with adjacent curve from a given sequence of data points. The choice of specific curve model depends on following factors:

1. Ease of implementation,
2. Computational efficiency,
3. Mathematical continuity,
4. Aesthetic smoothness,
5. Uniformness of flow rate.

Composite curve can be generated by fitting either evenly spaced data points or unevenly spaced data points.

1. Composite Curve fitting using evenly spaced data points is discussed here under following cases

   (a) Cubic spline fitting using Ferguson curve model and,

   (b) Uniform B-Spline fitting.

For evenly spaced data point fitting, parametric continuity conditions are best option to apply at joining point of two pieces of curves for generating smooth composite curve:

2. Composite Curve fitting for unevenly spaced data points is discussed here for following cases.

   (a) Chord length spline fitting,

(*b*) Non-uniform B-spline fitting.

When the physical spacing of the data points becomes uneven, composite curve obtained by parametric continuity conditions tends to show local flatness and kinks. To avoid this, geometric continuity conditions is better option to apply at joining points

6.1 CONTINUITY CONDITIONS

For joining two successive curve segments, there are two types of continuity conditions. They are:

(1) Parametric continuity condition.

(2) Geometric continuity condition.

6.1.1 Parametric Continuity Condition

In fitting, Positional continuous means co-ordinates of first segment end will be same as the coordinates of second segments starts. Let us consider two curve segments.

$\vec{r}^{a}(u)$ and $\vec{r}^{b}(u)$ in Fig. 6.1, each defined on the unit interval for $0 \leq u \leq 1$. In order for the two curve segments to be connected the following position continuity condition should hold at the common joints.

$$\vec{r}^{a}(1) = \vec{P}_1 = \vec{r}^{a}(0) \qquad \qquad ...(6.1)$$

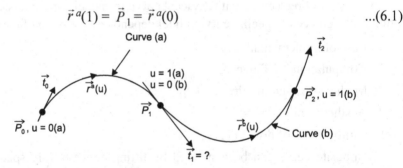

Fig. 6.1 Parametric continuity at common joints of two curve segments.

Equation (6.1) is called zeroth order continuity condition and represented as C^0. Similarly,

$$\dot{\vec{r}}^{a}(1) = \vec{t}_1 = \dot{\vec{r}}^{b}(0) \qquad \qquad ...(6.2)$$

Equation (6.2) is called first order parametric continuity condition and represented as C^1 and

$$\ddot{\vec{r}}^{a}(1) = \ddot{\vec{r}}^{b}(0) \qquad \qquad ...(6.3)$$

Equation (6.3) is called 2nd order continuity condition and represented as C^2.

The continuity conditions (6.1), (6.2) and (6.3) are collectively called a parametric C^2 condition.

Zero order parametric continuity means the values of x, y and z evaluated at u_2 for the first curve section are equal to the values of x, y and z evaluated at u_1 for the next curve section. First order continuity means that the tangent lines of two successive curve sections are equal at their joint points P_i. Finally, second order continuity condition means that the both the first and second parametric derivatives of the two curve sections are the same at the intersection point. Similarly. higher order parametric continuity conditions can be defined and used whenever required. [Fig. 6.2 (a) (b) and (c)] shows examples of C^0, C^1 and C^2 continuity respectively.

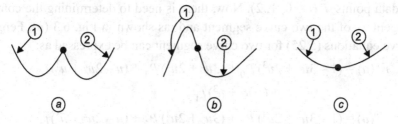

Fig. 6.2 Curve by joining two piecewise curve segments.

Fig. 6.2 suggested that Fig. 6.2(c) is more smooth that Fig. 6.2(b). it means higher order continuity conditions will give smoother curve. However, first order continuity is generally used to digitize drawings and for simple design applications while second order continuity is useful in any application such as designing, animation and simulation of free form products generation in CAD.

6.2 CUBIC SPLINE FITTING

Let we have two Ferguson curve segments (a) and (b) fitted as shown in Fig. 6.3(a) and its vector valued position vector of points of each curve segment is represent by $\vec{r}^a(u)$ and $\vec{r}^b(u)$ respectively,

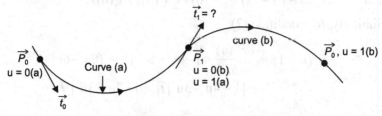

Fig. 6.3 (a) Two successive piecewise cubic spline segments.

Here $\vec{P}_0$, $\vec{P}_1$, $\vec{t}_0$, $\vec{t}_1$ and u are the position vectors, tangent vectors and value of parameter respectively for curve (a) and similarly $\vec{P}_1, \vec{P}_2, \vec{t}_1, \vec{t}_2$ and u are the position vector tangent vectors and value of parameter respectively for curve (b). When $\vec{P}_0, \vec{P}, \vec{t}_2, \vec{t}_0, \vec{t}_1$ and $\vec{t}_2$ parametric variable value u are known. Then these two Ferguson curve segments yields useful shape after fitting at common joint and results called composite curve. While constructing smooth curve, generally tangents are not given. Thus, one has a problem to determine unknown tangents at common join. Generally, for smooth fitting of a piece wise curve segments of degree n, continuity condition of order $n–1$ must satisfied at the common joints or internal joints. Similarly, for fitting of cubic spline, continuity condition of second order must satisfied at the common joints or internal joints.

It is assumed that start tangent $\vec{t}_0$ of the first curve segment (a) and end tangent $\vec{t}_2$ of the last curve segment are known in addition to the co-ordinates of data points $\vec{P}$ ($i = 0, 1, 2$). Now, there is need to determining the common tangent $\vec{t}_1$ of the two curve segment and as shown in Fig. 6.3 (a). Ferguson curve equations (5.25) for two curve segment can be expressed as:

$$\vec{r}^{\,a}(u) = (1 - 3u^2 + 2u^3)\,\vec{P}_0 + (3u^2 + 2u^3)\,\vec{P}_1 + (u - 2u^2 + u^3)\vec{t}_0$$
$$+ (- u^2 + u^3)\vec{t}_1 \qquad\qquad ...(6.4)$$

$$\vec{r}^{\,b}(u) = (1 - 3u^2 + 2u^3)\,\vec{P}_1 + (3u^2 + 2u^3)\,\vec{P}_2 + (u - 2u^2 + u^3)\vec{t}_1$$
$$+ (- u^2 + u^3)\vec{t}_2 \qquad\qquad ...(6.5)$$

For curve fitting, we can apply following C^2 – continuity condition at common joint.

(1) $\vec{r}^{\,a}(u = 1) = \vec{r}^{\,b}(u = 0)$ ...(a)

(2) $\dot{\vec{r}}^{\,a}(u = 1) = \dot{\vec{r}}^{\,b}(u = 0)$ ...(b)

(3) $\ddot{\vec{r}}^{\,a}(u = 1) = \ddot{\vec{r}}^{\,b}(u = 0)$ ...(c)

As per condition 1 putting value of u in Eqn. (6.4) and (6.5) gives

$$\vec{r}^{\,a}(u = 1) = (0)\,\vec{P}_0 + (1)\,\vec{P}_1 + (0)\vec{t}_0 + (0)\vec{t}_1 = \vec{P}_1$$

and $\vec{r}^{\,b}(u = 0) = (1)\,\vec{P}_1 + (0)\,\vec{P}_2 + (0)\vec{t}_1 + (0)\vec{t}_2$

Similarly, for condition (2)

$$\dot{\vec{r}}^{\,a}(u = 1) = \frac{d\vec{r}^{\,a}(u)}{du} = [-6u + 6u^2]\vec{P}_0 + (6u - 6u^2)\vec{P}_1$$
$$+ [1 - 4u - 3u^2]\vec{t}_0 + [- 2u - 3u^2]\,\vec{t}_1$$
$$= \vec{t}_1$$

$$\dot{\vec{r}}^{\,b}(u = 0) = \vec{t}_1$$

From above results, we can get generalized equations or first and last curve as:

$$\dot{\vec{r}}^{\,a}(u = 0) = \vec{t}_0 \quad \text{and} \quad \dot{\vec{r}}^{\,n}(u = 1) = \vec{t}_n \qquad ...(6.5(a))$$

Again similarly for condition (3),

$$\ddot{\vec{r}}^{\,a}(1) = \frac{d^2\vec{r}^{\,a}(u=1)}{du^2} = 6\vec{P}_0 - 6\vec{P}_1 + 2\vec{t}_0 + 4\vec{t}_1$$

and $\qquad \ddot{\vec{r}}^{\,b}(0) = \dfrac{d^2\vec{r}^{\,a}(u=0)}{du^2} = -6\vec{P}_1 + 6\vec{P}_2 - 4\vec{t}_1 - 2\vec{t}_2$

From above continuity conditions we observed that condition (1) and condition (2) gives same value but condition (3) gives following relation,

$$\ddot{\vec{r}}^{\,a}(1) = \ddot{\vec{r}}^{\,b}(0)$$

$$\Rightarrow 6\,\vec{P}_0 - 6\,\vec{P}_1 + 2\vec{t}_0 + 4\vec{t}_1 = -6\,\vec{P}_1 + 6\,\vec{P}_2 - 4\vec{t}_1 - 2\vec{t}_2$$

$$\Rightarrow \qquad \vec{t}_0 + 4\vec{t}_1 + \vec{t}_2 = 3(\vec{P}_2 - \vec{P}_0) \qquad\qquad \text{...(6.6)}$$

From equation (6.6) the unknown tangent $\vec{t}_1$ can be determined by following equation 6.8.

$$\vec{t}_1 = \frac{1}{4}[3(\vec{P}_2 - \vec{P}_0) - \vec{t}_0 - \vec{t}_2] \qquad\qquad \text{...(6.7)}$$

6.2.1 Composite Curve from Sequence of n+1 Data Points

For constructing composite cubic curve passing through a sequence of $n + 1$ data point as shown in [Fig. 6.3 (b)], one can apply a C^2 continuous condition. The process of fitting curve from a sequence of point data is sometime called the inversion process. In this case, unknown tangents at joining points can be determined under two cases. First when starting tangent of first curve and end tangent of last curve is known. Second, when these tangents are not known.

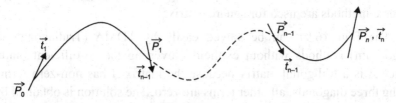

Fig. 6.3 (b) Composite curve from sequence of $n+1$ data points (Interpolated).

6.2.1.1 When Tangent $\vec{t}_0$ and $\vec{t}_n$ are Known

Initially it is assumed that start tangent ($\vec{t}_0 = \hat{t}_0$) of first curve segment and end tangent of last curve segment ($\vec{t}_n = \hat{t}_n$) are known in addition to the $n + 1$ data points ($\vec{P}_i$). Therefore, here boundary conditions are called clamped end condition. Let unknown tangent $\vec{t}_i$ holds well for each pair of neighboring curve segments $\vec{r}^{\,i-1}(u=1)$ and $\vec{r}^{\,i}(u)$ and is obtained as obtained in equation (6.6). Then the following set of linear equation are obtained

$$\vec{t}_{i-1} + 4\vec{t}_i + 4\vec{t}_{i+1} = 3(\vec{P}_{i+1} + \vec{P}_{i-1}) \text{ for } i = 1, 2, \ldots\ldots\ldots (n-1) \quad \text{...(6.8)}$$

Equation (6.8) can be used for determining unknown tangents of intermediate curves (except $\vec{t}_0$ of first and $\vec{t}_n$ of last curve). The equation (6.8) gives $(n-1)$ linear equations. But there is a $(n+1)$ data points thus we must have $(n+1)$ linear equations. These two additional linear equation can be obtained from equation 6.5 (a). Here, $\vec{t}_0$ and $\vec{t}_n$ are known. Thus, we have set of three equations as:

$$\vec{t}_0 = \vec{t}_0$$

$$\vec{t}_{i-1} + 4\vec{t}_i + 4\vec{t}_{i-1} = 3(\vec{P}_{i+1} + \vec{P}_{i-1})$$

$$\vec{t}_n = \vec{t}_n$$

The above three equations can be written in matrix form as

$$\begin{bmatrix} 1 & 0 & 0 & 0 & \vdots & \vdots & \cdots & & \cdots \\ 1 & 4 & 1 & 0 & \vdots & \vdots & \cdots & & \cdots \\ 0 & 1 & 4 & 1 & \vdots & \vdots & \cdots & & \cdots \\ \cdots & \cdots & & & \vdots & \vdots & \cdots & & \cdots \\ \cdots & \cdots & & & \vdots & \vdots & \cdots & & \cdots \\ \cdots & \cdots & & & \vdots & \vdots & 1 & 4 & 1 \\ \cdots & \cdots & & & \vdots & \vdots & 0 & 0 & 1 \end{bmatrix} \begin{bmatrix} \vec{t}_0 \\ \vec{t}_1 \\ \vec{t}_2 \\ \vdots \\ \vdots \\ \vec{t}_{n-1} \\ \vec{t}_n \end{bmatrix} = \begin{bmatrix} \hat{t}_0 \\ 3(\vec{P}_2 - \vec{P}_1) \\ 3(\vec{P}_3 - \vec{P}_1) \\ \vdots \\ \vdots \\ 3(\vec{P}_n - \vec{P}_{n-2}) \\ \hat{t}_n \end{bmatrix} \qquad \ldots(6.9)$$

$$\qquad\qquad [A] \qquad\qquad\qquad [X] \qquad\qquad [d]$$

$$\Rightarrow \qquad\qquad Ax = d \text{ (let)}$$

A general solution for unknown tangent vectors is given by $x = A^{-1}d$. This method is not convenient for determining large unknown values. Generally inverse methods are used for square matrix.

The Eqn. (6.9) can be solved easily by TDMA (Tridiagonal Matrix Algorithm) methods without explicitly inverting the co-efficient matrix A. Since A is a tridigonal matrix because the matrix A has non-zero term only along three diagonals, all other terms are zero. The solution is obtained by one forward substitution followed by a backward substitution. Spath (1974), has developed Tridiagonal matrix algorithms (TDMA) which solve such problems without inverting the matrix. This method is computationally very convenient and is used for such matrix.

6.2.1.2 Tridiagonal Matrix Algorithm

This algorithm is used to solve a linear equation system whose co-efficients matrix is "tridiagonal". This technique is given by Spath (1974) as below.

Let us consider a systems of "$n+1$" linear equations of the from

$$Ax = d \qquad\qquad \ldots(6.10)$$

Where

$$
A = \begin{bmatrix}
b_0 & c_0 & 0 & & \vdots & \vdots & \cdots & & \cdots \\
a_1 & b_1 & c_1 & & \vdots & \vdots & \cdots & & \cdots \\
0 & a_2 & b_2 & c_2 & \vdots & \vdots & \cdots & & \cdots \\
\cdots & \cdots & & & \vdots & \vdots & \cdots & & \cdots \\
\cdots & \cdots & & & \vdots & \vdots & \cdots & & \cdots \\
\cdots & \cdots & & & \vdots & \vdots & a_{n-1} & b_{n-1} & c_{n-1} \\
\cdots & \cdots & & & \vdots & \vdots & 0 & a_n & b_n
\end{bmatrix}_{(n+1)(n+1)}
\quad
x = \begin{bmatrix} x_0 \\ x_1 \\ x_2 \\ \vdots \\ \vdots \\ \vdots \\ x_n \end{bmatrix}
\quad
d = \begin{bmatrix} d_0 \\ d_1 \\ d_2 \\ \vdots \\ \vdots \\ \vdots \\ d_n \end{bmatrix}
$$

In order to meet the diagonal dominance condition

We need to have

$$|b_i| \ge |c_{(i-1)}| + |a_{(i+1)}|$$

With the inequality holding for at least one "i".

The tridiagonal matrix A can be decomposed into a product of two "diagonal" matrices L and U as follows

$$A = LU \qquad \qquad ...(6.11)$$

$\therefore$ Eqn. (6.10) becomes $LUx = d$ $\qquad$ ...(6.12)

Then, $\qquad$ let $Ux = y$ $\qquad \qquad$ ...(6.13)

Then $\qquad \qquad Ly = d$ $\qquad \qquad$ ...(6.14)

Therefore, solution to equation (6.10) can be obtained by solving the two linear equation systems (6.13) and (6.14).

Now let the bi-diagonal matrices, L and U have the following forms.

$$
L = \begin{bmatrix}
\beta_0 & 0 & 0 & 0 & \vdots & \vdots & \cdots & & \cdots \\
\alpha_1 & \beta_1 & 0 & 0 & \vdots & \vdots & \cdots & & \cdots \\
0 & \alpha_2 & \beta_2 & 0 & \vdots & \vdots & \cdots & & \cdots \\
0 & 0 & \alpha_3 & \beta_3 & \vdots & \vdots & \cdots & & \cdots \\
\cdots & \cdots & & & \vdots & \vdots & \cdots & & \cdots \\
\cdots & \cdots & & & \vdots & \vdots & \alpha_{n-1} & \beta_{n-1} & 0 \\
\cdots & \cdots & & & \vdots & \vdots & 0 & \alpha_n & \beta_n
\end{bmatrix} \quad \text{and}
$$

$$U = \begin{bmatrix} 1 & r_1 & 0 & 0 & \vdots & 0 & 0 \\ 0 & 1 & r_2 & 0 & \vdots & 0 & 0 \\ 0 & 0 & 1 & r_3 & \vdots & 0 & 0 \\ 0 & 0 & 0 & 1 & \vdots & 0 & 0 \\ & \cdots & & \cdots & \vdots & \cdots & \cdots \\ & \cdots & & \cdots & \vdots & 1 & r_n \\ & \cdots & & \cdots & \vdots & 0 & 1 \end{bmatrix}$$

$$L.U = \begin{bmatrix} \beta_0 & \beta_0 r_1 & 0 & 0 & \cdots & & \cdots & & \cdots \\ \alpha_1 & \alpha_1 r_1 + \beta_1 & \beta_1 r_2 & \cdots & & i^{th} & & \cdots & & \alpha_1 \\ & & & & & column & & & \\ 0 & \alpha_2 & \alpha_2 r_2 + \beta_2 & \beta_2 r_3 & \cdots & & \cdots & & \cdots \\ \cdots & \cdots & \cdots & \cdots & \cdots & & \cdots & & \cdots \\ \cdots & i^{th} row & \cdots & & \alpha_{i-1} & \alpha_{i-1} r_{i-1} + \beta_{i-1} & \beta_{i-1} r_i & & \cdots \\ \cdots & \cdots & \cdots & \cdots & \cdots & & \cdots & & \cdots \\ \cdots & \cdots & \cdots & \cdots & \cdots & & \alpha_n & \alpha_n r_n + \beta_n \end{bmatrix}$$

$$...(6.15)$$

Using following matric multiplication method as

$$\begin{bmatrix} a_{11} & a_{12} & a_{13} \\ a_{21} & a_{22} & a_{23} \\ a_{31} & a_{32} & a_{33} \\ a_{41} & a_{42} & a_{43} \end{bmatrix}_{4\times4} \begin{bmatrix} b_{11} & b_{12} & b_{13} \\ b_{21} & b_{22} & b_{23} \\ b_{31} & b_{32} & b_{33} \end{bmatrix}_{3\times3}$$

$$= \begin{bmatrix} a_{11}b_{11} + a_{12}b_{21} + a_{13}b_{31} & a_{11}b_{12} + a_{12}b_{22} + a_{13}b_{32} & a_{11}b_{13} + a_{12}b_{23} + a_{13}b_{33} \\ a_{21}b_{11} + a_{22}b_{21} + a_{23}b_{31} & a_{21}b_{12} + a_{22}b_{22} + a_{23}b_{32} & a_{21}b_{13} + a_{22}b_{23} + a_{23}b_{33} \\ a_{31}b_{11} + a_{32}b_{21} + a_{33}b_{31} & a_{31}b_{12} + a_{32}b_{22} + a_{33}b_{32} & a_{31}b_{13} + a_{32}b_{23} + a_{33}b_{33} \\ a_{41}b_{11} + a_{42}b_{21} + a_{43}b_{31} & a_{41}b_{12} + a_{42}b_{22} + a_{43}b_{32} & a_{41}b_{13} + a_{42}b_{23} + a_{43}b_{33} \end{bmatrix}$$

Comparing LU, with A, we obtained

(1) $\beta_0 = b_0$ ...(6.16)

(2) $\alpha_{i-1} = a_{i-1}$ for $i = 2$........ $(n+1)$

or $\alpha_1 = a_1,$

or $\alpha_i = a_i$ for $i = 1, 2$ .... n ...(6.17)

(3) $\alpha_{i-1} r_{i-1} + \beta_{i-1} = b_{i-1}$ for $i = 2, \ldots (n+1)$

   or $\beta_{i-1} = b_{i-1} - \alpha_{i-1} r_{i-1}$

   or $\beta_{i+1} = b_{i+1} - \alpha_{i+1} r_{i+1}$ for $i = 0, \ldots (n-1)$ ...(6.18)

   or $\beta_i = b_i - \alpha_i r_i$ ...(6.19)

(4) $\beta_{i-1} r_{i-1} = c_{i-1}$ for $i = 1, \ldots n$

   or $r_i = \dfrac{c_{i-1}}{\beta_{i-1}}$

   or $r_{i+1} = \dfrac{c_i}{\beta_i}$ ...(6.20)

From equation (6.18) and (6.20)

$$\beta_{i+1} = b_{i+1} - a_{i+1} \cdot \frac{c_i}{\beta_i} \qquad ...(6.21)$$

Here, we have to find out α_1 to α_n, β_0, to β_1 and r_1 to r_n, given a_1 to a_n, b_0 to b_n and c_o to c_{n-1}.

Now we are ready to solve Eqn. (6.13) and Eqn. (6.14). The solution of equation (6.13) is obtained after a forward substitution pass where $\beta_0 y_0 = d_0$

$$\therefore \qquad y_0 = \frac{d_0}{\beta_0} \qquad ...(6.22)$$

Similarly, i^{th} equation

    $\alpha_{i-1} y_{i-2} + \beta_{i-1} y_{i-1} = d_{i-1}$ for $i = 2, \ldots (n+1)$

   or, $\beta_{i-1} y_{i-1} = d_{i-1} - \alpha_{i-1} y_{i-2}$

$$\therefore \qquad y_{i-1} = \frac{d_{i-1} - \alpha_{i-1} y_{i-2}}{\beta_{i-1}}$$

   or, $y_{i+1} = \dfrac{1}{\beta_{i+1}} (d_{i+1} - \alpha_{i+1} y_i)$ for $i = 0, \ldots, n$

   or, $y_i = \dfrac{1}{\beta_i} (d_i - \alpha_i y_{i-1})$ ...(6.22a)

From equation (6.19) $\beta_i = b_i - \alpha_i r_i$

$$y_i = \frac{d_i - \alpha_i y_{i-1}}{(b_i - \alpha_i r_i)} \qquad \text{for} \quad i = 1, \ldots n \qquad ...(6.23)$$

$$\text{with } r_i = \frac{c_0}{b_0} \quad \text{and} \quad y_i = \frac{d_0}{b_0}$$

Similarly, from Eqn. $[Ux = y]$ is similarly solved by "backward substitution" pass with $x_n = y_n$

$$x_i = (y_i - r_{i+1} x_{i+1}) \qquad ...(6.24)$$
$$\text{for} \quad i = n-1 \ldots 0$$

Thus, solution of A matrix is obtained from Eqn. (6.23) and (6.24)

Thus, for TDMA

When $(n+1) \times (n+1)$ matrix is given

$$\alpha_i = a_i \qquad \text{for } i = 1 \text{ to } \ldots\ldots n$$

$$\beta_0 = b_0 \qquad \text{for } i = 0 \ldots\ldots n-1$$

$$\beta_{i+1} = b_{i+1} - a_{i+1} \frac{c_i}{\beta_i} \qquad i = 0 \text{ to } n-1$$

$$r_{i+1} = \frac{c_i}{\beta_i} \qquad \text{for } i = 1 \text{ to } \ldots\ldots n-1$$

from forward substitution

$$y_0 = \frac{d_0}{\beta_0}$$

$$y_{i+1} = \frac{1}{\beta_{i+1}}[d_{i+1} - \alpha_{i+1} y_i] - (2)\, i = 0 \ldots\ldots, n-1$$

From backward substitution

$$x_n = y_n$$

$$x_{i-1} = y_{i-1} - r_i x_i \quad \ldots \text{ for } i = n \text{ to } 1$$

Thus, from above methods we can find all x value. Similarly, having determined all the tangent vector $\vec{t}_i$, each Fergusson curve segment $\vec{r}^i(u)$ at a span $[\vec{P}_{i,\,d}]$ is expressed as

$$\vec{r}^i(u) = \text{UCS}' \qquad \text{For } i = 0,\, 1,\, 2, \ldots\ldots., n-1$$

Where

$$s^i = \begin{bmatrix} \vec{P}_i & \vec{P}_{i+1} & \vec{t}_i & \vec{t}_{i-1} \end{bmatrix}^T \qquad \ldots(6.26)$$

The composite curve segment (6.26) called cubic spline curve because it is defined by "cubic" polynomial function and the resulting curve is similar to the one obtained from a physical spline where the data points $\vec{P}i$ corresponds to "ducks".

Example 1: Consider the following set of linear equation.

$$x_0 + 2x_1 = 1$$

$$2x_0 + x_1 + 2x_2 = 2$$

$$2x_1 + x_2 = 3$$

or $\qquad$ [A]   [x] = [d]

$$\begin{bmatrix} 1 & 2 & 0 \\ 2 & 1 & 2 \\ 0 & 2 & 1 \end{bmatrix} \begin{bmatrix} x_0 \\ x_1 \\ x_2 \end{bmatrix} = \begin{bmatrix} 1 \\ 2 \\ 3 \end{bmatrix}$$

Where [A] being a Tridigonal matrix

Solution: Here, $a_1 = 2, a_2 = 2$

$$b_0 = 1, b_1 = 1, b = 1$$

$$c_0 = 2, c_1 = 2$$

To find out $\alpha_1, \alpha_2, \beta_0, \beta_1, \beta_2, r_1, r_2$

Comparing from following matrix for quartic equation

$$\underset{A}{\begin{bmatrix} b_0 & c_0 & 0 \\ a_1 & b_1 & c_1 \\ 0 & a_2 & b_2 \end{bmatrix}} = \underset{L}{\begin{bmatrix} \beta_0 & 0 & 0 \\ \alpha_1 & \beta_1 & \gamma_2 \\ 0 & \alpha_2 & \beta_2 \end{bmatrix}} \underset{U}{\begin{bmatrix} 1 & \gamma_1 & 0 \\ 0 & 1 & \gamma_2 \\ 0 & 0 & 1 \end{bmatrix}} = \begin{bmatrix} 1 & 2 & 0 \\ 2 & 1 & 2 \\ 0 & 2 & 1 \end{bmatrix}$$

Since from TDMA solution at equ (6.17) $\alpha_i = a_i$: $\alpha_1 = a_1 = 2$

At Eqn. (6.15) $\beta_0 = b_0 = 1$

At Equ. (6.19) $\beta_1 = b_1 - \alpha_1, c_0/\beta_0 = 1 - 2.2/1 = -3$

$$\beta_2 = b_2 - \alpha_2, c_1/\beta_1 = 1 - 2 \times 2/(-3) = 7/3$$

at (6.20) for $i = 0$ to 1

$$r_1 = \frac{c_0}{\beta_0} = \frac{2}{1} = 2$$

$$r_2 = \frac{c_1}{\beta_1} = \frac{2}{-3} = -\frac{2}{3}$$

$$[L] = \begin{bmatrix} \beta_0 & 0 & 0 \\ \alpha_1 & \beta_1 & 0 \\ 0 & \alpha_2 & \beta_2 \end{bmatrix} = \begin{bmatrix} 1 & 0 & 0 \\ 2 & -3 & 0 \\ 0 & 2 & 7/3 \end{bmatrix}$$

$$[L] = \begin{bmatrix} 1 & r_1 & 0 \\ 0 & 1 & r_2 \\ 0 & 1 & 1 \end{bmatrix} = \begin{bmatrix} 1 & 2 & 0 \\ 0 & 1 & -2/3 \\ 0 & 0 & 1 \end{bmatrix}$$

with $d = \begin{bmatrix} d_0 \\ d_1 \\ d_2 \end{bmatrix} = \begin{bmatrix} 1 \\ 2 \\ 3 \end{bmatrix}$

Solving for y_0, y_1 and y_2 for forward substitution

from eqn (6.22), $y_0 = \dfrac{d_0}{\beta_0} = \dfrac{1}{1} = 1$

From eqn (6.22a) $y_{i+1} = \dfrac{1}{\beta_{i+1}}[d_{i+1} - a_{i+1} \ y_i]$

$$y_1 = \frac{1}{\beta}[d_1 - \alpha_1 y_0]$$

$$y_1 = \frac{1}{\beta_1}[d_1 - \alpha_1 \ y_0] = \frac{1}{-3}[-2 \times 1] = 0$$

$$y_2 = \frac{1}{\beta_2}[d_2 - \alpha_2 \ y_1] = \frac{3}{7}[3 - 2 \times 0] = \frac{9}{7}$$

Now solving for x_0, x_1, x_2 by backward substitution

Where $x_n = y_n$ \qquad for $i = 2$ to 0

$$x_2 = y_2 = \frac{9}{7}$$

From eqn (6.24) $x_1 = y_1 - r_2 x_2 = 0 + \dfrac{2}{3} \times \dfrac{9}{7} = \dfrac{6}{7}$

$$x_0 = y_0 - r_1 x_1 = 1 - 2 \times \frac{6}{7} = -\frac{5}{7}$$

$$\therefore \qquad x = \begin{bmatrix} x_0 \\ x_1 \\ x_2 \end{bmatrix} = \begin{bmatrix} -5/7 \\ 6/7 \\ 9/7 \end{bmatrix}$$

Thus, \qquad $[x] = \begin{bmatrix} x_0 \\ x_1 \\ x_2 \end{bmatrix} = \begin{bmatrix} -5/7 \\ 6/7 \\ 9/7 \end{bmatrix}$ \hfill **Ans.**

Verification:

Verification (1) eqn : $x_0 + 2x_1 = 1$

or \qquad $\dfrac{-5}{7} + \dfrac{12}{7} = 1$ \hfill Satisfied

Eqn. (2) - $2x_0 + x_1 + 2x_2 = 2$

$$\frac{-10}{7} + \frac{6}{7} + \frac{18}{7} + \frac{18}{7} = 2$$ \hfill Satisfied

Eqn (3) \quad $2x_1 + x_2 = 2$

$$\frac{12}{7} + \frac{9}{7} = 3 = \frac{21}{7}$$ \hfill Satisfied

Example 2: Solve the following equation.

$$\begin{bmatrix} 2 & 1 & 0 & 0 & 0 \\ 1 & 2 & 1 & 0 & 0 \\ 0 & 1 & 2 & 1 & 0 \\ 0 & 0 & 1 & 2 & 1 \\ 0 & 0 & 0 & 1 & 2 \end{bmatrix} \begin{bmatrix} x_0 \\ x_1 \\ x_2 \\ x_3 \\ x_4 \end{bmatrix} = \begin{bmatrix} 3 \\ 4 \\ 4 \\ 4 \\ 3 \end{bmatrix}$$

$$2x_0 + x_1 = 3$$
$$x_0 - 2x_1 + x_2 = 4$$
$$x_1 + 2x_2 + x_3 = 4$$
$$x_2 + 2x_3 + x_4 = 4$$
$$x_3 + 2x_4 = 3$$

Solution: Solving by using TDMA method, one can get following solution.

where

$$x_0 = x_1 = x_2 = x_3 = x_4 = 1$$

and Intermediate results are

$$[L] = \begin{bmatrix} 2 & 0 & 0 & 0 & 0 \\ 1 & 3/2 & 0 & 0 & 0 \\ 0 & 1 & 4/3 & 0 & 0 \\ 0 & 0 & 1 & 5/4 & 0 \\ 0 & 0 & 0 & 1 & 6/5 \end{bmatrix}, [U] = \begin{bmatrix} 1 & 1/2 & 0 & 0 & 0 \\ 0 & 1 & 2/3 & 0 & 0 \\ 0 & 0 & 1 & 3/4 & 0 \\ 0 & 0 & 0 & 1 & 4/5 \\ 0 & 0 & 0 & 0 & 1 \end{bmatrix} [y] = \begin{bmatrix} 3/2 \\ 5/3 \\ 7/4 \\ 4/5 \\ 1 \end{bmatrix}$$

Other method is less efficient than TDMA when no of Eqn. is more.

(Two-D, examples are used throughout this chapter to simplify the calculation and the presentation of results. Three–D is simple extension]

Example 3: Considering the for two-dimensional position vectors $\vec{P}_0(0,0)$, $\vec{P}_1[1, 1]$, $\vec{P}_2[2 - 1]$ and $\vec{P}_3[3, 0]$ [See Fig. 6.1]. The tangent vectors at the ends are $\vec{t}_0(1, 1)$ and $\vec{t}_3(1, 1)$. Find normalized piecewise cubic spline curve through them.

Solution : The internal tangent vectors are obtained using eqn (6.5).

$$\begin{bmatrix} 1 & 0 & 0 & 0 \\ 1 & 4 & 1 & 0 \\ 0 & 1 & 4 & 1 \\ 0 & 0 & 0 & 1 \end{bmatrix} \begin{bmatrix} \vec{t}_0 \\ \vec{t}_1 \\ \vec{t}_2 \\ \vec{t}_3 \end{bmatrix} = \begin{bmatrix} 1 & 1 \\ 6 & -3 \\ 6 & -3 \\ 1 & 1 \end{bmatrix} \begin{bmatrix} 1 & 0 & 0 & 0 \\ 1 & 4 & 1 & 0 \\ 0 & 1 & 4 & 1 \\ 0 & 0 & 0 & 1 \end{bmatrix} \begin{bmatrix} \vec{t}_0 \\ \vec{t}_1 \\ \vec{t}_2 \\ \vec{t}_3 \end{bmatrix} = \begin{bmatrix} 1 & 1 \\ 6 & -3 \\ 6 & -3 \\ 1 & 1 \end{bmatrix}$$

$$\begin{bmatrix} 1 & 0 & 0 & 0 \\ 1 & 4 & 1 & 0 \\ 0 & 1 & 4 & 1 \\ 0 & 0 & 0 & 1 \end{bmatrix} \begin{bmatrix} \vec{t_0} \\ \vec{t_1} \\ \vec{t_2} \\ \vec{t_3} \end{bmatrix} = \begin{bmatrix} 1 & 1 \\ 6 & -3 \\ 6 & -3 \\ 1 & 1 \end{bmatrix}$$

After calculation by above methods

$$\begin{bmatrix} \vec{t_0} \\ \vec{t_1} \\ \vec{t_2} \\ \vec{t_3} \end{bmatrix} = \begin{bmatrix} 1 & 1 \\ 1 & -0.8 \\ 1 & -0.8 \\ 1 & 1 \end{bmatrix}$$

Using equation (a), the Hermit blending function matrix as 5.26 and 5.27 for the first segments at $u = 1/3$ is

$$UC = \begin{bmatrix} 1 & u & u^2 & u^3 \end{bmatrix} \begin{bmatrix} 1 & 0 & 0 & 0 \\ 0 & 0 & 1 & 0 \\ -3 & 3 & -2 & -1 \\ 2 & -2 & 1 & 1 \end{bmatrix}$$

$$= \begin{bmatrix} 1 & \dfrac{1}{3} & \dfrac{1}{9} & \dfrac{1}{27} \end{bmatrix} \begin{bmatrix} 1 & 0 & 0 & 0 \\ 0 & 0 & 1 & 0 \\ -3 & 3 & -2 & -1 \\ 2 & -2 & 1 & 1 \end{bmatrix}$$

$$= \begin{bmatrix} \dfrac{-2}{27} & \dfrac{4}{27} & \dfrac{7}{27} & \dfrac{20}{27} \end{bmatrix}$$

Similarly, at $u = 2/3$

$$UC = \begin{bmatrix} \dfrac{-4}{27} & \dfrac{2}{27} & \dfrac{20}{27} & \dfrac{7}{27} \end{bmatrix}$$

The point on the first line segment at $U = 1/3$

$$\vec{r}(u) = \begin{bmatrix} \dfrac{-2}{27} & \dfrac{4}{27} & \dfrac{7}{27} & \dfrac{20}{27} \end{bmatrix} \begin{bmatrix} \vec{P_0} \\ \vec{P_1} \\ \vec{t_0} \\ \vec{t_1} \end{bmatrix} = \begin{bmatrix} 0 & 0 \\ 1 & 1 \\ 1 & 1 \\ 1 & -0.8 \end{bmatrix}$$

$$\vec{r}(u) = \begin{bmatrix} -2/27 & 4/27 & 7/27 & 20/27 \end{bmatrix} \begin{bmatrix} 0,0 \\ 1,1 \\ 1,1 \\ 1,-0.8 \end{bmatrix}$$

$$\vec{r}\,(u) = \begin{bmatrix} \dfrac{1}{3} & \dfrac{63}{135} \end{bmatrix}$$

$$= [0.333 \quad 0.467]$$

at $u = 2/3$

$$\vec{r}\,(u) = \begin{bmatrix} \dfrac{-4}{27} & \dfrac{2}{27} & \dfrac{20}{27} & \dfrac{7}{27} \end{bmatrix} \begin{bmatrix} \vec{P}_0 \\ \vec{P}_1 \\ \vec{t}_0 \\ \vec{t}_1 \end{bmatrix}$$

$$= \begin{bmatrix} \dfrac{-4}{27} & \dfrac{2}{27} & \dfrac{20}{27} & \dfrac{7}{27} \end{bmatrix} \begin{bmatrix} 0 & 0 \\ 1 & 1 \\ 1 & 1 \\ 1 & -0.8 \end{bmatrix}$$

$$= \begin{bmatrix} \dfrac{2}{3} & \dfrac{26}{135} \end{bmatrix}$$

Complete results are shown in table and result curve is shown in [Fig. 6.3(c)]

Segment	u	$r_x(u)$	$r_y(u)$
1	1/3	0.333	0.467
	2/3	0.667	0.933
2	1/3	1.333	0.422
	2/3	1.667	-0.422
3	1/3	2.333	-0.933
	2/3	2.667	-0.467

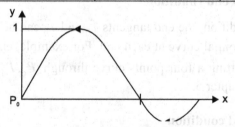

Fig. 6.3 (c) Composite curve.

6.2.2.1.2 *When end Targets of Curves are not Known*

Generally in most of the practical applications, the end tangents $\vec{t}_0$ and $\vec{t}_1$ are not given. In these cases, they need to be estimated by some means. There is various methods to estimate end tangents such as (*a*) Circular end condition

(*b*) Polynomial end condition and

(*c*) Natural end condition

(*a*) Circular end condition

Under circular end condition an end tangent of curve is estimated by fitting a circle through the three points at end and its end tangent is given by:

$$\vec{t}_0 = \frac{|\vec{a}|(\vec{r} \times \vec{c})}{|\vec{r} \times \vec{c}|} \qquad \text{where} \quad \vec{r} = \text{radius of circle}$$

$$= \vec{Q} - \vec{P}_0$$

$$= \frac{|\vec{a}|^2 (\vec{b} \times \vec{c}) + |\vec{b}|^2 (\vec{c} \times \vec{a})}{2|\vec{c}|^2}$$

Where $\vec{a} = \vec{P}_1 - \vec{P}_0, \vec{b} = \vec{P}_2 - \vec{P}_0, \vec{c} = \vec{a} \times \vec{b}, \vec{r} = \vec{Q} - \vec{P}_0$

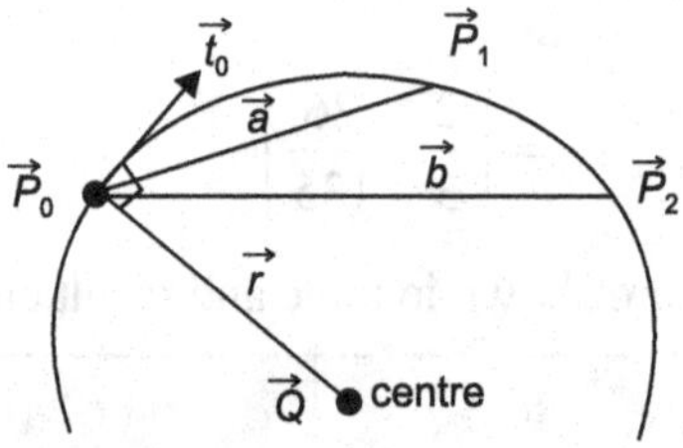

Fig. 6.4 End tangent estimation method under circular end condition.

Here, direction of end tangent must be perpendicular to line joining between $\vec{P}_0$ and $\vec{Q}$. Similarly we can find to $\vec{t}_1$ by fitting end condition $\vec{P}_1, \vec{P}_2$ and $\vec{P}_3$ in circle and so on.

(*b*) Polynomial end condition

Under this condition, the end tangents $\vec{t}_0$ and $\vec{t}_n$ can be estimated by fitting a standard polynomial curve at each end. For example, end tangents $\vec{t}_0$ may be estimated by fitting a four points curve through $\vec{P}_0, \vec{P}_1, \vec{P}_2$ and $\vec{P}_3$ which is discussed in chapter 5.

(*c*) Natural end condition

This condition is also called free or relaxed end condition. Free end condition corresponds to the situation where the composite curve is not subjected to any external local at its ends. This condition is obtained by setting zero curvature at the end points $\vec{P}_0$ and $\vec{P}_n$ such that curvature of the curve defined as (see equation).

$$kB = \frac{\dot{r}(u) \times \ddot{r}(u)}{|\dot{r}|^3}$$

$\therefore \quad k = 0$ in this case

$$\dot{r}(u) \times \ddot{r}(u) = 0 \qquad \qquad ...(6.27)$$

Equation (6.27) is the condition for zero curvature at any point on the curve segment. Then form the Ferguson curve segment.

$$\vec{r}(u) = (1 - 3u^2 + 2u^2)\vec{P_0} + (3u^2 - 2u^3)\vec{P_1} + (u - 2u^2 + u^3)\vec{t_0} + (-u^2 + 2u^3)\vec{t_1}$$

$$\Rightarrow \dot{r}(u) = (-6u + 6u^2)\vec{P_0} + (6u - 2u^2)\vec{P_1} + (1 - 4u + 3u^2)\vec{t_0} + (-2u + 3u^2)\vec{t_1}$$

and

$$\ddot{r}(u) = (-6 + 126u)\vec{P_0} + (6 + 12u)\vec{P_1} + (-4 + 6u)\vec{t_0} + (-2 + 6u)\vec{t_1}$$

Then for first curve at $u = 0$ *i.e.*, starting point of first curve

$$\dot{r}(u = 0) = \vec{t_0}$$

$$\ddot{r}(u = 0) = -6\vec{P_0} + 6\vec{P_1} - 4\vec{t_0} - 2\vec{t_1}$$

$$= 6(\vec{P_1} - \vec{P_0}) - 2(2\vec{t_0} + \vec{t_1})$$

Similarly, for the last curve at $u = 1$, *i.e.*, end point of last curve

$$\dot{r}(u = 0) = \vec{t_n}$$

$$\ddot{r}(u = 1) = -6\vec{P}_{n-1} - 6\vec{P_n} + 2\vec{t}_{n-1} + 4\vec{t_n}$$

$$= 6(\vec{P}_{n-1} - \vec{P_n}) + 2(\vec{t}_{n-1} + 2\vec{t_n})$$

Putting above results in equation (6.27), it gives

$$\vec{t_0} \times [6(\vec{P_1} - \vec{P_0}) - 2(2\vec{t_0} + \vec{t_1})] = 0$$

Since, $\vec{t_0} \neq 0$ because $\vec{t_0}$ to be calculated

$$6(\vec{P_1} - \vec{P_0}) - 2(2\vec{t_0} + \vec{t_1}) = 0$$

or $\quad 2\vec{t_0} + \vec{t_1} = 3(\vec{P_1} - \vec{P_0}) \qquad \qquad ...(6.28)$

Similarly

$$\vec{t_n} \times [6(\vec{P}_{n-1} - \vec{P_n}) + 2(\vec{t}_{n-1} + \vec{t_n})]$$

$\therefore \quad \vec{t_n} \neq 0 = 0$, because $\vec{t_n}$ to be calculated

$$\vec{t}_{i-1} + 2\vec{t_n} = 3(\vec{P_n} - \vec{P}_{n-1}) \qquad \qquad ...(6.29)$$

From section 6.2.1.1, we obtained on expression shown in eqn. (6.8) for estimating tangents of intermediate points (where t_0 and t_1 are known) which is

$$4\vec{t}_{i-1} + 4\vec{t_i} + \vec{t}_{i+1} = 3(\vec{P}_{i+1} - \vec{P}_{i-1}) \qquad \qquad ...(6.30)$$

For $i = 1, 2, 3, ... (n - 1)$

Thus, we have three equation as

$$2\vec{t}_0 + \vec{t}_1 = 3(\vec{P}_1 - \vec{P}_0) \text{ for first curve}$$

$$\vec{t}_{i-1} + 4\vec{t}_i + \vec{t}_{i+1} = 3(\vec{P}_{i+1} - \vec{P}_{i-1}) \text{ for intermediate curves}$$

$$\vec{t}_{i-1} + 2\vec{t}_n = 3(\vec{P}_n - \vec{P}_{n-1}) \text{ for last curves}$$

Above three equation make a system of $n + 1$ linear equations for $n + 1$ unknowns $\vec{t}_0$, $\vec{t}_1$, $\vec{t}_2$ ....$\vec{t}_n$. A matrix representation of the above said linear equations for free end condition case is given as :

$$\begin{bmatrix} 2 & 1 & 0 & 0 & \cdots & & \cdots \\ 1 & 4 & 1 & 0 & \cdots & & \cdots \\ 0 & 1 & 4 & 1 & \cdots & & \cdots \\ \cdots & \cdots & & \cdots & & & \cdots \\ \cdots & \cdots & & \cdots & & & \cdots \\ \cdots & \cdots & & 1 & 4 & 1 \\ \cdots & \cdots & & & 1 & 4 & 1 \\ \cdots & \cdots & & & 0 & 1 & 2 \end{bmatrix} \begin{bmatrix} \vec{t}_0 \\ \vec{t}_1 \\ \vec{t}_2 \\ \\ \\ \\ \vec{t}_{n-1} \\ \vec{t}_n \end{bmatrix} = \begin{bmatrix} 3(\vec{P}_1 - \vec{P}_0) \\ 3(\vec{P}_2 - \vec{P}_0) \\ 3(\vec{P}_3 - \vec{P}_1) \\ \\ \\ \\ 3(\vec{P}_n - \vec{P}_{n-2}) \\ 3(\vec{P}_n - \vec{P}_{n-1}) \end{bmatrix} \qquad ...(6.31)$$

The equation (6.31) can be solved easily by TDMA method for estimating all tangents.

Example 4: Draw Ferguson type (cubic spline model) curve through the four given points as shown in Fig 6.5. Assume free end condition

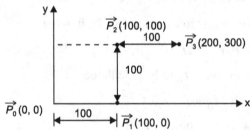

Fig. 6.5 Four coordinate points on xy plane.

Solution : From Fig. 6.5, we have

$$\vec{P}_0 = 0\hat{i} + 0\hat{j}$$

$$\vec{P}_1 = 100\hat{i} + 0\hat{j}$$

$$\vec{P}_2 = 100\hat{i} + 100\hat{j}$$

$$\vec{P}_3 = 200\hat{i} + 100\hat{j}$$

We have $n = 3$ in this problem ($n + 1 = 4$ data points)

So the matrix eqn takes the form using eqn (6.31)

$$\begin{bmatrix} 2 & 1 & 0 & 0 \\ 1 & 4 & 1 & 0 \\ 0 & 1 & 4 & 1 \\ 0 & 0 & 1 & 2 \end{bmatrix} \begin{bmatrix} \vec{t}_0 \\ \vec{t}_1 \\ \vec{t}_2 \\ \vec{t}_3 \end{bmatrix} = 3 \begin{bmatrix} \vec{P}_1 - \vec{P}_0 \\ \vec{P}_2 - \vec{P}_0 \\ \vec{P}_3 - \vec{P}_1 \\ \vec{P}_3 - \vec{P}_2 \end{bmatrix} = 3 \begin{bmatrix} 100i \\ 100i + 100j \\ 100i + 100j \\ 100i \end{bmatrix}$$

Therefore $2\vec{t}_0 + \vec{t}_1 = 300i$ ...(i)

$\vec{t}_0 + 4\vec{t}_1 + \vec{t}_2 = 300i + 300j$ ...(ii)

$\vec{t}_1 + 4\vec{t}_2 + \vec{t}_3 = 300i + 300j$ ...(iii)

$\vec{t}_2 + 2\vec{t}_3 = 300i$ ...(iv)

$\vec{t}_0 = \dfrac{300}{9}(4i - j), \vec{t}_1 = \dfrac{300}{9}(i + 2j), \vec{t}_2 = \dfrac{300}{9}(i + 2j), \vec{t}_3 = \dfrac{300}{9}(4i - j)$

Thus, for curve 1, $\vec{P}_0 = 0$, $\vec{P}_1 = 100i$, $\vec{t}_0 = \dfrac{300}{9}(4i - j)$,

$$\vec{t} = \frac{300}{9}(i + 2j)$$

For curve 2, $\vec{P}_1 = 100i$, $\vec{P}_2 = 100i + 100j$, $\vec{t}_1 = \dfrac{300}{9}(i + 2j)$,

$$\vec{t}_2 = \frac{300}{9}(i + 2j)$$

For curve 3, $\vec{P}_2 = 100i + 100j$, $\vec{P}_3 = 200i + 100j$, $\vec{t}_2 = \dfrac{300}{9}(i + 2j)$

and $\vec{t}_3 = \dfrac{300}{9}(4i + j)$

We can convert all in explicit form (in terms of x and y) and can plot for say, $u = 0, 0.25, 0.5, 0.75$ for all these curve using Ferguson equation.

Example 5: For following data set $(1, 1)$, $(1.5, 2)$, $(2.5, 1.75)$ and $(3.0, 3.25)$. Find the parameter cubic spline assuming a relaxed condition at both ends of the data.

Solution: We have $\vec{P}_0 = i + j$, $\vec{P}_1 = 1.5i + 2j$

$$\vec{P}_2 = 2.5i + 1.75j, \quad \vec{P}_3 = 3i + 3.25j$$

First, we compute

$$\vec{P}_1 - \vec{P}_0 = 0.5i + j$$

$$\vec{P}_2 - \vec{P}_0 = 1.5i + 0.75j$$

$$\vec{P}_3 - \vec{P}_1 = 0.5i + 1.25j$$

$$\vec{P}_3 - \vec{P}_2 = 0.5i + 1.5j$$

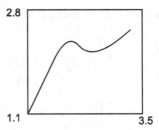

Fig. 6.6 Cubic Spline.

$$\therefore \quad \begin{bmatrix} 2 & 1 & 0 & 0 \\ 1 & 4 & 1 & 0 \\ 0 & 1 & 4 & 1 \\ 0 & 0 & 1 & 2 \end{bmatrix} \begin{bmatrix} \vec{t}_0 \\ \vec{t}_1 \\ \vec{t}_2 \\ \vec{t}_3 \end{bmatrix} = 3 \begin{bmatrix} \vec{P}_1 - \vec{P}_0 \\ \vec{P}_2 - \vec{P}_0 \\ \vec{P}_3 - \vec{P}_1 \\ \vec{P}_3 - \vec{P}_2 \end{bmatrix} = 3 \begin{bmatrix} 0.5i + j \\ 1.5i + 0.75j \\ 1.5i + 1.25j \\ 0.5i + 1.5j \end{bmatrix}$$

$$\Rightarrow \qquad 2\vec{t}_0 + \vec{t}_1 = 3(0.5i + j)$$

$$\vec{t}_0 + 4\vec{t}_1 + \vec{t}_2 = 3(1.5i + 0.75j)$$

$$\vec{t}_1 + 4\vec{t}_2 + \vec{t}_3 = 3(1.5i + 1.25j)$$

$$\vec{t}_2 + 4\vec{t}_3 = 3(0.5i + 1.5j)$$

After calculating $\vec{t}_0$, $\vec{t}_1$, $\vec{t}_2$ and $\vec{t}_3$ from above four equations. We can generate cubic spline curve as shown in fig 6.6 by fixing points and its respective tangents.

Example 6: Assume that the three position vectors $\vec{P}_0(1, 1)$, $\vec{P}_1(1, 2)$, and $\vec{P}_2(3, 2)$, are known. Determine the cubic spline curve through these points using relaxed end condition.

Solution :

We have

$$\vec{P}_1 - \vec{P}_0 = [1 \ 2]$$

$$\vec{P}_2 - \vec{P}_0 = [3 \ 2]$$

$$\vec{P}_2 - \vec{P}_1 = [2 \ 0]$$

Fig. 6.7 Composite Fergusion curve

Which can be written in matrix form for relaxed end condition as

$$\begin{bmatrix} 2 & 1 & 0 \\ 1 & 4 & 1 \\ 0 & 1 & 2 \end{bmatrix}\begin{bmatrix} \vec{t}_0 \\ \vec{t}_1 \\ \vec{t}_2 \end{bmatrix} = \begin{bmatrix} \vec{P}_1 - \vec{P}_0 \\ \vec{P}_2 - \vec{P}_0 \\ \vec{P}_2 - \vec{P}_0 \end{bmatrix} = \begin{bmatrix} 1 & 2 \\ 3 & 2 \\ 2 & 0 \end{bmatrix}$$

$$2\vec{t}_0 + \vec{t}_1 = 1i + 2j$$

$$\vec{t}_0 + 4\vec{t}_1 + \vec{t}_2 = 3i + 2j$$

$$\vec{t}_1 + 2\vec{t}_2 = 2i + 0j$$

$$\Rightarrow \vec{t}_0 + 4[1i + 2j - 2\vec{t}_0] + \frac{[2i + 0j - \vec{t}_1]}{2} = 3i + 2j$$

$$\Rightarrow \vec{t}_0 + 4[1i + 2j - 2\vec{t}_0] + \frac{[2i + 0j - [(1 + 2j) - 2\vec{t}_0]]}{2} = 3i + 2j$$

$$\vec{t}_0 = \frac{3i + 14j}{16}$$

$$\vec{t}_1 = \frac{5i + 30j}{8}$$

$$\vec{t}_2 = \frac{i - 30j}{16}$$

Above solution suggest that we have composite curve of two cubic spline curve let (a) and (b) because we have three points $\vec{P}_0$, $\vec{P}_1$, $\vec{P}_2$ and three tangents $\vec{t}_0$, $\vec{t}_1$ and $\vec{t}_2$.

Since cubic spline curve is represented as

$$\vec{r}^a(u) = (1 - 3u^2 + 2u^3)\vec{P}_0 + (3u^2 - 2u^3)\vec{P}_1 + (u - 2u^2 + u^3)\vec{t}_0 + (-u^2 + u^3)\vec{t}_1$$

$$\vec{r}^b(u) = (1 - 3u^2 + 2u^3)\vec{P}_1 + (3u^2 - 2u^3)\vec{P}_2 + (u - 2u^2 + u^3)\vec{t}_1 + (-u^2 + u^3)\vec{t}_2$$

After putting position vector of points P_i and t_i tangents, for $u = 0$, $u = 1/3$, $u = 2/3$ and $u = 1$, we can get co-ordinates of each points for two curve segment which is shown in Fig. 6.7.

6.3 UNIFORM B-SPLINE FITTING

Let us, we have one B-spline curve segment (a) which is shown in Fig. 6.8 and its mathematical model is represented as (equation 5.38 and 5.39 of section 5.9.1 of chapter 5)

$$\vec{r}^a(u) = \frac{1}{6}[1 \quad u \quad u^2 \quad u^3]\begin{bmatrix} 1 & 4 & 1 & 0 \\ -3 & 0 & 3 & 0 \\ 3 & -6 & 3 & 0 \\ -1 & 3 & -3 & 1 \end{bmatrix}\begin{bmatrix} \vec{V}_0^a \\ \vec{V}_1^a \\ \vec{V}_2^a \\ \vec{V}_3^a \end{bmatrix}$$

$$= \frac{1}{6}[(1 - 3u + 3u^2 - u^3)\vec{V}_0^a + (4 - 6u^2 + 3u^3)\vec{V}_1^a$$

$$+(1 - 3u + 3u^2 - 3u^3)\vec{V}_2^a + u^3\vec{V}_3^a] \qquad ...(6.32)$$

If we are interested to fit another B-spline curve (b) with curve (a) it make composite B-spline curve. This new B-spline curve (b) can be created by adding new control vertex $\vec{V}_3^b$ to the B-spline curve segment (a). This new curve can be represented mathematically as

$$\vec{r}^b(u) = \frac{1}{6}[1 \ u \ u^2 \ u^3] \begin{bmatrix} 1 & 4 & 1 & 0 \\ -3 & 0 & 3 & 0 \\ 3 & -6 & 3 & 0 \\ -1 & 3 & -3 & 1 \end{bmatrix} \begin{bmatrix} \vec{V}_0^b \\ \vec{V}_1^b \\ \vec{V}_2^b \\ \vec{V}_3^b \end{bmatrix} \qquad ...(6.33)$$

$$= \frac{1}{6}[(1 - 3u + 3u^2 - u^3)\vec{V}_0^b + (4 - 6u^2 + 3u^3)\vec{V}_1^b$$

$$+(1 - 3u + 3u^2 - 3u^3)\vec{V}_2^b + u^3\vec{V}_3^b]$$

Where, the control vertices of the two curve segment (a) and (b) are overlapped as (Fig. 6.8).

$$\vec{V}_0^b = \vec{V}_1^a, \vec{V}_1^b = \vec{V}_2^a, \vec{V}_2^b = \vec{V}_3^a$$

The fitting of above two curve (a) and (b) is continuous or not, this can be verify at the common join in the following way.

$$(1) \ \vec{r}^a(u = 1) = \vec{V}_1^a + 4\vec{V}_2^a + \vec{V}_3^a \Bigg\} \qquad ...(6.34)$$

$$\text{and} \quad \vec{r}^b(u = 0) = \frac{\vec{V}_1^b + 4\vec{V}_2^b + \vec{V}_3^b}{b} \Bigg\}$$

$$(2) \quad \dot{\vec{r}}^a(u = 1) = \frac{\vec{V}_3^a - \vec{V}_1^a}{2} \Bigg\} \qquad ...(6.35)$$

$$\text{and} \quad \dot{\vec{r}}^b(u = 1) = \frac{\vec{V}_2^a - \vec{V}_0^a}{2} \Bigg\}$$

$$(2) \quad \ddot{\vec{r}}^a(u = 1) = \vec{V}_1^a - 2\vec{V}_2^a + \vec{V}_3^a \Bigg\} \qquad ...(6.36)$$

$$\text{and} \quad \ddot{\vec{r}}^b(u = 0) = \vec{V}_3^a - 2\vec{V}_1^b + \vec{V}_2^b \Bigg\}$$

From Fig 6.8 we have $\vec{V}_0^b = \vec{V}_1^a, \vec{V}_1^b = \vec{V}_2^a$ and $\vec{V}_2^b = \vec{V}_3^a$. Putting these values in result 6.34, 6.35 and 6.36 we immediately have the following continuity condition which is identical to the parametric C^2-continuity.

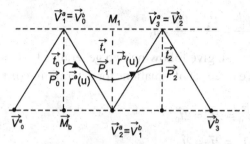

Fig. 6.8 Construction of composite B-spline curve from curve (a) and (b).

$\vec{r}^{\,b}(0) = \vec{r}^{\,a}(1)$ Positional continuity condition

$\dot{\vec{r}}^{\,b}(0) = \dot{\vec{r}}^{\,a}(1)$ Tangent line continuity condition

$\ddot{\vec{r}}^{\,b}(0) = \ddot{\vec{r}}^{\,a}(1)$ Curvature continuous at common joint

In other words a composite B-spline curve automatically guarantees parametric C^2-continuity.

Now for constructing a C^2 continuous composite B-spline curve from a sequence of given $(n+1)$ data points P_i $(i = 0\ 1,\text{---}\ n)$ from figure 6.8(a) we see that sequence of $(n+1)$ data points P_i is equivalent to $(n+3)$ control vertices $V_i(i = 0, 1, n+2)$.

To determine unknown control vertices for constructing composite B-spline, we can use positional continuity condition. This is

$$\vec{r}^{\,b}(0) = \vec{r}^{\,a}(1)\ \vec{P}_i$$

$$= \vec{P}_1 = \frac{\vec{V}_1^{\,a} + 4\vec{V}_2^{\,a} + \vec{V}_3^{\,a}}{6} = \frac{\vec{V}_0^{\,b} + 4\vec{V}_1^{\,b} + \vec{V}_2^{\,b}}{6}$$

Similarly, since a curve segment $r^i(u)$ spans from $\vec{P}_i$ to $\vec{P}_{i+1}$, the following relation holds at each data points P_i (for $i = 0.1.\text{-------}n$). Above both relation gives following generalized relation. They are

$$\vec{r}^{\,i}(0) = \vec{P}_i \quad \text{and}$$

$$\vec{r}^{\,i}(1) = \vec{P}_{i+1}$$

$$\vec{V}_i + 4\vec{V}_{i+1} + \vec{V}_{i+2} = 6P_i \quad \text{for}\quad i = 0, 1, \dots n \qquad \dots(6.37)$$

There is need of two additional linear equations in order to determine the $n+3$ control vertices in equation (6.37). These can be determined under two conditions. First is fixed end condition and second is relaxed or free end condition.

(a) Fixed end condition

When the end tangents $\hat{t}_0$ and $\hat{t}_n$ are known $[\vec{t} = \hat{t}\,]$ *i.e.*, fixed the two additional equations are obtained from tangent line continuity condition as:

$$\because \qquad \dot{\vec{r}}^{\,b}(1) = \dot{\vec{r}}^{\,a}(0) = \vec{t}_1 \qquad\qquad \text{(at the common join)}$$

$$\therefore \quad \frac{V_2^b - V_0^b}{2} = \frac{V_3^a - V_1^a}{2} = \vec{t_1}$$

These results can give following two generalized relation.

Thus we have three set of equations for determining $(n + 3)$ control vertices as:

$$\vec{V}_2 - \vec{V}_0 = 2\vec{t}_0 = 2\hat{t}_0 \qquad \qquad \text{... (6.38)} \ \{\vec{t}_0 = \hat{t}_0\}$$

$$\vec{V}_{n+2} - \vec{V}_n = 2\vec{t}_n = 2\hat{t}_n \qquad \qquad \text{... (6.39)} \ \{\vec{t}_n = \hat{t}_n\}$$

Thus, we have three set of equations for determining $(n + 3)$ control vertices as

$$\vec{V}_2 - \vec{V}_0 = 2\hat{t}_0 \qquad \text{for first curve}$$

$$\text{or,} \qquad -\vec{V}_0 + \vec{V}_2 = 2\hat{t}_0$$

$$\vec{V}_i + 4\vec{V}_{i+1} + \vec{V}_{i+2} = 6\vec{P}_i \qquad \text{for intermediate curve}$$

$$\vec{V}_{n+2} - \vec{V}_n = 2\hat{t}_n \qquad \text{for last curve}$$

$$\text{or,} \qquad -\vec{V}_n + \vec{V}_{n+2} = 2\hat{t}_n$$

Above three equations can make a set of $(n + 3)$ linear equations for estimating $(n + 3)$ unknown control vertices $V_i(i = 0, 1, ..., n +2)$. A matrix representation of the above said linear equations for free end condition case is given as

$$\begin{bmatrix} -1 & 0 & 1 & 0 & \vdots & \vdots & ... & & ... \\ 1 & 4 & 1 & 0 & \vdots & \vdots & ... & & ... \\ 0 & 1 & 4 & 1 & \vdots & \vdots & ... & & ... \\ ... & ... & & \vdots & \vdots & ... & & ... \\ ... & ... & & \vdots & \vdots & ... & & ... \\ ... & ... & & \vdots & \vdots & 1 & 4 & 1 \\ ... & ... & & \vdots & \vdots & -1 & 0 & 1 \end{bmatrix} \begin{bmatrix} V_0 \\ V_1 \\ V_2 \\ \vdots \\ \vdots \\ \vdots \\ V_{n+2} \end{bmatrix} = \begin{bmatrix} 2\hat{t}_0 \\ 6\vec{P}_0 \\ 6\vec{P}_1 \\ \vdots \\ \vdots \\ 6\vec{P}_n \\ 2\hat{t}_n \end{bmatrix} \qquad ...(6.40)$$

The above equation can be solved easily by TDMA method for estimating all vertices.

(b) Free end condition

If end tangents are not given, they may be estimated by following three conditions

1. Circular end condition
2. Polynomial end condition
3. Free end condition.

Above two conditions is similar to that procedure which was discussed in previous section (6.2.2).

In free end condition, the curvature at both ends of the composite curve are set to be zero. Let the starting curve is assigned (0) and end curve is assigned $(n-1)$. Then applying curvature continuous as

$$\dot{\vec{r}}^0(u=0) \times \ddot{\vec{r}}^0(u=0) = 0 \quad : \quad \text{Zero curvature at start at curve}$$

$$\dot{\vec{r}}^{n-1}(u=0) \times \ddot{\vec{r}}^{n-1}(u=0) = 0 \quad : \quad \text{Zero curvature at end of curve}$$

Putting results of equations (6.35) and (6.36) in the first of above vector product forms becomes (Here in place of curve a, we assigned curve 0)

$$\dot{\vec{r}}^0(u=0) \times \ddot{\vec{r}}^0(u=0) = \frac{1}{2}(\vec{V}_2 - \vec{V}_0) \times (\vec{V}_2 - 2\vec{V}_1 + \vec{V}_0) = 0$$

The above relation is satisfied by one at the following relations:

$$\vec{V}_2 - \vec{V}_0 = 0$$

or $\vec{V}_2 - 2\vec{V}_1 + \vec{V}_0 = 0$

or $(\vec{V}_2 - \vec{V}_0) = (\vec{V}_2 - 2\vec{V}_1 + \vec{V}_0)$

From above three solutions, the last one is commonly adopted which is represented in other form.

$$\vec{V}_2 - \vec{V}_0 = \vec{V}_2 - 2\vec{V}_1 + \vec{V}_0$$

or $-2\vec{V}_0 = -2\vec{V}_1$

or $\vec{V}_0 = \vec{V}_1$ ...(6.41)

This relation gives us multiple vertices condition. Thus at beginning of curve, we can set $\vec{V}_0 = \vec{V}_1$

Similarly, for the end curve we can set

$$\vec{V}_{n+1} = \vec{V}_{n+2}$$

These two linear equations in addition to equation (6.37) is sufficient to solve $(n+3)$ unknown vertices V_i $(i = 0, 1, 2, \text{---} \ n+1)$. These three equations are as for first curve

$$\vec{V}_0 - \vec{V}_1 = 0 \quad \text{for first curve}$$

$$\vec{V}_i + 4\vec{V}_{i+1} + \vec{V}_{i+2} = 6\vec{P}_i \quad \text{for last curve}$$

$$\vec{V}_{n+1} + \vec{V}_{n+2} = 0 \quad \text{for last curve}$$

Above three equation can be written in matrix form as :

$$\begin{bmatrix} 1 & -1 & 0 & 0 & \vdots & \vdots & \cdots & & \cdots \\ 1 & 4 & 1 & 0 & \vdots & \vdots & \cdots & & \cdots \\ 0 & 1 & 4 & 1 & \vdots & \vdots & \cdots & & \cdots \\ \cdots & \cdots & & & \vdots & \vdots & \cdots & & \cdots \\ \cdots & \cdots & & & \vdots & \vdots & \cdots & & \cdots \\ \cdots & \cdots & & & \vdots & \vdots & 1 & 4 & 1 \\ \cdots & \cdots & & & \vdots & \vdots & 0 & -1 & 1 \end{bmatrix} \begin{bmatrix} \vec{V}_0 \\ \vec{V}_1 \\ \vec{V}_2 \\ \vdots \\ \vdots \\ \vec{V}_{n+1} \\ \vec{V}_{n+2} \end{bmatrix} = \begin{bmatrix} 0 \\ 6\vec{P}_0 \\ 6\vec{P}_1 \\ \vdots \\ \vdots \\ 6\vec{P}_n \\ 0 \end{bmatrix} \qquad \ldots(6.42)$$

The unknown vertices can be determined by TDMA methods

Example 7: Draw uniform B-spline curve segments for the four given points. Assume free end conditions?

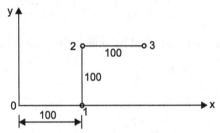

Solution: There are 4 data points. So we have to locate ($n + 2 = 4 + 2 = 6$) 6 control points. Here data points are

$$\vec{P}_0 = 0, \ \vec{P}_1 = 100i, \ \vec{P}_2 = 100i + 100j, \ \vec{P}_3 = 200i + 100j$$

The matrix eqn. will be

$$\begin{bmatrix} 1 & -1 & 0 & 0 & 0 & 0 \\ 1 & 4 & 1 & 0 & 0 & 0 \\ 0 & 1 & 4 & 1 & 0 & 0 \\ 0 & 0 & 1 & 4 & 1 & 0 \\ 1 & 0 & 0 & 1 & 4 & 1 \\ 1 & 0 & 0 & 0 & -1 & 1 \end{bmatrix} \begin{bmatrix} \vec{V}_0 \\ \vec{V}_1 \\ \vec{V}_2 \\ \vec{V}_3 \\ \vec{V}_4 \\ \vec{V}_5 \end{bmatrix} = 6 \begin{bmatrix} 0 \\ 0 \\ 100i \\ 100i + 100j \\ 200i + 100j \\ 0 \end{bmatrix}$$

$$\therefore \qquad \vec{V}_0 - \vec{V}_1 = 0 \qquad \qquad \ldots(1)$$

$$\vec{V}_0 + 4\vec{V}_1 + \vec{V}_2 = 0 \qquad \qquad \ldots(2)$$

$$\vec{V}_1 + 4\vec{V}_2 + \vec{V}_3 = 600i \qquad \qquad \ldots(3)$$

$$\vec{V}_2 + 4\vec{V}_3 + \vec{V}_4 = 600i + 600j \qquad \qquad \ldots(4)$$

$$\vec{V}_3 + 4\vec{V}_4 + \vec{V}_5 = 1200i + 600j \qquad \qquad \ldots(5)$$

$$-\vec{V}_4 + \vec{V}_5 = 0 \qquad \qquad \ldots(6)$$

This gives

$$\vec{V}_0 = \vec{V}_1 = -2857i + 7.14j$$
$$\vec{V}_2 = 142.86i - 35.71j$$
$$\vec{V}_3 = 57.17i + 135.72j$$
$$\vec{V}_4 = \vec{V}_5 = 228.57i + 92.86j$$

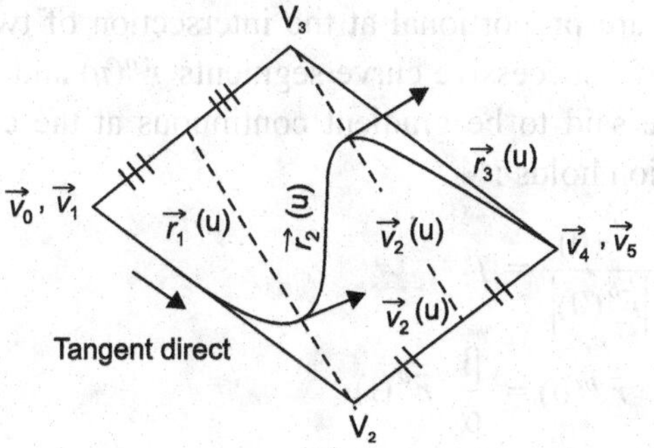

Fig. 6.9 Composite B-spline curve.

After solving above equations one can draw composite B-Spline curve for u-laying between 0 and 1 for 3 segments a shown in Fig. 6.9.

6.4 CURVE FITTING FOR UNEVENLY SPACED DATA POINTS

In this case, physical spacing (called chord length) of the successive data points will be taken into account for constructing smooth composite curve. Curve fitting in this case can be done by using any one of following two methods.

1. Chord-length spline fitting which is based on spline curve model.

2. Non-uniform B-spline (NUB) fitting which is based on NUB curve model.

First method is similar to cubic spline fitting method for evenly spaced data points (Section 6.2), only difference is that chord-length information is taken into account in determining tangents $\vec{t}_i$ and data point $\vec{P}_i$ because its data points is not evenly spaced.

Similarly, in second method we take knot span (∇) in place of chord-length information.

6.5 GEOMETRIC CONTINUITY CONDITIONS

This is the alternative methods in place of parametric continuity condition for joining two successive curve segments. This is more suitable when physical spacing of data points is unevenly spaced.

Similar, to zero order parametric continuity, zero order geometric continuity is represented by G^0, This is also called positional continuity in which two curve segments have the same co-ordinates at the joining points.

$$\vec{r}^{\,a}(1) = \vec{r}^{\,b}(0) \qquad\qquad ...(6.43)$$

Equation 6.43 is called first order geometric continuity [or first order gradient continuity or G^1 continuity condition]. This means the parametric first derivatives are proportional at the intersection of two successive curve segments. The two successive curve segments $\vec{r}^{\,a}(u)$ and $\vec{r}^{\,b}(u)$, satisfying $\vec{r}^{\,a}(1) = \vec{r}^{\,b}(0)$ are said to be gradient continuous at the common joint if the following equation holds :

$$\frac{\dot{\vec{r}}^{\,a}(1)}{\left|\dot{\vec{r}}^{\,a}(1)\right|} = \frac{\dot{\vec{r}}^{\,b}(0)}{\left|\dot{\vec{r}}^{\,b}(0)\right|} = T \qquad\qquad ...(6.44)$$

$$\Rightarrow \qquad \dot{\vec{r}}^{\,b}(0) = \frac{\beta}{\alpha} \cdot \dot{\vec{r}}^{\,a}(1) \qquad\qquad ...(6.44)$$

or $\qquad \dot{\vec{r}}^{\,b}(0) = \omega \cdot \dot{\vec{r}}^{\,a}(1) \qquad\qquad ...(6.44)$

Where $\alpha = \left|\dot{\vec{r}}^{\,a}(1)\right|$ and $\beta = \left|\dot{\vec{r}}^{\,b}(0)\right|$

and $\qquad \omega = \beta/\alpha = $ Tangent magnitude ratio.

See equation (5.10) of section 5.4 of chapter 5, where T is the unit tangent at the join.

Second order geometric continuity or G^2 continuity condition means that both the first and second parametric derivatives of the two successive curve segments are proportional at their boundary. Under G^2 continuity, curvatures of two curve segments will match at the joining point.

In order to join two successive curve segments $\vec{r}^{\,a}(u)$ and $\vec{r}^{\,b}(u)$ satisfying $\vec{r}^{\,a}(1) = \vec{r}^{\,b}(1)$ will be curvature continuous at their common joints if following condition [eqn (5.12) sec 5.4 of chapter 5] satisfied. They are

$$\frac{\dot{\vec{r}}(1) \times \ddot{\vec{r}}(1)}{\left|\dot{\vec{r}}^{\,a}(1)\right|^3} = \frac{\dot{\vec{r}}^{\,b}(0) \times \ddot{\vec{r}}^{\,b}(0)}{\left|\dot{\vec{r}}^{\,b}(0)\right|^3}$$

Putting equation (6.44) into equation (6.45), we have

$$\frac{\dot{\vec{r}}^{\,a}(1) \times \ddot{\vec{r}}^{\,a}(1)}{\left|\ddot{\vec{r}}^{\,a}(1)\right| \cdot \left|\ddot{\vec{r}}^{\,a}(1)\right|^2} = \frac{\dot{\vec{r}}^{\,b}(0) \times \ddot{\vec{r}}^{\,b}(0)}{\left|\dot{\vec{r}}^{\,b}(0)\right| \cdot \left|\dot{\vec{r}}^{\,b}(0)\right|^2}$$

$$\Rightarrow \qquad T.\ddot{\vec{r}}^{\,a}(1) = T.\frac{\left|\dot{\vec{r}}^{\,a}(1)\right|^2}{\left|\dot{\vec{r}}^{\,b}(1)\right|^2} \cdot \ddot{\vec{r}}^{\,b}(0)$$

$$\Rightarrow \qquad \ddot{\vec{r}}^{\,a}(1) = \ddot{\vec{r}}^{\,b}(0).\left(\frac{\alpha}{\beta}\right)^2$$

$$\text{or} \qquad \ddot{\vec{r}}^{\,b}(0) = \left(\frac{\beta}{\alpha}\right)^2 \ddot{\vec{r}}^{\,a}(1)$$

$$\ddot{\vec{r}}^{\,b}(0) = \omega^2 \ddot{\vec{r}}^{\,a}(1) \qquad \qquad ...(6.46)$$

Where $\alpha = |\dot{\vec{r}}^{\,b}(1)|$ and $\beta = |\dot{\vec{r}}^{\,a}(0)|$ ratio $\omega(=\beta/\alpha)$ is called tangent magnitude ratio.

The relation (6.46) is called geometric G^2-condition or simply G^2-condition.

6.6 CHORD LENGTH SPLINE FITTING

Let us we have two Ferguson curve segments $\vec{r}^{\,a}(u)$ and $\vec{r}^{\,b}(u)$ fitted as shown in figure 6.10, which is passing through three point data's $\vec{P}_0$, $\vec{P}_1$ and $\vec{P}_2$ and its, tangents is $\vec{t}_0$, $\vec{t}_1$ and $\vec{t}_2$ respectively. When all data points and its tangents are known, it will yield useful shape of composite curve after fitting (*i.e.*, putting values).

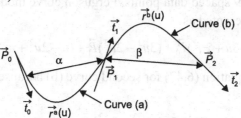

Fig. 6.10 Composite curve of chord–length spline curve.

In this section we want to construct a composite Ferguson curve by employing the G^2 condition. Using G^2 condition, we solve the problem of determining unknown tangent vectors t_1 at the common join.

Let t_1 be equal to the end tangent at the end of the first curve segment (*a*) which can be represented as

$$\vec{t}_1 = \dot{\vec{r}}^{\,a}(1)$$

Then, in order to meet the G^2 condition, the end tangent at the beginning of the second curve segment (*b*) should be given by [Using Eqn. (6.44)].

$$\dot{\vec{r}}^{\,b}(1) = \omega \vec{t}_i \qquad \qquad ...(6.47)$$

where $\quad \omega = \dfrac{\beta}{\alpha}$

$$= \frac{\left|\ddot{\vec{r}}^b(0)\right|}{\left|\ddot{\vec{r}}^a(1)\right|} \quad \text{Called tangent magnitude ratio}$$

It is important to note that in chord length fitting, the magnitudes of the end tangents at the common join are set to the chord-lengths of the curve segments which is given by

$$\dot{\vec{r}}^a(1) = \alpha = \left|\vec{P}_1 - \vec{P}_0\right|$$

and $\quad \dot{\vec{r}}^b(0) = \beta = \left|\vec{P}_2 - \vec{P}_1\right|$

$$\Rightarrow \quad \omega = \frac{\left|\vec{P}_2 - \vec{P}_1\right|}{\left|\vec{P}_1 - \vec{P}_0\right|}$$

Here, we notice that the tangent magnitude ratio ω now becomes a chord length ratio. Keeping ω as a chord length ratio, second order geometric continuity condition (i.e., G^2 continuity condition) eqn. (6.46) is represents as

$$\ddot{\vec{r}}^b(0) = \omega \ddot{\vec{r}}^b(1) \qquad \qquad ...(6.48)$$

Were ω is chord-length ratio.

For unevenly spaced data points, Ferguson curve model for curve (a) and curve (b) is represented as

$$\vec{r}^a(u) = (1 - 3u + 2u^3)\vec{P}_0 + (3u^2 - 2u^3)\vec{P}_1 + (u - 2u^2 + u^3)\vec{wt}_0 + (-u^2 + u^3)\vec{t}_1$$

and using equation (6.47) for second curve (b) because chord length is not equal.

$$\vec{r}^b(u) = (1 - 3u + 2u^3)\vec{P}_1 + (3u^2 - 2u^3)\vec{P}_2 + (u - 2u^2 + u^3)\omega\vec{t}_1 + (-u^2 + u^3)\vec{t}_2$$

$$\Rightarrow \quad \ddot{\vec{r}}^a(1) = 6\vec{P}_0 - 6\vec{P}_1 + 2\vec{t}_0 + 4\vec{t}_1 \quad \text{and}$$

$$\ddot{\vec{r}}^b(0) = -6\vec{P}_1 + 6\vec{P}_2 - 4\omega\vec{t}_1 - 2\vec{t}_2$$

Putting above results in equation (6.48) gives following relation

$$\Rightarrow \quad (-6\vec{P}_1 + 6\vec{P}_2 - 4\omega\vec{t}_1 - 2\vec{t}_2) = \omega^2(6\vec{P}_0 - 6\vec{P}_1 + 2\vec{t}_0 + 4\vec{t}_1)$$

$$\Rightarrow \quad -6\vec{P}_1 + 6\vec{P}_2 - 4\omega\vec{t}_1 - 2\vec{t}_2 = \omega^2(6\vec{P}_0 - 6\vec{P}_1 + 2\vec{t}_0 + 4\vec{t}_1)$$

$$\Rightarrow \quad \omega^2 2\vec{t}_0 + \omega^2 4\vec{t}_1 + 4\omega\vec{t}_1 + 2\vec{t}_2 = 6\vec{P}_2 + \omega^2 6\vec{P}_1 - 6\vec{P}_1 - \omega^2 6\vec{P}_0$$

$$\Rightarrow \quad \omega^2 2\vec{t}_0 + 4\vec{t}_1\,\omega(1 + \omega) + 2\vec{t}_2 = 6\vec{P}_2 + 6\vec{P}_1(\omega^2 - 1) - \omega^2 6\vec{P}_0$$

$$\Rightarrow \quad \omega^2 2\vec{t}_0 + \omega(1 + \omega)\,4\vec{t}_1 + 2\vec{t}_2 = 6\vec{P}_2 + 6\vec{P}_1(\omega^2 - 1) - \omega^2 6\vec{P}_0$$

$$\Rightarrow \quad \omega^2\vec{t}_0 + \omega(1 + \omega)\,2\vec{t}_1 + \vec{t}_2 = 3\vec{P}_2 + 3\vec{P}_1(\omega^2 - 1) - \omega^2 3\vec{P}_0$$

$$\Rightarrow \quad \omega^2\vec{t}_0 + \omega(1 + \omega)\,2\vec{t}_1 + \vec{t}_2 = 3[\vec{P}_2 + \vec{P}_1(\omega^2 - 1) - \omega^2\vec{P}_0] \qquad ...(6.49)$$

From equation (6.49), we can determine unknown tangent , when

$\vec{t}_0$, $\vec{t}_2$, $\vec{P}_0$, $\vec{P}_1$ and $\vec{P}_2$ and its ω are known.

Now we consider the problem of fitting a G^2 continues curve through a sequence of $(n + 1)$ data points P_i $(i + 0, 1, ..., n)$. The curve fitting problem can be study under two conditions:

(a) Fixed or clamped end condition

This is used when starting tangent of first curve $\vec{t}_0$ and end tangent of last curve $\vec{t}_n$ is known. Let for first curve

$$\vec{t}_0 = \hat{t}_0$$

And for last curve

$$\vec{t}_n = \hat{t}_n$$

Similar, to relation (6.49), for two curve joining using G^2 condition, we can obtain the following set of $(n - 1)$ linear equations (for $i = 1, 2, 3, \text{---} \ n-1$)

$$\omega_{i-1} \cdot \omega_i^2 \cdot \vec{t}_{i-1} + 2\omega_i(1+\omega_i)\vec{t}_i + \vec{t}_{i+2} = 3[\vec{P}_{i+1} + (\omega_i^2 - 1)P_i - \omega_i^2 P_{i-1} \quad ...(6.50)$$

Where $\omega_0 = 1$, and $\omega_i = \dfrac{\left|\vec{P}_{i+1} - \vec{P}_i\right|}{\left|\vec{P}_i - \vec{P}_{i-1}\right|}$ for $i = 1, 2, ... , (n - 1)$

Equation (6.50) can be used for determining intermediate tangents t_i, (for $i = 1.2, ... n - 1$)

Thus we have a set of following equations to determine tangents for $(n + 1)$ data points P_i, they are:

$$\vec{t}_0 = \hat{t}_0 \qquad\qquad \text{(Known or fixed)}$$

$$\vec{t}_n = \hat{t}_n \qquad\qquad \text{(Known or fixed) and}$$

$$\omega_{i-1} \cdot \omega_i^2 \cdot \vec{t}_{i-1} + 2\omega_i(1+\omega_i)\vec{t}_i + \vec{t}_{i+1} = 3[\vec{P}_{i+1} + (\omega_i^2 - 1)\vec{P}_i - \omega_i^2 \vec{P}_{i-1}]$$

Above equations can be written in matrix form as given below

$$\begin{bmatrix} 1 & 0 & 0 & 0 & : & : & \cdots & & \cdots \\ \omega_1^2 & 2\omega_1 + 2\omega_1^2 & 1 & 0 & : & : & \cdots & & \cdots \\ 0 & \omega_1\omega_2^2 & 2\omega_2 + 2\omega_2^2 & 1 & : & : & \cdots & & \cdots \\ \cdots & \cdots & & : & : & \cdots & & \cdots \\ \cdots & \cdots & & : & : & \cdots & & \cdots \\ \cdots & \cdots & & : & : & 2\omega_{n-2}\omega_{n-1}^2 & 2\omega_{n-1} + 2\omega_{n-1}^2 & 1 \\ \cdots & \cdots & & : & : & 0 & 0 & 1 \end{bmatrix}$$

$$
= \begin{bmatrix} \vec{t}_0 \\ \vec{t}_1 \\ \vdots \\ \vdots \\ \vdots \\ \vec{t}_{n-1} \\ \vec{t}_n \end{bmatrix} = \begin{bmatrix} \hat{t}_0 \\ \vec{b}_1 \\ \vec{b}_2 \\ \vdots \\ \vdots \\ \vec{b}_{n-1} \\ \hat{t}_n \end{bmatrix} \qquad \qquad \text{...6.51}
$$

Where $\vec{b}_i = 3[\vec{P}_{i+1} + (\omega_i^2 + 1)\vec{P}_i - \omega_i^2 \vec{P}_{i-1}]$ and $\omega_0 = 1$

The values of internal tangents can be determined by using TDMA. We observe that the linear equation (6.50) can be converted into the cubic spline fitting case equation (6.9) when $\omega_i = 1$, for all i. In other words, the chord length spline curve becomes a cubic spline curve if all the chord length is equal.

(b) Free end condition

This condition is used when $\vec{t}_0$ and $\vec{t}_n$ is also not given. Generally, we use three methods to determine all tangents of composite curve. They are

(a) Circular end conditions

(b) Polynomial end condition

(c) Free end condition.

These three conditions are similar to conditions discussed in preview sections.

Example 8: The position vector of four data points are $\vec{P}_0[0\ 0\ 0]$, $\vec{P}_1[1\ 1\ 1]$, $\vec{P}_2[2\ -1\ -1]$ and $\vec{P}_3[3\ 0\ 0]$. The tangent vectors at the ends are to and $\vec{t}_0[1\ 1\ 1]$ and $\vec{t}_3[1\ 1\ 1]$. Determine and draw the cubic spline curve passing through above data points, using chord-length spline fitting.

Solution: Using relation given in matrix form equation (6.50) for four data points $P_i\ (i = 0,1,2,3)$, the matrix form will be given as

$$
\begin{bmatrix} 1 & 0 & 0 & 0 \\ \omega_1^2 & 2\omega_1 + 2\omega_1^2 & 1 & 0 \\ 0 & \omega_1\omega_2^2 & 2\omega_2 + 2\omega_2^2 & 1 \\ 0 & 0 & 0 & 1 \end{bmatrix} \begin{bmatrix} \vec{t}_0 \\ \vec{t}_1 \\ \vec{t}_2 \\ \vec{t}_3 \end{bmatrix} = \begin{bmatrix} \hat{t}_0 \\ \vec{b}_1 \\ \vec{b}_2 \\ \hat{t}_n \end{bmatrix}
$$

Here, $\alpha = |\vec{P}_1 - \vec{P}_0|$

$= |[1 \quad 1 \quad 1]|$

$= \sqrt{3}$

$\beta = |\vec{P}_2 - \vec{P}_1| = 3$

$\therefore \ \alpha = \sqrt{3}$, $\beta = 3$, here $\alpha \neq \beta$. Thus, this problem can be solved by chord length spline fitting method.

Here, $\omega_i = \dfrac{|\vec{P}_{i+1} - \vec{P}_i|}{|\vec{P}_i - \vec{P}_{i-1}|}$ for $i = 1, 2, \text{---} \ n$

Where $\omega_0 = 1$ and

$$\omega_1 = \frac{|\vec{P}_2 - \vec{P}_1|}{|\vec{P}_0 - \vec{P}_1|} = \frac{|[1 - 2 \ -2]|}{|[1 \ 1 \ 1]|} = \frac{3}{\sqrt{3}} = \sqrt{3}$$

$$\omega_2 = \frac{|\vec{P}_3 - \vec{P}_1|}{|\vec{P}_2 - \vec{P}_1|} = \frac{|[1 \ 1 \ 1]|}{|[1 \ -2 \ -2]|} = \frac{\sqrt{3}}{3} = \frac{1}{\sqrt{3}}$$

$$= \frac{|\vec{P}_3 - \vec{P}_1|}{|\vec{P}_2 - \vec{P}_1|} = \frac{|[1 \ 1 \ 1]|}{|[1 \ 1 \ 1]|} = \frac{\sqrt{3}}{3} = \frac{1}{\sqrt{3}}$$

$\vec{t}_0 = [1 \quad 1 \quad 1]$, $\vec{t}_3 = [1 \quad 1 \quad 1]$

Given $= \hat{t}_0$, $= \hat{t}_3$ for $i = 1, 2, \dots n - 1$

and $\vec{b}_i = 3[\vec{P}_{i+1} + (\omega_i^2 + 1)\vec{P}_i - \omega_i^2 P_{i-1}]$ for $i = 1, 2, \dots n - 1$

$\vec{b}_1 = 3[\vec{P}_2 + (\omega_1^2 + 1)\vec{P}_1 - \omega_1^2 \vec{P}_0]$

$= 3\{[2 - 1 \ -1] + (3 + 1)[1 \ 1 \ 1] - 3[0 \ 0 \ 0]$

$= \{[6 - 3 - 3] + [4 \ 4 \ 4]\}$

$= [10 \ 1 \ 1]$

$\vec{b}_2 = 3[\vec{P}_3 + (\omega_2^2 + 1)\vec{P}_2 - \omega_2^2 \vec{P}_1]$

$= 3\left\{[3 \ 0 \ 0] + \left(\dfrac{1}{3} + 1\right)[2 \ -1 \ -1] - \dfrac{1}{3}[1 \ 1 \ 1]\right\}$

$= 3\left\{[3 \ 0 \ 0] + \left(\dfrac{4}{3}\right)[2 \ -1 \ -1] - \dfrac{1}{3}[1 \ 1 \ 1]\right\}$

$= [3 \ 0 \ 0] + [8 \ -4 \ -4] - [1 \ 1 \ 1]$

$= [11 \ -4 \ -4] - [1 \ 1 \ 1]$

$= [10 \ -3 \ -3]$

$\therefore$ Putting all values in matrix form.

$$\begin{bmatrix} 1 & 0 & 0 & 0 \\ 3 & 2\cdot\sqrt{3}+2\cdot 3 & 1 & 0 \\ 0 & \dfrac{1}{3}\cdot\sqrt{3} & 2\cdot\dfrac{1}{\sqrt{3}}+2\cdot\dfrac{1}{3} & 1 \\ 0 & 0 & 0 & 1 \end{bmatrix}\begin{bmatrix} \vec{t_0} \\ \vec{t_1} \\ \vec{t_2} \\ \vec{t_3} \end{bmatrix} = \begin{bmatrix} 1 & 1 & 1 \\ 10 & 1 & 1 \\ 10 & -3 & -3 \\ 1 & 1 & 1 \end{bmatrix}$$

$\therefore$ $\qquad\qquad \vec{t}_0 = [1\ \ 1\ \ 1]$

$3\vec{t}_0 + (2.\ \sqrt{3}+6)\vec{t}_1 + \vec{t}_2 = [10\ \ 1\ \ 1]$

$\dfrac{\sqrt{3}}{3}\vec{t_1} + \left(\dfrac{2}{\sqrt{3}}+\dfrac{2}{3}\right)\vec{t_2} + \vec{t_3} = [10\ \ -3\ \ -3]$ and $\vec{t}_3 = [1\ \ 1\ \ 1]$

$\Rightarrow\qquad 9.5\vec{t}_1 + \vec{t}_2 = [9\ \ 0\ \ 0]$

$0.577\ \vec{t}_1 + 1.82\vec{t}_2 = [3\ \ 0\ \ 0]$

$\therefore\qquad\qquad \vec{t}_1 = [0.8\ \ 0\ \ 0]$ and

$\qquad\qquad\qquad \vec{t}_2 = [1.4\ \ 0\ \ 0]$

Therefore, using cubic spline curve

$\vec{r}^{\,1}(u) = (1-3u^2+2u^3)\,\vec{P}_0 + (3u^2-2u^3)\,\vec{P}_1 + (u-2u^2+u^3)\vec{t}_0 + (-u^2+u^3)\vec{t}_1$

$\qquad = (1-3u^2+2u^3)\,[0\ \ 0\ \ 0] + (3u^2-2u^3)\,[1\ \ 1\ \ 1] +$

$\qquad\qquad (u-2u^2+u^3)[1\ \ 1\ \ 1] + (-u^2-u^3)\,[0.8\ \ 0\ \ 0]$

$\vec{r}^{\,1}(u) = (u+0.2u^2-0.2u^3)\hat{i} + (u+u^2-u^3)\hat{j} + (u+u^2-u^3)\hat{k}$

By putting suitable value of parameter, $0 \le u \le 1$ we can get equation for the points of curve segments $\vec{r}^{\,1}(u)$ for data points $\vec{P}_0$, $\vec{P}_1$ and $\vec{P}_2$ similarly we can get for second curve segment $\vec{r}^{\,2}(u)$ for data point $\vec{P}_1$, $\vec{P}_2$ and $\vec{P}_3$. After finding different points we can draw final composite curve.

6.7 NON-UNIFORM B-SPLINE FITTING

This section gives explanation for how one can approach for constructing a smooth cubic NUB curve posing through a know sequence of 3D data points $\vec{P}_i$ (for $i - 0, 1, 2, --n$) when at $\vec{P}_0$, tangent is $\vec{t}_0$ and at $\vec{P}_n$ tangents is $\vec{t}_n$ are given. From these data points one can construct a composite curve of n cubic NUB curve segments $r^i(u)$ {for $i = 0, 1... (n-1)$} and $u \in [0\ 1]$, as shown in Fig. 6.12 , which is defined by $(n+3)$ control vertices $\vec{V}_i$ {for $i = 0, 1, ... (n+2)$}, and $(n+4)$ knot spans ∇_i [for $i = -2, -1, --, (n+1)$].

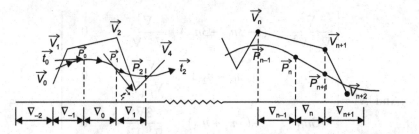

Fig. 6.12 Non-Uniform cubic p-spline curve fitting.

Since, shape of the NUB curve is controlled by knot span ∇_1 and control vertices $\vec{V}_i$. Therefore, there is need to determine or assign each knot spans and control vertices. The overall curve fitting procedure is similar to that of constructing a composite uniform B-spline curve discussed in providers section (6.3).

A shown in Fig. 6.12, the composite curve is supported n knot spans, ∇_0 through ∇_{n-1} which we call supporting knot spans. The rest knot spans are called extended knot spans. A reasonable choice for the supporting knot spans is to make them equal to corresponding chord length. They are

$$\nabla_i = |\vec{P}_{i+1} - \vec{P}_i| \quad \text{for } i = 0, 1 \text{ ----- } (n-1) \quad ...(6.52)$$

Again we notice that the choice for the extended knot does not affect the quality of the resulting NUB curve. They could be set to zero as in equation (6.53) or to be assign a uniform value as in (6.54). They are

$$\nabla_{-2} = \nabla_{-1} = \nabla_{n+1} = \nabla_n = 0 \qquad ...(6.53)$$

or $\qquad \nabla_{-2} = \nabla_{-1} = \nabla_0$.and

$$\nabla_{n-1} = \nabla_n = \nabla_{n+1} \qquad ...(6.54)$$

When we set zero to all extended knot spans. Then it is called multiple knots. After determining the knot spans the next step is to determine control vertices V_i. For this we have to obtain a set of linear equation systems by using cubing NUB curve model. The cubic NUB curve model [eqn. (5.47) from section 5.9.2.2] is represented as

$$r^i(u) = UN_c^i R^i \quad \text{for } i = 0, 1, \text{ ------ } (n-1),$$

Where $U = U = \begin{bmatrix} 1 \\ u \\ u^2 \\ u^3 \end{bmatrix}$, $R^i = \begin{bmatrix} \vec{V}_i \\ \vec{V}_{i+1} \\ \vec{V}_{i+2} \\ \vec{V}_{i+3} \end{bmatrix}$

$$\text{And } N_c^i = \begin{bmatrix} \dfrac{\nabla_i^2}{\nabla_{i-1}^2 \nabla_{i-2}^3} & (1-3n_{11}-3n_{13}) & \dfrac{\nabla_{i-1}^2}{\nabla_{i-1}^3 \nabla_{i-2}^2} & 0 \\[2ex] -3n_{11} & (3n_{11}-n_{23}) & \dfrac{3\nabla_i \nabla_{i-1}}{\nabla_{i-1}^3 \nabla_{i-1}^2} & 0 \\[2ex] 3n_{11} & -(3n_{11}+n_{33}) & \dfrac{3\nabla_i^2}{\nabla_{i-1}^3 \nabla_{i-1}^2} & 0 \\[2ex] n_{11} & (n_{11}-n_{43}-n_{44}) & n_{43} & \dfrac{\nabla_i^2}{\nabla_i^3 \nabla_i^2} \end{bmatrix}$$

where
$$n_{43} = -\left[\frac{1}{3}n_{33} + n_{44} + \frac{\nabla_i^2}{\nabla_i^2 \nabla_{i-1}^2}\right]$$

$$\nabla_i^k = \nabla_i + \nabla_{i+1} + \ldots\ldots + \nabla_{i+k-1}$$

n_{ij} = element in row i and column j

Since, a curve segment $r^i(u)$ spans from to $\vec{P}_i$ to $\vec{P}_{i+1}$, the following relation holds at each data points P_i (for $i = 0,1, --- (n-1)$). They are

$$r^i(0) = \vec{P}_i \qquad\qquad\qquad ...(6.56a)$$

and
$$r^i(1) = \vec{P}_{i+1} \qquad\qquad\qquad ...(6.56b)$$

form relation 6.56(a) using cubic NUB curve equation 6.55, we can generate following set of linear equations. They are

$$f_i\vec{V}_i + h_i \cdot \vec{V}_{i+1} + g_i\vec{V}_{i+2} = \vec{P}_i \qquad \text{for } i = 0,1,-----,n$$

Where $f_i = \dfrac{\nabla_i^2}{\nabla_{i-1}^2 \nabla_{i-2}^3}$, $g_i = \dfrac{\nabla_i^2}{\nabla_{i-1}^2 \nabla_{i-1}^3}$.

$$h_i = (1-f_i-g_i)$$

The equation (6.57) gives $(n+1)$ linear equations for determining $(n+1)$ control vertices. But there is need of two more equations for determining total $(n+3)$ control vertices. These two more linear equations can be obtained by evaluating the curve derivatives at the very ends of the composite curve in Fig 6.12. That is the end tangent at the beginning of the composite curve $i.e.$, starting tangent of the first curve is evaluated as

$$\hat{t}_0 = \dot{\vec{r}}^{\,0}(0)$$

$$= a_0\vec{V}_2 + (b_0 - a_0)\vec{V}_1 - b_0\vec{V}_0 \qquad\qquad ...(6.58)$$

Where $a_0 = \dfrac{3\nabla_0\nabla_{-1}}{\nabla_{-1}^2 \nabla_{-1}^3}$, $a_0 = \dfrac{3\nabla_0^2}{\nabla_{-1}^2 \nabla_{-2}^3}$

Similarly, the end tangent of last curve of the composite curve is given by

$$\hat{t}_n = \dot{\vec{r}}^{\,n-1}(0)$$

$$= a_1 \vec{V}_{n+2} + (b_1 - a_1)\vec{V}_{n+1} - b_1 \vec{V}_n \qquad \qquad ...(6.58)$$

Where $b_1 = \dfrac{3\nabla_n \nabla_{n-1}}{\nabla_{n-1}^2 \nabla_{n-2}^3}, a_1 = \dfrac{3\nabla_{n-1}^2}{\nabla_{n-1}^2 \nabla_{n-1}^3}$

if we use equation (6.53), then some of the co-efficient in (6.57) and (6.58) can be easily obtained as

$$f_0 = 1, g_0 = 1, f_n = 0, \ g_n = 1 \text{ and}$$

$$a_0 = 0, b_0 = 3, a_1 = 3, b_1 = 0$$

From above values and using linear equations (6.58), (6.57) and (6.59), we can obtain following linear equation where its matrix form is represented as

$$\begin{bmatrix} -3 & -3 & 0 & 0 & \vdots & \vdots & ... & & ... \\ 1 & 0 & 0 & 0 & \vdots & \vdots & ... & & ... \\ 0 & f_1 & h_1 & g_1 & \vdots & \vdots & ... & & ... \\ ... & ... & & \vdots & \vdots & ... & & ... \\ ... & ... & & \vdots & \vdots & f_{n-1} & h_{n-1} & g_{n-1} \\ ... & ... & & \vdots & \vdots & 0 & 0 & 1 \\ ... & ... & & \vdots & \vdots & 0 & -3 & 3 \end{bmatrix} \begin{bmatrix} \vec{V}_0 \\ \vec{V}_1 \\ \vdots \\ \vdots \\ \vdots \\ \vec{V}_{n+1} \\ \vec{V}_{n+2} \end{bmatrix} = \begin{bmatrix} \hat{t}_0 \\ \vec{P}_0 \\ \vdots \\ \vdots \\ \vdots \\ \vec{P}_n \\ \hat{t} \end{bmatrix} \qquad ...(6.60)$$

Where $f_i = \dfrac{\nabla_i^2}{\nabla_{i-1}^2 \nabla_{i-2}^3}, g_i = \dfrac{\nabla_i^2}{\nabla_{i-1}^2 \nabla_{i-1}^3}$

$$h_i = (1 - f_i - g_i)$$

The equation (6.60) can be solved for determining $(n + 3)$ control vertices V_i by TDMA method but care must be taken because the co-efficient matrix of equation (6.60) has some diagonal element where values are zero. Therefore there is need to row operations to make zero diagonal elements to non zero. We notice that equation (6.60) is similar to uniform B-spline composite curve when all supporting knot spans are equal.

UNSOLVED PROBLEMS

Problem 1: If four two dimensional position vectors of data points are $\vec{P}_0[0\ 0]$, $\vec{P}_1[1\ 1]$, $\vec{P}_2[2\ 2]$ and $\vec{P}_3[3\ 0]$ as shown in Fig 6.11. The tangent vector at their ends are $\vec{t}_0[1\ 1]$ and $\vec{t}_3[1\ 1]$. Determine the piecewise cubic spline curve passing through them using the chord length fitting by taking intermediate points at $u = 1/13$ and $u = 2/3$ for each segments.

Solution :

Segments	at u =	x	Y
1	1/3	0.416	0.484
	2/3	0.740	0.876
2.	1/3	1.343	0.457
	2/3	1.657	-0.457
3.	1/3	0.260	-0.876
	2/3	2.548	0.489

Problem 2: If three position vector are $\vec{P}_0$ [0 0], $\vec{P}_1$ [1 2] and $\vec{P}_2$[3 2]. Determine the cubic spline curve through these points using relaxed end condition. Use the Chord-length approximation.

$$\textbf{Solution:} \quad \begin{bmatrix} \vec{t}_0 \\ \vec{t}_1 \\ \vec{t}_2 \end{bmatrix} = \begin{bmatrix} 0.301 & 1.131 \\ 0.739 & 0.422 \\ 1.131 & -0.211 \end{bmatrix}$$

❑❑❑

7

Surface Modelling
and Surface Fitting

7.0 INTRODUCTION

Imagine moving the set of control points of the Ferguson (or Bezier or B-Spline) curves in three dimensions. As they move in space, new curves will be generated. If they are moved smoothly in a proper way as desired then the curves formed create a surface, which may be thought as a bundle of curves. If each of the control point moves along a Ferguson curves of its owns, then a Ferguson surface patch will be created. Similarly, if each of the control points moves along Bazier curves of its own, then a Brazier surface patch will be created. Creating and representation of surface patch is discussed in this chapter. After knowing surface patch creation, surface fitting is also discussed in this chapter so that objects can be generated with the help of programming in CAD/CAM system.

7.1 SURFACE REPRESENTATION

Surface representation is an extension of curves representation discussed in the previous section. Representation and shape designs of sculptured objects such as car, ship, airplane and rocket propulsion bodies cannot be achieved by curves generation covered in chapter 5 and 6. In such cases, surfaces must be utilized to describe sculptured objects precisely and accurately. In CAD/CAM, we create surfaces, and then we use them to cut and grim as per solid features and primitives to obtain the models of the sculptured/complex objects. The parametric form of curves can be used in surface construction. The treatment of curves surfaces and solids in computer graphics and CAD/CAM requires developing the proper equation and algorithms for both computation and programming purposes. Using suitable program in CNC machine, one can generate tool path for generation of line, curves, surface of the solid. Similar, to curve, surface can be defined mathematically in three-dimensional space by either non-parametric or parametric equation. There are several methods to fit non-parametric surface to a given set of data points. This fall in two categories. In the first, one equation is fitted to pass through all the points while in second, the data points are used to develop as series of surface patches that are connected together for at least position and first-derivative continuity. In both categories, the non-parametric equations of the surfaces or surface patch is given by following equations.

Implicit form for equation of surface will be represented as

$$f(x, y, z) = 0 \qquad \qquad ...7.0(a)$$

In above form, equation of a sphere at (x_0, y_0, z_0) as centre with radius r will be represented as

$$f(x, y, z) = (x - x_0)^2 + (y - y_0)^2 (z - z_0)^2 - r^2 = 0 \qquad ...7.0(b)$$

The explicit form for equation of surface will be represented as

$$Z = f(x, y) = \sum_{i=0}^{m} \sum_{i=0}^{n} a_i x^i y^i \qquad \qquad ...7.0(c)$$

where the surface is described by an XY grid of size $(m + 1) \times (n + 1)$ points as shown in Fig 7.1. In Fig 7.1, $\vec{P}$ is the position vector of a point on the surface but non-perametric surface representation is not efficient in *CAD/CAM*. Thus parametric surface is used in graphics and *CAD/CAM*. The parametric representative of a surface means a continuous, vector valued function $\vec{r}\,(u, v)$ of two variables (or parameter u and v) where $\vec{r}\,(u, v)$ assumes every position on the surface. The most general way to represent the parametric equation of a three-dimensional curved surface in space is given as

$$\vec{r}\,(u, v) = [x\,(u, v)\ \ y\,(u, v)\ \ z\,(u, v)] \qquad \qquad ...(7.1)$$

For $u_{min} \leq u \leq u_{max}$

and $v_{min} \leq v \leq v_{max}$

Here most of the surfaces are created with interval are [0,1].

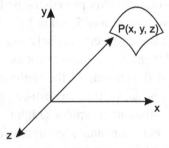

Fig. 7.1 Point P on a non-parametric Surface Path.

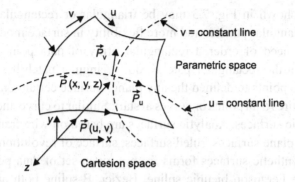

Fig 7.2 Parametric representation of a 3D surface.

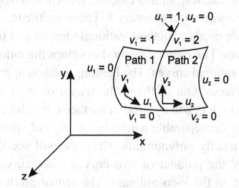

Fig 7.3 Two patch parametric surface.

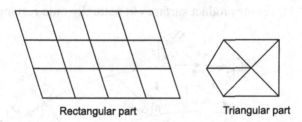

Rectangular part   Triangular part

Fig 7.4.

Surface equation 7.1 gives the co-ordinates of a point on the surface. It uniquely maps the parametric space (in u and v values) to the Cartesian space (on x, y and z) as shown in Fig. 7.2. The parametric variables u and v are constrained to intervals bonded by minimum and maximum values. In most surface, these intervals are [0, 1] for both u and v. The equation (7.1) suggest that a general three-dimensional surface (Composite Surface) may be modelled by dividing it into an assembly of topological patches. A patch is considered the basic mathematical element to create a composite surface. Patch is small region of surface which is mesh of curves. Some surface may consist of one patch only while others may be a few patches connected together. Fig. 7.3 shows a two patch surface where the u and v values are (0.1). The topology of a patch shown in Fig. 7.3 may be triangular or rectangular as shown in Fig. 7.4. Triangular patches add more flexibility in surface modelling because there is no need of ordered rectangular array of data points to create the surface as in the rectangular patches do. Triangular patch has the minimum co-ordinates points to defined the any plane. Surface certain on CAD systems usually requires data points or curves at start. Similar to curve, there are analytic and synthetic surfaces. Analytic surfaces are based on wire frame entities and include the plane surfaces, ruled surfaces, surface of revolution and tabulated cylinder. Synthetic surfaces forms from a given set of data points or curves (include the Ferguson bicubic spline, Bezier, B-spline both uniformed non-uniform and coons patches). In this chapter, we will discuss about the surfaces only made by curves given in chapters 5. These synthetic surfaces can also be generated by tensor product method, rational method and blending method as discussed for curves. The rational method develops the rational surfaces which is an extension of rational curves. The bending method approximates a surface by piece wise surfaces. Out of them, the tensor product method is the most popular method which is widely used in surface modelling and also discussed here due to its simple, separable nature involving only products of univariate basis functions, usually polynomials. Here we will see that tensor product surface is literally the product of two curves : one curves in u co-ordinate and another curve in the v-co-ordinate. The tensor product formulation is a mapping of a rectangular patches described by the u and v values; ($0 \leq u \leq 1$ and $0 \leq v < 1$). Tensor product surfaces fit naturally onto rectangular patches.

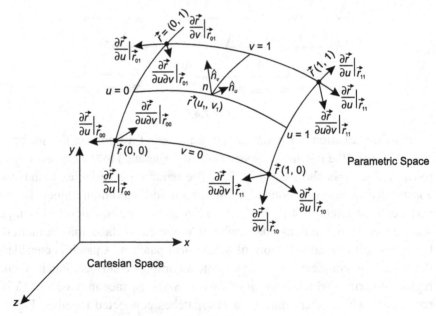

Fig 7.5 Representation of different vector points in patches.

There are sixteen vectors (4 position vectors + 8 tangent vectors + 4 twist vectors) for the composite surface made by four boundary curves as shown in Fig. 7.5.

From Fig. 7.5, it is clear that there are four position vectors for the four corner points $\vec{r}\,(0, 0)$ $\vec{r}\,(1, 0)$ $\vec{r}\,(1, 1)$ and $\vec{r}\,(0, 1)$, eight tangent vectors (two at each corner); and four twist vectors at the corner points (the definition of twist vectors is given in section 7.1.2). All these vectors must be known for generation of surface patch. Position vectors is needed to fix for starting and ending limit of objects at various points. Knowing the tangent vectors to a surface enables driving a cutting tool along the surface to machine it and knowing the normal vectors to the surfaces provides the proper directions for the tool to approach and retract from the surface.

7.1.1 Tangent Vectors

The tangent at any point $\vec{r}\,(u, v)$ on the surface is obtained by holding one parameter constant and differentiating with respect to the others. Therefore, there are two tangent vectors, a tangent to each of the intersecting curves passing through the point as shown in Fig. 7.5. Since surface is represented in parametric form as

$$\vec{r}\,(u, v) = [x\,(u, v)\ y\,(u, v)\ z\,(u, v)]$$

then tangent vector will be represented as

$$\frac{d\vec{r}(u,v)}{du} = \frac{\partial x}{\partial u}\hat{i} + \frac{\partial y}{\partial u}\hat{j} + \frac{\partial z}{\partial u}\hat{k}, u_{min} \le u \le u_{max}$$

$$v_{min} \le v \le v_{max}$$

$$= \vec{t}_{ij} \qquad\qquad ...7.2$$

above equation 7.2 is along v = constant curve and it is also called v-direction tangent vector and

$$\frac{d\vec{r}(u,v)}{dv} = \frac{\partial x}{\partial v}\hat{i} + \frac{\partial y}{\partial v}\hat{j} + \frac{\partial z}{\partial v}\hat{k}, u_{min} \le u \le u_{max}$$

$$= \vec{s}_{ij} \qquad\qquad v_{min} \le v \le v_{max} \qquad ...7.3$$

above equation 7.3 is tangent vector along u = constant curve and called u-direction tangent vector.

Similarly, unit vectors of the tangent vectors are given by

$$\hat{n}_u = \left.\frac{\dfrac{\vec{r}(u,v)}{du}}{\left|\dfrac{\vec{r}(u,v)}{du}\right|}\right|_{v\,=\,constant} = \frac{\vec{t}_{ij}}{|\vec{t}_{ij}|}$$

and $\qquad \widehat{n}_v = \left. \dfrac{\dfrac{\vec{r}(u,v)}{dv}}{\left| \dfrac{\vec{r}(u,v)}{dv} \right|} \right|_{u = constant} = \dfrac{\vec{s}_{ij}}{|\vec{s}_{ij}|}$

where $\qquad |\vec{t}_{ij}| = \left| \dfrac{\vec{r}(u,v)}{du} \right| = \sqrt{\left(\dfrac{dx}{du}\right)^2 + \left(\dfrac{dy}{du}\right)^2 + \left(\dfrac{dz}{du}\right)^2}$

and $\qquad |\vec{s}_{ij}| = \left| \dfrac{\vec{r}(u,v)}{dv} \right| = \sqrt{\left(\dfrac{dx}{dv}\right)^2 + \left(\dfrac{dy}{dv}\right)^2 + \left(\dfrac{dz}{dv}\right)^2}$

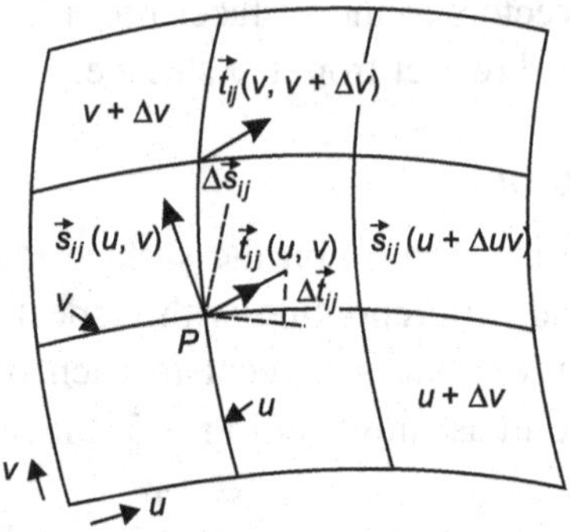

Fig. 7.6 Twist Vector Interpretation in Geometric form.

7.1.2 Twist and Normal Vector

The twist vector at a point on a surface is said to measure the twist in the surface at that point. Knowing twists or links is very important during generation of surface so that during modelling one can avoid any twist on surface for longer life. Twist is the rate of range of the tangent vector $\vec{t}_{ij}$ with respect to v or $\vec{s}_{ij}$ with respect to u, or it is the cross (mixed) derivative vector at the point. Fig. 7.6. shows the geometric interpretation of the twist vector in geometric form. If we increase u and v by Δu and Δv respectively and the draw the tangent vectors as shown in Fig. 7.6, the incremental changes in $\vec{t}_{ij}$ and $\vec{s}_{ij}$ at point P whose position vector are $\vec{r}$ (u, v) are obtained by translating $\vec{t}_{ij}(u, v + \Delta v)$ and $\vec{s}_{ij}(u + \Delta v, v)$ to P'. The incremental rate of change of the two tangent vectors become $\dfrac{\partial \vec{t}_{ij}}{\partial v}$ and $\dfrac{\partial \vec{s}_{ij}}{\partial u}$, and the infinitesimal rate of change is given by the following limits.

$$\underset{\Delta v \to 0}{\text{limit}} \ \dfrac{\partial \vec{t}_{ij}}{\partial v} = \left. \dfrac{\partial^2 \vec{r}(u,v)}{\partial u \, \partial v} \right|_{u=0} = \vec{x}_{ij} \qquad \text{(Twist vector along } u = 0 \text{ line)}$$

$$\underset{\Delta u \to 0}{\text{limit}} \ \dfrac{\partial \vec{s}_{ij}}{\partial v} = \left. \dfrac{\partial^2 \vec{r}(u,v)}{\partial u \, \partial v} \right|_{v=0} = \vec{x}_{ij} \qquad \text{(Twist vector along } v = 0 \text{ line)}$$

The twist vector can be written in terms of its Cartesian component as

$$\vec{x}_{ij} = \left[\frac{\partial^2 x}{\partial u \partial v} \frac{\partial^2 y}{\partial u \partial v} \frac{\partial^2 z}{\partial u \partial v} \right]^r$$

$$= \frac{\partial^2 x}{\partial u \partial v} \hat{i} + \frac{\partial^2 y}{\partial u \partial v} \hat{j} + \frac{\partial^2 z}{\partial u \partial v} \hat{k} \qquad \text{...7.4}$$

For $u_{min} \leq u \leq u_{max}$, $v_{min} \leq v \leq v_{max}$

Equation 7.4 indicate that twist vector is the second derivatives with respect to u and v. The twist vector depends on both the surface geometric characteristics and its parameterization.

The normal vector to a surface can be used to calculate cutter offsets for three dimensional NC programming to machine surface, volume calculation and shading of a surface model. The surface normal to a point vector which is perpendicular to both tangent vectors at the point (Fig. 7.6) is given as

$$\vec{N} (u, v) = \frac{\partial \vec{r}(u,v)}{\partial u} \times \frac{\partial \vec{r}(u,v)}{\partial v} = \vec{t}_{ij} \times \vec{s}_{ij} \qquad \text{...7.5}$$

Surface normal will be zero when $\vec{t}_{ij} \times \vec{s}_{ij} = 0$

and the unit normal vector is given by

$$\hat{n}_n = \frac{N}{|N|} = \frac{\vec{t}_{ij} \times \vec{s}_{ij}}{|\vec{t}_{ij} \times s_{ij}|} \qquad \text{...7.6}$$

In machining, the sense of $\hat{n}_n$ is usually chosen such that $\hat{n}_n$ points must be away from the surface being machined. In volume calculation, the sense of $\hat{n}$ is chosen positive when pointing toward existing material and negative when pointing to holes in the part. Here the terms "surface" and "patch" are used interchangeably. However, in a more general sense, a surface is considered the superset since a surface can contain one or more patches.

7.2 SURFACE PATCH MODEL CONSTRUCTION

Simple Portions of curved surfaces can be represented as surface patch simple portions modelled by bivariate (two-variable) polynomials of simple plane surface equation given below

$$z = a_0 + a_1 x + a_2 y \qquad \text{...7.7}(a)$$

and curved surface patches can be represented by higher order. Polynomials which are given below

1. Bilinear patches: $-z = a_0 + a_1 x + a_2 y + a_3 xy$ ...7.7(b)

2. Biquadratic patches: $-z = a_0 + a_1x + a_2y + a_3xy + a_4x^2 + a_5y^2$ ...7.7(c)

3. Bicubic patches: $-z = a_0 + a_1x + a_2y + a_3xy + a_4x^2 + a_5y^2 + a_6x^3 + a_7x^2y + a_8xy^2 + a_9y^3$ ...7.7(d)

Above polynomial surface patches are good for modelling portions of a surface but surface patches are not convenient for modelling an entire complicated surfaces.

Therefore, there is need of more complex surfaces or free form surfaces which can be modelled using Ferguson, Bazier, B-spline curves which discussed in next sections for their generation. In next sections, various types of surfaces patch are discussed that will be used as building blocks in constructing complex surface shapes. The types of surface models are given below.

1. Ferguson, Bezier and B-spline uniform and non-uniform surface patches.

2. Ruled, Lofted, Coons (for rectangular patch) and Gregory for triangle surface patch.

3. Sweep surface patches.

4. Quadratic surface primitives.

There are practically large number of surface models available in the literature, but we limit our discussion to surfaces made from curves model covered in chapter 5 and 6. From this curve model, one can generate synthetic surface such as.

1. Standard polynomial surface patches.

2. Ferguson surfaces patches

3. Bezier surface patches (rectangular)

4. Uniform B-spline surfaces patches

5. Non-uniform B-spline surface patches

6. Ruled and lotted surface etc.

Above synthetic surface patch can obtain by either tensor product method or by rational method or by blending methods, but here we used tensor product method only. A tenior product surface representation is formed from the combination of two curve representations, one in each parametric co-ordinate. Surface made tewor product is literally the product of two curves. One curve in the u-co-ordinate and another curve in the v-co-ordinate. It means, if one co-ordinate is fixed, the curve will generate with other parameter.

7.3 STANDARD POLYNOMIAL PARAMETRIC SURFACES PATCHES

Let equation of surfaces defined by vector valued polynomial function $\bar{r}(u, v)$ whose degrees are cubic in both u and v with co-efficient d_{ij} (for u^1, v^1).

Using tensor product method and two standard cubic curves, a standard bicubic polynomial patch is defined as

$$\vec{r}\,(u, v) = \sum_{i=0}^{3} \sum_{j=0}^{3} \vec{d}_{ij}\, u^i v^j \text{ with } 0 \le u, v \le 1 \qquad\qquad ...7.8(a)$$

$$= 1.[\vec{d}_{00}.1 + \vec{d}_{01}.v + \vec{d}_{02}.v^2 + \vec{d}_{03}.v^3] + u.[\vec{d}_{10}.1 + \vec{d}_{11}.v$$

$$+ \vec{d}_{12}.v^2 + \vec{d}_{13}.v^3 + u^2[\vec{d}_{20}.1 + \vec{d}_{21}.v + \vec{d}_{22}.v^2 + \vec{d}_{23}.v^3]$$

$$+ u^3[\vec{d}_{30}.1 + \vec{d}_{31}.v + \vec{d}_{32}.v^2 + \vec{d}_{33}.v^3] \quad ...7.8(b)$$

Above expression 7.8 (b) have 16 unknown vectors $\vec{d}_{ij}$. One way to generate surface patch from equation 7.8 (a) is that each 16 unknown vectors must be assigned by 16 position vectors of three diamensional point each. Thus, we must have $16 \times 3 = 48$ known points $\vec{p}_{ij}$ to generate surface patch as shown in Fig. 7.7.

Above equation 7.8 b can be is expressed in matrix form as

$$\vec{r}\,(u, v) = U \vec{D} ij\, V^T \qquad\qquad ... 7.8(b)$$

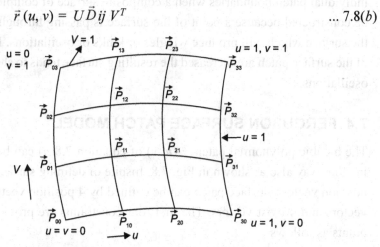

Fig. 7.7 Standard Bicubic Polynomial surface patch.

where

$$\vec{D}_{ij} = \begin{vmatrix} \vec{d}_{00} & \vec{d}_{01} & \vec{d}_{02} & \vec{d}_{03} \\ \vec{d}_{10} & \vec{d}_{11} & \vec{d}_{12} & \vec{d}_{13} \\ \vec{d}_{20} & \vec{d}_{21} & \vec{d}_{22} & \vec{d}_{23} \\ \vec{d}_{30} & \vec{d}_{31} & \vec{d}_{32} & \vec{d}_{33} \end{vmatrix} : \text{co-efficients matrix.}$$

Here $\vec{D}_{ij}$ are the vectors of coefficient for each coordinate in the parametric surface.

$$V = [1 \; v \; v^2 \; v^3]$$

$$U = [1 \; u \; u^2 \; u^3]$$

Thus, the bicubic polynomial surface patch (7.8*b*) may be used in constructing a smooth surface interpolating to 4×4 arrays of 3*D* points $\{P_{ij}\}$. Therefore this patch is called interpolated patch. Fig. 7.7 shows a bicubic polynomial patch defined by 16 positional data points in vector valued form.

If 16 unknown vectors of co-efficients for each co-ordinate are known, after putting and solving equation 7.8(*b*), a bicubic polynomial surface patch equation will evolve in terms of *u* and *v*. The parameter values at the corners may be assigned as follows:

$$u = v = 0 \text{ at } \vec{P}_{00};\ u = o,\ v = 1 \text{ at } \vec{P}_{03};\ u = 1,\ v = 0 \text{ at } \vec{P}_{30};\ u = v = 1 \text{ at } \vec{P}_{33}$$

After putting all values, a surface patch can be generated which passes through all point called bicubic surface patch.

A major drawback of the standard polynomial model given in equation (7.8 *c*) is that it is difficult to maintain a desired level of continuity across individual patch boundaries when a composite surface of complex shape is to be constructed because a point of the surface is passing through all points of the surface which will produce wiggles or kinks or oscillations. If the degrees of the surface patch are increased the resulting surface tends to show unwanted oscillations.

7.4 FERGUSON SURFACE PATCH MODEL

The bicubic polynomial patch $\vec{r}\,(u,\ v)$ of equation 7.8(*a*) can be interpolated in other way also as shown in Fig. 7.8. Inspite of defining surface patch by 16 position vectors, surface patch can be defined by 4 position vectors, 8 tangent vectors and 4 twist vectors. The first four constraints are provided by corner points as follows:

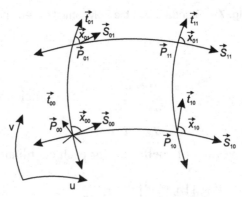

Fig. 7.8 Furguson Surface patch.

$\vec{p}_{ij}$ = position vectors at corners for $i, j = 0, 1$

$$\vec{P}_{00} = (x_{00}\ y_{00}\ z_{00}) \qquad ...(7.9a)$$
$$\vec{P}_{10} = (x_{10}\ y_{10}\ z_{10})$$
$$\vec{P}_{01} = (x_{01}\ y_{01}\ z_{01})$$
$$\vec{P}_{11} = (x_{11}\ y_{11}\ z_{11})$$

Other twelve constrains (8 tangents vectors + 4 twist vectors) can be defined by corner conditions as shown in Fig. 7.8 are given as

$\vec{s}_{ij}$ = u-direction tangent vector at P_{ij}

$$\vec{s}_{00} \qquad ...(7.9b)$$
$$\vec{s}_{10}$$
$$\vec{s}_{01}$$
$$\vec{s}_{11}$$

$\vec{t}_{ij}$ = v-direction tangent vector at P_{ij}

$$\vec{t}_{00} \qquad ...(7.9c)$$
$$\vec{t}_{10}$$
$$\vec{t}_{01}$$
$$\vec{t}_{11}$$

$\vec{x}_{ij}$ = twist vector at P_{ij}

$$\vec{x}_{00} \qquad ...(7.9d)$$
$$\vec{x}_{10}$$
$$\vec{x}_{01}$$
$$\vec{x}_{11}$$

where $\qquad \vec{t}_{ij} = \dfrac{\partial \vec{r}(u,v)}{\partial u}$ and $\vec{s}_{ij} = \dfrac{\partial \vec{r}(u,v)}{\partial v}$

$$\vec{x}_{ij} = \frac{\partial^2 r(u,v)}{\partial u\ \partial v} \qquad ...(7.10)$$

Then $\vec{t}$ and $\vec{s}$ are called tangent vectors and $\vec{x}$ is called twist vector.

$\therefore$ from eqn. 7.8(a) and 7.9(a)

$$\overline{P_{00}} = \vec{r}(0,0) = \vec{d}_{00} \qquad ...(7.11)$$
$$\overline{P_{01}} = \vec{r}(0,1) = \vec{d}_{01} \qquad ...(7.12)$$
$$\overline{P_{10}} = \vec{r}(1,0) = \vec{d}_{10} \qquad ...(7.13)$$
$$\overline{P_{11}} = \vec{r}(1,1) = \vec{d}_{11} \qquad ...(7.14)$$

From (7.8a) and (7.9c)

$$\vec{t}_{00} = \frac{\partial \vec{r}(u,v)}{\partial v} = \frac{\partial \vec{r}(0,0)}{\partial v} \qquad ...(7.15)$$
$$\vec{t}_{10} = \frac{\partial \vec{r}(u,v)}{\partial v} = \frac{\partial \vec{r}(1,0)}{dv} \qquad ...(7.16)$$

$$\vec{t_{01}} = \frac{\partial \vec{r}(u,v)}{\partial v} = \frac{\partial \vec{r}(0,1)}{dv} \qquad \text{...(7.17)}$$

$$\vec{t_{11}} = \frac{\partial \vec{r}(u,v)}{\partial v} = \frac{\partial \vec{r}(1,1)}{dv} \qquad \text{...(7.18)}$$

From (7.8a) and (7.9b)

$$\vec{s_{00}} = \frac{\partial \vec{r}(u,v)}{\partial v} = \frac{\partial \vec{r}(0,0)}{du} \qquad \text{...(7.19)}$$

$$\vec{s_{10}} = \frac{\partial \vec{r}(u,v)}{\partial v} = \frac{\partial \vec{r}(1,0)}{du} \qquad \text{...(7.10)}$$

$$\vec{s_{01}} = \frac{\partial \vec{r}(u,v)}{\partial v} = \frac{\partial \vec{r}(0,1)}{du} \qquad \text{...(7.11)}$$

$$\vec{s_{11}} = \frac{\partial \vec{r}(u,v)}{\partial v} = \frac{\partial \vec{r}(1,1)}{du} \qquad \text{...(7.12)}$$

From (7.8a) and (7.9d)

$$\vec{x_{00}} = \frac{\partial^2 \vec{r}(u,v)}{\partial v \partial v} = \frac{\partial^2 \vec{r}(0,0)}{\partial u \partial v} \qquad \text{...(7.13)}$$

$$\vec{x_{10}} = \frac{\partial^2 \vec{r}(u,v)}{\partial v \partial v} = \frac{\partial^2 \vec{r}(1,0)}{\partial u \partial v} \qquad \text{...(7.14)}$$

$$\vec{x_{01}} = \frac{\partial^2 \vec{r}(u,v)}{\partial v \partial v} = \frac{\partial^2 \vec{r}(0,1)}{\partial u \partial v} \qquad \text{...(7.15)}$$

$$\vec{x_{11}} = \frac{\partial^2 \vec{r}(u,v)}{\partial v \partial v} = \frac{\partial^2 \vec{r}(1,1)}{\partial u \partial v} \qquad \text{...(7.16)}$$

After solving the above 16 linear equations (from 7.11 to 7.16) for the unknown co-efficient $\vec{d_{ij}}$ (after finding $\vec{d_{ij}}$ in terms of $\vec{P_{ij}}$, $\vec{s_{ij}}$, $\vec{t_{ij}}$, $\vec{x_{ij}}$), the bicubic polynomial surface equation (7.8a) will be converted into Ferguson patch equation in geometric form.

$$\vec{r}(u,v) = U D V^T \qquad \text{...(7.17)}$$

$$= U C Q C^T V^T : 0 \le u, v \le 1 \qquad \text{...(7.18)}$$

where $U = [1\ u\ u^2\ u^3]$,

$V = [1\ v\ v^2\ v^3]$, $D = CQC^T$

$$C = \begin{bmatrix} 1 & 0 & 0 & 0 \\ 0 & 0 & 1 & 0 \\ -3 & 3 & -2 & -1 \\ 2 & -2 & 1 & 1 \end{bmatrix}$$

Ferguson co-efficient matrix of geometric co-efficient

$$Q = \begin{bmatrix} \overrightarrow{P_{00}} & \overrightarrow{P_{01}} & \overrightarrow{t_{00}} & \overrightarrow{t_{01}} \\ \overrightarrow{P_{10}} & \overrightarrow{P_{11}} & \overrightarrow{t_{10}} & \overrightarrow{t_{11}} \\ \overrightarrow{S_{00}} & \overrightarrow{S_{01}} & \overrightarrow{x_{00}} & \overrightarrow{x_{01}} \\ \overrightarrow{S_{10}} & \overrightarrow{S_{11}} & \overrightarrow{x_{10}} & \overrightarrow{x_{11}} \end{bmatrix} : \text{Corner conditions}$$

Equation (7.18) represents Furguson patch equation.

7.5 BEZIER SURFACE PATCH MODEL

Since standard Bezier cubic curve as discussed in preview chapter is represented as

$$\vec{r}(u) = (1-u)^3 \overrightarrow{V_0} + 3u(1-u)^2 \overrightarrow{V_1} + 3u^2(1-u)\overrightarrow{V_2} + u^3 \overrightarrow{V_3}$$

$$\vec{r}(u) = \begin{bmatrix} 1 & u & u^2 & u^3 \end{bmatrix} \begin{bmatrix} 1 & 0 & 0 & 0 \\ -3 & 3 & 0 & 0 \\ 3 & -6 & 3 & 0 \\ -1 & 3 & -3 & 1 \end{bmatrix} \begin{bmatrix} \overrightarrow{V_0} \\ \overrightarrow{V_1} \\ \overrightarrow{V_2} \\ \overrightarrow{V_3} \end{bmatrix}$$

$$= \sum_{i=0}^{3} B_i^3.(u).\overrightarrow{V_i} \qquad ...(7.19)$$

where $B_i^3.(u)$ is called cubic Bernstien function (also called Bezier power basis function), similarly for order n,

$$B_i^n.(u) = \frac{n1}{(n-1)!i!} u^i (1-u)^{n-i} \text{ is called polynomial Bernsteing}$$
function then,

$$\vec{r}^n(u_i) = \sum_{i=0}^{n} B_i^n.(u).\overrightarrow{V_i}$$

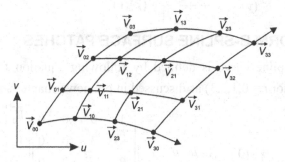

Fig. 7.9 Bicubic Bezier patch.

A bicubic Bezier patch (Fig 7.9) is defined here as a tensor product surface (*i.e.*, products of univariate basis function) of Bazier curves (Eq. 7.19) which is mathematically represented as

$$\vec{r}(u, v) = \sum_{i=0}^{3}\sum_{j=0}^{3} B_i^3(u) B_j^3(v).\overrightarrow{V_{ij}}$$

$$= \sum_{i=0}^{3}\sum_{j=0}^{3} \frac{3!}{(3-i)!i!} u^i (1-u)^{3-i} \times \frac{3!}{(3-j)!j!} v^i (1-v)^{3-j} .\overrightarrow{V_{ij}}$$

Putting all the values, we get

$$\vec{r}(u, v) = U M B M^T V^T \qquad \qquad ...(7.20)$$

Equation (7.20) is called bicubic Bezier patch equation where patch is shown in Fig. 7.9.

where $U = [1 \ u \ u^2 \ u^3]; V = [1 \ v \ v^2 \ v^3]$

$$M = \begin{bmatrix} 1 & 0 & 0 & 0 \\ -3 & 3 & 0 & 0 \\ 3 & -6 & 3 & 0 \\ -1 & 3 & -3 & 1 \end{bmatrix}; B = \begin{bmatrix} \overrightarrow{V_{00}} & \overrightarrow{V_{01}} & \overrightarrow{V_{02}} & \overrightarrow{V_{03}} \\ \overrightarrow{V_{10}} & \overrightarrow{V_{11}} & \overrightarrow{V_{12}} & \overrightarrow{V_{13}} \\ \overrightarrow{V_{20}} & \overrightarrow{V_{21}} & \overrightarrow{V_{22}} & \overrightarrow{V_{23}} \\ \overrightarrow{V_{30}} & \overrightarrow{V_{31}} & \overrightarrow{V_{32}} & \overrightarrow{V_{33}} \end{bmatrix}$$

Here, the matrix M is called a cubic Bezier co-efficient matrix and B is called a control point matrix.

Similar, to Bezier curves, the bicubic Bezier patch model can be generalized to a degrees m, n as given below.

$$\vec{r}(u, v) = \sum_{i=0}^{m}\sum_{j=0}^{n} B_1^m(u) B_j^n(v) \vec{V}_{ij} \qquad \qquad ...(7.21)$$

where $B_i^m(u) = \dfrac{m!}{(m-i)|i|} u^i (1-u)^{m-i}$,

$B_j^n(v) = \dfrac{n!}{(n-i)|i|} v^i (1-v)^{n-i}$

7.6 UNIFORM B-SPLINE SURFACE PATCHES

Uniform *B*-spline curve is defined by following equation for four control vertices $\overrightarrow{V_{ij}}$ (for $i = 0,1,2,3$) as discussed in previews chapter/section.

$$\vec{r}(u) = [1 \ u \ u^2 \ u^3] \begin{bmatrix} 1 & 0 & 0 & 0 \\ -3 & 3 & 0 & 0 \\ 3 & -6 & 3 & 0 \\ -1 & 3 & -3 & 1 \end{bmatrix} \begin{bmatrix} \overrightarrow{V_0} \\ \overrightarrow{V_1} \\ \overrightarrow{V_2} \\ \overrightarrow{V_3} \end{bmatrix} \qquad ...(7.22)$$

Similar, to Bezier patch, a bicubic B-spline patch is defined as a tensor product surface of the uniform cubic B-spline curves equation (7.22). Then by using curve equation 7.22, we can express uniform B-spline surface patch mathematically as given below:

$$\vec{r}\ (u, v) = \sum_{i=0}^{3} \sum_{i=1}^{3} N_i^3(u) N_j^3(u) \vec{V}_{ij}$$

$$\vec{r}\ (u, v) = U N \vec{B} N^T V^T \text{ with } 0 \le u \le 1 \qquad \qquad ...(7.23)$$

where $U = [1\ u\ u^2\ u^3]$,

$$V = [1\ v\ v^2\ v^3],$$

$$B = \begin{bmatrix} \vec{V}_{00} & \vec{V}_{01} & \vec{V}_{02} & \vec{V}_{03} \\ \vec{V}_{10} & \vec{V}_{11} & \vec{V}_{12} & \vec{V}_{13} \\ \vec{V}_{20} & \vec{V}_{21} & \vec{V}_{22} & \vec{V}_{23} \\ \vec{V}_{30} & \vec{V}_{31} & \vec{V}_{32} & \vec{V}_{33} \end{bmatrix}$$

$$N = \frac{1}{6} \begin{bmatrix} 1 & 4 & 1 & 1 \\ -3 & 0 & 3 & 0 \\ 3 & -6 & 3 & 0 \\ -1 & 3 & -3 & 1 \end{bmatrix}$$

Here, $N_0^3(u) = \dfrac{(1 - 3u + 3u^2 - u^3)}{6}$

$$N_1^3(u) = \frac{(4 - 6u^2 + 3u^3)}{6}$$

$$N_2^3(u) = \frac{(1 + 3u + 3u^2 - 3u^3)}{6}$$

$$N_3^3(u) = \frac{1}{6} u^3$$

Above equation (7.23) is called bicubic uniform B-spline surface patch equation.

There are also several types of surface patches such as (1) NURB patches and (2) Triangular Bezier patches. They are usually more flexible and smooth and hence commonly used in commercial CAD/CAM software. At some places for shape of dome, triangular Bezier patches are useful.

7.7 NON-UNIFORM B-SPLINE SURFACE PATCHES MODEL (NUB patches)

Similar, to B-spline surface patch, A NUB (Non-uniform B-spline) surface is also defined as a tensor product surfaces of NUB curves given in section 7.6. Here we limit our discussion with biquadratic NUB surface due long equations in cubic NUB curves as expressed in equations (5.41 to 5.44c) in chapter 5. Quadratic curve is sufficient to generate smooth surface for understanding of beginners. For example with knot span vectors $\{\nabla_i\}$ and $\{\nabla_j\}$, a biquaratic NUB surface patch can be constructed by quadratic NUB curve model as given below:

$$\vec{r}\ (u,\ v) = \ \overrightarrow{U\ N_s}\ \overrightarrow{B N_t^T}\ \overrightarrow{V^T} \qquad\qquad ...(7.24)$$

Where,

$$U = [1 \quad u \quad u^2]$$

$$V = [1 \quad v \quad v^2]$$

$$\vec{B} = \begin{bmatrix} \overrightarrow{V_{00}} & \overrightarrow{V_{01}} & \overrightarrow{V_{02}} \\ \overrightarrow{V_{10}} & \overrightarrow{V_{11}} & \overrightarrow{V_{12}} \\ \overrightarrow{V_{20}} & \overrightarrow{V_{22}} & \overrightarrow{V_{23}} \end{bmatrix} : \text{control vertices,}$$

$$N_S = \begin{bmatrix} (\nabla_i/\nabla_{i-2}^2) & (\nabla_i/\nabla_{i-1}^2) & 0 \\ (-2\nabla_i/\nabla_{i-1}^2) & (-2\nabla_i/\nabla_{i-1}^2) & 0 \\ (\nabla_i/\nabla_{i-1}^2) & \dfrac{\nabla_i}{\nabla_{i-1}}\left\{\dfrac{\nabla_i}{\nabla_{i-1}^2}-\dfrac{\nabla_{i-1}^3}{\nabla_i^2}\right\} & \dfrac{\nabla_i}{\nabla_i^2} \end{bmatrix}$$

$$N_t = \begin{bmatrix} (\nabla_j/\nabla_{j-1}^2) & (\nabla_j/\nabla_{j-1}^2) & 0 \\ (-2\nabla_j/\nabla_{j-1}^2) & (-2\nabla_j/\nabla_{j-1}^2) & 0 \\ (\nabla_j/\nabla_{j-1}^2) & \dfrac{\nabla_j}{\nabla_{j-1}}\left\{\dfrac{\nabla_j}{\nabla_{j-1}^2}-\dfrac{\nabla_{j-1}^3}{\nabla_j^2}\right\} & \dfrac{\nabla_j}{\nabla_j^2} \end{bmatrix}$$

$\{\nabla_i\}$: u-direction knot spans,

$\{\nabla_j\}$: v-direction knot spans.

7.8 TRIANGULAR BEZIER PATCHES

This is generated by blending methods. Blending surfaces made by blending method is a surface that connects two non-adjacent surfaces or patches. The blending surface is usually created to manifest C^0 and C^1 continuity with the two given patches. Here, triangular polynomial patch model is called a triangular Bezier patch which can be expressed in terms of control vertices and bivariate polynomials. Let us first define triangular Bezier patch by use of barycentric concepts.

Let $\vec{P_0}$, $\vec{P_1}$ and $\vec{P_2}$ be four co-planar points as shown in Fig 7.10 such that

$$\vec{P} = u\vec{P_0} + v\vec{P_1} + u\vec{P_2} \text{ with } u+v+w = 1, 0 < u, v, w < 1 \quad \ldots(7.25)$$

Then u, v, w becomes barycentric co-ordinates with respect to $\vec{P_0}$, $\vec{P_1}$ and $\vec{P_2}$. In this case the barycentric co-ordinates corresponds to area rates. If all the co-ordinates are positive, the point $\vec{P}$ is located inside the triangle formed by three vertices $\vec{P_0}$, $\vec{P_1}$ and $\vec{P_2}$ is shown in Fig. 7.10, the big triangle is decomposed into three sub triangles by a point $\vec{P}$ and area ratios of the sub triangles are denoted by u, v and w as shown in Fig 7.10.

Let us now define bivariate Bernstein polynomial in terms of the barycentric co-ordinates (u, v, w) then

$$B_i^n.(u) = \frac{n!}{i!j!k!} u^i v^j w^k \text{ for } 0 \leq i, j, k \leq n, \quad \ldots(7.27)$$

where $\qquad u = (u, v, w)$

and $\qquad i = (i, j, k)$ with $|i| = i + j + k = n$

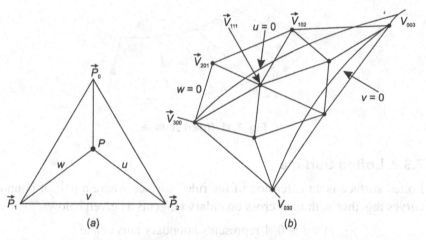

Fig. 7.10 Triangular cubic Bezier patch.

Then, with the 10 control vertices $\{\vec{V}_{ijk}\}$ as shown in Fig. 7.10(b) cubic ($n = 3$) triangular Bezier patch is defined as follows :

$$\vec{r}(u) = \Sigma_{|i|=3} \, \vec{V_i} \, B_i^3(u) \quad \ldots 7.28$$

Where, $\qquad i = (i, j, k)$

$\qquad u = (u, v, w),$

$\qquad \vec{V_i}$ = Bezier control points,

$\qquad B_i^3(u)$ = bivariate cubic bersnstein polynomial.

7.9 CURVED BOUNDARY INTERPOLATING SURFACE PATCHES

This type of surface can be made both by analytic and synthetic method. The well defined analytic surface patch are cone, parabola, cylinder, hyperbola, ellipse etc., on which students are assumed to be familier. This surfaces are frequency used as primitives in CAD/CAM. Some of the synthetic surface patches are ruled, lofted, and sweep surface etc., are discussed here.

7.9.1 Ruled Surface

Ruled surface is linear blending of the two parametric curves $\vec{r}_0(u)$ and $\vec{r}_1(u)$ with $0 \le u \le 1$, as shown in Fig. 7.11. Equation of ruled surface is given below

$$\vec{r}\ (u, v) = (1 - v)\ \vec{r}_0(u) + v\vec{r}_1(u) : 0 \le u, v \le 1, \qquad ...(7.29a)$$

This is the simplest possible ruled surface that can be defined from boundary curves and widely used in engineering products such as the transition surface in CRT monitors (the surface between the CRT screen and the front face of the monitor) and a wing of an airplane.

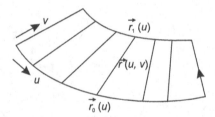

Fig. 7.11 Ruled surface.

7.9.2 Lofted Surface

Lofted surface is an extension of the ruled surface where a pair of boundary curves together with their cross boundary tangents as given below:

$\vec{r}_i(u)$ for $i = 0, 1$ represents boundary curves and

$\vec{t}_i(u)$ for $i = 0, 1$ represents cross-boundary tangents.

The situation is exactly the same as the Fergusson curve generation with the difference that this time we have vector valued functions (instead of vectors). Thus a lofted surface is constructed by blending the input data with cubic *Hermite blending function* $H_i^3(v)$:

$$\vec{r}\ (u, v) = H_0^3(v)\ \vec{r}_0(u) + H_1^3(v)\ \vec{t}_0(u) + H_2^3(v)\ \vec{t}_1(u) + H_0^3(v)\ \vec{r}_1(u)$$

$$...7.29(b)$$

where, $H_0^3(v) = (1 - 3v^2 + 2v^3)$

$$H_1^3(v) = (v - 2v^2 + v^{3,}),$$

$$H_2^3(v) = (-v^2 + v^{3,}),$$

$$H_3^3(v) = (3v^2 + 2v^{3,}),$$

Above surface patch is sometimes also called a cubic hermite Lofted surface.

There are also useful patches used in CAD/CAM such as Coons surface patches, sweep surface patches (translation and rotational which are used for generation of solid).

7.10 SURFACE FITTING

Surfaces are the most important elements for constructing complex, free formed and sculptured objects. There are various methods available for constructing composite surfaces (surface fitting) but surface models discussed in previous sections of this chapter are only used for constructing larger/ composite surfaces. One way for construction composite curve is shown in Fig 7.12.

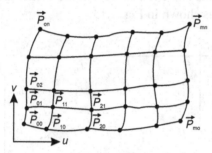

Fig. 7.12 Input data points $(\vec{P}_{ij})$ so be interpolated
for constructing composite surface.

In Fig. 7.12, there are an array of 3D data points $(\vec{P}_{ij}$ where $i = 0, 1,$ ..., m, and $j = 0,1, 2, ...n)$ connected to form a composite surface. If the input data are regularly arranged, rectangular interpolants are employed. If we have a set of scattered data points, they are first triangulated to obtain a triangular grid and the triangular interpolants are constructed. One way of fitting the data points in Fig. 7.12 is to use the standard polynomial models of the surface given in equation (7.8a) which are reproduced below for degree m and n in place of degree 3 and 3 i.e., bicubic

$$\vec{r}(u, v) = \sum_{i=0}^{n}\sum_{j=0}^{n} \vec{d}_{ij}\, u^i v^j \qquad\qquad ...(7.30)$$

for $\vec{P}_{ij} : i = 0, 1, ... m$ and $j = 0, 1, ... n$

Where $\vec{r}$ (u, v) is the equation of parametric surface for parameter u and v associated with the indices i and j of the input data points as shown in Fig. 7.12 and $\vec{d}_{ij}$ are vector co-efficients. However the resulting surface using equation (7.30) may process undesirable properties when the degree m and n becomes too large. Therefore, there is need to use a low degree (generally cubic) polynomial patch model to form a composite surfaces. For this, we can use Ferguson patch model (Eqn. 7.18), Bezier patch model (Eqn. 7.20) and uniform B-spline surface patch model (Eqn. 7.24). By using these models, a composite surface can be constructed by satisfying the geometric and continuity boundary conditions at the patch boundaries. The surface fitting methods to be discussed in this chapter are given below.

1. The FMILL method.

2. Composite Ferguson fitting method.

3. Uniform B-spline fitting method.

4. Non-uniform B-spline fitting methods.

In all the four methods, it is necessary to know the boundary tangent at the boundary mesh points and twist vectors at the corner mesh points in addition to the mesh points as shown in Fig. 7.13.

$\vec{x}_{00}$	$\vec{s}_{00}$	$\vec{s}_{01}$	$\vec{s}_{02}$	$\cdots$	$\vec{s}_{0j}$	$\cdots$	$\vec{s}_{0n}$	$\vec{x}_{0n}$
$\vec{t}_{00}$	$\vec{P}_{00}$	$\vec{P}_{01}$	$\vec{P}_{02}$	$\cdots$	$\vec{P}_{0j}$	$\cdots$	$\vec{P}_{0n}$	$\vec{t}_{0n}$
$\vec{t}_{10}$	$\vec{P}_{10}$	$\vec{P}_{11}$	$\vec{P}_{10}$	$\cdots$	$\vec{P}_{1j}$	$\cdots$	$\vec{P}_{1n}$	$\vec{t}_{1n}$
$\vdots$	$\vdots$	$\vdots$	$\vdots$	$\cdots$	$\vdots$	$\cdots$	$\vdots$	$\vdots$
$\vec{t}_{i0}$	$\vec{P}_{i0}$	$\vec{P}_{i1}$	$\vec{P}_{i2}$	$\cdots$	$\vec{P}_{ij}$	$\cdots$	$\vec{P}_{in}$	$\vec{t}_{in}$
$\vdots$	$\vdots$							
$\vec{t}_{m0}$	$\vec{P}_{m0}$	$\vec{P}_{m1}$	$\vec{P}_{m2}$	$\cdots$	$\vec{P}_{mj}$	$\cdots$	$\vec{P}_{mn}$	$\vec{t}_{mn}$
$\vec{x}_{m0}$	$\vec{s}_{m0}$	$\vec{s}_{m1}$	$\vec{s}_{m2}$	$\cdots$	$\vec{s}_{mj}$	$\cdots$	$\vec{s}_{mn}$	$\vec{x}_{mn}$

Fig. 7.13 Input data for composite surface construction.

For construction composite surfaces, following boundary data are discussed to be given.

1. $\vec{s}_{oj}, \vec{s}_{mj}$: u-direction corresponding tangents at boundary mesh points.

2. $\vec{t}_{io}, \vec{t}_{in}$: v-direction cross boundary tangents at boundary mesh points.

3. $\vec{x}_{oo}, \vec{x}_{mo}, \vec{x}_{on}$ $\vec{x}_{mn}$: twist vectors at corner mesh points.

The FMILL, Ferguson and uniform B-spline surface fitting method are applicable only to evenly spaced data points because they tend to produce surfaces having local flatness or bulges for unevenly spaced data points.

The Δ non-uniform B-spline (NUB) surface fitting method can be used for data array whose physical spacings are semi-even, meaning that rows and columns of input data are parallel but uneven with each other.

When physical spacing is completely uneven, the first order geometric Bezier method (G^1 Bezier method) can be used in order to obtain a smooth surface which is free from local flatness or bulges.

7.10.1 FMILL surface fitting

In FMILL surface fitting method, cubic Ferguson surface patch (shown in Fig. 7.14) is used as a basis equation as given below (refer equation 7.18).

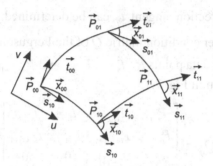

Fig. 7.14 Ferguson surface patch.

$$\vec{r}\ (u, v) = UCQ\ C^T\ V^T \qquad \qquad ...(7.31)$$

$$U = [1 \quad u \quad u^2 \quad u^3]$$

$$V = [1 \quad v \quad v^2 \quad v^3]$$

$$C = \begin{bmatrix} 1 & 0 & 0 & 0 \\ 0 & 0 & 1 & 0 \\ -3 & 3 & -2 & -1 \\ 2 & -2 & 1 & 1 \end{bmatrix} \qquad \begin{array}{l} \text{called Ferguson} \\ \text{co-efficient metric} \end{array}$$

and $\quad Q = \begin{bmatrix} \vec{P}_{00} & \vec{P}_{01} & \vec{t}_{00} & \vec{t}_{10} \\ \vec{P}_{10} & \vec{P}_{11} & \vec{t}_{10} & \vec{t}_{11} \\ \vec{s}_{00} & \vec{s}_{01} & \vec{x}_{00} & \vec{x}_{01} \\ \vec{s}_{10} & \vec{s}_{11} & \vec{x}_{10} & \vec{x}_{11} \end{bmatrix} \qquad$ called corner condition

Ferguson surface 7.31, it is clear that the Ferguson surface path is completely specified by position vectors ($\vec{P}_{ij}$), tangent vectors ($\vec{s}_{ij}$ and $\vec{t}_{ij}$: tangent vectors in u and v direction respectively) and twist vectors $\vec{x}_{ij}$ at the four corner points. In the FMILL method, [which is a surface fitting routine in the APT system (Automatic Programming tool) is a high level computer programming language used to generate instruction for Numerically controlled machine tools (CNC)], the twist vectors $\vec{x}_{ij}$ at the array of data points are set to zero (in other words, twist vectors are assumed to zero). Then the u-direction tangents $\vec{s}_{ij}$ are evaluated from the following equation:

$$\vec{s}_{ij} = c_i \frac{(\vec{P}_{j+1, j} - \vec{P}_{i-1, j})}{|(\vec{P}_{j+1, j} - \vec{P}_{i-1, j})|} \qquad \qquad ...(7.32)$$

for $\qquad\qquad i = 1, 2, ..., (m-1)$ and $j = 0, 1, ..., n$

where $\qquad\qquad c_i = \min \{| \vec{P}_{i, j} - \vec{P}_{i-1, j} |, | \vec{P}_{i+1, j} - \vec{P}_{i, j} |\}$

Similarly, v-direction tangent $\vec{t}_{ij}$ can be determined.

Then, the corner condition matric Q of the Ferguson patch (7.31) in terms of i, j, over the four data points $\vec{P}_{ij}$, $\vec{P}_{i+1, j}$, $\vec{P}_{i, j+1}$ and $\vec{P}_{i+1, j+1}$ is given by following equation and shown in Fig. 7.15.

$$Q_{ij} = \begin{bmatrix} \vec{P}_{i, j} & \vec{P}_{i, j+1} & \vec{t}_{i, j} & \vec{t}_{i, j+1} \\ \vec{P}_{i+1, j} & \vec{P}_{i+1, j+1} & \vec{t}_{i+1, j} & \vec{t}_{i+1, j+1} \\ \vec{s}_{i, j} & \vec{s}_{i+ j+1} & 0 & 0 \\ \vec{s}_{i+1, j} & \vec{s}_{i+1, j+1} & 0 & 0 \end{bmatrix} \qquad ...(7.33)$$

If the corner condition matrix Q_{ij} is fixed, the rectangular region will be represented as a Ferguson patch. In this way, a FMILL composite surface composed of $m \times n$ Ferguson patches is obtained.

FMILL surface fitting method is very easy to implement for composite surface construction and the resulting surface will be visually smooth. Composite surface generated by FMILL fitting method will be aesthetically smooth as long as the date points are evenly spaced. But it may produce undesirable surface normal at mesh points due to the assumption of zero twist vectors.

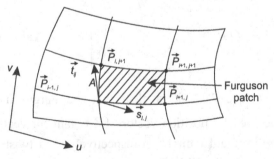

Fig 7.15 A Ferguson patch in the mesh of data points.

7.10.2 Composite Ferguson Surface Fitting

In this method, as per Faux and Pratt (1980), if we remove the assumption of "zero twist vector" from the FMILL method, then the *twist vectors* $\vec{x}_{ij}$ at mesh points have to be determined. One way of determining twist vectors $\vec{x}_{ij}$ is to impose the *parametric C^2-condition* across patch boundaries.

Consider three Ferguson patches, $\vec{r}^1(u, v)$, $\vec{r}^2(u, v)$, $\vec{r}^3(u, v)$, sharing the mesh point $\vec{t}_{ij}$ as shown in Fig. 7.16. As discussed in previous section, Ferguson patch $\vec{r}^1(u, v)_0$ can be expressed as given below:

$$r^1(u, v) = U C Q^1 C^T V^T : 0 \le u, v \le 1 \qquad\qquad 7.34$$

where
$$C = \begin{bmatrix} 1 & 0 & 0 & 0 \\ 0 & 0 & 1 & 0 \\ -3 & 3 & -2 & -1 \\ 2 & -2 & 1 & 1 \end{bmatrix}$$

$$Q^1 = \begin{bmatrix} \vec{P}_{i-1, j-1} & \vec{P}_{i-1, j} & \vec{t}_{i-1, j-1} & \vec{t}_{i-1, j} \\ \vec{P}_{i, i-1} & \vec{P}_{i, j} & \vec{t}_{i, i-1} & \vec{t}_{i, j} \\ \vec{s}_{i-1, j-1} & \vec{s}_{i-1, j} & \vec{x}_{i-1, j-1} & \vec{x}_{i-1, j} \\ \vec{s}_{i, j-1} & \vec{s}_{i, j} & \vec{x}_{i, j-1} & \vec{x}_{i, j} \end{bmatrix}$$

where parametric c^2 – condition are:

$$\vec{r}^a(1) = \vec{P}_1 = \vec{r}^b(0) \qquad\qquad ...(a)$$

$$\vec{r}^1(u, v) = \vec{t}_i = \vec{r}^b(0) \qquad\qquad ...(b)$$

$$\vec{r}^1(u, v) = \vec{r}^b(0) \qquad\qquad ...(c)$$

An application of the C^2-condition at the common boundary of $\vec{r}^1(u, v)$ and $\vec{r}^2(u, v)$ and that of $\vec{r}^1(u, v)$ and $\vec{r}^3(u, v)$ would give

$$\vec{r}^1(1, v) = \vec{r}^2(0, v) \qquad\qquad ...(7.35a)$$

$$\vec{r}^1(u, 1) = \vec{r}^2(u, 0) \qquad\qquad ...(7.35b)$$

Since, the u-direction second derivative of the Ferguson patch equation is expressed as

$$\ddot{\vec{r}}(u, v) = U C Q C^T V^T$$

$$= [0\ 0\ 2\ 6]\, C Q C^T V^T,$$

and the right-hand side of (7.35a) is evaluated as

$$\ddot{r}^2(1, v) = [0\ 0\ 2\ 6]\ C\ Q^1\ C^T\ V^T$$

$$= [6\ -6\ 2\ 4]\ Q^1\ C^T\ V^T$$

and the right-hand side would become

$$\ddot{r}^2(0, v) = [0\ 0\ 2\ 0]\ C\ Q^2\ C^T\ V^T$$

$$= [-6\ 6\ -4\ -2]\ Q^2\ C^T\ V^T$$

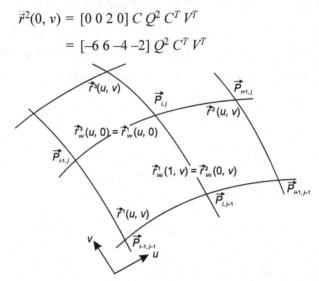

Fig. 7.16 C^2-Conditions among Ferguson Patches.

Thus, the u-direction C^2-condition (7.35a) is rewriting as follow :

$$[6\ -6\ 2\ 4]\ Q^1 = [-6\ 6\ -4\ -2]\ Q^2 \qquad ...(7.35(c)$$

where,

$$Q^1 = \begin{bmatrix} \vec{P}_{i-1,\,j-1} & \vec{P}_{i-1,\,j} & \vec{t}_{i-1,\,j-1} & \vec{t}_{i-1,\,j} \\ \vec{P}_{i,\,i-1} & \vec{P}_{i,\,j} & \vec{t}_{i,\,j-1} & \vec{t}_{i,\,j} \\ \vec{s}_{i-1,\,j-1} & \vec{s}_{i-1,\,j} & \vec{x}_{i-1,\,j-1} & \vec{x}_{i-1,\,j} \\ \vec{s}_{i,\,j-1} & \vec{s}_{i,\,j} & \vec{x}_{i,\,j-1} & \vec{x}_{i,\,j} \end{bmatrix}$$

$$Q^2 = \begin{bmatrix} \vec{P}_{i,\,j-1} & \vec{P}_{i,\,j} & \vec{t}_{i,\,j-1} & \vec{t}_{i,\,j} \\ \vec{P}_{i+1,\,j-1} & \vec{P}_{i+1,\,j} & \vec{t}_{i+1,\,j-1} & \vec{t}_{i+1,\,j} \\ \vec{s}_{i,\,j-1} & \vec{s}_{i,\,j} & \vec{x}_{i,\,j-1} & \vec{x}_{i,\,j} \\ \vec{s}_{i+1,\,j-1} & \vec{s}_{i+1,\,j} & \vec{x}_{i+1,\,j-1} & \vec{x}_{i+1,\,j} \end{bmatrix}$$

It is noted that the relation (7.35c) gives four linear (vector) equations, one from each column of the Q-matrix. The 2nd equation in (7.35c) is rearranged as (*for i* = 1, ..., *m* – 1)

$$\vec{s}_{i-1,\,j} + 4\vec{s}_{i,\,j} + \vec{s}_{i+1,\,j} = 3(\vec{P}_{i+1,\,j} - \vec{P}_{i-1,\,j}) \qquad ...(7.36a)$$

and the last equation in (7.35) is expressed as (for $i = 1, ..., m-1$)

$$\vec{x}_{i-1,j} + 4\vec{x}_{i,j} + \vec{x}_{i+1,j} = 3(\vec{t}_{i+1,j} - \vec{t}_{i-1,j}) \qquad ...(7.36b)$$

Similarly, the u-direction C^2-condition (7.35b) would produce for $j = 1, 2,$ .... $n-1$.

$$\vec{t}_{i,j-1} + 4\vec{t}_{i,j} + \vec{t}_{i,j+1} = 3(\vec{P}_{i,j+1} - \vec{P}_{i,j-1}) \qquad ...(7.37a)$$

$$\vec{x}_{i,j-1} + 4\vec{x}_{i,j} + \vec{x}_{i,j+1} = 3(\vec{s}_{i,j+1} - \vec{s}_{i,j-1}) \qquad ...(7.37b)$$

Above tangent vectors and twist vectors at the mesh points can be determined by solving the linear equation in 7.36a, 7.36b, 7.37a and 7.37b as follows :

(a) $\{\vec{s}_{ij} : j = 0, 1, ..., n\}$ are determined by solving

Eqn. (7.36a) for $i = 1, ..., m-1$ together with $\vec{s}_{oj} = \vec{s}_{oj}$, $\vec{s}_{mj} = \vec{s}_{mj}$ ...(7.38)

(b) $\{\vec{t}_{ij} : i = 0, 1, ..., m\}$ are determined by solving

Eqn. (7.37 − a) for $j = 1, ..., n-1$ together with $\vec{t}_{oj} = \vec{t}_{oji}$ $\vec{t}_{mj} = \vec{t}_{mj}$ ...(7.39)

(a) $\{\vec{x}_{ij} : j = 0 \, \& \, j = n\}$ are determined by solving

Eqn. (7.36b) for $i = 1, ..., m-1$ together with $\vec{x}_{oj} = \vec{x}_{oji}$ $\vec{x}_{mj} = \vec{x}_{mj}$ ...(7.40)

4. $\{\vec{x}_{ij} : i = 0, 1, ..., m\}$ are determined by solving

Eqn. (7.36b) for $j = 1, ..., n-1$ together with $\vec{x}_{i0} = \vec{x}_{i0i}$ $\vec{x}_{in} = \vec{x}_{in}$ ...(7.41)

After solving above linear equation system 7.38, 7.39, 7.40 and 7.41 we can get each data.

After determining all the tangent and twist vectors, the next step is to form a *corner condition matrix* Q^{ij} for each rectangular region. After putting all values, the resulting surface is a C^2 surface of $m \times n$ Ferguson patches which is called a composite Ferguson surface. The major drawback of the composite Ferguson surface is that it may not be *aesthetically smooth* when the data points are unevenly spaced (the same is true for the FMILL surface patch).

Fergusons composite surface fitting methods are widely used in automatic surface fitting from an array of 3D points, are second order continuous (C^{-2}), but they suffer from local flatness and bulges when physical spacing of data points becomes uneven.

7.10.3 Uniform and Non-Uniform B-Spline Surface Fitting

Similar to Ferguson surface fitting method, one can use geometric conditions to generate composite uniform B-spline and non uniform B-spline surfaces. After determing various geometric entities such as control vertices, knot vectors in u and v directions, knot spans, intermedial control points and boundary vectors with application of continuity and geometric condiyions at common points, one can generate equations for Uniform and non-uniform composite surfaces. The resulting surfaces will be called C^2 composite surfaces. Composite from Uniform B-spline surface fitting will be aesthetically smooth when the physical spaciny of data points is even otherwise composite surface from Non-Uniform B-spline will give better results when the physical spacing of data points is not even for application in CAD/CAM.

❏❏❏

8

Solid Modelling and Animation

8.0 SOLID MODELLING

Solid modelling is a relatively new comer. It is intended to overcome the limitations of the 2D/3D wire frame and surface modelling when representing and analyzing 3D objects. The aim of solid modelling is to create unambiguous objects and its complete geometric representation in Computer Graphics and CAD. The methods used in geometric modelling to represent object/solids in CAD system are wireframe (2D and 3D), surface and constructive solid geometric modelling. In other words, wireframe (2D and 3D), surface and constructive solid geometric modelling are three classical methods to represent solid objects.

Wireframe model is the first method to represent the solid objects. Wireframe have only vertices and their co-ordinate values and edges information but does not have face information. In wire frame modelling, complex objects with many edges become confusing. Wireframe modelling are especially well suited for drafting (which is heart of any CAD system). Wireframe models are limited use in CAD because volume and mass properties, NC tool path generation, cross sectioning and interference detections cannot calculate. Shading is time consuming and provides general feeling of the final product. For making simple object wire frame modelling is used in many industries till date for low cast and easy construction. All existing CAD/CAM system provides users with basic wireframe entities which can be divided into analytic and synthetic entities. Analytic entities are points, lines, arcs, circle, fillets and chamfers, conics (ellipses, parabolas and hyperbolas). Synthetic entities include type of Splines and Bazier curves. In previous chapter, we have seen that surface modelling is construction of surface using series of points, lines or curves. Surface/boundary representation is the extension of wireframe modelling by adding face information for solid construction. A solid is bounded by its surfaces and has its interior and exterior information. It has two types of information such as topological (relationships among vertices, edges, faces and orientations of faces and edges) and geometric information (the graphical information of dimension, length, angle, area, transformation and equations of edges and faces). Similar, to wireframe entities, existing CAD/CAM system provides engineers with both analytic and synthetic surface entities. Analytic entities include plane surface, ruled surface, surface of revolution, cylinders. Synthetic entities include spline surface, Bezier patches, coon's patches etc.

Unlike wireframe and surface modelling, uses invisible topological information like connectivity, neighbuorhoods, associatively and relationships in addition to above said geometric and visible topological information to represent the solid object unambiguously and completely. Thus, solid modelling results accurate design, helps to further the goal of CAD/CAM like CIM (Computer Aided Manufacturing) and FM (Flexible Manufacturing) leading to better automation (for tool path generation, material handling etc.) of the manufacturing process. Once the solid object is created, one can reflect, rotate, shear, shade or even section the object to show interior details using CAD/CAM software. Solid modelling software are IDEA, CATIA, Solid works, Pro-E etc. which provides mass, volume, type of materials and moment of inertia of the parts. Using software, one can accelerate their designing time, increase productivity and reduce cost of products. Solid objects can also be combined with the other object stored in the database to form a complex assembly of the objects whose design has to be carried out. Thus solid modelling using CAD/CAM software and hardware is better for product design and manufacturing such as CNC machining.

Third method used in geometric modelling to represent object/solids in CAD system is constructive solid geometric modelling (CSG). Constructive solid geometric modelling method is the solid construction technique in 3D and also called primitive Instancing. In this method, a number of 3D solids are provided as primitives. Some typical primitive are blocks, wedges, cylinders, cones, tours, pipes and so on. Using solid modelling software, solid models can be created by joining together or unioning above basic primitive shapes or by defining a shape as a polyline and extruding it into solid shapes. Solid primitives may also be subtracted from one another. For example, to create a hole in a solid box, draw a solid cylinder of suitable length and diameter, then subtract by cylinder of same length and small diameter from the box. The result will be an open volume in the shape of a hole. Thus, complex objects can create by adding/subtracting the primitive. To make a complex objects, Boolean operations like union, intersection and differences are also used. The advantage of solid modelling is that each body is represented as a single object and not as a complex collection of surfaces. As information is stored in their database, due to which there models are complete and unambiguous.

8.1 SOLID MODELLING TECHNIQUES

There are several techniques used for the construction and editing of solid objects. Some of them are analytical solid modelling technique and construction techniques. Construction techniques include Boolean operation, sweeping, automated filleting and chamfering, tweaking and fleshing out of wireframe and projection. None of above techniques seems to be adequate by them. Ideal solid model system should support all of above alongwith other existing modular. It is observed that designing representations for solid is a difficult job, however, some are given below.

8.1.1 Analytical Solid Modelling

Analytical solid modelling is an extension of the well defined tensor product method using parametric space u, v and w. Using method used in previous chapters, one can easily derive the representations of tricubic, Bezier and B-spline (Uniform as well as non-uniform) solids similar to bicubic, Bezier and B-spline surfaces in two dimensional parametric space $i.e.$, u and v and w similar to cubic Bezier and B-spline curves in one dimensional parametric space $i.e.$, u.

The tensor product formulation in 3D parametric space is a mapping of a cubical parametric domain described by u, v, w values into a solid object where parametric values are function of x, y, and z in the Cartesian space as shown in Fig. 8.1. The resulting solid is called a parametric solid or a hyperpatch because hyperpatches are extensions of and bounded by surface patches whose points in the interior or on the boundary are given by

$$\vec{r}\,(u, v, w) = [x(u, v, w) \; y\,(u, v, w)\, z(u, v, w)$$

$$\text{for } u_{min} \leq u \leq u_{max} \leq v_{min}, \; \leq \; v \leq v_{max}, \; w_{min} \leq w \leq w_{max}$$

$$\vec{r}\,(u, v, w) = \sum_{i=0}^{3} \sum_{j=0}^{3} \sum_{k=0}^{3} \vec{d}_{ijk}\, u^i v^j w^k \qquad \qquad ... \; 8.1$$

Equation 8.1 is the parametric cubic equation of solid. For generation of cube, normalized parameter can be used $i.e.$, $0 \leq u \leq 1$, $0 \leq v \leq 1$, $0 \leq w \leq 1$

There are 64 $\vec{d}_{ijk}$. vector co-efficients that must be determined by utilizing a given set of boundary conditions of a given solid/hyperpatch.

There will be 8 position vectors [one $\vec{r}$ (u, v, w) at each corner vertex], 24 tangent vectors [Three $\dfrac{\partial \vec{r}}{\partial u}, \dfrac{\partial \vec{r}}{\partial v}$ and $\dfrac{\partial \vec{r}}{\partial w}$ at each corner vertex), 24 Owist vectors $\left[\text{Three} \left(\dfrac{\partial^2 \vec{r}}{\partial u \partial v}, \dfrac{\partial^2 \vec{r}}{\partial u, \partial w} \text{ and } \dfrac{\partial^2 \vec{r}}{\partial v \partial w} \right) \right]$ at each corner vertex and 8 triple mixed partial derivatives $\left(\text{one} \dfrac{\partial^2 \vec{r}}{\partial u \, \partial v \partial w} \right)$ at each corner vertex.

However, analytical solid modelling is not adequate for manufacturing applications such as tool path generation because face surfaces of hyperpatches are not explicitly stored and are not orientable. In this case, normal to the face surfaces cannot indicate the interior or exterior of the objects.

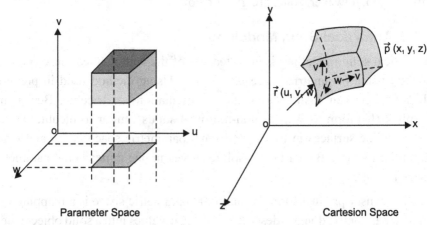

Parameter Space   Cartesion Space

Fig. 8.1 Hyperpatch representation.

8.1.2 Constructive Solid Modelling Techniques

In construction techniques, 'solid Modelling' is a method used to design objects by combining various 'solid objects or by evolving some base object, often called primitives. Primitives are simple basic shapes and are considered the solid modelling entities which can be combined by a mathematical set of Boolean operations to create the solid. Primitives themselves are considered valid "off–the-shelf" solid. Generally, solid modelers has database of primitive shapes such as a cone, torus, cylinder, sphere, and so on. Some of the primitives and instancing (a scaled/transformed replica of original primitives) are given in Fig. 8.2. These primitives could evolved into other solid objects being created and formed from swept, lofted, rotated, and extruded 2D wireframe or sketch geometry etc. For this purposes, some solid modelers have stock' library of objects for providing the designer with a similar shape to begin the design with, eliminating some of the initial tedious design work.

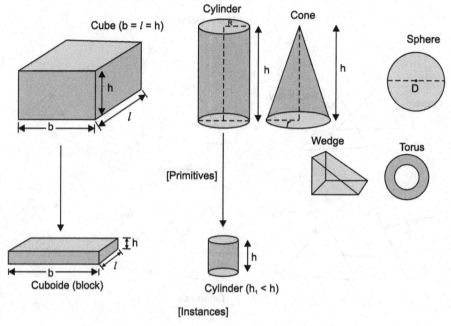

Fig. 8.2 Primitives and Instances.

8.1.2.1 Boolean Operation

Intersecting, joining, and subtracting solid objects together is called a Boolean operation. Although Boolean operation does not create new solid from scratch but create new shape of solid from other solid. When we use Boolean operation, the validity of third object is ensured. Fig. 8.3 illustrates three Boolean operations. Boolean operation do not support general union operation but allow for the joining (*i.e.*, gluing) of two objects that have disjointed interiors that meet in a common face because it required little computation. Most solid modelers keep a history list of the procedures, parameters, and geometry used to create each solid object in the order that they were created. Most solid modelers will also store the Boolean operations, and selected objects for the operation, in the same history tree. From Fig. 8.3, indicate that Boolean operations form a very natural constructive technique. Intersection and differences (*i.e.*, subtraction) operation is similar to material removal process and union operation is similar to bounding processes such as welding and gluing.

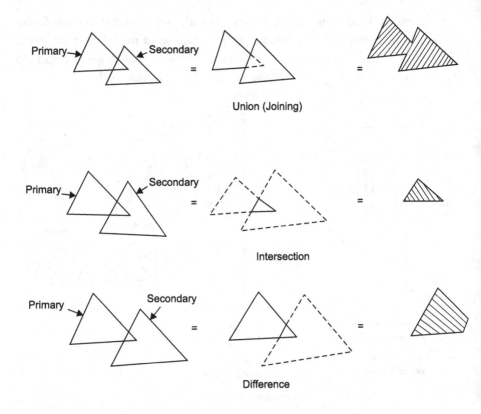

Fig. 8.3 Booleon Operation.

8.1.3 Sweeping

Sweeping is used to create a model with a contact cross-section along a non-linear axis. It is a generalization of the extrusion feature. In solid modelling, when an object (*i.e.* generator) is moved along a curve (*i.e.* a trajectory) in order to sweep out a new object is called sweep operation. [Fig. 8.4(*a*)]. shows a simple example in which a face representing a cross section is swept along a linear trajectory in order to create the new object. The generator can be curve, a face, or a solid object, whereas the trajectory can only be a curve or a strip of curves. Sweeping is a very convenient input technique for solid generation. For many objects, most of the parts can be created with just a few sweep operations. For example, intruded or projected parts can be easily modeled using sweep operations in which the trajectory is a straight line in case of generation of cylinders. Also, curved parts can be modeled using sweep operations in which the trajectory is a circle lying in a plane perpendicular to the center line. A turned part, modelled using a rotational sweep may be helical spring, wheels, sprocket etc.

8.1.4 Lofting

A loft feature is used to create a model with a variant cross-section along a linear/non-linear axis. It is a generalization is not sweep feature. It requires a set of cross-sections as shown in Fig. 8.4(*b*). A guide curve may be used to blend the cross-section.

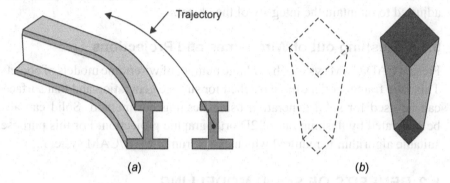

Trajectory

(a)   (b)

Fig. 8.4 (*a*) Sweeping Operation, (*b*) Lefted Surface.

8.1.4 Automated Filleting and Chamfering

A rounding of an interior or exterior corner of a designed part is called filleting and an interior or exterior corner with an angle or type of bevel, is called a chamfering. The linear edges whose vertices are trihedral can often be filleted fairly easily. For filleting, edge and fillet radius must be known. Then CAD/CAM system can create a cylindrical face with its four edges and then it automatically modifies all adjoining faces and edges as shown in Fig 8.5. Similar, function can also be performed for chamfering. The algorithms

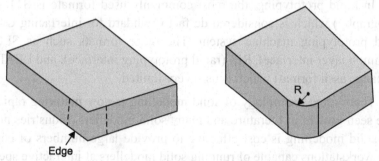

R

Edge

Fig. 8.5 Filleting Operation.

for both operations are very similar, but only planar faces should be created. In constructive solid modelling, chambering and filleting can be done using Boolean operations. Sometimes, special primitives are created to facilitate this operation using CAD/CAM software.

8.1.5 Tweaking

For small adjustments to an existing shape, Boolean operations are expensive. Therefore, there is need of simple operation which can edit the existing shape of the object. Tweaking is an editing operation in which a face of an object is moved in some way. The tweaked face and the faces adjacent to it are then adjusted to maintain the integrity of the object.

8.1.6 Fleshing out of Wireframes and Projections

Present CAD/CAM systems have large number of wireframe models of objects. This wire frame model can be patched for surface generation and that surfaces can be used for solid generation using fleshing out method. Solid can also be generated by fleshing out of 2D orthographic projection. For this purpose, suitable algorithm is required which can be run in CAD/CAM system.

8.2 BENEFITS OF SOLID MODELLING

Once solid modelling is over in CAD as per desired, one can make a model by the use of Rapid Prototyping Machine or actual object by the use of CNC machine. For CNC machines, most software available such as Pro-E, IDEA, CATIA, SOLID WORKS etc., has a facility to convert geometric interties of the object modeled into code (Fanuc code such as G and N code). The code decides the path of tool to remove the undesirable material from the raw object to cut the desired shape in CNC lathe, CNC drilling, CNC milling etc. Some special software generates code for Robot command used in industry for manufacturing products.

In rapid prototyping, the most commonly used formate is STL (Stereo lithography) which is considered de facto standard for interfacing CAD and rapid prototyping machine system. The other formats such as SLC, CLI (common layer interface), RPI (rapid prototyping interface), and LEAF (layer exchange assii format) which is uses very limited.

Theory and technology of solid modelling is now maturing rapidly. We have seen growth in literature and many solid modellers. Industries now find that solid modelling is cost effective to provide large numbers of engineers with workstations capable of running solid modellers at interactive speeds for complex objects. Now, there is facility to run algorithm prepared for cutter path generation. Boolean operation continue to be fundamental in solid modelling but other operations like sweep are equally important. Developers are now using techniques from artificial intelligence to build more flexible and automatic CAD/CAM system. Thus, main aim of any modelling system is to develop products for human being.

8.3 ANIMATION & ITS APPLICATION: INTRODUCTION

To better understand computer animation first we have to understand animation. The word animation is Japanese word **'anime'** which means life. Animation is way to create motion and shape change illusion. Animation is the method of displaying images in a quick succession to create illusion of movement and these images can be hand drawn, generated by computer, or films of 3D objects. Animation is created by specialized artist called animators. Although most of us relate animation with cartoons only but it has lots of application in industrial and scientific research. For decades, animation has been a skill that rested exclusively in the hands of the entertainment industry. The practice requisite a great deal with time, manpower and difficult apparatus to complete. However, with the help of computer generated animation, this process becomes increasingly simpler. The task which was earlier done with pen and paper and paint by a group of animators can now be performed by a single person with a home computer alongwith the right software

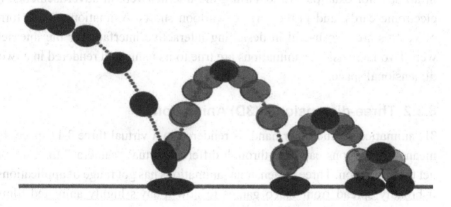

Fig. 8.6 Effect of Computer Animation in Bouncing Ball.

Computer animation mostly uses 3D computer graphics, eventhough 2D computer graphics are used for stylistic, low bandwidth and more rapid real-time renderings. Computer animation is fundamentally a digital descendant of the stop motion techniques used in traditional animation with 3D models and frame-by-frame animation of 2D illustrations. Animators displayed an image in computer and constantly replaced by a new image which is similar to it, to create illusions. However, it is advanced in respect of time with similar technology used in televisions and motion picture. In animation trapping of the eye and brain occurs when we are watching a smoothly moving object, the images should be drawn at nearly 12 frames per second (frame/second) or faster. Fig. 8.6, shows how computer animation comes into play when we represent 3D real object into 2D screen, here bouncing ball can be represented by number of balls to create illusion in the viewers mind. Conformist hand-drawn animators frequently uses 15 frames/second in order to save on the number of drawings needed, but this is generally accepted for the stylized nature of cartoons. However, to produce more realistic imagery, computer animation demands advanced frame rates to strengthen this realism.

The word "computer animation" itself generally covers a broad range of genres and applications, however the simplest approach is to break it down into the categories of 2D and 3D animation.

8.3.1 Two-dimensional (2D) Animation

It is from time to time also called vector animation and is typically done in programs like Macromedia Flash and Macromedia Director. The most well-known form of two dimensional animations can be found just by turning on your TV on a Saturday morning: conventional comics, which was making progress into the digital territory. One can most likely see easier animations in all day, for example while surfing the internet/web, in advertisements, in electronic cards, and in the form of cartoon shorts. Animations in the form of vectors are also useful in designing interactive interface for the internet/web. Two Dimensional animations are true to its name and rendered in a two-dimensional space.

8.3.2 Three-dimensional (3D) Animation

3D animation on the other hand, is rendered in a virtual three 3-D space, by means of polygons captured through different virtual "cameras" to "film" to get the animation. Three dimensional animations has got range of applications, it broadly spread from video games to now-a-day's highly animated films. Most commonly, three dimensional animations are used to get a number of unique sound/special effects generally seen in live action films and removing the requirements for balance model set. Both types of computer animation can be accomplished by either frame-by-frame animation or by mathematical interpolation among key frames, the early steps before animation are drastically different and two separate processes are also required for different software packages. With that in mind, the tutorials provided here have been grouped into the categories of 2D and 3D animation.

8.4 ANIMATION SYSTEM

Animation system is basically divided into four sub groups; High level animation system, Medium level animation system, Low level animation system, and High level command (Fig. 8.7).

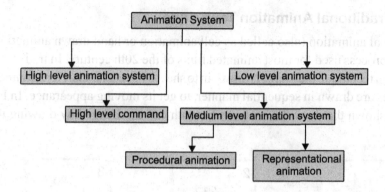

Fig. 8.7 Flow chart of Animation System.

High Level Animation System: High level animation systems allow the animator to specify the motion in abstract general terms.

Low Level Animation System: Low level animation systems require animator to specify individual moving parameters.

High Level Command: High level command describes behaviour implicitly in terms of events and relationships.

Medium Level Animation System: Medium level animation system may generally be placed in one or more of the following categories:

- *Procedural Animation:* Procedural animation has control over motion specification achieved through the use of procedures that explicitly define the movement as a function of time.

- *Representational Animation:* Representational animations not only can an object move through space, but also the shape of the object itself may change.

8.5 ANIMATION TECHNIQUES

Animation is the rapid display of a sequence of images of 2D or 3D artwork or model positions in order to create an illusion of movement. There are various techniques available to get animated object or animation and few of them we are going to discuss here.

1. Traditional animation.

2. Stop motion animation.

3. Computer animation (2D and 3D).

4. Soft animation.

5. Other animation techniques.

8.5.1 Traditional Animation Technique

Traditional animation (also called as cell animation or hand drawn animation) was the process used for most animated films of the 20th century. In traditional animation technique the image is drawn in to sheet by using hands. Here numbers of images are drawn in sequential manner, to get its moving appearance. In Fig 8.8 it is shown that how the posture of mouth can be changed by drawing the images.

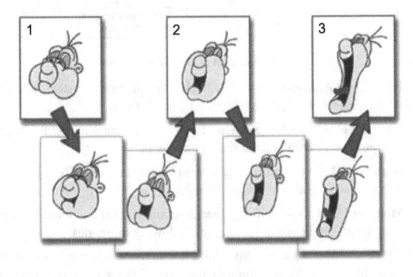

Fig 8.8 Traditional Animation Technique.

Traditional animation can further be divided into four sub-parts which are given below:

1. **Full animation** is a process of drawing high quality image or animated film which generally uses detailed drawing and possible motion.

2. **Limited animation** uses less detailed drawings and method of movement.

3. **Rot scoping** is a technique which traces live action frame by frame.

4. **Live action animated film** is a technique, which combines hand-drawn characters into live action shots.

8.5.2 Stop Motion Technique

Stop-motion animation is used to describe animation created by physically manipulating real-world objects and photographing them one frame of film at a time to create the illusion of movement. Fig. 8.9 represents stop motion animation where objects are trying to move by own after manipulating motion initially.

Fig. 8.9 Basic representation of stop motion animation.

In the study number of stop motion animation were found, some of those given below:

1. Puppet
2. Clay animation
3. Cutout animation
4. Silhouette animation
5. Model animation
6. Go motion
7. Object animation
8. Pixilation

8.5.3 Computer Animation

When the animation is performed by using the capability of computer then it is termed as computer animation. It contains a variety of techniques, and the unifying factor being that of the animation is formed digitally on a computer. Computer animation is the integration of traditional animation, here to generate moving object or picture, one object is quickly replaced by another similar object which is shifted by some distance. Computer animation is faster and more accurate technique than traditional one. It is generally used for entertainment, education and for science and technology. Computer animation is broadly divided into two parts *i.e.*, 2D and 3D animations which is already discussed in introduction part.

8.5.4 Soft Animation Technique

Soft animation is defined as an object that can be deformed by the user or during the process of animation, such as shape deformation to show the dynamic interaction with the environment. For example an animator may want to create a basketball that will deform when it bounces on the ground or deformation of the shape of a car during a collision in a racing simulation.

8.5.5 Other Animation Techniques

Beyond the above discussed animation techniques, there are some other techniques which are important as well. So here we will discuss some of them:

1. **Flip Book:** A flip book (sometimes, especially in British English, called a flick book) is a book with a string of pictures that varies step by step from one page to the next page, such that when the pages are turned quickly the pictures come into sight to animate by simulating motion or some other change. Flip books are frequently illustrated as books for children, but now it is not only limited to children, it may also attract adults and employ a series of photographs rather than drawings. Flip books are not always separate books, but may come into view as a supplementary part in ordinary books or magazines, frequently in the page corners. Software packages and websites are also available that convert digital video files into custom-made flip books.

2. **Sand animation:** Sand is moved around on a back or front-lighted piece of glass to create each frame for an animated film. These create an attractive effect when animated, because of the light contrast.

3. **Pin screen animation:** Pin screen animation makes use of a screen filled with variable pins, which can be moved in or out by pressing an object onto the screen.

8.6 Computer Graphics

Computer is a machine which is used for information processing like data storing, manipulating and correlating data. Computer graphics is most effective way to communicate information data with the user. It also facilitate graphical user interface, which is able to display information in the form of graphics objects such as charts, graphs, pictures and diagrams instead of simple text. The picture or graphics object displayed by computer may be an engineering drawing, architectural structures, business graphs, a single frame from an animated movie or a machine parts illustrated for a service manual. Picture or graphics in a screen is represented by the collection of pixel which is smallest addressable unit of picture. Pixel is defined as number of dots per inch. If number of dots will be higher than density will be higher and picture quality will be good and *vice versa*. Computer graphics can be classified according to their uses, which is shown in Fig. 8.10.

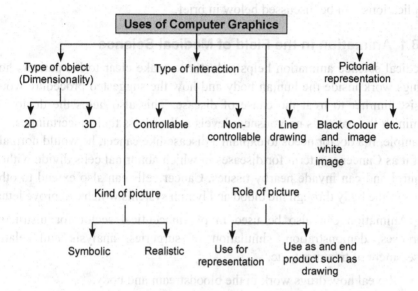

Fig. 8.10 Classification of Computer Graphics on the basis of Applications.

8.7 SOFTWARE USED TO PERFORM ANIMATION

Today animation is mostly performed by using computer ability, but this can be achieved by computer software. There are number of software available and some of them are discussed here-

(*i*) Autodesk 3D max	(*x*) Final Cut Pro
(*ii*) Autodesk Maya	(*xi*) Eyeon Fusion
(*iii*) Z-Brush	(*xii*) Nuke
(*iv*) Motion Builder	(*xiii*) Game Brayo
(*v*) Stop Motion Pro	(*xiv*) Flipbook
(*vi*) V-ray	(*xv*) Cinema 4D Prime
(*vii*) Adobe after effect	(*xvi*) Illustrator CC
(*viii*) Adobe Photoshop	(*xvii*) Unity Pro 4
(*ix*) Adobe Premiere	

8.8 APPLICATION OF COMPUTER ANIMATION

Computer animation can also be classified on the basis of their application in various fields, like medical animation, architectural animation, forensic animation, animation in education, and mechanical animation. All these applications will be discussed below in brief.

8.8.1 Animation in the Field of Medical Science

Medical science animation helps a doctor to make clear to his patients how things work inside the human body and how the suggested procedure would assist him/her to treat the cause of disease. This also helps the doctors to diminish the patient's nervousness levels and address their uncertainties. For example, if a doctor needs to explain a disease like cancer, he would normally put it as Cancer is a term for diseases in which abnormal cells divide without control and can invade nearby tissues. Cancer cells can also extend to other parts of the body through the blood and lymph systems which can prove lethal.

Animation can also be used in pharmaceutical sector for instructive purposes, demonstration, simulation of surgeries, analysis and relative assessment of treatment, etc.

- Reveal how drugs work in the bloodstream and body.
- Design of macroscopic and microscopic interactive models of the human body.
- Current patient data in the form of three dimensional visual descriptions.
- Design instructions and materials for medical students.
- Explain with the help of animation that how a medical equipment, surgical process or technique will work.

8.8.2 Architectural Animation

A small architectural film formed on a computer screen is called Architectural Animation. A computer-generated building is formed alongwith landscaping and sometimes moving vehicles and people. Unlike an architectural interpretation, which is a single image from a single point of outlook, an architectural animation is a series of hundreds or even thousands of motionless images. When these images are assembled and played back quickly it produces a moving effect like a real movie camera except all images are synthetically created by computer. It is possible to put in a computer produced environment around the building to enhance reality and to better convey its relationship to the surrounding area; this can all be done before the project is built giving designers and stakeholders a realistic view of the accomplished project. Architectural renderings are frequently used alongside architectural animation.

Commercial requirement for computer generated description is on the rise, but 3D scale models are still popular. Typically members of the AIA (American Institute of Architects) and NAHB (National Association of Home Builders) prefer to use 3D animations and single renderings for their customers before starting on a building project. These professionals generally found their clients and unable to grasp the complexity and spatial qualities of large projects without the help of computer generated visual aids. The animations and renderings are usually supplied by small animation studios.

8.8.3 Forensic Animation

A number of applications for medical animations have been developed in the field of forensic science. These include the so-called "virtuosi," or MRI-assisted virtual autopsy of remains that are too damaged to be otherwise inspected or reconstructed. Likewise, medical animations can appear in the courtrooms, be used as forensic "reconstructions" of crime scenes or recreate the crimes themselves. The admissibility of such evidence is questionable. **Forensic animation** is a branch of forensics in which animated recreation of incidents are created to aid investigators and help solve cases. Examples include the use of computer animation, stills, and other audio visual aids. Check out this video to understand how animation helps forensic experts.

8.8.4 Animation in Education

Today, computer animation reached out at every field of life and education field is one of the most important areas where it found wide applications. In a study it was found that teaching with animated videos or picture or presentation is more effective than traditional and/or conventional method of teaching. In recent days animated books are also available which also increases interest and motivation of learner. Many companies and production houses are in progress of producing teaching content in the form of animation. As the training and education industry is massive and the content delivered is huge, there is a great demand for content taught with the help of animation.

8.8.5 Mechanical Animation

Using computer animation and modelling to produce mechanical designs and virtual or actual model of products can save companies millions of dollars and time, by cutting down the development costs and processes. The mechanical department of "The City College", University of New York has introduced the utilization of computer animated modules in its undergraduate dynamics course which are intended to help the students visualize and obtain a better understanding of important concepts covered in the course. The software's on which these modules are based are known as Working Models and are commercially available in the form of knowledge revolution. The software which allows the user to generate two dimensional mechanical systems on the screen containing devices like springs, pulleys, dampers, motors, masses and actuators. There are various types of forces which may be simulated including frictional, gravitational and electrostatic forces. The experiment to animate the object can be simply performed by clicking a RUN button. The system contains some varying physical parameters like magnitude and direction of applied forces, initial position of object, velocity and acceleration of objects and torques which may be obtained by introducing controls in system by animator. Some basic physical quantities (velocity, acceleration, linear and angular momentum and kinetic energy) may also be measured and displayed on the screen during an animation development.

8.8.5.1 Mechanical 3D Product Animation

CGI (Computer Generated Imagery) can be created by Mechanical 3D product animation method of creating realistic 3D animation to visually indicate the design, assembly and models of various mechanical products and their components. With the fast growing world and developing technologies like CGI (Computer Generated Image) animation technologies in the latest years, 3D product animation has emerged as a point of reference for the mechanical engineering group of people worldwide. It is increasingly being used to test products and implement real-time changes for maximum performance and efficiency.

8.8.5.2 Product Development through Mechanical Animation

3D animation of mechanical products provides easy and precise wire-frame geometry creation, monitoring of kinetics and easy verification of designs according to the design rules and specifications. Such product simulations also provide a superior analysis of the final product, its performance and efficiency. Mechanical 3D product animation is also a resourceful way to display the virtual prototype to the potential trade and help them to understand the model of a product and its features. It gives presentations, an added essence of reality which is quite impossible by the conventional methods. More prominently, mechanical design engineers favour resorting to three dimensional product animations, during early designing phases. These complicated and detailed animations are favourable for visualizing a concept or product even before the project goes into the potentially costly prototype stage. Doing so also helps designers diminish the monotonous and sometimes frustratingly repetitive assignment of product redesign during the afterward stages.

Visual or computer graphics facilitate viewers to understand the core concept and features after the design, even if they are not belonging to technical background. Having an operational virtual prototype, when the product is in the design and development stage, helps engineers to bring the process of manufacturing stage in a reasonably much shorter duration. However the most stimulating phase of mechanical product 3-D animations is that it allows the engineering team to design multiple prototypes with least cost and maximum efficiency. Before the age of three dimensional animations, mechanical engineers generally resorted to traditional prototyping techniques which, unnecessary to say, were costly, time and resource consuming and prone to errors. Some of the key benefits of using three dimensional animations for mechanical products are:

- Exceptionally effective three dimensional virtualization technology that allow developed mechanical drawings
- Quicker authentication of product design against design guidelines and specifications
- Simple design of assemblies and sub-assemblies
- Three dimensional sectional views are possible
- Proper monitoring of kinetics, clearance and interference in the assemblies

8.8.5.3 Three Dimensional Animation Procedure for Mechanical Product

Mechanical product three dimensional animation techniques need to be of the peak quality to make sure that the final result is realistic and free from error. Also, it is pretty essential that the progress is strictly monitored at each and every stage during the project cycle to discard any scope for flaw. In most cases, three dimensional animation procedures commence with an input from the client that may include animation narration or a storyboard. These inputs may also be accompanied through hand drawing and/or 2D CAD models. The animation team first creates three dimensional models as per the customers' preference. In the next stage, the animation team defines all the camera angles and sets the lightning. The completed combinations are then dispatched to the client for approval. If approved, then team alongwith the design engineers renders final three dimensional product animation. The computer animation and visualization technique allow the acquirement of essential information which could assist the designer in correct design and control of the product from early conceptual design phase to the final assembly design stage. The computer assembly animation of a mechanical product allows the utilization of a profitable CAD system. By utilizing properly some features of the CAD (Computer-aided design) system, a general trajectory can be assigned for each mating product component that allows us to analyze the local and global product assimilability or disassemblability or to analyze possible disassembling trajectories which guarantee that no collisions would happen.

CAD is the use of computer systems to support in the creation, modification analysis, or optimization of product design. CAD software is used to increase the productivity of the designer, to get better quality of the design, enhanced interactions through records and to create a record for manufacturing. CAD output is generally in the form of electronic files for print, machining or other manufacturing operations.

REFERENCES

1. Marek Balazinski & Aleksander, (2005), "Teaching Manufacturing Process Using Computer Animation", Journal of Manufacturing System.

2. Ning Fang, (2012), "Using Computer Simulation and Animation to Improve Student Learning of Engineering Dynamics", International Conference on Teaching and Learning in Higher Education (ICTLHE 2012) in conjunction with RCEE & RHED, Social and Behavioral Sciences 56, 504-512.

3. Can Cemal Cingi, (2013), "Computer animation in teaching surgical procedures", Social and Behavioral Sciences 103, 230 – 237.

4. Principles of traditional animation applied to 3D computer animation (1989), International Conference on Computer Graphics and Interactive Techniques, Proceedings of the 14th annual conference on Computer graphics and interactive techniques, 35-40.

5. Michalis Raptis, Darko Kirovski, Hugues Hoppe, (2011), Real-Time Classification of Dance Gestures from Skeleton Animation, Eurographics ACM SIGGRAPH Symposium on Computer Animation.

9

Finite Element Analysis

9.1 INTRODUCTION

In machine design and CAD/CAM, various engineering objects are studied for their behaviour under different loading conditions. The stress produced is checked for the reliability of that object (machine part) under these loading conditions.

In some cases the stress distribution not uniform due to some discontinuity. This discontinuity can be a geometrical or a meteorological discontinuity. The geometrical discontinuity can be due to the holes, notches, grooves, corners, abrupt change of section etc. These discontinuities give rise to increase in stress near its periphery. Under the frequent loading condition this stress irregularity can lead to progressive crack resulting in fracture of that part.

This stress irregularity should therefore, be considered as a major factor while designing a machine part (specially, when there is cyclic loading). In dealing with axial loading, bending and torsion it was possible to make certain general assumption regarding the internal behaviour of the structure, however, these assumptions are considered satisfactory only when saint Venant's principle can be applied, that is, when the section being analyzed were not close to a point of local load application or sharp discontinuity in the flow path of the forces. The effect of the localized increase in stress depends upon the type of loading, the geometry and material of the component. This stress rise can be mathematically represented by a factor called stress concentration factor (k_t) which is the ratio of maximum stress at a point to average or normal stress on that component.

Method of analysis:

1. Analytical Method
2. Experimental Method
3. Numerical Method

1. **Analytical Method:** In this method, governing differential equation is to be solved.

2. **Experimental Method:** In this method, experimental models are developed (experimentations are done to find the roots).

3. **Numerical Method:** In this method analysis is done with the help of numerical analysis tool. This method is classified as

   (*a*) Finite difference method.

   (*b*) Finite element method.

Difference between finite difference and finite element method

1. Finite difference method gives point wise approximation through the governing equation. Where as in FEM it is piece wise approximation.

2. FDM consist of finite difference equation obtained from governing differential equation whereas in finite element method (FEM) formulation of element properties is done resulting in linear simultaneous equation.

3. Irregular and complex loading and complex material properties can be incorporated in FEM only.

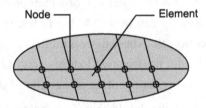

Fig. 9.1 The representation of node and element.

Fig. 1 represents the information about node and element. Finite element method is the best numerical method used for the analysis of stress, strain and their effect on a structure. The discretization of component and/or structure is done, which gives very accurate values of stress and strains at various elements. Due to acceptance by the computer the FEM is now widely used in various industries.

Example: A plate with hole

Here the stress concentration factor infinite width plate having two unequal elliptical holes under uniaxial tension has been determined, by the use of ANSYS software (a design purpose computer package), which uses 'Finite Element Method' as a tool.

Outlines of FE analysis work: Here the finite element analysis is done in two phases:

1. The drawing of whole plate has been developed in AUTO-CAD 12 and then further processing was done on this drawing.

2. For stress analysis of this plate which is having two elliptical holes, ANSYS package is used.

9.1.1 What is Finite Element Method

Engineering problems are solved by various analytical methods, however, sometimes, it becomes very difficult to obtain analytical solution for various engineering problems. An analytical solution is also called mathematical expression, which can be used to calculate the value of field variables or also calculate the unknown quantity in the body at any point. Only certain simplified problems are used to derive the analytical solution. If a given problem maintains the different boundary conditions and complex material properties, then numerical methods provide the approximate solution which is an acceptable solution.

Automatic computation is useful for such big amount of data. This method of discretization of a body in a finite number of smaller parts (or elements) is known as 'Finite Element Method' and is one of the most powerful tools for the solution of complicated problems of machine design, structural analysis and vibration analysis etc., in this era of high speed digital computers.

In FEM continuum model is divided into small region is called elements, and the elements are interconnected through discrete points called nodes. The properties of elements are formulated and assembled, resulting in a set of linear simultaneous equation. Solution of these equations gives the results.

Why FEM is used:

• Complicated geometric problem.

• Complex loading.

• Complicated material properties.

9.1.2 Areas of Applications of FEM

The basis of FEM is the division of a body into smaller regions called elements. These elements are inter-connected with neighbouring elements at discrete and finite number of points called nodes. The transmission of force between elements could thus, takes place only through these node points. In these elements, the behaviour is described by a set of assumed function which describes its stresses and displacements. Considering equilibrium of elements and then of whole continuum, analysis can be performed. Any rigid and flexible body/fluid or structure such as machine part, plate or pin can be treated as a link and connected like in nature every thing is connected. FEM is used in two types of problems:

1. **Structural problem,** like stress analysis, vibration analysis, buckling analysis, fracture analysis etc.

2. **Non-Structural problem,** like heat transfer, temperature problem, fluid flow, magnetic problem etc.

Software's used in two ways:

1. General software commercially available like ANSYS, NASTRAN, NISA, LSDYNA etc.

2. Special purpose software, developed by researchers.

   Matrix Analysis

   A matrix is a set of number in order:

   $$[A] = A \text{ is a matrix}$$

   $$|A| = A \text{ is a determinants}$$

   Terminology

   • **Discretization:** The region is divided into a set of small sub-regions, which is called discretization of region.

   • **Mesh:** The discretized region is called mesh.

   • **Element:** Each sub-region is called as element.

   • **Node:** All the elements are connected through only node.

   • **Degree of freedom:** Number of independent displacement required to define the behaviour of node is called degree of freedom.

9.1.3 General Steps in Finite Element Analysis (Procedure)

(1) Discretization of the continuum

In the discretization the region is divided into a set of small sub regions the problem is called discretization of region *i.e.,* the body is divided into smaller parts (the size may be as the pre-requirement of the problem). These smaller parts which are termed as finite elements may be of various shapes like triangular, rectangular, group of triangles or even 2D bar like shape etc., for a 2-dimensional continuum. For a 3-dimensional analysis, the elements may be tetrahedral, rectangular prisms or hexahedral.

(2) Selection of displacement modals

The assumed displacement function or models represent only approximate distribution of the displacement. There are three factors which governs the selection of displacement modals:

- The type and degree of displacement model must be choosen.
- The particular displacement magnitude, that describe the model must be selected.
- The model should satisfy certain requirements, which ensures that the numerical results approach the correct solutions.

Nodal displacement vector

A vector representing all possible displacement/degree of freedom for an element/mesh is called nodal displacement.

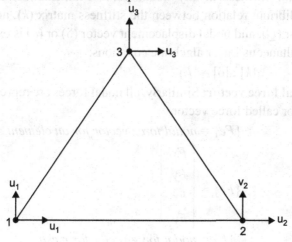

Fig. 9.2 Element.

Number of node 3,

u_1 and v_1 are nodal displacement in x and y direction of node 1 respectively.

u_2 and v_2 are nodal displacement in x and y direction of node 2 respectively.

u_3 and v_3 are nodal displacement in x and y direction of node 3 respectively.

$\{\delta e\}$ is a nodal displacement vector for an element.

$$\{\delta_e\} = \begin{bmatrix} u_1 \\ v_1 \\ u_2 \\ v_2 \\ u_3 \\ v_3 \end{bmatrix}$$

$\{\delta\}$ is a nodal displacement vector for the mesh.

$$\{\delta\} = \begin{bmatrix} u_1 \\ v_1 \\ \vdots \\ \vdots \\ u_x \\ v_x \end{bmatrix}$$

(3) Derivation of the element stiffness matrix using variational principle
The stiffness matrix consists of the equilibrium equations. These equilibrium equations derived from geometric and material properties of an element and these equations obtained by the use of the principle of minimum potential energy. Force and displacement vector are used to find stiffness at any nodal point. Mathematical equation and the equilibrium relation between the stiffness matrix (k), nodal force vector (F) or (Q), and nodal displacement vector (δ) or (q) is expressed as set of simultaneous linear algebraic equations:

$$[k] \cdot [\delta] = [F]$$

Nodal force vector: Similarly, all nodal forces are represented in form of vector called force vector.

$\{Fe\}$ = *nodal force vector for an element.*

$$\{Fe\} = \begin{bmatrix} Fx_1 \\ Fy_1 \\ Fx_2 \\ Fy_2 \end{bmatrix}$$

$\{F\}$ = *nodal force vector for mesh.*

$$\{F\} = \begin{bmatrix} Fx_1 \\ Fy_1 \\ Fx_2 \\ Fy_2 \end{bmatrix}$$

$[Ke]6 * 6 \{\delta e\}6 * 1 = \{Fe\} 6 * 1$

$[Ke]$ = *element stiffness matrix, which is always square matrix.*

$$\begin{bmatrix} k_{11}k_{12} & \cdots & \cdots & \cdots & \cdots & \cdots & k_{16} \\ k_{21}k_{22}k_{23} & \cdots & \cdots & \cdots & \cdots & \cdots & k_{26} \\ \cdots & \cdots & \cdots & \cdots & \cdots & \cdots & \cdots \\ \cdots & \cdots & \cdots & \cdots & \cdots & \cdots & \cdots \\ \cdots & \cdots & \cdots & \cdots & \cdots & \cdots & \cdots \\ k_{61}k_{62} & \cdots & \cdots & \cdots & \cdots & \cdots & k_{66} \end{bmatrix} \begin{bmatrix} \delta_1 \\ \delta_2 \\ \delta_3 \\ \delta_4 \\ \delta_5 \\ \delta_6 \end{bmatrix} = \begin{bmatrix} F_1 \\ F_2 \\ F_3 \\ F_4 \\ F_5 \\ F_6 \end{bmatrix}$$

k_{23} is the required value of 2nd force to produce unit value of 3rd displacement where all other displacements are zero.

$$k_{23}\, \delta_3 = F_2$$

k_{ij} is the required value of 'i'th force to produce unit value of 'j'th displacement when all other displacements are zero.

So, $k_{ij} = k_{ij}$ [ke] *always square matrix.*

The elements of the stiffness matrix are the influence co-efficients. Stiffness of a structure is an influence co-efficient that gives the force at one point on a structure associated with a unit displacement of the same or a different points.

The stiffness matrix of elements depends upon

(1) The displacement nodal.

(2) The geometry of the element.

(3) The local material properties.

Since material properties are assigned to a particular finite element, it is possible to account for non-homogeneity by assigning different material properties to different finite elements in the assemblage.

(4) Assembly of the algebraic equations for the overall discretized continuum

In this step individual stiffness matrices are assembled in the form of global stiffness matrix of the entire body and the element nodal, load vectors or force vectors are assembled to get global force vector or load vector. The most common technique to find stiffness is a direct stiffness method, in this method nodal interconnections requires the displacement at a node should be same for all elements adjacent to that node.

The overall equilibrium equation or relation between total load vector {R}, local stiffness matrix [K], and the entire body nodal displacement vector {V} is given below:

$$[K] . \{V\} = \{R\}$$

(5) Unknown displacements solution

The algebraic equations assembled in step (4) above are solved for unknown displacement. This is done by matrix algebra technique.

(6) Computation of element stresses and strains from the nodal displacements

After getting the nodal displacements, strains and stresses at the nodes are evaluated. In general the strains and stresses are proportional to the derivatives of the displacements.

9.1.4 Examples of Finite Element Modelling

General method to evaluate element stiffness matrix:

(1) Assume displacement function and determine shape function. Express interior displacement in term of nodal displacement as:

$$\{u\} = [N]\,[\delta e]$$

Strains are evaluated and express in terms of nodal displacement.

$$\{\varepsilon\} = [B]\,[\delta e]$$

Where $[B]$ is strain displacement matrix.

Stress is expressed in terms of nodal displacement/strain as,

$$[\sigma] = [D]\,[\delta e]$$

$[D]$ is elastic matrix.

$$[\sigma] = [D]\,\{\varepsilon\}$$

$$[\sigma] = [D]\,[B]\,[\delta e]$$

Now, strain energy is given as

$$U = \int \frac{1}{2}[\sigma]^T \{\varepsilon\}\, d\,\text{vol.}$$

$$U = \int \frac{1}{2}[\delta e]^T [B]^T [D]^T [B]\,[\delta e]\, d\,\text{vol}$$

Using cartilaginous theorem,

$\partial u/\partial \delta e = [Fe][D]$ is elastic matrix which is symmetrical.

So, $[Fe] = 2/2 \int \ [B]^T [D]\,[B]\,[\delta e]\, d\,\text{vol.}$

Comparing with element equation $[Ke]\,[\delta e] = [F_e]$

So,

$$K_e = \int [B]^T [D]\,[B]\, d\,\text{vol.}$$

$$K_e = \int_0^1 1 \begin{bmatrix} -1/L \\ 1/L \end{bmatrix} E \begin{bmatrix} -\dfrac{1}{L}, \dfrac{1}{L} \end{bmatrix} A\, dx$$

$$K_e = EA \begin{bmatrix} \dfrac{1}{l} & -\dfrac{1}{l} \\[2mm] -\dfrac{1}{l} & \dfrac{1}{l} \end{bmatrix} \qquad \text{Element stiffness matrix.}$$

Question (1) Determine the stress, and strain in given bar.

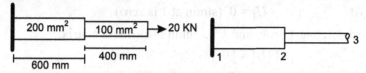

Fig. 9.3 Stepped bar under axial load.

Given: $E = 200 \text{ GN/m}^2$

Solution: Element stiffness matrix:

$$K_e = EA \begin{bmatrix} \dfrac{1}{l} & -\dfrac{1}{l} \\ -\dfrac{1}{l} & \dfrac{1}{l} \end{bmatrix}$$

$$K_{e_1} = EA1 \begin{bmatrix} \dfrac{1}{l} & -\dfrac{1}{l} \\ -\dfrac{1}{l} & \dfrac{1}{l} \end{bmatrix}$$

$$= 200 \times 2 \times 10^5/600 \begin{bmatrix} 1 & -1 \\ -1 & 1 \end{bmatrix}$$

$$= 10^5 \begin{bmatrix} 2/3 & -2/3 \\ -2/3 & 2/3 \end{bmatrix}$$

$$K_{e_2} = EA2 \begin{bmatrix} \dfrac{1}{l} & -\dfrac{1}{l} \\ -\dfrac{1}{l} & \dfrac{1}{l} \end{bmatrix}$$

$$= 100 \times 2 \times 10^5/400 \begin{bmatrix} 1 & -1 \\ -1 & 1 \end{bmatrix}$$

$$= 10^5 \begin{bmatrix} 1/2 & -1/2 \\ -1/2 & 1/2 \end{bmatrix}$$

So, stiffness matrix:

$$[K] = \begin{bmatrix} \dfrac{2}{3} & -\dfrac{2}{3} & 0 \\ -\dfrac{2}{3} & \dfrac{2}{3}+\dfrac{1}{2} & -\dfrac{1}{2} \\ 0 & -\dfrac{1}{2} & \dfrac{1}{2} \end{bmatrix}$$

Now apply boundary condition:

At $U_1 = 0$ (strain at 1 is zero)

So deleting 1st row and 1st column in stiffness matrix.

$$[K]\,[U] = [Fe]$$

$$105 = \begin{bmatrix} 7/6 & -1/2 \\ -1/2 & 1/2 \end{bmatrix}\begin{bmatrix} u2 \\ u3 \end{bmatrix}$$

$$7/6U_2 - 1/2U_3 = 0$$

$$-1/2 + 1/2U_3 = 0.2$$

So, $U_2 = 0.2 \times 3/2 = 0.3$ mm

And $U_3 = 0.7$ mm

Strain: $\{\varepsilon\} = [B]\,[\delta e]$

$$= \begin{bmatrix} -\dfrac{1}{l} & \dfrac{1}{l} \end{bmatrix}[\delta e]$$

So, $$\{\varepsilon 1\} = \begin{bmatrix} -\dfrac{1}{600} & \dfrac{1}{600} \end{bmatrix}\begin{bmatrix} u1 \\ u2 \end{bmatrix}$$

$$\{\varepsilon 1\} = \begin{bmatrix} -\dfrac{1}{600} & \dfrac{1}{600} \end{bmatrix}\begin{bmatrix} 0 \\ u2 \end{bmatrix}$$

$$\{\varepsilon 1\} = \begin{bmatrix} -\dfrac{1}{600} & \dfrac{1}{600} \end{bmatrix}\begin{bmatrix} 0 \\ 0.3 \end{bmatrix}$$

$$\varepsilon 1 = 0.0005$$

And $$\{\varepsilon 2\} = \begin{bmatrix} -\dfrac{1}{400} & \dfrac{1}{400} \end{bmatrix}\begin{bmatrix} u2 \\ u3 \end{bmatrix}$$

$$\{\varepsilon 2\} = \begin{bmatrix} -\dfrac{1}{400} & \dfrac{1}{400} \end{bmatrix}\begin{bmatrix} 0.3 \\ 0.7 \end{bmatrix}$$

$$\{\varepsilon 2\} = \varepsilon 2 = 0.001$$

Stress: $\{\sigma\} = E\{\varepsilon\}$

Element 1. $\{\sigma 1\} = E\{\varepsilon 1\}$

$$\{\sigma 1\} = 2 \times 10^5 \times 0.0005$$

$$= 1000 \text{ N/mm}^2$$

Element 2. $\{\sigma 2\} = E\{\varepsilon 2\}$

$$\{\sigma 2\} = 2 \times 10^5 \times 0.001$$

$$= 200 \text{ N/mm}^2$$

Tapered bar elements

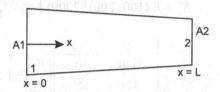

Fig. 9.4 Tapered bar elements.

$$Ax = A_1 - (A_1 - A_2)/L \times X$$

$$K_e = \int [B]^T [D] [B] \, d \, \text{vol.}$$

$$= E \int \begin{bmatrix} -\dfrac{1}{l} \\[2mm] 1/l \end{bmatrix} \begin{bmatrix} -\dfrac{1}{l} & \dfrac{1}{l} \end{bmatrix} Ax \ dx$$

$$= E \int_0^1 1 \begin{bmatrix} \dfrac{1}{l} \times \dfrac{1}{l} & -\dfrac{1}{l} \times \dfrac{1}{l} \\[3mm] -\dfrac{1}{l} \times \dfrac{1}{l} & \dfrac{1}{l} \times \dfrac{1}{l} \end{bmatrix} \left[A_1 - \dfrac{A_1 - A_2}{L} x \right] dx$$

$$= E \begin{bmatrix} \dfrac{1}{l} \times \dfrac{1}{l} & -\dfrac{1}{l} \times \dfrac{1}{l} \\[3mm] -\dfrac{1}{l} \times \dfrac{1}{l} & \dfrac{1}{l} \times \dfrac{1}{l} \end{bmatrix} \left[A_1 L - \dfrac{A_1 - A_2}{2} L \right]$$

$$K_e = E (A_1 + A_2)/(2L) \begin{bmatrix} 1 & -1 \\ -1 & 1 \end{bmatrix}$$

Element stiffness matrix for tapered bar.

Question 2: Determine the stress and strain in tapered bar.

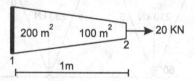

Fig. 9.5 Tapered bar under axial load.

Solution: $\quad K_e = E (A_1 + A_2)/(2L) \begin{bmatrix} 1 & -1 \\ -1 & 1 \end{bmatrix}$

$$K_e = E\,(100+200)/(2000) \begin{bmatrix} 1 & -1 \\ -1 & 1 \end{bmatrix}$$

$$= \begin{bmatrix} \dfrac{150}{1000} & -\dfrac{150}{1000} \\[2mm] -\dfrac{150}{1000} & \dfrac{150}{1000} \end{bmatrix} \begin{bmatrix} u_1 \\ u_2 \end{bmatrix} = \begin{bmatrix} 0 \\ 20000 \end{bmatrix}$$

Apply boundary conditions, $U_1 = 0$

So delete 1st row and 1st column.

$E\,150\,U_2/1000 = 20000$

$$U_2 = 133333.33/E$$

Stress: $\{\sigma\} = E\{\varepsilon\}$

$$\{\sigma\} = E \begin{bmatrix} -\dfrac{1}{l} & \dfrac{1}{l} \end{bmatrix} \begin{bmatrix} u_1 \\ u_2 \end{bmatrix}$$

$$\{\sigma\} = E \begin{bmatrix} -\dfrac{1}{10000} & \dfrac{1}{1000} \end{bmatrix} \begin{bmatrix} 0 \\ 133333.333 / E \end{bmatrix}$$

$$\sigma = 133.33\ \text{N/mm}^2 \quad \textbf{Ans.}$$

9.1.5 Two Dimensional Truss

To solve the two dimensional truss problem using ANSYS program.

In the 2D truss problem, we determine the reaction force, nodal reaction forces, stress and value of E and A for a truss system shown in following figure: $(E = 200\ \text{GPa},\ A = 3250\ \text{mm}^2)$.

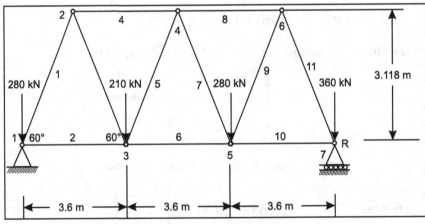

Fig. 9.6 Two dimensional truss.

9.1.6 Effect of Self Weight on a Cantilever Beam

This problem was completed using ANSYS. The purpose of this problem is to show the required steps to account for the weight of an object in ANSYS.

Loads will not be applied to the beam shown below in order to observe the deflection caused by the weight of the beam itself. The beam is to be made of steel and modulus of elasticity of the beam is 200 GPa.

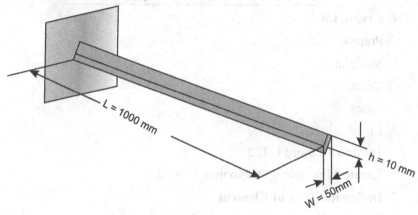

Fig. 9.7 The cantilever beam.

Preprocessing: Defining the Problem

1. **Give a Title example**

   Utility Menu

   File

   Change

   Titl ...

   /title, Effects of Self Weight for a Cantilever Beam

2. **Open preprocessor menu**

   ANSYS

   Main Menu

   Preprocessor

   PREP7

3. **Define Key points**

   Preprocessor

   Modeling

   Create

   Key points

In Active CS...K,

#, x, y, z

Now to define 2 key points of the beam as given in the following table:

Key point	Co-ordinates (x, y, z)
1	(0, 0)
2	(1000, 0)

4. Create Lines

Preprocessor

Modeling

Create

Lines

Lines

In Active Co-ord L,1, 2

Create a line joining Keypoints 1 and 2

5. Define the Type of Element

Preprocessor

Element Type

Add/Edit/Delete...

For this problem we will use the BEAM3 (Beam 2 Dimensional elastic) element. This element has 3 degrees of freedom (translation and rotation along the *X, Y* axis and *Z* axis respectively).

6. Define Real Constants

Preprocessor

Real Constants...

Add...

In the 'Real Constants for BEAM3' window, enter the value of geometric properties:

• Value of cross-sectional area AREA: 500

• Value of area of moment of inertia IZZ: 4166.67

• Value of total beam height: 10

This defines a beam with a width of 50 mm and a height of 10 mm.

7. Define Material Properties of an Element

Preprocessor

Material Props

Material Models

Structural

Linear

Elastic

Isotropic

In the window that appears, insert the value of geometric properties of steel:

- Value of Young's modulus EX: 200000
- Value of Poisson's Ratio PRXY: 0.3

8. Define Density of element

Preprocessor

Material Props

Material Models

Structural

Linear

Density

In the window that appears, insert the value of density for steel:

- Value of Density DENS: 7.86e-6

9. Define Mesh Size

Preprocessor

Meshing

Size Cntrls

Manual Size

Lines

All Lines...

In this example insert the value of element edge length of 100 mm.

10. Mesh the frame

Preprocessor

Meshing

Mesh

Lines

click 'Pick All'

Solution phase: In this step loads are applied to the beam and solving

1. Define Analysis Type

Solution

Analysis

Type

New

Analysis

Static

ANTYPE, 0

2. Apply Constraints

Solution

Define Loads

Apply

Structural

Displacement

On Keypoints

Fix key point 1 (*i.e.* all DOF constrained)

3. Define Gravity

In this step, need to define the magnitude and direction of gravity.

❖ Select Solution

- Define Loads

- Apply

- Structural

- Inertia

- Gravity...

❖ In an appeared window, insert the value of acceleration 9.81 m/s^2 in the direction of y.

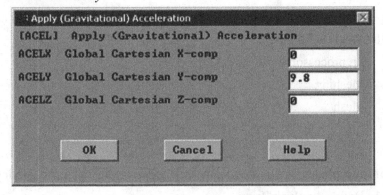

Note: insert the value of acceleration in term of meters. Also note that gravity in the negative Y direction stimulates a positive acceleration in the y direction.

In the given figure, red arrow pointing shows the positive y direction. This indicates that an acceleration has been defined in the y direction.

DK,1, ALL,0,

ACEL, 9.8

The applied loads and constraints should now appear as shown in the figure below.

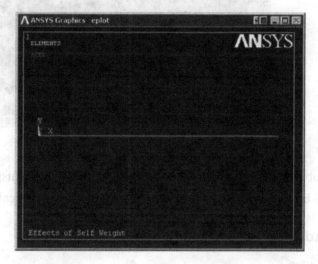

4. Solve the System

Solution

Solve

Current LS SOLVE

Postprocessing: Viewing the Results

1. Hand calculations

   Hand calculations were performed to verify the solution obtained from ANSYS:

   The maximum deflection was shown to be 5.777 mm

2. Show the deformation of the beam

   • General Postproc

   • Plot Results

- Deformed Shape ...
- Def + undef edge

PLDISP,2

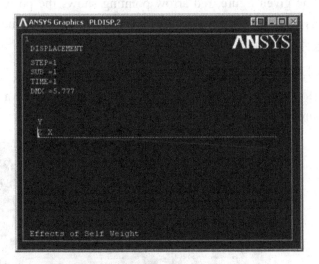

As observed in the upper left hand corner, the maximum displacement was found to be 5.777 mm. This is in agreement with the theoretical value.

9.1.7 Advantages and Limitation of FEM

Advantages

- As FEM, like other numerical approximation technique is base on the concept of discretization, so no separate interpolation technique is required to extend the solution to every point within the continuum.
- The use of separate sub regions or finite element permits a greater flexibility in considered continuum of complex shape. It doesn't require trial solutions which must be applied to the entire multi dimensional continuum.
- Due to the technique of introducing boundary conditions, one can use the same field variable models for both internal and external elements.
- Irregular boundaries/bodies can be handled easily.
- General loading problem can be handled easily.
- Unlimited number of boundaries can be analyses.

- Size of element can be varies in single model.

- Alternation or modification can be done easily.

- FEM readily accounts for non-homogeneity by assigning different properties to different elements.

- Finally programme's developed for one field of engineering can be used successfully for problems in a different field with little or no modification.

Limitations

- The basic process of sub-dividing the continuum and of generating error free input data for the computer are varied, tedious and error prone; consequently checks are needed to detect errors.

- Certain complex phenomenon are not accommodated adequately by FEM, *e.g.* cracking and fracture criteria, contact problems etc.

9.2 BENDING OF BEAMS

9.2.1 Introduction

Beam

A beam is a rod or bar of uniform cross-section (circular or rectangular) whose length is very much greater than its thickness as shown in Figure 8.

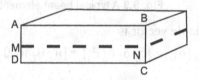

Fig. 9.8 A simple beam.

A beam is considered to be made up of a large number of thin plane layers called surfaces placed one above the other.

Types of beams

The beams are of several types:

1. **Simply supported:** A beam supported on the ends which are free to rotate and have no moment resistance.

2. **Fixed:** A beam supported on both ends and restrained from rotation.

3. **Over hanging:** A simple beam extending beyond its support on one end.

4. **Double overhanging:** A simple beam with both ends extending beyond its supports on both ends.

5. **Continuous:** A beam extending over more than two supports.

6. **Cantilever:** A projecting beam fixed only at one end.

7. **Trussed:** A beam strengthened by adding a cable or rod to form a truss.

9.2.2 The Potential Energy Approach

The typical beam element is shown in fig below:

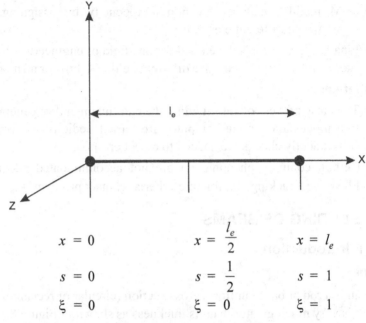

$$x = 0 \qquad x = \frac{l_e}{2} \qquad x = l_e$$

$$s = 0 \qquad s = \frac{1}{2} \qquad s = 1$$

$$\xi = 0 \qquad \xi = 0 \qquad \xi = 1$$

Fig. 9.9 A typical beam element.

The nodal variable vector is

$$\{\delta\}^T = [\delta_1 \ \delta_2 \ \delta_3 \ \delta_4] = [w_1 \ \theta_1 \ w_2 \ \theta_2]$$

Where

$$w_i = \text{Lateral displacement at node } i.$$
$$\theta_i = \text{Rotation at node } i.$$

The shape functions for such element is,

$$N_1 = 1 - \frac{3x^2}{l^2} - \frac{2x^3}{l^3} ; N_4 = \frac{-2x^2}{l} + \frac{x^3}{l^2}$$

$$N_3 = \frac{3x^2}{l^2} - \frac{2x^3}{l^3} ; N_4 = \frac{-x^2}{l} + \frac{x^3}{l^2} \qquad \text{...(9.1)}$$

If non-dimensioning is done using $s = \dfrac{x}{l_e}$, the shape functions are,

$$N_1 = 1 - 3s^2 + 2s^2$$
$$N_2 = l_e \, s(s-1)^2$$
$$N_3 = s \, (3 - 2s)$$
$$N_4 = l_e s^2 \, (s-1) \qquad \text{....(9.2)}$$

If we use non-dimensioning concept as in isoparametric formulation *i.e.* ξ varying from -1 to 1, then the shape function are

$$N_1 = \frac{2 - 3\xi + \xi^3}{4}$$

$$N_2 = \frac{l_e}{2} \frac{1 - \xi - \xi^2 + \xi^3}{4}$$

$$N_3 = \frac{2 + 3\xi - \xi^3}{4}$$

$$N_4 = \frac{l_e}{2} \frac{-1 - \xi + \xi^2 + \xi^3}{4}$$

Where,

$$\xi = \frac{2x}{l_e} - 1$$

Moment Curvature Relation

From basic solid mechanics we know

$$M = EI \frac{\partial^2 y}{\partial x^2}$$

Since

$$y = [N]\{\delta\}_e = [N_1\ N_2\ N_3\ N_4]\{\delta\}_e$$

$$\frac{\partial^2 y}{\partial x^2} = \left[\frac{\partial^2 N_1}{\partial x^2}\ \frac{\partial^2 N_2}{\partial x^2}\ \frac{\partial^2 N_3}{\partial x^2}\ \frac{\partial^2 N_4}{\partial x^2} \right]\{\delta\}_e = [B]\{\delta\}_e$$

we get

$$M = EI \left[\frac{\partial^2 N_1}{\partial x^2}\ \frac{\partial^2 N_2}{\partial x^2}\ \frac{\partial^2 N_3}{\partial x^2}\ \frac{\partial^2 N_4}{\partial x^2} \right]\{\delta\}_e$$

$$= [D][B]\{\delta\}_e$$

Where,

$$[D] = EI$$

$$[B] = \left[\frac{\partial^2 N_1}{\partial x^2}\ \frac{\partial^2 N_2}{\partial x^2}\ \frac{\partial^2 N_3}{\partial x^2}\ \frac{\partial^2 N_4}{\partial x^2} \right]$$

which is stress resultant curvature matrix.

Strain Energy

From basic solid mechanics, we know strain energy dU_e in an element length dx is given by

$$dU_e = \frac{1}{2} \frac{M^2}{EI} dV$$

$$U_e = \frac{1}{2} \int_0^{l_e} \left\{ EI \frac{\partial^2 y}{\partial x^2} \right\} \frac{1}{EI} dx$$

$$= \frac{1}{2} \int_0^{l_e} \left\{ \frac{\partial^2 y}{\partial x^2} \right\}^2 dx = \frac{1}{2} \int_0^{l_e} EI ([B]\{\delta\}_e)^T [B]\{\delta\}_e dx$$

$$= \frac{1}{2} \{\delta\}_e^T \int_0^{l_e} EI [B]^T [B]\{\delta\}_e \frac{l_e}{2} d\xi$$

Since,

$$\xi = \frac{2x}{l_e} - 1$$

$\therefore$
$$U_e = EI \frac{l_e}{2} \{\delta\}_e^T [B]^T [B]\{\delta\}_\mathbf{e} \, d\xi \qquad \qquad ...(9.3)$$

$$[B] = \left[\frac{\partial^2 N_1}{\partial x^2} \quad \frac{\partial^2 N_2}{\partial x^2} \quad \frac{\partial^2 N_3}{\partial x^2} \quad \frac{\partial^2 N_4}{\partial x^2} \right]$$

Since,

$$\xi = \frac{2x}{l_e} - 1$$

$$\frac{\partial N_i}{\partial x} = \frac{\partial N_i}{\partial \xi} \frac{\partial \xi}{\partial x} = \frac{\partial N_i}{\partial \xi} \frac{2}{l_e}$$

$\therefore$
$$\frac{\partial^2 N_i}{\partial x^2} = \frac{\partial}{\partial x} \left(\frac{\partial N_i}{\partial x} \right) = \frac{2}{l_e} \frac{\partial}{\partial \xi} \left(\frac{2}{l_e} \frac{\partial N_i}{\partial \xi} \right)$$

$$= \frac{4}{l_e^2} \left(\frac{\partial^2 N_i}{\partial \xi^2} \right)$$

$\therefore$
$$[B] = \frac{4}{l_e^2} \left[\frac{\partial^2 N_i}{\partial \xi^2} \quad \frac{\partial^2 N_2}{\partial \xi^2} \quad \frac{\partial^2 N_3}{\partial \xi^2} \quad \frac{\partial^2 N_4}{\partial \xi^2} \right]$$

$$= \frac{4}{l_e^2} \left[\frac{6\xi}{4} \quad -\frac{(1-3\xi)}{4} l_e \quad -\frac{6\xi}{4} \quad \frac{(1+3\xi)}{4} l_e \right]$$

$$= \frac{1}{l_e^2}[6\xi - (1-3\xi)l_e - 6\xi\ (1+3\xi)\,l_e]$$

$$\therefore \quad [B]^T\,[B] = \frac{1}{l_e^2}\begin{bmatrix} 6\xi \\ -(1-3\xi)l_e \\ -6\xi \\ (1+3\xi)l_e \end{bmatrix} \frac{1}{l_e^2}[6\xi - (1-3\xi)l_e - 6\xi\ (1+3\xi)l_e]$$

$$= \frac{1}{l_e^4}\begin{bmatrix} 36\xi^2 & (1-3\xi)l_e\,(6\xi) & -36\xi^2 & 6\xi(1+3\xi)l_e \\ & l_e^2(1-3\xi)^2 & 6\xi(1-3\xi)l_e & -(1+3\xi)(1-3\xi)l_e^2 \\ & SYM & 36\xi^2 & -6\xi(1+3\xi)l_e \\ & & & l_e^2(1+3\xi)^2 \end{bmatrix}$$

Now noting that

$$\int_{-1}^{1} c\,d\xi = 2C,\quad \int_{-1}^{1}\xi\,d\xi = \int_{-1}^{1}\xi^3\,d\xi = 0 \text{ and } \int_{-1}^{1}\xi^2\,d\xi = \frac{2}{3}$$

we can write

$$U_e = EI\,\frac{l_e}{2}\{\delta\}_e^T\,\frac{1}{l_e^4}\begin{bmatrix} 24 & 12l_e & -24 & 12l_e \\ & 8l_e^2 & -12l_e & 4l_e^2 \\ & SYM & 24 & -12l_e \\ & & & 8l_e^2 \end{bmatrix}\{\delta\}_e$$

$$= \frac{1}{2}\{\delta\}_e^T\,\frac{EI}{l_e^3}\begin{bmatrix} 12 & 6l_e & -12 & 6l_e \\ & 4l_e^2 & -6l_e & 2l_e^2 \\ & SYM & 24 & -6l_e \\ & & & 4l_e^2 \end{bmatrix}\{\delta\}_e$$

$$= \tfrac{1}{2}\{\delta\}_e^T\,[K]_e\,\{\delta\}_e$$

Where $[k]_e$ is element stiffness matrix and is equal to:

$$[K]_e = \frac{EI}{l_e^3}\begin{bmatrix} 12 & 6l_e & -12 & 6l_e \\ & 4l_e^2 & -6l_e & 2l_e^2 \\ & SYM & 24 & -6l_e \\ & & & 4l_e^2 \end{bmatrix}$$

Potential Energy

Potential energy of an element is equal to strain energy minus the work done by the external forces acting on the element. Thus,

$$\Pi_e = \frac{1}{2}U_e - \int_0^{l_e} pydx - \Sigma P_m Y_m = \int M_x \left(\frac{dy}{dx}\right)_k \qquad \ldots(9.4)$$

Where,

$$p - \text{Distributed load per unit length}$$

$$P_m - \text{Concentrated load at point } m$$

$$M_k - \text{External moment applied at } k.$$

The strain energy term U_e has been already derived. The work done by external loads can be assembled as explained below:

Due to uniformly Distributed load P per unit length:

$$\oint pydx = \oint p[N_1 \quad N_2 \quad N_3 \quad N_4]\{\delta\}_e \frac{l_e}{2} d\xi$$

$$= \frac{pl_e}{2} \int_{-1}^{1} \begin{bmatrix} \dfrac{2-3\xi+\xi^3}{4} & \dfrac{l_e}{2} \dfrac{1-\xi-\xi^2+\xi^3}{4} \\[2mm] \dfrac{2+3\xi-\xi^3}{4} & \dfrac{l_e}{2} \dfrac{-1-\xi+\xi^2+\xi^3}{4} \end{bmatrix} \{\delta\}_e d\xi$$

Noting that

$$\int_{-1}^{1} cd\xi = 2C, \int_{-1}^{1} \xi d\xi = \int_{-1}^{1} \xi^3 d\xi = 0 \text{ and } \int_{-1}^{1} \xi^2 d\xi = \frac{2}{3}$$

$$\int_{-1}^{1} pydx = \frac{pl_e}{8}\left[4 \quad \frac{pl_e}{6} \quad 4 \quad -\frac{4l_e}{6}\right]\{\delta\}_e$$

$$= \left[\frac{pl_e}{2} \quad \frac{pl_e^2}{12} \quad \frac{pl_e}{2} \quad -\frac{pl_e^2}{12}\right]\{\delta\}_e$$

This equivalent load on the element is shown below. The point loads like P_m and M_k are readily taken care by introducing nodes at the points of application.

Thus work done by external load is assembled. Let it be represented by

$$\Sigma F_i \delta_i = F_1 \delta_1 + F_2 \delta_2 + F_3 \delta_3 + F_4 \delta_4$$

$$= \{\delta\}_e^T \{F\}_e$$

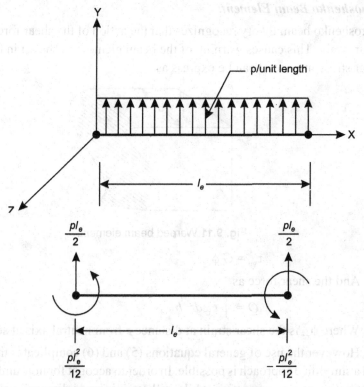

Fig. 9.10 Equivalent nodal loads of UDL.

Minimization of Potential Energy:

In finite element analysis the total potential energy of the system is considered as the summation of total potential energy of the elements. Thus

$$\Pi = \sum \Pi_e$$

$$= U_e - \sum \{\delta\}_e^T \{F\}_e = \frac{1}{2} \{F\}^T [k] \{\delta\} - \{\delta\}^T \{F\}$$

where, $\{\delta\}$ and $\{F\}$ are nodal unknown vector and load vector respectively. From the principle of minimization of potential energy we get

$$\frac{d\Pi}{d\delta} = 0$$

$$[k] \{\delta\} = 0$$

$$[k] \{\delta\} = F$$

In finite element analysis, element stiffness matrix $[k]_e$ is assembled and placed in global matrix at appropriate place. When this process is completed for all the elements, we get global stiffness matrix $[k]$. Similarly global load vector $\{F\}$ is assembled.

Timoshenko Beam Element:

Timoshenko beam theory recognizes that the action of the shear force causes a shear strain. This causes warping of the beam element as shown in figure. The shear stress in general can be express as

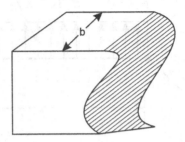

Fig. 9.11 Warped beam element.

$$\tau_{xy} = G\,\phi_{xz} \qquad\qquad ...(5)$$

And the shear force as

$$Q = \oint \tau_{xz}\,dz\ b \qquad\qquad ...(9.6)$$

Where ϕ_{xz} is the shear strain at distance z from neutral axis at section x.

However the use of general equations (5) and (6) complicates the problem and a simplified approach is possible. In order to account for non-uniform stress distribution at a cross-section while still retaining one dimensional approach, the equations (5) and (6) are modified using a shear correction factor as follow:

$$\tau_{xy} = \alpha\,G\phi_x$$

and

$$Q = \tau_{xz}\,A = \alpha\,AG\phi_x$$

The shear correction factor α is a function of the cross-sectional shape and poisson ratio μ. The term αA is the 'shear area' of the section associated with shear and may be denoted as A_s. Thus

$$A_s = \alpha A \qquad\text{where}\qquad \alpha < 1$$

Values of α for various cross-sectional shapes are given in the solid mechanics books. The value of α for a rectangular section is $\dfrac{5}{6}$. Hence,

$$\phi = \frac{Q}{G\,A_s} \qquad\qquad ...(9.7)$$

$$\phi = \theta - \frac{\partial w}{\partial x} \qquad\qquad ...(9.8)$$

Where θ is the angle through which the face of the cross section rotates after deformation as shown in Fig. 9.12.

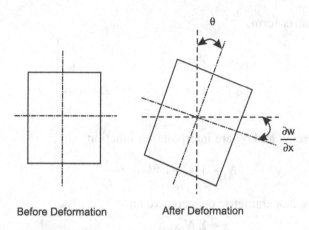

Before Deformation   After Deformation

Fig. 9.12 Deformation after application of force.

Now, in a beam element

$$M = EI \frac{d\theta}{dx}$$

$\therefore$ Strain energy due to flexure $= \int \frac{M^2}{2EI} dx = \frac{EI}{2} \int_0^{l_e} \left(\frac{d\theta}{dx} \right)^2 dx$

and strain energy due to shear $= \oint \frac{1}{2} \times$ shear stress $\times$ shear strain $\times dV$

$$= \oint \frac{1}{2} \tau_{xy} \phi \, dV$$

$$\oint \frac{1}{2} G \, \phi^2 \, dV = \frac{1}{2} G \, A_s \int_0^{l_e} \left(\theta - \frac{\partial w}{\partial x} \right)^2 dx$$

$\therefore$ Total strain energy of the element is

$$U = \frac{1}{2} EI \int_0^{l_e} \left(\frac{d\theta}{dx} \right)^2 dx + \frac{1}{2} GA_s \int_0^{l_e} \left(\theta - \frac{\partial w}{\partial x} \right)^2 dx \qquad ...(9.9)$$

9.2.3 Finite Element Formulation

Since, according to Timoshenko theory $\theta = \begin{Bmatrix} w \\ \theta \end{Bmatrix}$, θ and w are decoupled *i.e.*
they are independent of each other, at every node there are two independent
displacements components θ and w. In a two noded beam element they vary
linearly. Thus,

$$w = N_1 w_1 + N_2 w_2$$
$$\theta = N_1 \theta_1 + N_2 \theta_2$$

In matrix form,

$$\begin{Bmatrix} w \\ \theta \end{Bmatrix} = \begin{bmatrix} N_1 & 0 & N_2 & 0 \\ 0 & N_1 & 0 & N_2 \end{bmatrix} \begin{Bmatrix} w_1 \\ \theta_1 \\ w_2 \\ \theta_2 \end{Bmatrix} \qquad ...(9.10)$$

Where N_1 and N_2 are interpolation functions *i.e.*

$$N_1 = 1 - \frac{x}{l_e} \text{ and } N_2 = \frac{x}{l_e}$$

Using isoparametric concept, we have

$$x = \Sigma N_i x_i$$

$$\frac{d\theta}{dx} = \sum_{i=1}^{2} \frac{\partial N_i}{\partial x} \theta_i$$

$$\therefore \qquad \phi = \theta - \frac{\partial w}{\partial x} = \sum_{i=1}^{2} N_i \theta_i - \sum_{i=1}^{2} \frac{\partial N_i}{\partial x} w_i$$

Strain vector,

$$\{\varepsilon\} = \begin{Bmatrix} k \\ \phi \end{Bmatrix}$$

Where k is curvature $= \dfrac{d\theta}{dx}$

$$\therefore \{\varepsilon\} = \begin{Bmatrix} k \\ \phi \end{Bmatrix} = \begin{bmatrix} 0 & \dfrac{dN_1}{dx} & 0 & \dfrac{dN_2}{dx} \\ \dfrac{-dN_1}{dx} & N_1 & \dfrac{-dN_2}{dx} & x \end{bmatrix} = \frac{1}{l_e} \begin{bmatrix} 0 & -1 & 0 & 1 \\ l & l_e - x & -1 & x \end{bmatrix}$$

The stress resultants M and Q are related to strain as

$$[\varepsilon] = \begin{Bmatrix} M \\ Q \end{Bmatrix} = [D] \{\varepsilon\}$$

Now $M = EI\,k$

For rectangular section $I = \dfrac{1}{12} bh^3$

$$\therefore \qquad D_{11} = \frac{E}{12} bh^3$$

$$Q = A_s \tau_{xy} = A_s h\phi = \alpha A \frac{E}{2(1+\mu)} \phi = \frac{\alpha bh}{2} E\phi$$

$$\therefore \quad [\sigma] = \begin{Bmatrix} M \\ Q \end{Bmatrix} = \begin{bmatrix} \dfrac{E}{12}bh^3 & 0 \\ 0 & \dfrac{\alpha bh}{2}E \end{bmatrix} \begin{Bmatrix} k \\ \varnothing \end{Bmatrix} = \dfrac{Ebh}{12}\begin{bmatrix} h^2 & 0 \\ 0 & 6\alpha \end{bmatrix} \begin{Bmatrix} k \\ \varnothing \end{Bmatrix}$$

Assuming $\mu = 0$, D matrix for rectangular section is

$$[D] = \frac{Ebh}{12}\begin{bmatrix} h^2 & 0 \\ 0 & 6\alpha \end{bmatrix}$$

$$\therefore \quad [k_e] = \int_0^{l_e} [B]^T [D][B]\, dx$$

$$= \frac{1}{l_e^2}\int_0^{l_e} \begin{bmatrix} 0 & 1 \\ -1 & l_e - x \\ 0 & -1 \\ 1 & x \end{bmatrix} \frac{Ebh}{12}\begin{bmatrix} h^2 & 0 \\ 0 & 6\alpha \end{bmatrix}\begin{bmatrix} 0 & -1 & 0 & 1 \\ l & l_e - x & -1 & x \end{bmatrix} dx$$

$$= \frac{Ebh}{12 l_e^2}\int_0^{l_e} \begin{bmatrix} 6\alpha & 6\alpha(l_e - x) & -6\alpha & 6\alpha x \\ 6\alpha(l_e - x) & h^2 + 6\alpha(l_e - x) & -6\alpha(l_e - x) & -h^2 + 6\alpha(l_e - x) \\ -6\alpha & -6\alpha(l_e - x) & 6\alpha & 6\alpha x \\ 6\alpha x & -h^2 + 6\alpha x(l_e - x) & -6\alpha x & h^2 + 6\alpha x^2 \end{bmatrix} dx$$

Separating bending and shear terms, we can write

$$[k]_e = \frac{Ebh}{12 l_e^2}\begin{bmatrix} 0 & 0 & 0 & 0 \\ 0 & h^2 & 0 & -h^2 \\ 0 & 0 & 0 & 0 \\ 0 & -h^2 & 0 & h^2 \end{bmatrix} dx + 6\alpha\, \frac{Ebh}{12 l_e^2}$$

$$\begin{bmatrix} l & l_e - x & -1 & x \\ l_e - x & (l_e - x^2) & -(l_e - x) & x(l_e - x) \\ -1 & -(l_e - x) & 1 & -x \\ x & x(l_e - x) & -x & x^2 \end{bmatrix} dx$$

i.e.

$$[k]_e = [k]_{be} + [k]_{se} \qquad\qquad \dots (9.11)$$

where $[k]_{be}$ and $[k]_{se}$ are the contributions of bending and shear to the total stiffness. The integration can be performed to get $[k]_{be}$ and $[k]_{se}$ as shown below:

$$[k]_{se} = \frac{Ebh}{12l_e^2}\begin{bmatrix} 0 & 0 & 0 & 0 \\ 0 & 1 & 0 & -1 \\ 0 & 0 & 0 & 0 \\ 0 & -1 & 0 & 1 \end{bmatrix}$$

$$[k]_{se} = \frac{Gh\alpha}{l_e}\begin{bmatrix} 1 & \dfrac{l_e}{2} & -1 & \dfrac{l_e}{2} \\ \dfrac{l_e}{2} & \dfrac{l_e^2}{3} & -\dfrac{l_e}{2} & \dfrac{l_e^2}{6} \\ -1 & -\dfrac{l_e}{2} & 1 & -\dfrac{l_e}{2} \\ \dfrac{l_e}{2} & \dfrac{l_e^2}{6} & -\dfrac{l_e}{2} & \dfrac{l_e^2}{3} \end{bmatrix}$$

The above formulation gives good results for moderately thick beams. For thin beams $\left(\dfrac{l_e}{h} \text{ very large}\right)$, the results obtained by this formulation are not correct. The shear term, which should tend to zero in such cases, do not tend to zero. This is called Shear locking. The shear stiffness is increasingly constrained. This is called spurious constraint. There are two popular remedies for the elimination of this type of errors

1. Reduced Integration Technique

2. Using field consistency element

Reduced Integration Technique:

If shear stiffness in equation (9.11) is integrated with one point Gaussian technique, we get

$$[k]_{se} = \frac{\alpha Gh}{l_e}\begin{bmatrix} 1 & \dfrac{l_e}{2} & -1 & \dfrac{l_e}{2} \\ \dfrac{l_e}{2} & \dfrac{l_e^2}{4} & -\dfrac{l_e}{2} & \dfrac{l_e^2}{4} \\ -1 & -\dfrac{l_e}{2} & 1 & -\dfrac{l_e}{2} \\ \dfrac{l_e}{2} & \dfrac{l_e^2}{4} & \dfrac{l_e}{2} & \dfrac{l_e^2}{4} \end{bmatrix}$$

Since $x = \dfrac{1+\xi}{2}, dx = \dfrac{1}{2}d\xi$

and $\qquad f(\xi)d\xi = 2f(\xi = 0)$

In case of two point integration sampling points are at $\pm \dfrac{1}{\sqrt{3}}$ and weight function: $W_i = 1$.

Hence

$$[k]^2_{se} = \frac{\alpha Gh}{l_e} \begin{bmatrix} 1 & \dfrac{l_e}{2} & -1 & \dfrac{l_e}{2} \\ \dfrac{l_e}{2} & \dfrac{l_e^2}{3} & -\dfrac{l_e}{2} & \dfrac{l_e^2}{6} \\ -1 & -\dfrac{l_e}{2} & 1 & -\dfrac{l_e}{2} \\ \dfrac{l_e}{2} & \dfrac{l_e^2}{6} & -\dfrac{l_e}{2} & \dfrac{l_e^2}{3} \end{bmatrix}$$

Now consider the analysis of cantilever beam with single element. The stiffness matrix of the beam is

$$[k] = [k]_e = [k]_{be} + [k]_{se}$$

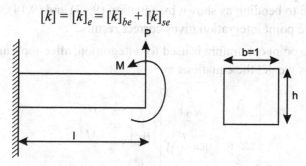

Fig. 9.13 Loading condition on cantilever beam.

Applying the boundary conditions that $w_1 = 0$, $\theta_1 = 0$ and defining

$$\psi = \frac{Eh^3}{12l_e} = \frac{Eh^3}{12l} \quad \text{and} \quad \beta = \frac{\alpha Gh}{l_e} = \frac{\alpha Gh}{l}, \quad \text{we get the equilibrium equation}$$

from one point quadrature as,

$$\begin{bmatrix} \beta & \dfrac{l}{2}\beta & -\beta & \dfrac{l}{2}\beta \\ \dfrac{l}{2}\beta & \Psi+\dfrac{l^2}{4}\beta & -\dfrac{l}{2}\beta & -\Psi+\dfrac{l^2}{4}\beta \\ -\beta & -\dfrac{l}{2}\beta & \beta & -\dfrac{l}{2}\beta \\ \dfrac{1}{2}\beta & -\Psi+\dfrac{l^2}{4}\beta & -\dfrac{1}{2}\beta & \Psi+\dfrac{l^2}{4}\beta \end{bmatrix} \begin{Bmatrix} 0 \\ 0 \\ w_2 \\ \theta_2 \end{Bmatrix} = \begin{Bmatrix} 0 \\ 0 \\ P \\ M \end{Bmatrix}$$

$$\begin{bmatrix} \beta & -\dfrac{l}{2}\beta \\ -\dfrac{l}{2}\beta & \Psi+\dfrac{l^2}{4}\beta \end{bmatrix} \begin{Bmatrix} w_2 \\ \theta_2 \end{Bmatrix} = \begin{Bmatrix} P \\ M \end{Bmatrix}$$

Solving the above equation, we get

$$w_2 = \left(\dfrac{l^2}{4\Psi}+\dfrac{1}{\beta}\right)P+\dfrac{1}{2\Psi}M \qquad \qquad ...(9.12)$$

$$\theta_2 = \dfrac{\dfrac{l}{2}P+M}{\Psi} \qquad \qquad ...(9.13)$$

In case of thin beam, $\beta \geq \Psi$. Hence equation (9.12) reduces to

$$w_2 = \dfrac{1}{2\Psi}\left[\dfrac{lP}{2}+M\right] \qquad \qquad ...(9.14)$$

And θ_2 remains same as equation (9.13). Thus the beam deformation is solely due to bending as shown by equation (9.13) and (9.14). Hence, for thin beams one point integration gives correct results.

If two point quadrature is used for integration, after applying the boundary conditions we get the equations as

$$\begin{bmatrix} \beta & -\dfrac{l}{2}\beta \\ -\dfrac{l}{2}\beta & \Psi+\dfrac{l^3}{3}\beta \end{bmatrix} \begin{Bmatrix} w_2 \\ \theta_2 \end{Bmatrix} = \begin{Bmatrix} P \\ M \end{Bmatrix}$$

Solving for w_2 and θ_2, we get

$$w_2 = \dfrac{\Psi+\dfrac{\beta l^2}{3}}{\beta\left(\Psi+\dfrac{\beta l^2}{12}\right)}P+\dfrac{lM}{2\left(\Psi+\dfrac{\beta l^2}{12}\right)}$$

$$\theta_2 = \dfrac{M+\dfrac{l}{2}P}{\left(\Psi+\dfrac{\beta l^2}{12}\right)}$$

In case of thin beams $\beta \geq \psi$. Hence we get

$$w_2 = \dfrac{4P+6\dfrac{M}{l}}{\beta} \qquad \qquad ...(9.15)$$

$$\theta_2 = \frac{6(lP + 2M)}{l^2\beta} \qquad \qquad \ldots(9.16)$$

The above two equations show that the free end deformation depends on the co-efficient β corresponding to shear deformation, which is not true in case of thin beams. Hence, two point integration (equation 15 and 16) lead to erroneous results.

Thus, the reduced integration (1 point Gaussian integration technique) is used to get good results for thin beams.

9.2.4 Field Consistent Element Formulation

Let us first see how the element formulation is field inconsistent in the case of very thin beams. In the formulation we have taken,

$$w = [N_1 \ N_2]\begin{Bmatrix} w_1 \\ w_2 \end{Bmatrix} = N_1 w_1 + N_2 w_2$$

$$\theta = [N_1 \ N_2]\begin{Bmatrix} \theta_1 \\ \theta_2 \end{Bmatrix} = N_1\theta_1 + N_2\theta_2$$

Where $\qquad N_1 = \dfrac{1-\xi}{2}$ and $N_2 = \dfrac{1+\xi}{2}$

$$\xi = \frac{2x}{l_e} - 1$$

Rearranging the terms, we get

$$w = \frac{1-\xi}{2}w_1 + \frac{1+\xi}{2}w_2 = \frac{w_1 + w_2}{2} + \frac{w_2 - w_1}{2}\xi = a_1 + a_2\xi$$

Where

$$a_1 = \frac{w_1 + w_2}{2} \text{ and } a_2 = \frac{w_2 - w_1}{2}$$

Similarly $\qquad \theta = b_1 + b_2 \xi$

Where $\qquad b_1 = \dfrac{\theta_1 + \theta_2}{2}$ and $b_2 = \dfrac{\theta_2 - \theta_1}{2}$

Now bending strain

$$k = \frac{d\theta}{dx} = \frac{d\theta}{d\xi}\frac{d\xi}{dx} = \frac{2}{l}b_2$$

And shear strain

$$\emptyset = \theta - \frac{dw}{dx} = b_1 + b_2\xi - \frac{d\xi}{dx}\frac{dw}{d\xi} = b_1 + b_2\xi - \frac{2}{l}a_2$$

Strain energy due to bending is given by,

$$U_b = \oint \frac{EI}{2}\left(\frac{d\theta}{dx}\right)^2 dx = \oint \frac{EI}{2}\left(\frac{2}{l}b_2\right)^2 dx$$

And strain energy due to shear is

$$U_s = \oint \frac{GA_s}{2}(\emptyset)^2 dx = \oint \frac{GA_s}{2}\left(b_1 - \frac{2}{l}a_2 + b_2\xi\right)^2 dx$$

As the thickness approaches zero, the strain energy should vanish and bending strain energy should exist.

i.e.,

$$b_1 - \frac{2}{l}a_2 + b_2\,\xi \rightarrow 0$$

$$b_1 - \frac{2}{l}a_2 \rightarrow 0 \qquad\qquad ...(9.17)$$

And

$$b_2 \rightarrow 0 \qquad\qquad ...(9.18)$$

The terms corresponding to condition (9.17) correspond to both the strain fields flexure and shear. Hence, it is called field consistent term. The constraint corresponding to equation (9.18) contains the term corresponding only to flexure field. If $b_2 \rightarrow 0$, the strain energy due to bending tends to zero, which should not happen. Hence, this constraint requirement in the limiting case is spurious and it is this requirement which causes shear locking.

To get rid of this situation in the limiting case, the function smoothening is required *i.e.* alter the terms to overcome this situation. This is achieved by making $b_2 = 0$ in the shear strain field *i.e.* by taking

$$\bar{\theta} = b_1 = \frac{\theta_1 + \theta_2}{2} \quad \text{in the shear field}$$

Thus,

$$\bar{\theta} = b_1 = \frac{\theta_1 + \theta_2}{2} = \begin{bmatrix} \frac{1}{2} & \frac{1}{2} \end{bmatrix}\begin{Bmatrix} \theta_1 \\ \theta_2 \end{Bmatrix} = \begin{bmatrix} \bar{N}_1 & \bar{N}_2 \end{bmatrix}\begin{Bmatrix} \theta_1 \\ \theta_2 \end{Bmatrix}$$

i.e. in shear field interpolation function for θ will be taken as $\begin{bmatrix} \bar{N}_1 & \bar{N}_2 \end{bmatrix} = \begin{bmatrix} \frac{1}{2} & \frac{1}{2} \end{bmatrix}$. Thus smoothening is required not only in the shear strain field but even in the shear stress field also.

9.2.5 Shape Function for a two Nodded Beam Element using Polynomial Function

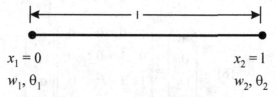

$$x_1 = 0 \qquad\qquad\qquad x_2 = 1$$
$$w_1, \theta_1 \qquad\qquad\qquad w_2, \theta_2$$

Fig. 9.14 A beam element.

The typical beam element is shown in figure 9.4. In this case C^1 – continuing is to be satisfied, since strain energy expression involves second differentiation term $\dfrac{d^2 w}{dx^2}$. Hence in this case at each node, unknowns are the displacement and slope. *i.e.*,

$$\{\delta\} = \begin{pmatrix} w_1 \\ \theta_1 \\ w_2 \\ \theta_2 \end{pmatrix}$$

$$\theta_1 = \frac{\partial w_1}{\partial x}$$

$$\theta_2 = \frac{\partial w_2}{\partial x}$$

Since, there are four nodal values, we select polynomial with four constants. Thus,

$$w = \alpha_1 + \alpha_2 x + \alpha_3 x^2 + \alpha_4 x^3 \qquad\qquad ...(9.19)$$

Equation (9.19) satisfies compatibility and completeness requirement. Now,

$$\theta = \frac{\partial w}{\partial x} = \alpha_2 + 2\alpha_3 x + 3\alpha_4 x^2$$

For convenience we select local co-ordinate system.

i.e.,

$$x_1 = 0$$
$$x_2 = l$$
$\therefore \qquad\quad w_1 = \alpha_1$
$$\theta_1 = \alpha_2$$

$$w_2 = \alpha_1 + \alpha_2 l + \alpha_3 l^2 + \alpha_4 x l^3$$
$$\theta_2 = \alpha_2 + 2\alpha_3 l + 3\alpha_4 l^2$$

i.e.,

$$\{\delta\} = \begin{pmatrix} w_1 \\ \theta_1 \\ w_2 \\ \theta_2 \end{pmatrix} = \begin{bmatrix} 1 & 0 & 0 & 0 \\ 0 & 1 & 0 & 0 \\ 1 & l & l^2 & l^2 \\ 0 & 1 & 2l & 3l^2 \end{bmatrix} \begin{pmatrix} \alpha_1 \\ \alpha_2 \\ \alpha_3 \\ \alpha_4 \end{pmatrix}$$

$$\begin{pmatrix} \alpha_1 \\ \alpha_2 \\ \alpha_3 \\ \alpha_4 \end{pmatrix} = \begin{bmatrix} 1 & 0 & 0 & 0 \\ 0 & 1 & 0 & 0 \\ 1 & l & l^2 & l^2 \\ 0 & 1 & 2l & 3l^2 \end{bmatrix}^{-1} \begin{pmatrix} w_1 \\ \theta_1 \\ w_2 \\ \theta_2 \end{pmatrix}$$

$$= \frac{1}{3l^4 - 2l^4} \begin{bmatrix} l^4 & 0 & -3l^2 & 2l \\ 0 & l^4 & -2l^2 & l^2 \\ 0 & 0 & 3l^2 & -2l \\ 0 & 0 & -l^3 & l^2 \end{bmatrix}^{T} \begin{pmatrix} w_1 \\ \theta_1 \\ w_2 \\ \theta_2 \end{pmatrix}$$

$$= \begin{bmatrix} 1 & 0 & 0 & 0 \\ 0 & 1 & 0 & 0 \\ \dfrac{-3}{l^2} & \dfrac{-2}{l} & \dfrac{3}{l^2} & \dfrac{-1}{l} \\ \dfrac{2}{l^3} & \dfrac{1}{l^2} & \dfrac{-2}{l^3} & \dfrac{1}{l^2} \end{bmatrix} \begin{pmatrix} w_1 \\ \theta_1 \\ w_2 \\ \theta_2 \end{pmatrix}$$

$$w = \alpha_1 + \alpha_2 x + \alpha_3 x^2 + \alpha_4 x^3$$

$$= [1 \ x \ x^2 \ x^3] \begin{pmatrix} \alpha_1 \\ \alpha_2 \\ \alpha_3 \\ \alpha_4 \end{pmatrix}$$

$$= [1 \ x \ x^2 \ x^3] \begin{bmatrix} 1 & 0 & 0 & 0 \\ 0 & 1 & 0 & 0 \\ \dfrac{-3}{l^2} & \dfrac{-2}{l} & \dfrac{3}{l^2} & \dfrac{-1}{l} \\ \dfrac{2}{l^3} & \dfrac{1}{l^2} & \dfrac{-2}{l^3} & \dfrac{1}{l^2} \end{bmatrix} \begin{pmatrix} w_1 \\ \theta_1 \\ w_2 \\ \theta_2 \end{pmatrix}$$

$$= \left[1 - \frac{3x^2}{l^2} + \frac{2x^3}{l^3} \quad x - \frac{2x^2}{l} + \frac{x^3}{l^2} \quad \frac{3x^2}{l^2} - \frac{2x^3}{l^3} \quad \frac{-x^2}{l} + \frac{x^3}{l^2} \right] \begin{pmatrix} w_1 \\ \theta_1 \\ w_2 \\ \theta_2 \end{pmatrix}$$

$$= [N_1 \ N_2 \ N_3 \ N_4] \{\delta\}_e$$

Where $[N] = [N_1 \ N_2 \ N_3 \ N_4]$

and $N_1 = 1 - \frac{3x^2}{l^2} + \frac{2x^3}{l^3}; \quad N_2 = x - \frac{2x^2}{l} + \frac{x^3}{l^2}$

$$N_3 = \frac{3x^2}{l^2} - \frac{2x^3}{l^3}; \quad N_4 = \frac{-x^2}{l} + \frac{x^3}{l^2}$$

9.2.6 Single Beam Element Stiffness Matrix Formulation

Consider a prismatic beam of length L loaded by shear force and moments at the ends as shown in figure 9.15. Distance along the beam is measured with a co-ordinate x, starting at the left end.

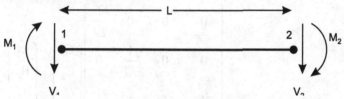

Fig. 9.15 Prismatic beam loaded with shear force and moments at the ends.

The shear force and moment at left end are V_1 and M_1 respectively.

Corresponding quantities at the right end are V_2 and M_2.

Assuming zero transverse distributed load, the load-differential equation can be integrated sequentially to yield expression for shear force, bending moment, slope and deflection.

$$EI \frac{d^4w}{dx^4} = 0$$

$$EI \frac{d^3w}{dx^3} = C_1 = -V(x)$$

$$EI \frac{d^3w}{dx^3} = C_1x + C_2 = -M(x)$$

$$EI \frac{dw}{dx} = C_1\frac{x^2}{2} + C_2x + C_3$$

$$EIw = C_1\frac{x^3}{6} + C_2\frac{x^2}{2} + C_3x + C_4$$

The displacement and rotation at left end are denoted by w_1 and θ_1, respectively. Corresponding quantities at right end are w_2 and θ_2. These four kinematic variables may then be expressed in terms of the constants C_1, C_2, C_3 and C_4 using the equation above, as follow:

$$w_1 = w(0) = \frac{1}{EI}C_4$$

$$\theta_1 = \frac{dw}{dx}(0) = \frac{1}{EI}C_3$$

$$w_2 = w(L) = \frac{1}{EI}\left[C_1\frac{L^3}{6} + C_2\frac{L^2}{2} + C_3L + C_4\right]$$

$$\theta_2 = \frac{dw}{dx}(L) = \frac{1}{EI}\left[C_1\frac{L^2}{2} + C_2L + C_3\right]$$

The equations can be written in matrix form, as follows:

$$
\begin{bmatrix}
0 & 0 & 0 & \dfrac{1}{EI} \\
0 & 0 & \dfrac{1}{EI} & 0 \\
\dfrac{L^3}{6EI} & \dfrac{L^2}{2EI} & \dfrac{L}{EI} & \dfrac{1}{EI} \\
\dfrac{L^2}{2EI} & \dfrac{L}{EI} & \dfrac{1}{EI} & 0
\end{bmatrix}
\begin{Bmatrix}
C_1 \\ C_2 \\ C_3 \\ C_4
\end{Bmatrix}
=
\begin{Bmatrix}
w_1 \\ \theta_1 \\ w_2 \\ \theta_2
\end{Bmatrix}
$$

Solving this system of linear algebraic equations for C_1, C_2, C_3 and C_4 gives

$$
\begin{Bmatrix}
C_1 \\ C_2 \\ C_3 \\ C_4
\end{Bmatrix}
=
\begin{bmatrix}
\dfrac{12EI}{L^3} & \dfrac{6EI}{L^2} & \dfrac{-12EI}{L^3} & \dfrac{6EI}{L^2} \\
\dfrac{-6EI}{L^2} & \dfrac{-4EI}{L} & \dfrac{6EI}{L^2} & \dfrac{-2EI}{L} \\
0 & EI & 0 & 0 \\
EI & 0 & 0 & 0
\end{bmatrix}
\begin{Bmatrix}
w_1 \\ \theta_1 \\ w_2 \\ \theta_2
\end{Bmatrix}
$$

The shear force and bending moment at the two ends of the beam can be expressed in terms of the constants C_1, C_2, C_3 and C_4. Then, using the result above the shear force and bending moments on the ends can be written in terms of the end displacements and rotations.

$$V(0) = -V_1 = C_1$$

$$V_1 = \frac{12EI}{L^3} w_1 + \frac{6EI}{L^2} \theta_1 - \frac{12EI}{L^3} w_2 + \frac{6EI}{L^2} \theta_2$$

$$M(0) = M_1 = C_2$$

$$M_1 = \frac{6EI}{L^2} w_1 + \frac{4EI}{L} \theta_1 - \frac{6EI}{L^2} w_2 + \frac{2EI}{L} \theta_2$$

$$V(L) = V_2 = -C_1$$

$$V_2 = \frac{-12EI}{L^3} w_1 - \frac{6EI}{L^2} \theta_1 + \frac{12EI}{L^3} w_2 - \frac{6EI}{L^2} \theta_2$$

$$M(L) = -M_2 = -C_1 L - C_2$$

$$M_2 = \frac{6EI}{L^2} w_1 + \frac{2EI}{L} \theta_1 - \frac{6EI}{L^2} w_2 + \frac{4EI}{L} \theta_2$$

The equations can be written in matrix form, as follows

$$\frac{EI}{L^3} \begin{bmatrix} 12 & 6L & -12 & 6L \\ 6L & 4L^2 & -6L & 2L^2 \\ -12 & -6L & 12 & -6L \\ 6L & 2L^2 & -6L & 4L^2 \end{bmatrix} \begin{pmatrix} w_1 \\ \theta_1 \\ w_2 \\ \theta_2 \end{pmatrix} = \begin{pmatrix} V_1 \\ M_1 \\ V_2 \\ M_2 \end{pmatrix}$$

Where;

$$\begin{pmatrix} w_1 \\ \theta_1 \\ w_2 \\ \theta_2 \end{pmatrix} = \text{Element displacement vector}$$

$$\begin{pmatrix} V_1 \\ M_1 \\ V_2 \\ M_2 \end{pmatrix} = \text{Element force vector}$$

$$\frac{EI}{L^3} \begin{bmatrix} 12 & 6L & -12 & 6L \\ 6L & 4L^2 & -6L & 2L^2 \\ -12 & -6L & 12 & -6L \\ 6L & 2L^2 & -6L & 4L^2 \end{bmatrix} = \text{Finite element stiffness matrix}$$

9.2.7 Boundary Conditions

The beam equation contains a fourth-order derivative in x. To find a unique solution we need four boundary conditions. The support or displacement boundary conditions are used to fix values of displacement (w) and rotations $\dfrac{dw}{dx}$ on the boundary. Load and moment boundary conditions involve higher derivatives of w.

A simple support (pin or roller) is equivalent to a point force on the beam which is adjusted in such a way as to fix the position of the beam at that point. A fixed support or clamp, is equivalent to the combination of a point force and a point torque which is adjusted in such a way as to fix both the position and slope of the beam at that point. Point forces and torques, whether from supports or directly applied, will divide a beam into a set of segments, between which the beam equation will yield a continuous solution, given four boundary conditions, two at each end of the segment. Assuming that the product EI is a constant, and defining $\lambda = F/EI$ where F is the magnitude of a point force, and $\tau = M/EI$ where M is the magnitude of a point torque, the boundary conditions appropriate for some common cases is given in the table below.

Table 9.1 Boundary conditions for beams

Boundary	w'''	w''	w'	w
Clamp			$\Delta w' = 0^*$	$\Delta w = 0^*$
Simple support		$\Delta w'' = 0$	$\Delta w' = 0$	$\Delta w = 0^*$
Point force	$\Delta w''' = \lambda$	$\Delta w'' = 0$	$\Delta w' = 0$	$\Delta w = 0$
Point torque	$\Delta w''' = 0$	$\Delta w'' = \tau$	$\Delta w' = 0$	$\Delta w = 0$
Free end	$\Delta w''' = 0$	$\Delta w'' = 0$		
Clamp at end			w' fixed	w fixed
Simple supported end		$w'' = 0$		w fixed
Point force at end	$w''' = \pm \lambda$	$w'' = 0$		
Point torque at end	$w''' = 0$	$w''' = \pm \tau$		

9.3. PLANE STRESS AND STRAIN

9.3.1 Plane Stress

Plane stress can be defined as a state of stress in which the normal stress and the shear stress that are perpendicular to the plane are assumed to be zero. Thus, the normal stress σz and shear stresses τ_{xz} and τ_{yz} are assumed to be zero in magnitude. Generally, the thin members (which have a small z dimension compared to the dimensions in x and y plane) and whose loads act only in the x-y plane can be considered to be under plane stress condition.

9.3.2 Plane Strain

Plane strain can be defined as a state of strain in which the strain normal to the x-y plane and the shear strains are assumed to be zero. Thus, the normal strain $\mathcal{E}z$ and the shear strains Υxz and Υyz are assumed to be zero in magnitude. The assumptions of plane strain are realistic for long bodies (say, in the z direction) with constant cross-sectional area subjected to loads that act only in the x and/or y directions and do not vary in the z direction.

9.3.3 Constant Strain Triangle (CST)

The triangular elements with a number of different nodes are used for solving two dimensional solid members. The first element type developed for the finite element analysis of 2D solids was the linear triangular element. However, the linear triangular element is less accurate than the linear quadrilateral elements as observed. However, the triangular element is still very useful element for its adaptability to complex geometries. If the geometry of 2D model is of complex nature then triangular element is used. Mathematically, it is simple to develop constant strain triangle (CST). In CST, strain has no variation inside the element and hence element size should be small enough to obtain correct and accurate results. In case of 2D solid elements, the displacement is expressed in two orthogonal directions. Thus the displacement field can be written as

$$\{d\} = \begin{Bmatrix} u \\ v \end{Bmatrix}$$

Here, u and v are the displacements parallel to x and y directions respectively.

Element Stiffness Matrix for CST

A typical triangular element assumed to represent a sub-domain of a plane body under plane stress/strain condition is represented in Fig 9.16. The displacement (u, v) of any point P is represented in terms of nodal displacements:

$$u = N_1u_1 + N_2 u_2 + N_3u_3 \qquad \text{... (9.19)}$$

$$v = N_1v_1 + N_2v_2 + N_3v_3 \qquad \text{...(9.20)}$$

Where, N_1, N_2, N_3 are the shape functions.

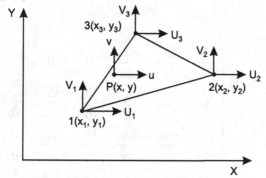

Fig. 9.16 Constant Strain Triangle.

9.3.4 Linear Triangular Element for Plane Stress/Strain

The strain-displacement relationship for 2 dimensional plane stress/strain problem can be simplified in the following form:

$$\varepsilon_x = \frac{\partial u}{\partial x} + \frac{1}{2}\left[\left(\frac{\partial u}{\partial x}\right)^2 + \left(\frac{\partial v}{\partial x}\right)^2\right] \qquad ...(9.21)$$

$$\varepsilon_y = \frac{\partial u}{\partial y} + \frac{1}{2}\left[\left(\frac{\partial u}{\partial y}\right)^2 + \left(\frac{\partial v}{\partial y}\right)^2\right] \qquad ...(9.22)$$

$$\gamma_x = \frac{\partial v}{\partial x} + \frac{\partial u}{\partial y} + \left[\frac{\partial u}{\partial x}\frac{\partial u}{\partial y} + \frac{\partial v}{\partial x}\frac{\partial v}{\partial y}\right] \qquad ...(9.23)$$

In case of small amplitude of displacement, the non-linear term of the above equation can be ignored and following expression will be reached.

$$\varepsilon_x = \frac{\partial u}{\partial x}$$

$$\varepsilon_y = \frac{\partial v}{\partial y}$$

$$\gamma_{xy} = \frac{\partial v}{\partial x} + \frac{\partial u}{\partial y}$$

Hence the element strain components can be represented as,

$$\varepsilon = \begin{cases} \varepsilon_x = \dfrac{\partial u}{\partial x} = \dfrac{\partial N_1}{\partial x}u_1 + \dfrac{\partial N_2}{\partial x_2}u_2 + \dfrac{\partial N_3}{\partial x}u_3 \\[3mm] \varepsilon_y = \dfrac{\partial v}{\partial y} = \dfrac{\partial N_1}{\partial y}v_1 + \dfrac{\partial N_2}{\partial y}v_2 + \dfrac{\partial N_3}{\partial y}v_3 \\[3mm] \gamma_{xy} = \dfrac{\partial u}{\partial y} + \dfrac{\partial v}{\partial x} = \dfrac{\partial N_1}{\partial y}u_1 + \dfrac{\partial N_2}{\partial y}u_2 + \dfrac{\partial N_3}{\partial y}u_3 + \dfrac{\partial N_1}{\partial x}v_1 + \dfrac{\partial N_2}{\partial x}v_2 + \dfrac{\partial N_3}{\partial x}v_3 \end{cases}$$

Or,

$$\varepsilon = \begin{Bmatrix} \varepsilon_x \\ \varepsilon_y \\ \gamma_{xy} \end{Bmatrix} = \begin{bmatrix} \dfrac{\partial N_1}{\partial x} & \dfrac{\partial N_2}{\partial x} & \dfrac{\partial N_3}{\partial x} & 0 & 0 & 0 \\[3mm] 0 & 0 & 0 & \dfrac{\partial N_1}{\partial y} & \dfrac{\partial N_2}{\partial y} & \dfrac{\partial N_3}{\partial y} \\[3mm] \dfrac{\partial N_1}{\partial y} & \dfrac{\partial N_2}{\partial y} & \dfrac{\partial N_3}{\partial y} & \dfrac{\partial N_1}{\partial x} & \dfrac{\partial N_2}{\partial x} & \dfrac{\partial N_3}{\partial x} \end{bmatrix} \begin{Bmatrix} u_1 \\ u_2 \\ u_3 \\ v_1 \\ v_2 \\ v_3 \end{Bmatrix}$$

Or,

$$\varepsilon = [B]\{d\}$$

In the above equation $[B]$ is called as strain displacement relationship matrix. In Cartesian co-ordinates, the shape functions for the 3 node triangular element is represented as,

$$\frac{\partial N_1}{\partial x} = \begin{cases} \dfrac{1}{2A}[(x_2 y_3 - x_3 y_2) + (y_2 - y_3)x + (x_3 - x_2)y] \\[2mm] \dfrac{1}{2A}[(x_3 y_1 - x_1 y_3) + (y_3 - y_1)x + (x_1 - x_3)y] \\[2mm] \dfrac{1}{2A}[(x_1 y_2 - x_2 y_1) + (y_1 - y_2)x + (x_2 - x_1)y] \end{cases}$$

Or,

$$\frac{\partial N_1}{\partial x} = \begin{cases} \dfrac{1}{2A}[\alpha_1 + \beta_1 x + \gamma_1 y] \\[2mm] \dfrac{1}{2A}[\alpha_2 + \beta_2 x + \gamma_2 y] \\[2mm] \dfrac{1}{2A}[\alpha_3 + \beta_3 x + \gamma_3 y] \end{cases}$$

Where,

$$\alpha_1 = (x_2 y_3 - x_3 y_2) \quad \beta_1 = (y_2 - y_3) \quad \gamma_1 = (x_3 - x_2)$$
$$\alpha_2 = (x_3 y_1 - x_1 y_3) \quad \beta_2 = (y_3 - y_1) \quad \gamma_2 = (x_1 - x_3)$$
$$\alpha_3 = (x_1 y_2 - x_2 y_1) \quad \beta_3 = (y_1 - y_2) \quad \gamma_3 = (x_2 - x_1)$$

Hence, the required partial derivatives of shape functions are,

$$\frac{\partial N_1}{\partial x} = \frac{\beta_1}{2A} \quad \frac{\partial N_2}{\partial x} = \frac{\beta_2}{2A} \quad \frac{\partial N_3}{\partial x} = \frac{\beta_3}{\partial x} = \frac{\beta_3}{2A}$$

$$\frac{\partial N_1}{\partial y} = \frac{\gamma_1}{2A} \quad \frac{\partial N_2}{\partial y} \quad \frac{\partial N_2}{\partial y} = \frac{\gamma_2}{2A} \quad \frac{\partial N_3}{\partial y} = \frac{\gamma_3}{2A}$$

Hence, the value of $[B]$ becomes:

$$[B] = \begin{bmatrix} \dfrac{\partial N_1}{\partial x} & \dfrac{\partial N_2}{\partial x} & \dfrac{\partial N_3}{\partial x} & 0 & 0 & 0 \\[3mm] 0 & 0 & 0 & \dfrac{\partial N_1}{\partial y} & \dfrac{\partial N_2}{\partial y} & \dfrac{\partial N_3}{\partial y} \\[3mm] \dfrac{\partial N_1}{\partial y} & \dfrac{\partial N_2}{\partial y} & \dfrac{\partial N_3}{\partial y} & \dfrac{\partial N_1}{\partial x} & \dfrac{\partial N_2}{\partial x} & \dfrac{\partial N_3}{\partial x} \end{bmatrix}$$

Or,

$$[B] = \frac{1}{2A}\begin{bmatrix} \beta_1 & b_2 & \beta_3 & 0 & 0 & 0 \\ 0 & 0 & 0 & \gamma_1 & \gamma_2 & \gamma_3 \\ \beta_1 & \beta_2 & \beta_3 & \gamma_1 & \gamma_2 & \gamma_3 \end{bmatrix}$$

The stiffness matrix is represented as,

$$[k] = \iiint_\Omega [B]^T [D][B]d\Omega$$

Since, $[B]$ and $[D]$ are constant matrices; the above expression can be expressed as

$$[k] = [B]^T [D][B] \iiint_V d\; \overline{\overline{V}}[B]^T [D][B]V$$

For a constant thickness (t) of the element, the volume will become $A*t$. Hence the above equation becomes,

$$[k] = [B]^T [D][B]\, At \qquad\qquad ...(9.24)$$

For plane stress condition, $[D]$ matrix will become:

$$[D] = \frac{E}{1-\mu^2}\begin{bmatrix} 1 & \mu & 0 \\ \mu & 1 & 0 \\ 0 & 0 & \dfrac{1-\mu}{2} \end{bmatrix}$$

Therefore, the element stiffness matrix for a plane stress problem becomes,

$$[k] = \frac{Et}{4A(1-\mu^2)}\begin{bmatrix} \beta_1 & 0 & \beta_1 \\ \beta_2 & 0 & \beta_2 \\ \beta_3 & 0 & \beta_3 \\ 0 & \gamma_1 & \gamma_1 \\ 0 & \gamma_1 & \gamma_2 \\ 0 & \gamma_3 & \gamma_3 \end{bmatrix}\begin{bmatrix} 1 & \mu & 0 \\ \mu & 1 & 0 \\ 0 & 0 & \dfrac{1-\mu}{2} \end{bmatrix}\begin{bmatrix} \beta_1 & \beta_2 & \beta_3 & 0 & 0 & 0 \\ 0 & 0 & 0 & \gamma_1 & \gamma_2 & \gamma_3 \\ \beta_1 & \beta_2 & \beta_3 & \gamma_1 & \gamma_2 & \gamma_3 \end{bmatrix}$$

Similarly, for plane strain condition, $[D]$ matrix is equal to,

$$[D] = \frac{E}{(1+\mu)(1-2\mu)}\begin{bmatrix} 1-\mu & \mu & 0 \\ \mu & 1-\mu & 0 \\ 0 & 0 & \dfrac{1-2\mu}{2} \end{bmatrix}$$

Nodal Load Vector for CST

From the principle of virtual work,

$$\int_\Omega d(\varepsilon)^T \{\sigma\} d\Omega = \int_\Gamma \delta\{u\}^T \{F_\Gamma\} d\Gamma + \int_\Omega \delta\{u\}^T \{F_\Omega\} d\Omega$$

Where, F_Γ and F_Ω are the surface and body forces respectively. Using the relationship between stress-stain and strain displacement, one can derive the following expressions:

$$\{\sigma\} = [D][B]\{d\}, \ \delta\{\varepsilon\} = [B]\delta\{d\} \quad \text{and} \quad \delta\{u\} = [N]\delta\{d\}$$

Hence, above equation can be rewritten as:

$$\int_\Omega \delta\{d\}^T [B]^T [D][B]\{d\} d\Omega$$

$$= \int_\Gamma \delta\{d\}^T [N^s]^T \{F_\Gamma\} d\Gamma + \int_\Omega \delta\{d\}^T [N]^T \{F_\Omega\} d\Omega$$

Or,

$$\int_\Omega [B]^T [D][B]\{d\} d\Omega = \int_\Gamma [N^s]^T \{F_\Gamma\} d\Gamma + \int_\Omega [N]^T \{F_\Omega\} d\Omega$$

Here, $[N^s]$ is the shape function along the boundary where forces are prescribed. This equation is equivalent to $[k]\{d\} = \{F\}$, and thus, the nodal load vector becomes

$$\{F\} = \int_\Gamma [N^s]^T \{F_\Gamma\} d\Gamma + \int_\Omega [N]^T \{G_\Omega\} d\Omega$$

For a constant thickness of the triangular element equation can be re-written as

$$\{F\} = t\int_s [N^s]^T \{F_\Gamma\} ds + t\int_A [N]^T \{F_\Omega\} dA$$

For a three node triangular two dimensional element, one can represent F_Ω and F_Γ as,

$$\{F_\Omega\} = \begin{Bmatrix} F_{\Omega x} \\ F_{\Omega y} \end{Bmatrix} \quad \text{and} \quad \{F_\Gamma\} = \begin{Bmatrix} F_{\Gamma x} \\ F_{\Gamma y} \end{Bmatrix}$$

For example, in case of gravity load on CST element,

$$\{F_\Omega\} = \begin{Bmatrix} F_{\Omega x} \\ F_{\Omega y} \end{Bmatrix} = \begin{Bmatrix} 0 \\ -\rho g \end{Bmatrix}$$

9.3.5 Isoparametric Representation

The isoparametric method may initially appear to be somewhat tedious (and confusing), but it will lead to the formulation of a simple computer program, and it is generally applicable for two and three-dimensional stress analysis and for non-structural problems. The isoparametric formulation allows to create the elements that are non-rectangular and have curved sides. The isoparametric formulation to develop element stiffness matrix of bar element is relatively easy to understand because of the resulting simple expressions. It is illustrated below:

Isoparametric Formulation of the Bar Element

The term isoparametric is derived from the use of same shape functions (or interpolation functions) $[N]$ to define the element's geometric shape as are used to define the displacements within the element. Thus, when the interpolation function is $u = a_1 + a_2 s$ for the displacement, we use $x = a_1 + a_2 s$ for the description of the nodal co-ordinate of a point on the bar element and, hence, the physical shape of the element.

Isoparametric element equations are formulated using a natural (or intrinsic) co-ordinate system s that is defined by element geometry and not by the element orientation in the global co-ordinate system. In other words, axial co-ordinate s is attached to the bar and remains directed along the axial length of the bar, regardless of how the bar is oriented in space. There is a relationship (called a *transformation mapping*) between the natural co-ordinate system and the global co-ordinate system x for each element of a specific structure.

First, the natural co-ordinate s is attached to the element, with the origin located at the center of the element. The s axis need not to be parallel to the x-axis-this is only for convenience.

Consider the bar element to have two degrees of freedom-axial displacements u_1 and u_2 at each node associated with the global x axis.

For the special case when the s and x axes are parallel to each other, the s and x co-ordinates can be related by:

$$x = x_c + \frac{L}{2} S$$

Using the global co-ordinates x_1 and x_2 with $x_c = (x_1 + x_2)/2$, we can express the natural co-ordinate s in terms of the global co-ordinates as:

$$s = \left[x - \frac{(x_1 + x_2)}{2} \right]\left[\frac{2}{(x_2 - x_1)} \right]$$

The shape functions used to define a position within the bar are found in a manner similar to that used to define displacement within a bar. We begin by relating the natural co-ordinate to the global co-ordinate by:

$$x = a_1 + a_2 s$$

Note that $-1 \leq s \leq 1$.

The relationship between x and s co-ordinates can be given by:

$$x = \frac{1}{2}[(1 - s)x_1 + (1 + s)x_2] \quad \text{(From the above figure)}$$

In matrix form:

$$\{x\} = [N_1 \quad N_2]\begin{Bmatrix} x_1 \\ x_2 \end{Bmatrix} \quad N_1 = \frac{1-s}{2} \quad N_2 = \frac{1+s}{2}$$

The linear shape functions map the s co-ordinate of any point in the element to the x co-ordinate. For instance, when $s = -1$, then $x = x_1$ and when $s = 1$, then $x = x_2$

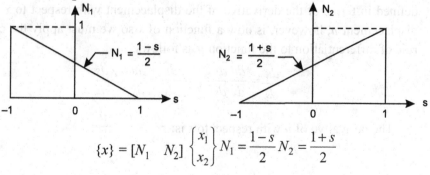

$$\{x\} = [N_1 \quad N_2]\begin{Bmatrix} x_1 \\ x_2 \end{Bmatrix} \quad N_1 = \frac{1-s}{2} \quad N_2 = \frac{1+s}{2}$$

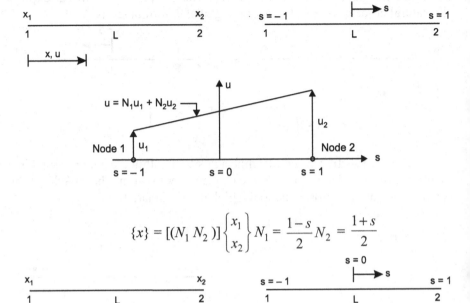

$$\{x\} = [(N_1\ N_2\ )]\begin{Bmatrix} x_1 \\ x_2 \end{Bmatrix}\quad N_1 = \frac{1-s}{2}\quad N_2 = \frac{1+s}{2}$$

When a particular co-ordinate s is substituted into $[N]$ yields the displacement of a point on the bar in terms of the nodal degrees of freedom u_1 and u_2. Since u and x are defined by the same shape functions at the same nodes, the element is called *isoparametric*.

9.3.6 Strain-Displacement and Stress-Strain Relationships

Now matrix $[B]$ need to be formulated, to evaluate $[k]$. We use the isoparametric formulation to illustrate its manipulations. For a simple bar element, there may be no evident real advantage. However, for higher-order elements, the advantage will become clear because of relatively simple computer program formulations.

To construct the element stiffness matrix, determine the strain, which is defined in terms of the derivative of the displacement with respect to x. The displacement u, however, is now a function of s so we must apply the chain rule of differentiation to the function u as follows:

$$\frac{du}{ds} = \frac{du}{dx}\frac{dx}{ds}\varepsilon_x = \frac{du}{dx} = \frac{du}{ds}\bigg/\frac{ds}{dx}$$

The derivative of u with respect to s is: $\dfrac{du}{ds} = \dfrac{u_2 - u_1}{2}$

The derivative of x with respect to s is: $\dfrac{dx}{ds} = \dfrac{x_2 - x_1}{2} = \dfrac{L}{2}$

Therefore the strain is: $\{\varepsilon_x\} = \begin{bmatrix} -\dfrac{1}{L} & \dfrac{1}{L} \end{bmatrix} \begin{Bmatrix} u_1 \\ u_2 \end{Bmatrix}$

Since, $\{\varepsilon\} = [B]\{d\}$, the strain-displacement matrix $[B]$ is:

$$[B] = \begin{bmatrix} -\dfrac{1}{L} & \dfrac{1}{L} \end{bmatrix}$$

Recall that use of linear shape functions results in a constant $[B]$ matrix, and hence, in a constant strain within the element. For higher-order elements, such as the quadratic bar with three nodes, $[B]$ becomes a function of natural co-ordinates.

The stress matrix is again given by Hooke's law as:

$$\{\sigma\} = E\{\varepsilon\} = E[B]\{d\}$$

The stiffness matrix is: $[k] = \int_0^L [B]^T E[B] A \, dx$

However, in general, we must transform the co-ordinate x to s because $[B]$ is, in general, a function of s.

$$\int_0^L f(x)\,dx = \int_{-1}^1 f(s)\,|[J]|\,ds$$

Where, $[J]$ is called the *Jacobian* matrix.

In the one-dimensional case, we have $|[J]| = J$.

9.3.7 Derive the Element Stiffness Matrix and Equations

For the simple bar element: $|[J]| = \dfrac{dx}{dx} = \dfrac{L}{2}$

The Jacobian determinant relates an element length (dx) in the global-co-ordinate system to an element length (ds) in the natural-co-ordinate system. In general, $|[J]|$ is a function of s and depends on the numerical values of the nodal co-ordinates. This can be seen by looking at the equations for a quadrilateral element.

The stiffness matrix in natural co-ordinates is:

$$[k] = \dfrac{L}{2} \int_{-1}^1 [B]^T E[B] A \, ds$$

For the one-dimensional case, we have used the modulus of elasticity $E = [D]$.

Performing the simple integration, we obtain:

$$[k] = \frac{AE}{L}\begin{bmatrix} 1 & -1 \\ -1 & 1 \end{bmatrix}$$

For higher-order one-dimensional elements, the integration in closed form becomes difficult if not impossible. Even the simple rectangular element stiffness matrix is difficult to evaluate in closed form. However, the use of numerical integration illustrates the distinct advantage of the isoparametric formulation of the equations. Determine the body-force matrix using the natural co-ordinate system s. The body-force matrix is:

$$\{f_b\} = \int_V [N]^T \{X_b\} dV \{f_b\} = \int_V [N]^T \{X_b\} A dx$$

Substituting for N_1 and N_2 and using $dx = \left(\frac{L}{2}\right) ds$

$$\{f_b\} = A \int_{-1}^{1} \begin{Bmatrix} \dfrac{1-s}{2} \\ \dfrac{1+s}{2} \end{Bmatrix} \{x_b\} \frac{L}{2} ds = \frac{ALX_b}{2} \begin{Bmatrix} 1 \\ 1 \end{Bmatrix}$$

The physical interpretation of the results for $\{f_b\}$ is that since AL represents the volume of the element and X_b the body force per unit volume, then ALX_b is the total body force acting on the element. The factor ½ indicates that this body force is equally distributed to the two nodes of the element.

$$\{f_b\} = A \int_{-1}^{1} \begin{Bmatrix} \dfrac{1-s}{2} \\ \dfrac{1+s}{2} \end{Bmatrix} \{x_b\} \frac{L}{2} ds = \frac{ALX_b}{2} \begin{Bmatrix} 1 \\ 1 \end{Bmatrix}$$

Determine the surface-force matrix using the natural co-ordinate system s. The surface-force matrix is:

$$\{f_s\} = \int_s [N_s]^T \{T_x\} ds$$

Assuming the cross section is constant and the traction is uniform over the perimeter and along the length of the element, we obtain:

$$\{f_s\} = \int_0^L [N_s]^T \{T_x\} dx$$

Where, we now assume $\{T_x\}$ is in units of force per unit length.

Substituting for N_1 and N_2 and using $dx = \left(\frac{L}{2}\right) ds$

$$\{f_s\} = \int_{-1}^{1} \begin{Bmatrix} \dfrac{1-s}{2} \\ \dfrac{1+s}{2} \end{Bmatrix} \{T_s\} \frac{L}{2} ds = \{T_x\} \frac{L}{2} \begin{Bmatrix} 1 \\ 1 \end{Bmatrix}$$

Since, $\{T_x\}$ is in force-per-unit length $\{T_x\}L$ is now the total force. The ½ indicates that the uniform surface traction is equally distributed to the two nodes of the element.

Substituting for N_1 and N_2 and using $dx = \left(\dfrac{L}{2}\right)ds$

$$\{f_s\} = \int_{-1}^{1} \begin{Bmatrix} \dfrac{1-s}{2} \\ \dfrac{1+s}{2} \end{Bmatrix} \{T_x\}\dfrac{L}{2}\,ds = \{T_x\}\dfrac{L}{2}\begin{Bmatrix} 1 \\ 1 \end{Bmatrix}$$

Note that if $\{T_x\}$ were a function of x (or s), then the amounts of force allocated to each node would generally not be equal and would be found through integration.

9.3.8 Potential Energy Approach–Element Stiffness and Force Terms

One of the alternative methods often used to derive the element equations and the stiffness matrix for an element is based on the *principle of minimum potential energy*. This method has the advantage of being more general than the methods involving nodal and element equilibrium equations, alongwith the stress/strain law for the element. The principle of minimum potential energy is more adaptable for the determination of element equations for complicated elements (those with large numbers of degrees of freedom) such as the plane stress/strain element, the axisymmetric stress element, the plate bending element, and the three dimensional solid stress element.

The total potential energy π_p is defined as the sum of the internal strain energy U and the potential energy of the external forces Ω:

$$\pi_p = U + \Omega$$

Strain energy is the capacity of the internal forces (or stresses) to do work through deformations (strains) in the structure.

The potential energy of the external forces Ω is the capacity of forces such as body forces, surface traction forces and applied nodal forces to do work through deformation of the structure.

Recall the force-displacement relationship for a linear spring:

$$F = kx$$

The differential internal work (or strain energy) dU in the spring is the internal force multiplied by the displacement:

$$dU = Fdx = (kx)dx$$

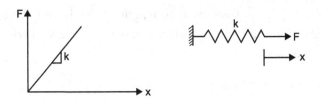

Fig. 9.17 A spring with stiffness K

The total strain energy is: $U = \int_L dU = \int_0^x (kx)dx = \frac{1}{2}kx^2$

The strain energy is the area under the force-displacement curve. The potential energy of the external forces is the work done by the external forces:

$$\Omega = -Fx \qquad\qquad\qquad ...(9.25)$$

Therefore, the total potential energy is: $\pi_p = \frac{1}{2}kx^2 - F_x$ ...(9.26)

The concept of a **stationary value** of a function G is shown below:

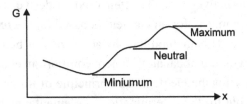

Fig. 9.18 The variation of stationary value function G with x

The function G is expressed in terms of x. To find a value of x yielding a stationary value of $G(x)$, we use differential calculus to differentiate G with respect to x and set the expression equal to zero.

We can replace G with the total potential energy π_p and the co-ordinate x with a discrete value d_i. To minimize π_p we first take the variation of π_p (we will not cover the details of variational calculus):

$$\delta\pi_p = \frac{\partial\pi_p}{\partial d_1}\delta d_1 + \frac{\partial\pi_p}{\partial d_2}\delta d_2 + ...+ \frac{\partial\pi_p}{\partial d_n}\delta d_n \qquad ...(9.27)$$

The principle states that equilibrium exist when the d_i define a structure state such that $\delta\pi_p = 0$ for arbitrary admissible variations δd_i from the equilibrium state.

To satisfy $\delta\pi_p = 0$, all co-efficients associated with δd_i must be zero independently, therefore:

$$\frac{\partial\pi_p}{\partial d_i} = 0 \quad i = 1, 2, ... n \quad or \quad \frac{\partial\pi_p}{\partial\{d\}} = 0$$

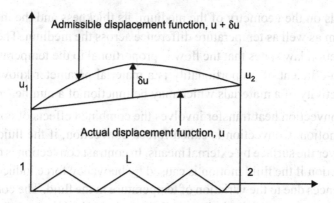

Fig. 9.19 The actual and admissible displacement functions

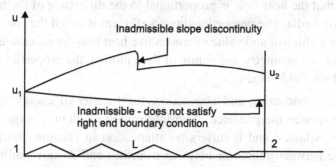

Fig. 9.20 The Inadmissible slope discontinuity

9.4 ONE DIMENSIONAL STEADY STATE HEAT TRANSFER

9.4.1 Introduction

The heat transfer may be defined as "The transmission of energy from one region to another as a result of temperature gradient". In heat transfer the driving potential is temperature difference. The main purpose of heat transfer analysis is:

1. To find out the temperature under both the steady state and transient conditions.

2. To estimate the rate of flow of energy as heat through the boundary of a system under study (both under steady state and transient condition).

Heat transfer may take place in one or more of its three basic forms: Conduction, Convection and Radiation. Conduction can take place in solids, liquids or gases. In gases and liquids; conduction is due to the collisions and diffusion of the molecules during their random motion but in solids, it is due to the combination of vibrations of the molecules in a lattice and the energy transport by free electrons. The rate of heat conduction through a medium depends on the geometry of the medium, its thickness and the material of the medium as well as temperature difference across the medium. The fourier heat conduction law states that the flow is proportional to the temperature gradient. The co-efficient of proportionality is a material parameter known as thermal conductivity of a materials which may be function of a number of variables.

Convection heat transfer involves the combined effects of conduction and fluid motion. Convection is called forced convection, if the fluid is forced to flow over the surface by external means. In contrast convection is called natural convection if the fluid motion is caused by buoyancy force induced by density differences due to the variation of temperature in the fluid. The convective heat transfer between two dissimilar media is governed by Newton's law of cooling. It states that the heat flow is proportional to the difference of the temperature of the two media. The proportionality co-efficient is called the convective heat transfer co-efficient and value of convective heat transfer co-efficient depends on the surface geometry, the nature of fluid motion, the properties of the fluid and the bulk fluid velocity.

Unlike conduction and convection, the transfer of energy by radiation does not require the presence of an intervening medium. Energy transfer by radiation is fastest and it suffers no attenuation in vacuum. Radiant energy exchange between region or between a surface and its surrounding with the help by Stefan-Boltzmann law.

9.4.2 Heat Transfer Analysis

In the steady state finite element analysis of heat transfer problems it is instructive to first recall the differential and variable equations that govern the heat transfer conditions to be analyzed. These equations provide the basis for the finite element formulation and solution of heat transfer problems.

Conduction

We present a finite element formulation for computation of the steady-state temperature distribution $T(x, y, z)$ and/or transient temperature distribution $T(x, y, z, t)$ for solids with general surface heat transfer. In following section we will have detailed discussion of the finite element solution of practical problems in heat transfer by conduction.

Fourier Law of Heat Conduction

$$Q = -kA \; \frac{dT}{dx} \qquad\qquad ...(9.28)$$

negative sign indicates the clausius statement of second law of thermodynamic which state that heat always transfer from higher temperature to lower temperature.

Where

(dT/dx) is the temperature gradient and it is always negative along positive x direction.

Importance of Fourier Law

1. It is based on experimental evidence and cannot be derived from first principle.

2. It is applicable to all matter (may be solid, liquid or gas).

3. It is a vector expression indicating that heat flow rate is in the direction of decreasing temperature and is normal to an isotherm.

9.4.3 Effects of Various Parameters on the Thermal Conductivity of Solids

The following are the effects of various parameters on the thermal conductivity of solids.

1. **Chemical composition:** Pure metals have very high thermal conductivity. Impurities or alloying elements reduce the thermal conductivity considerably. The thermal conductivity (k) of pure copper is 385 W/m°C, and that for pure nickel is 93 W/m°C. But monel metal (an alloy of 30% Ni and 70% Cu) has thermal conductivity of 24 W/m°C. Again for copper containing traces of Arsenic the value of k is reduced to 142 W/m°C.

2. **Mechanical forming:** Forging, drawing and bending or heat treatment of metals causes considerable variation in thermal conductivity. For example, the thermal conductivity of hardened steel is lower than that of annealed state.

3. **Temperature rise:** The value of k for most metals decreases with temperature rise since at elevated temperatures the thermal vibrations of the lattice become higher, that retard the motion of free electrons.

4. **Non-metallic solids:** Non-metallic solids have thermal conductivity (k) much lower than that for metals. For many of the building materials (concrete, stone, brick, fire brick, glass, wool, cork etc.) the thermal conductivity may vary from sample to sample due to variation in structure, composition, density and porosity.

5. **Presence of air:** The thermal conductivity is reduced due to the presence of air filled pores or cavities.

6. **Dampness:** Thermal conductivity of a damp material is considerably higher than that of dry material.

7. **Density:** Thermal conductivity of insulating powder, asbestos etc. increases with increase of density. The thermal conductivity of snow is also proportional to its density.

Thermal Resistance: (Rth)

The thermal resistance is analogous to electrical resistance in the flow of electricity. As per Ohm's Law:

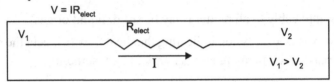

Fig. 9.21 The representation of electrical resistance

Voltage Drop = Current flow × Resistance

Thermal Analogy to Ohm's Law:

$$\Delta T = q R_{th}$$

Temperature Drop = Heat Flow × Resistance

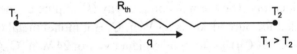

Fig. 9.22 The thermal resistance analogous to electrical resistance

A. Conduction Thermal Resistance:

(i)   Slab $R_{th} = \dfrac{L}{KA}$

(ii) Hollow cylinder $R_{th} = \dfrac{\ln(r_2 / r_1)}{2\pi KL}$

(iii) Hollow sphere $R_{th} = \dfrac{(r_2 - r_1)}{4\pi k r_2 r_1}$

B. Convection Thermal Resistance: $R_{th} = \dfrac{1}{hA}$

C. Radiation Thermal Resistance: $R_{th} = \dfrac{1}{\sigma FA(T_1 + T_2)(T_1^2 + T_2^2)}$.

9.4.4 One Dimensional Heat Conduction through a Plane Wall

$$\Sigma Rt = (1/h_1 A) + (L/kA) + (1/h_2 A) \qquad \ldots (9.29) \text{ (thermal resistance)}$$

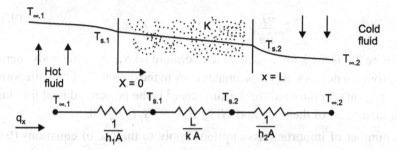

Fig. 9.23 The representation of thermal resistance

9.4.5 Governing Heat Transfer Equation

Consider a three dimensional body in the heat transfer condition as shown in figure and consider first steady-state conditions. For the heat transfer analysis we assume that the material obeys Fourier Law of heat conduction. The figure 9.24 shows prescribed temperature T^s on S_T and prescribed heat flow input q^s on S_q.

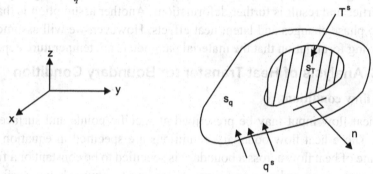

Fig. 9.24 Body subjected to heat transfer.

$$q_x = -k_x \frac{\partial T}{\partial x}; \qquad q_y = -k_y \frac{\partial T}{\partial y}; \qquad q_z = -k_z \frac{\partial T}{\partial z};$$

Where $q_x, q_y,$ and q_z are the heat flow conducted per unit area, k_x, k_y, k_z are the thermal conductivities corresponding to the principal axes in the direction of x, y, and z. T is the temperature of the body. Considering the heat flow equilibrium in the interior body, now we get

$$\frac{\partial}{\partial x}\left(K_x \frac{\partial T}{\partial x}\right) + \frac{\partial}{\partial y}\left(K_y \frac{\partial T}{\partial y}\right) + \frac{\partial}{\partial z}\left(K_z \frac{\partial T}{\partial z}\right) = -q^B \quad \dots (9.30)$$

Where q^B is said to be the rate of heat generated per unit volume. Following conditions must be satisfied on the surface of the body.

$$T\big|_{S_T} = T^S \qquad \qquad \dots(9.31)$$

$$k_n \frac{\partial T}{\partial n}\Big|_{S_q} = q^s \qquad \qquad ...(9.32)$$

Where T^s is the known surface temperature on S_T, k_n is the body thermal conductivity, n denotes the co-ordinates axes in the direction of the unit normal vector n (pointing outward) to the surface, q^s is the prescribed heat flux input on the surface s^q of the body and $S_T \cup S_q = S$, $S_T \cap S_q = 0$.

A number of important assumptions apply to the use of equations (9.30) to (9.32). A primary assumption is that the material particles of the body are at rest and thus we consider the heat conduction conditions in solids and structures. If the heat transfer in a moving fluid is to be analyzed, it is necessary to include in Eq. 9.30 a term allowing for the convective heat transfer through the medium. Another assumption is that the heat transfer condition can be analyzed decoupled from the stress conditions. This assumption is valid in many structural analyses, but may not be appropriate, for example, in the analysis of metal forming processes where the deformation may generate heat and change the temperature field. Such a change in turn may affect the material properties and result is further deformations. Another assumption is that there are no phase changes and latent heat effects. However, we will assume in the following formulation that the material parameters are temperature dependent.

9.4.6 Analysis of Heat Transfer for Boundary Condition

Heat flow condition

The heat flow input may be prescribed at specific points and surface of the body. These heat flow boundary conditions are specified in equation (9.32). The rate of heat flow across a boundary is specified to be constant or a function of a boundary co-ordinate and time. According to Fourier's law surface heat flow equation expresses for isotropic solid as

$$k \frac{\partial T}{\partial n} = q_s \qquad \qquad ... (9.33)$$

Where q_s denote the rate of surface heat flow per area and n shows normal to the boundary.

Neumann boundary condition specifies the normal derivative of the dependent variable and show prescribed heat flow example.

Temperature condition

The temperature may be prescribed at specific points and surfaces of the body, denoted by S_T in equation (9.31).

The surface temperature of a boundary is specified to be constant at a boundary co-ordinate and/or time. Dirichlet boundary conditions show the example of prescribed temperature.

Convection boundary conditions

Included in equation (9.32) are convection boundary condition where

$$q^s = h(T_e - T^s) \qquad \ldots (9.34)$$

Here h is the convection co-efficient, which may be temperature dependent. Here surface temperature T^s is unknown and this calculate environmental known temperature T_e.

Radiation boundary conditions

Equation (9.32) specified the radiation boundary condition

$$q^s = k(T_r - T_s) \qquad \ldots (9.35)$$

Where k is a co-efficient and temperature of the external radiative source T_r is the known.

$$k = h^r[T_r^2 - (T^s)^2](T_e - T^s) \qquad \ldots (9.36)$$

h_r is the variable and it is determined with the help of Stefan-Boltzmann constant, the geometric view factors and absorbisng materials and the emissivity of the radiant.

Here, we assume T^r is known and on the other hand considered, situation of two bodies radiating heat to each other and then the analysis is considerably more complicated. In the transient analysis initial temperature is also specified as additional boundary condition. Heat transfer problem is solved with the help of finite element method, in which we use principle of virtual temperature as given below:

$$\int_v \bar{T}'^T kT' dv = \int_v \bar{T} d^B dv + \int_{s_q} \bar{T}^s d^s ds + \Sigma_i \bar{T}^I \qquad \ldots (9.37)$$

$$T^T = \begin{bmatrix} \dfrac{\partial T}{\partial x} & \dfrac{\partial T}{\partial y} & \dfrac{\partial T}{\partial z} \end{bmatrix}$$

$$k = \begin{bmatrix} k_x & 0 & 0 \\ 0 & k_y & 0 \\ 0 & 0 & k_z \end{bmatrix}$$

The Q^i is said to be concentrated heat flow input and each Q^i is equivalent to a surface heat flow input over a very small area. The bar over the temperature T indicates that a virtual temperature distribution is being considered.

The heat flow equilibrium equation follow the principal of virtual temperature in which T is consideration as solution of the body temperature, equation (9.37) must hold for arbitrary virtual (continuous) temperature distributions that are zero on S_T.

The expression of 'principle of virtual temperature' is same like that principle of virtual displacements which is used in stress analysis. So, in this expression we use the principle of virtual temperatures in the same way as the principle of virtual displacements and indeed all procedures, whereas in the previous discussion we solved for the vector of unknown displacements.

9.4.7 Heat Transfer Under Steady State Conditions

Consider steady-state and/ or transient heat transfer in a three dimensional anisotropic solid Ω bounded by a surface Γ (Figure 9.25). The problem is governed by the energy equation.

$$\left(\frac{\partial q_x}{\partial x} + \frac{\partial q_y}{\partial y} + \frac{\partial qz}{\partial z}\right) + Q = \rho c \frac{\partial T}{\partial t} \qquad \dots (9.38)$$

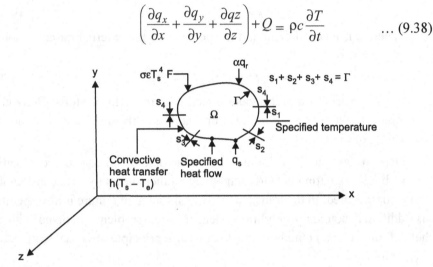

Fig. 9.25 Three-dimensional solution domain for general heat conduction

Where q_x, q_y and q_z are components of the heat flows vector per unit are in Cartesian co-ordinates (x, y, z), $Q(x, y, z, t)$ is the heat generation rate per unit volume, ρ is the density and c is the specific heat. For an anisotropic medium Fourier's law is

$$q_x = -\left(k_{11}\frac{\partial T}{\partial x} + k_{12}\frac{\partial T}{\partial y} + k_{13}\frac{\partial T}{\partial z}\right) \qquad \dots (9.39)$$

$$q_y = -\left(k_{21}\frac{\partial T}{\partial x} + k_{22}\frac{\partial T}{\partial y} + k_{23}\frac{\partial T}{\partial z}\right) \qquad \dots (9.40)$$

$$q_z = -\left(k_{31}\frac{\partial T}{\partial x} + k_{32}\frac{\partial T}{\partial y} + k_{33}\frac{\partial T}{\partial z}\right) \qquad \dots (9.41)$$

Where k_{ij} is the symmetric conductivity tensor. The material properties ρ, c and k_{ij} may be temperature dependent. If we substitute Fourier's law, equations (9.39 to 9.41) into the energy equation, (equation 9.38), we obtain the parabolic heat conduction equation. The heat conduction equation is solved, subject to an initial condition and boundary conditions on all portions of the surface Γ. The initial condition specifies the temperature distribution at time zero,

$$T(x, y, z, 0) = T_0(x, y, z) \qquad \ldots(9.42)$$

Heat conduction boundary conditions take several forms. Consider the frequently encountered conditions of specified surface temperature, specified surface heat flow, convective heat exchange and radiation heat exchange. The boundary condition (figure 9.38) are

$$T_s = T_1(x, y, z, t) \text{ on } S_1 \qquad \ldots(9.43a)$$

$$q_x n_x + q_y n_y + q_z n_z = -q_s \text{ on } S_2 \qquad \ldots(9.43b)$$

$$q_x n_x + q_y n_y + q_z n_z = h(T_s - T_e) \text{ on } S_3 \qquad \ldots(9.43c)$$

$$q_x n_x + q_y n_y + q_z n_z = \sigma \varepsilon T_s^4 - \alpha \varepsilon q_r \text{ on } S_4 \qquad \ldots(9.43d)$$

Where T_{1x} is the specified surface temperature, which may vary with position and time n_x, n_y, and n_z are the direction cosines of the outward normal to the surface, q_s is the specified heat flow rate per unit area (positive into the surface), h is a convective heat transfer co-efficient that may be function of the convective exchange temperature T_e, T_s is the unknown surface temperature, σ is the Stefan-Boltzmann constant ε, is the surface emissivity, which may be a function of surface temperature, α is the surface absorptivity, and q is the incident radiant heat flow rate per unit area.

The governing equation and boundary conditions are similar to the time dependent field problem formulated. The principal differences are that this formulation permits temperature dependent anisotropic material properties. The boundary conditions include temperature dependent convection co-efficients and non-linear radiation boundary conditions. Temperature dependent material properties and non-linear boundary conditions signify that the problem is inherently non-linear. Element equations are derived by the method of weighted residuals with galleria's criteria. However, non-linear terms arise from the radiation boundary conditions. After assembly of the element matrices the non-linear equation has to be solved iteratively. In the following sections we present a derivation of heat conduction finite elements in terms of general interpolation function N_i and element matrices frequently used in heat conduction elements. Solution methods for steady-state and transient heat conduction and illustrative examples also appear.

9.4.8 Finite Element Formulation

The three dimensional anisotropic solid Ω is shown to the solution domain and divided into element 'M' which have 'r' nodes each. With the help of procedure we express the temperature gradients and temperature within each element as

$$T^{(e)}(x, y, z, t) = \sum_{i=1}^{r} N_i(x, y, z) T_i(t) \qquad \ldots (9.44a)$$

$$\frac{\partial T^{(e)}}{\partial x}(x, y, z, t) = \sum_{i=1}^{r} \frac{\partial N_i}{\partial x}(x, y, z) T_i(t) \qquad \ldots (9.44b)$$

$$\frac{\partial T^{(e)}}{\partial y}(x, y, z, t) = \sum_{i=1}^{r} \frac{\partial N_i}{\partial y}(x, y, z) T_i(t) \qquad \ldots (9.44\ c)$$

$$\frac{\partial T^{(e)}}{\partial z}(x, y, z, t) = \sum_{i=1}^{r} \frac{\partial N_i}{\partial z}(x, y, z) T_i(t) \qquad \ldots (9.44\ d)$$

In the form of matrix we denote

$$T^{(e)}(x, y, z, t) = |N(x, y, z)| \{T(t)\}$$

$$\begin{bmatrix} \dfrac{\partial T}{\partial x}(x, y, z, t) \\[2mm] \dfrac{\partial T}{\partial y}(x, y, z, t) \\[2mm] \dfrac{\partial T}{\partial z}(x, y, z, t) \end{bmatrix} = [B(x, y, z)] \{T(t)\} \qquad \ldots (9.45b)$$

$[B]$ shows the temperature gradient interpolation matrix $[N]$ shows the temperature interpolation matrix.

$$|N(x, y, z)| = [N_1\ N_2 \ldots \ldots \ldots N_r] \qquad \ldots (9.4\ 6a)$$

$$B(x, y, z)] = \begin{bmatrix} \dfrac{\partial N_1}{\partial x} & \dfrac{\partial N_2}{\partial x} & \dfrac{\partial N_r}{\partial x} \\[2mm] \dfrac{\partial N_1}{\partial y} & \dfrac{\partial N_2}{\partial y} & \dfrac{\partial N_r}{\partial y} \\[2mm] \dfrac{\partial N_1}{\partial z} & \dfrac{\partial N_2}{\partial z} & \dfrac{\partial N_r}{\partial z} \end{bmatrix} \qquad \ldots (9.46b)$$

$\{T(t)\}$ is the vector of element nodal temperatures and $T_i(t)$ is the value of the temperature at each node. Only C^0 continuity is used for second order heat conduction equation, when nodal temperature is unknown, then it may be used. Only single element is focused and superscript (e) is omitted for the simplicity. The element equations starting with the energy equation are required to be derived by the method of weighted residuals. The one and two-dimensional heat conduction problems are solved by the equation 9.38. The weighted residuals method requires:

$$\int_{\Omega} (e) \left(\frac{\partial q_x}{\partial x} + \frac{\partial q_y}{\partial y} + \frac{\partial q_z}{\partial z} - Q\ \rho c \frac{\partial T}{\partial t} \right) N_i d\Omega = 0 \qquad \ldots (9.47)$$

Where, $\Omega^{(e)}$ is the domain for element (e) and integrate the term step by step:

$$\int_{\Omega^{(e)}} \left(\frac{\partial q_x}{\partial x} + \frac{\partial q_y}{\partial y} + \frac{\partial q_z}{\partial z} \right) N_i d\Omega = 0$$

According to Gauss's theorem that introduces surface integrals of the heat flow across the element boundary $\Gamma^{(e)}$. Now write the result in the form:

$$\int_{\Omega^{(e)}} \rho c \frac{\partial T}{\partial t} N_i d\Omega - \int_{\Omega^{(e)}} \left[\frac{\partial N_i}{\partial x} \quad \frac{\partial N_i}{\partial y} \quad \frac{\partial N_i}{\partial z} \right] \begin{bmatrix} q_x \\ q_y \\ q_z \end{bmatrix} d\Omega$$

$$= \int_{\Omega^{(e)}} Q N_i d\Omega - \int_{\Gamma^{(e)}} (q \cdot \hat{n}) \ N_i d\Gamma, \quad i = 1, 2, \dots r \qquad \dots(9.48)$$

The surface integral is expressed by the sum of integrals over S_1, S_2, S_3 and S_4 and boundary conditions also introduce equation 9.43. Thus,

$$\int_{\Omega^{(e)}} \rho c \frac{\partial T}{\partial t} N_i d\Omega - \int_{\Omega(e)} \left[\frac{\partial N_i}{\partial x} \quad \frac{\partial N_i}{\partial y} \quad \frac{\partial N_i}{\partial z} \right] \begin{bmatrix} q_x \\ q_y \\ q_z \end{bmatrix} d\Omega$$

$$= \int_{\Omega(e)} Q N_i d\Omega - \int_{S_1} (q \cdot \hat{n}) N_i d\Gamma$$

$$+ \int_{S_2} q_s N_i d\Gamma - \int_{S_3} h(T_s - T_e) N_i d\Gamma - \int_{S4} (\sigma \in T_S^4 - \alpha q_r) \ N_i \ d\Gamma$$

$$i = 1, 2, \dots \dots r \qquad \dots(9.49)$$

As the last step introduces the element temperatures from equation [9.45(a)] and heat flow components from Fourier's law, equations 9.39 to 9.41. For convenience we first write these equations in matrix form.

$$\begin{Bmatrix} q_x \\ q_y \\ q_z \end{Bmatrix} = \begin{bmatrix} k_{11} & k_{12} & k_{13} \\ k_{21} & k_{22} & k_{23} \\ k_{31} & k_{32} & k_{33} \end{bmatrix} \begin{Bmatrix} \dfrac{\partial T}{\partial x} \\ \dfrac{\partial T}{\partial y} \\ \dfrac{\partial T}{\partial z} \end{Bmatrix}$$

Where $[k]$ is the thermal conductivity matrix, and then express the temperature gradients in terms of nodal temperature through equation [9.45(b)].

$$\begin{Bmatrix} q_x \\ q_y \\ q_z \end{Bmatrix} = -[K][B]\{T\}$$

After some manipulation the resulting element equations become

$$[C]\left\{\frac{dT}{dt}\right\} + [[K_c] + [K_h]]\,\{T\} = \{R_T\} + \{R_Q\} + \{R_q\} + \{R_h\} + \{R_\sigma\} + \{R_r\}$$
$$\dotfill (9.50)$$

Where,

$$[C] = \int_{\Omega(e)} \rho c \{N\}[N]\,d\Omega$$

$$[K_c] = \int_{\Omega(e)} \rho c [B]^T [k][B]\,d\Omega$$

$$[K_h] = \int_{S_3} h\{N\}[N]\,d\Gamma$$

$$[R_T] = \int_{S_1} (q\cdot\hat{n})\{N\}\,d\Gamma$$

$$\{R_Q\} = \int_{\Omega} (Q\{N\}\,d\Omega$$

$$\{R_q\} = \int_{S_2} q_S\{N\}\,d\Gamma$$

$$\{R_h\} = \int_{S_3} hT_e\{N\}\,d\Gamma$$

$$\{R_\sigma\} = \int_{S_4} \sigma \in T_s^4 \{N\}\,d\Gamma$$

$$\{R_r\} = \int_{S_4} \alpha q_r\{N\}\,d\Gamma$$

The co-efficient matrix $[C]$ of the time derivative of the nodal temperature is the element capacitance matrix. The co-efficient matrices $[K]_c$ and $[K]_h$ are element conductance matrices and related to conduction and convection respectively. The convection matrix is computed only for elements with surface convection. The vectors $\{R\}T, \{R\}Q, \{R\}_q$ and $\{R\}_h$ are heat local vectors arising from specified nodal temperatures, internal heat generation, specified surface heating and surface convection respectively. The vectors $\{R_\sigma\}$ and $\{R_r\}$ arise from surface radiation. The vectors $\{R_T\}$ represent unknown nodal heat loads applied to maintain the nodes on the surface S_1 at specified temperatures. These heat loads may be computed, if desired, after the assembly of the element equations. The integral definition of $\{R_T\}$, is not evaluated and is not considered in subsequent discussions. The convection and radiation heat load vectors are computed only for elements with surface convection and/or radiation.

Equation 9.50 is a general non-linear formulation of element equations for transient heat conduction in an anisotropic medium. Assembly of the element equations to obtain the system equations follows the standard procedure. Note that since the nodal unknowns T_i are scalars, no transformations of matrices computed in local co-ordinates are necessary before assembly of the global matrices.

For analysis of practical heat conduction problems special cases of the general equations are usually considered because solution algorithms depend on whether a problem is steady or transient, linear or non-linear. For subsequent discussion the following cases are identified:

Linear steady-state analysis:

$$[[K_c] + [K_h]]\{T\} = \{R_Q\} + \{R_q\} + \{R_h\} \qquad ... (9.51)$$

Linear transient analysis:

$$[C]\{T(t)\} + [[K_c] + [K_h(t)]] \{T(t)\} = \{R_Q(t)\} + \{R_q(t)\} + \{R_h(t)\} \qquad ... (9.52)$$

Non-linear steady-state analysis:

$$[[K_c(T)] + [K_h(T)]] \{T\} = \{R_Q(T)\} + \{R_q(T)\} + \{R_h(T)\} + \{R_\sigma(T)\} + \{R_r(T)\} \qquad ... (9.53)$$

Non-linear transient analysis:

$$[C(T)]\{T\} + [[K_c(T)] + [K_h(T, t)]] \{T(t)\}$$
$$= \{R_Q(T, t)\} + \{R_q(T, t)\} + \{R_h(T, t)\} + \{R_\sigma(T, t)\} + \{R_r(T, t)\} \qquad ...(9.54)$$

For linear steady-state analysis equation 9.51 shows that the element conductance matrix has contributions from conduction and convection and the heat load vector has contributions from internal heat generation, surface heating and surface convection. For a linear steady-state analysis, element matrices and heat load vectors are contend and a linear solution of a set of simultaneous equation is required. For a linear transient analysis, equation 9.52 shows that element capacitance matrices are also required, element convection matrices and local vectors are time dependent, and a solution of the equations by a time-marching scheme is required. For a non steady-state analysis, equation 9.53 shows that element matrices and heat load vectors have contributions from radiation and the matrices and vectors are temperature dependent, thus the equations are non-linear and require solution by an iterative scheme. For the general non-linear transient case, equation 9.54 shows that element matrices and heat load vectors are both temperature and time dependent, and solution by a time-marching scheme is required. The details of each of these analyses appear in subsequent sections. However, before we consider solution methods, the next sections present typical element matrices employed in many of these analysis.

Element Equations

To illustrate application of the foregoing element equations we consider one and two dimensional conduction elements with specified heating and surface convection and develop element capacitance and conduction matrices and heat load vectors. Element thermal properties, internal heat generation, surface heating and surface convections are assumed constant for an element.

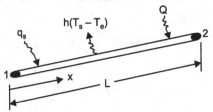

Fig. 9.26 Rod heat transfer element

One-dimensional rod element

A one-dimensional two-node rod element with conduction, internal heat generation, specified surface heating, and surface convection is shown in figure 9.26. The rod has cross-sectional area A and perimeter p in local co-ordinates the element interpolation function.

$$N_1(x) = L_1(x) = 1 - \frac{x}{L}$$

$$N_2(x) = L_2(x) = \frac{x}{L}$$

And by equation [9.45(b)]

$$B_1 = \frac{\partial N_1}{\partial x} = -\frac{1}{L}$$

$$B_2 = \frac{\partial N_2}{\partial x} = \frac{1}{L}$$

Element matrices and heat load vectors are readily evaluated using $[k] = k$, $d\Omega = A\,dx$, and $d\Gamma = p\,dx$:

$$[C] = \int_0^L \rho c \{N\}[N] A\,dx = \frac{\rho c A L}{6}\begin{bmatrix} 2 & 1 \\ 1 & 2 \end{bmatrix} \quad \text{(Consistent)} \dots (9.55a)$$

$$[K_c] = \int_0^L k\{B\}[B] A\,dx = \frac{kA}{L}\begin{bmatrix} 1 & -1 \\ -1 & 1 \end{bmatrix} \dots (9.55b)$$

$$[K_h] = \int_0^L h\{N\}[N] p\,dx = \frac{hpL}{6}\begin{bmatrix} 2 & 1 \\ 1 & 2 \end{bmatrix} \dots (9.55c)$$

$$\{R_Q\} = \int_0^L Q\{N\}\{N\}A\,dx = \frac{AQL}{2}\begin{Bmatrix}1\\1\end{Bmatrix} \qquad (9.55d)$$

$$\{R_q\} = \int_0^L q_s\{N\}p\,dx = \frac{qspL}{2}\begin{Bmatrix}1\\1\end{Bmatrix} \qquad \dots (9.55e)$$

$$\{R_h\} = \int_0^L hT_e\{N\}p\,dx = \frac{hT_epL}{2}\begin{Bmatrix}1\\1\end{Bmatrix} \qquad \dots (9.55f)$$

The rod element capacitance matrix, equation [9.55(a)], is known as a consistent capacitance matrix, because it is derived using the general finite element matrix equation, which is consistent with the other element matrix definitions, an alternative approach is to "lump" the capacitance at each node, thereby a diagonal capacitance matrix is produced. A diagonal capacitance matrix is convenient in transient analysis because it permits the use of an explicit time integration algorithm. The lumped-capacitance matrix for a rod element is

$$[C] = \frac{\rho cAL}{2}\begin{bmatrix}1 & 0\\0 & 1\end{bmatrix} \qquad \text{(Lumped)} \quad \dots(9.55g)$$

Which physically means that the element capacitance ρcAL is divided equally between the two nodes.

9.4.9 Temperature Boundary Conditions

When fixed temperature condition are applied at the wall, the wall heat flux is calculated from a fluid cell as:

$$q = h_f(Tw - T_f) + q_{rad} \qquad \dots (9.56)$$

Where,

q_{rad} is the radiative heat flux.

T_f is the temperature of local fluid.

T_w is the surface temperature of wall.

h_f is co-efficient of convective heat transfer and also called fluid-side local heat transfer co-efficient.

Calculate the fluid-side heat transfer co-efficient on the basis of local flow-field conditions such as temperature, velocity profile and turbulence level.

Calculate heat transfer to the wall boundary from a solid cell as:

$$q = \frac{k_s}{\Delta n}(T_w - T_s) + q_{rad} \qquad \dots (9.57)$$

Where,

k_s is the thermal conductivity of given solid.

Δ_n is the distance between wall surface and the solid cell center.

T_s is the temperature of local solid.

9.4.10 Heat Flux Boundary Conditions

When heat flux boundary condition is defined at a wall then wall surface specify the heat flux. Fluent uses Equation 9.56 and determine the wall surface temperature at adjacent to a fluid cell with the help of input of heat flux.

$$T_w = \frac{q - q_{rad}}{h_f} + T_f \qquad \qquad ... (9.58)$$

In the above equation calculate the fluid-side heat transfer co-efficient on the basis of local flow-field conditions.

$$T_w = \frac{(q - q_{rad})\Delta_n}{k_s} + T_s \qquad \qquad ... (9.59)$$

If the wall surrounds a solid region then wall surface temperature is calculated by the equation 9.59.

SOLVED EXAMPLES

Example 1: Analyze the beam as shown below in Fig. 9.27 by finite element method and calculate the end reactions. Also calculate the deflection at mid span.

Take, $E = 2 \times 105$ N/mm^2 and $1 = 5 \times 10^6$ mm^5

Solution:

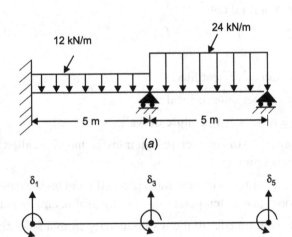

Fig. 9.27

Using kN and unit throughout,

$$E = 2 \times 10^5 \text{ N/mm}^2 = 2 \times 10^5 \times \frac{10^6}{10^3}$$
$$= 2 \times 10^8 \text{ kN/m}^2$$

and

$$l = 5 \times 10^6 \text{ mm}^4 = 5 \times 10^{-6} \text{ m}^4$$

∴

$$El = 2 \times 8 \times 5 \times 10^{-6} = 1000 \text{ kN-m}^2$$

Let the two elements be numbered as shown in [Fig. 9.27 (b)]. The nodal displacement vector is

$$[\delta]^T = [\delta_1 \ \delta_2 \ \delta_3 \ \delta_4 \ \delta_5 \ \delta_6]$$
$$= [w_1 \ \theta_1 \ w_2 \ \theta_2 \ w_3 \ \theta_3]$$

$$k_1 = \frac{E_1 l_1}{l_1^3} \begin{bmatrix} 12 & 6l_1 & -12 & 6l_1 \\ 6l_1 & 5l_1^2 & -6l_1 & 2l_1^2 \\ -12 & -6l_1 & 12 & -6l_1 \\ 6l_1 & 2l_1^2 & -6l_1 & 5l_1^2 \end{bmatrix}$$

$$k_1 = \frac{1000}{5^3} \begin{bmatrix} 12 & 30 & -12 & 30 \\ 30 & 100 & -30 & 50 \\ -12 & -30 & 12 & -30 \\ 30 & 50 & -30 & 100 \end{bmatrix}$$

$$k_1 = 8 \begin{bmatrix} 12 & 30 & -12 & 30 \\ 30 & 100 & -30 & 50 \\ -12 & -30 & 12 & -30 \\ 30 & 50 & -30 & 100 \end{bmatrix}$$

Similarly,

$$k_2 = 8 \begin{bmatrix} 12 & 30 & -12 & 30 \\ 30 & 100 & -30 & 50 \\ -12 & -30 & 12 & -30 \\ 30 & 50 & -30 & 100 \end{bmatrix}$$

$$= 8 \begin{bmatrix} 12 & 30 & -12 & 30 & & \\ 30 & 100 & -30 & 50 & & \\ -12 & -30 & 12+12 & -30+30 & -12 & 30 \\ 30 & 50 & -30+30 & 100+100 & -30 & 50 \\ & & -12 & -30 & 12 & -30 \\ & & 30 & 50 & -30 & 100 \end{bmatrix}$$

$$= 8 \begin{bmatrix} 12 & 30 & -12 & 30 & 0 & 0 \\ 30 & 100 & -30 & 50 & 0 & 0 \\ -12 & -30 & 24 & 0 & -12 & 30 \\ 30 & 50 & 0 & 200 & -30 & 50 \\ 0 & 0 & -12 & -30 & 12 & -30 \\ 0 & 0 & 30 & 50 & -30 & 100 \end{bmatrix}$$

$$F = \begin{Bmatrix} \dfrac{pl_e}{2} \\ \dfrac{pl_e^2}{12} \\ \dfrac{pl_e}{2} \\ \dfrac{-pl_e^2}{12} \end{Bmatrix} = \begin{Bmatrix} \dfrac{-12 \times 5}{2} \\ \dfrac{-12 \times 5^2}{12} \\ \dfrac{-12 \times 5}{2} \\ \dfrac{12 \times 5^2}{12} \end{Bmatrix} = \begin{Bmatrix} -30 \\ -25 \\ -30 \\ 25 \end{Bmatrix}$$

$$F = \begin{Bmatrix} \dfrac{-24 \times 5}{2} \\ \dfrac{-24 \times 5^2}{12} \\ \dfrac{-24 \times 5}{2} \\ \dfrac{24 \times 5^2}{12} \end{Bmatrix} = \begin{Bmatrix} 60 \\ -50 \\ -60 \\ 50 \end{Bmatrix}$$

$$F = \begin{Bmatrix} -30 \\ -25 \\ -90 \\ -25 \\ -60 \\ 50 \end{Bmatrix}$$

∴   The stiffness equation is

$$8 \begin{bmatrix} 12 & 30 & -12 & 30 & 0 & 0 \\ 30 & 100 & -30 & 50 & 0 & 0 \\ -12 & -30 & 24 & 0 & -12 & 30 \\ 30 & 50 & 0 & 200 & -30 & 50 \\ 0 & 0 & -12 & -30 & 12 & -30 \\ 0 & 0 & 30 & 50 & -30 & 100 \end{bmatrix} \begin{Bmatrix} \delta_1 \\ \delta_2 \\ \delta_3 \\ \delta_4 \\ \delta_5 \\ \delta_6 \end{Bmatrix} = \begin{Bmatrix} -30 \\ -25 \\ -90 \\ -25 \\ -60 \\ 50 \end{Bmatrix}$$

Boundary conditions are:

$$\delta_1 = \delta_2 = \delta_3 = \delta_5 = 0$$

Imposing them by elimination method, we get

$$8\begin{bmatrix} 200 & 50 \\ 50 & 100 \end{bmatrix} \begin{Bmatrix} \delta_4 \\ \delta_6 \end{Bmatrix} = \begin{Bmatrix} -25 \\ 50 \end{Bmatrix}$$

$$400\begin{bmatrix} 4 & 1 \\ 1 & 2 \end{bmatrix} \begin{Bmatrix} \delta_4 \\ \delta_6 \end{Bmatrix} = \begin{Bmatrix} -25 \\ 50 \end{Bmatrix}$$

$$\begin{Bmatrix} \delta_4 \\ \delta_6 \end{Bmatrix} = \frac{1}{400}\begin{bmatrix} 4 & 1 \\ 1 & 2 \end{bmatrix}^{-1} \begin{Bmatrix} -25 \\ 50 \end{Bmatrix}$$

$$\begin{Bmatrix} \delta_4 \\ \delta_6 \end{Bmatrix} = \frac{1}{400} \times \frac{1}{8-1}\begin{bmatrix} 2 & -1 \\ -1 & 4 \end{bmatrix} \begin{Bmatrix} -25 \\ 50 \end{Bmatrix}$$

$$\begin{Bmatrix} \delta_4 \\ \delta_6 \end{Bmatrix} = \frac{1}{2800}\begin{bmatrix} -100 \\ 225 \end{bmatrix} \quad \textbf{Ans.}$$

Since, $\delta_1 = \delta_2 = \delta_3 = 0$ and $\delta_5 = -\dfrac{100}{2800}$

End reactions are

$$\begin{Bmatrix} R_1 \\ R_2 \\ R_3 \\ R_4 \end{Bmatrix} = 8\begin{bmatrix} 12 & 30 & -12 & 30 \\ 30 & 100 & -30 & 50 \\ -12 & -30 & 12 & -30 \\ 30 & 50 & -30 & 100 \end{bmatrix} \begin{Bmatrix} 0 \\ 0 \\ 0 \\ \dfrac{-100}{2800} \end{Bmatrix} - \begin{Bmatrix} -30 \\ -25 \\ -30 \\ 25 \end{Bmatrix}$$

$$\begin{Bmatrix} R_1 \\ R_2 \\ R_3 \\ R_4 \end{Bmatrix} = \begin{Bmatrix} 21.429 \\ 10.714 \\ -38.571 \\ -53.571 \end{Bmatrix} \quad \textbf{Ans.}$$

For element 2,

$$\delta_3 = \delta_5 = 0 \text{ and } \delta_5 = -\frac{100}{2800} \text{ and } \delta_6 = \frac{225}{2800}$$

End reactions are

$$\begin{Bmatrix} R_3 \\ R_4 \\ R_5 \\ R_6 \end{Bmatrix} = 8\begin{bmatrix} 12 & 30 & -12 & 30 \\ 30 & 100 & -30 & 50 \\ -12 & -30 & 12 & -30 \\ 30 & 50 & -30 & 100 \end{bmatrix} \begin{Bmatrix} 0 \\ \dfrac{-100}{2800} \\ 0 \\ \dfrac{225}{2800} \end{Bmatrix} - \begin{Bmatrix} -60 \\ -50 \\ -60 \\ 50 \end{Bmatrix}$$

$$\begin{Bmatrix} R_3 \\ R_4 \\ R_5 \\ R_6 \end{Bmatrix} = \begin{Bmatrix} 70.714 \\ 53.571 \\ 49.286 \\ 0 \end{Bmatrix} \quad \textbf{Ans.}$$

Deflection at mid span

$y = [N_1 \ N_2 \ N_3 \ N_5]\{\delta\}_e$

$$= \left[\frac{2 - 3\xi + \xi^3}{5} \quad \frac{l_e}{2}\frac{1 - \xi - \xi^2 + \xi^3}{5} \quad \frac{2 + 3\xi - \xi^3}{5} \quad \frac{l_e}{2}\frac{-1 - \xi + \xi^2 + \xi^3}{5} \right]\{\delta\}$$

For mid span $\xi = 0$

$\therefore y$ Centre $= [0.5 \ \ 0.125 \ l_e \ \ 0.5 \ -0.125 \ l_e]\{\delta\}$

For element 1,

$$\therefore y_1 \text{ Centre} = [0.5 \ \ 0.125 \times 5 \ \ 0.5 \ -0.125 \times 5] \begin{Bmatrix} 0 \\ -\dfrac{100}{2800} \\ 0 \\ \dfrac{225}{2800} \end{Bmatrix}$$

$$y_2 = -0.02790 \text{ m}$$

$$y_2 = 27.90 \text{ mm, downward } \textbf{Ans.}$$

Example 4: Find the steady state heat flux through the composite slab as shown in Figure 9.28 and the interface temperature. The thermal conductivities of the two materials vary with temperature as given below:

$k_A = 0.05(1 + 0.0065 \, t)$ W/m°C; $k_B = 0.04 \, (1 + 0.0076 \, t)$ W/m°C, where temperature are in °C.

Solution:

$t_1 = 600 \text{ °C}; t_3 = 300 \text{ °C}$

$L_A = 50 \text{ mm} = 0.05 \text{ m}; L_B = 100 \text{ mm} = 0.1 \text{ m}$

$$k_{mA} = k_{OA}\left[1 + \alpha_A\left(\frac{t_1 + t_2}{2}\right)\right] = 0.05\left[1 + 0.0065\left(\frac{t_1 + t_2}{2}\right)\right]$$

$$k_{mB} = k_{OB}\left[1 + \alpha_B\left(\frac{t_2 + t_3}{2}\right)\right] = 0.04\left[1 + 0.0075\left(\frac{t_2 + t_3}{2}\right)\right]$$

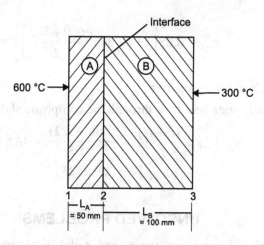

Fig. 9.28

Interface temperature: t_2

Rate of heat transfer per m^2,

$$q = \frac{Q}{A} = \frac{(t_1 - t_2)}{\left(\dfrac{L_A}{k_{mA}}\right)} = \frac{(t_2 - t_3)}{\left(\dfrac{L_B}{k_{mB}}\right)}$$

Now substituting the values of k_{mA} and k_{mB} in above equation, we get

$$\frac{(600 - t_2)}{0.05\left[1 + 0.0065\left(\dfrac{600 + t_2}{2}\right)\right]} = \frac{(t_2 - 300)}{0.04\left[1 + 0.0075\left(\dfrac{t_2 + 300}{2}\right)\right]}$$

$$\text{or, } (600 - t_2)\left[1 + 0.0065\left(\frac{600 + t_2}{2}\right)\right] = 0.4(t_2 - 300)\left[1 + 0.0075\left(\frac{t_2 + 300}{2}\right)\right]$$

$$\text{or, } (600 - t_2)\left[\frac{5.9 + 0.0065\,t_2}{2}\right] = (t_2 - 300)\left[\frac{4.25 + 0.0075\,t_2}{2}\right] \times 0.4$$

or, $(600 - t_2)(5.9 + 0.0065\,t_2) = (t_2 - 300)(1.7 + 0.003\,t_2)$

or $3540 + 3.9\,t_2 - 5.9\,t_2 - 0.0065\,t_2^2 = 1.7\,t_2 + 0.003\,t_2^2 - 510 - 0.9\,t_2$

or $0.0095\,t_2^2 + 2.8\,t_2 - 4050 = 0$

or $t_2^2 - 294.7\,t_2 - 426315 = 0$

or

$$t_2 = \frac{-294.7 \pm \sqrt{294.7^2 + 4 \times 426316}}{2}$$

$$= \frac{-294.7 \pm 1338.7}{2} = 522 \ °C$$

$$k_{mA} = 0.05\left[1+0.0065\left(\frac{600+522}{2}\right)\right] = 0.2323 \text{ W/m}°\text{C}$$

Rate of heat transfer per m^2, q :

The steady state heat flow through the composite slab,

$$q = \frac{(t_1 - t_2)}{\left(\dfrac{L_A}{k_{mA}}\right)} = \frac{(600-522)}{\left(\dfrac{0.05}{0.2323}\right)} = 362.39 \text{ W/m}^2 \text{ Ans.}$$

UNSOLVED PROBLEMS

1. Determine the stresses, strain, and nodal displacement in the steeped beam as shown in Fig. 9.29.

Element	Length	Area(cross section)	Young modulas (E)
ab	500 mm	150 mm²	200 GPa
bc	500 mm	100 mm²	140 GPa

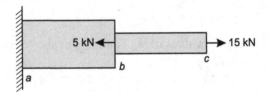

Fig. 9.29

2. Determine the stresses, strain and nodal displacements in the tapered bar as shown in Fig. 9.30 ($ab = bc = 500$ mm).

Element (cross section)	Area (cross section)
aa1	300 mm²
bb2	200 mm²
cc3	100 mm²

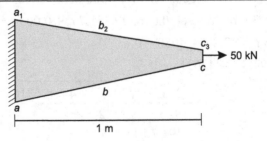

Fig. 9.30

3. A beam of length 10 m, fixed at one end and supported by a roller at the other end as shown in Fig. 9.31 carries a 25 kN concentrated load at the centre of the span. By taking the modulus of elasticity of material as 200 GPa and moment of inertia as 24×10^{-6} m^4, determine:

1. Deflection under load

2. Shear force and bending moment at mid span

3. Reactions at supports

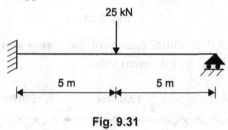

Fig. 9.31

4. Analyze the beam as shown in Fig. 9.32 by FEM and determine the end reactions.

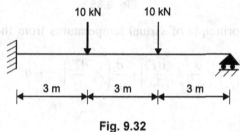

Fig. 9.32

5. Determine the consistent nodal vector due to loads acting on the beam as shown in Fig. 9.33.

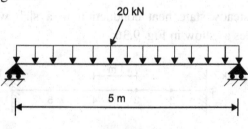

Fig. 9.33

6. For the four-noded linear plane quadrilateral element shown below (Fig. 9.34) with a uniform surface traction along the side 2-3, evaluate the force matrix using the energy equivalent nodal forces. Take thickness of the element be 5 mm.

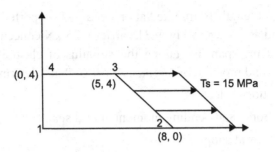

Fig. 9.34

7. Obtain the total potential energy of the spring system shown below in Fig. 9.35 and find its minimum value.

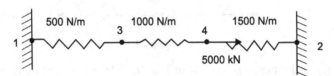

Fig. 9.35

8. Derive the principle of virtual temperatures from the basic differential equations:

1. $\dfrac{\partial}{\partial x}\left(k_x \dfrac{\partial T}{\partial x}\right) + \dfrac{\partial}{\partial y}\left(k_y \dfrac{\partial T}{\partial y}\right) + \dfrac{\partial}{\partial z}\left(k_z \dfrac{\partial T}{\partial z}\right) = -q^B$

2. $T\,|S_T = T^s$

3. $k_n \dfrac{\partial T}{\partial n}\bigg| S_q$

9. Consider steady state heat conduction in a slab with specified wall temperatures as show in Fig. 9.36:

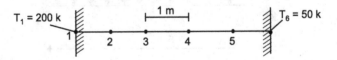

Fig. 9.36

(a) Write the matrix equation for computing nodal temperature using the central finite difference approximation for the governing equation.

(b) Write a similar matrix equation using linear finite elements.

(c) Compare and discuss the result.

10. Consider heat transfer in the three – member truss as shown in Fig. 9.37. In a crude finite element model each member of the truss is represented by a single- conduction, two-node rod element. Member 2 experiences internal heat generation, and member 3 experiences convective heat transfer to a surrounding medium. Compute the following:

(*a*) Temperatures at nodes 2 and 3.

(*b*) Nodal heat flow at node 1.

(*c*) The heat fluxes in all elements.

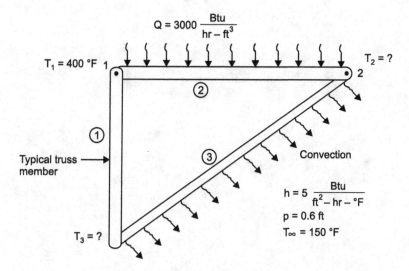

Fig. 9.37

Element	K (Btu/hr-ft-°F)	A (ft²)	L(ft)
1	60	0.02	4
2	60	0.02	4
3	80	0.02	6

◻◻◻

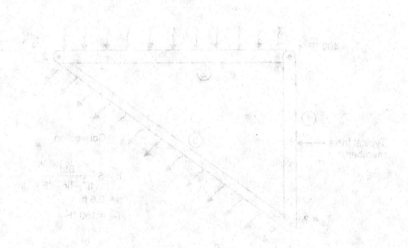

Index

□□□